THE
END OF THE WAR
IN ASIA

LOUIS ALLEN

THE
END OF THE WAR
IN ASIA

c. 1

BEEKMAN/ESANU PUBLISHERS, INC.
38 Hicks Street
Brooklyn Heights, New York U.S.A. 11201

Published in the United States in 1979 by

BEEKMAN/ESANU PUBLISHERS, INC.
38 Hicks Street
Brooklyn Heights, New York U.S.A. 11201

ISBN 0 8464 0034 X
LCC 79 51655

To Margaret
(who else?)

CONTENTS

LIST OF MAPS

ACKNOWLEDGEMENTS

I have received help from many colleagues in this country, in the United States, and in various countries of Asia. The Very Rev. J. S. Wild allowed me the use of his brother's papers on Singapore. Professor Stanley Falk obtained for me a scarce copy of the State Department's papers on China in 1945. Dr Kalyan Ghosh and Professor Joyce Lebra sent me books and papers on the Indian National Army which deepened my knowledge of that movement. Many other people wrote to me or talked to me about it: Philip Mason, Hugh Toye, Field-Marshal Lord Auchinleck, Sisir K. Bose, Arabinda Basu. For the knowledge of what happened in Japanese headquarters in Burma I am indebted to Mr Tsuchiya Eiichi, one of the first peace envoys from 28th Army, and his friends – and mine – Mr Hachisuka Mitsuo, the late Mr Iuchi Kikuji and Mr Wakō Kōtarō. To them, and to Mr Tsutsumi Shinzō, once of the Imperial Japanese Navy and now head of Mitsui's London branch, my debt is one of hospitality as well as information. To Mr Tsuchiya I am grateful also for an introduction to Mr Fuwa Hiroshi of the War History Room at the Defence Agency in Ichigaya, who led me to a variety of sources in print and manuscript. I must thank, too, a former major on the Army General Staff, Mr Fujishima Kōsaku, not merely for unfailing cooperation in the busy days in Indo-China, but for correspondence which began then and continues to this day, thirty years later. For similar reasons, my grateful memory goes to the late Colonel Komatsubara Yukio, with whom I exchanged letters until his death, and to Lieutenant-General Fujiwara Iwaichi, surely one of the ablest men the Japanese Army has produced in this century, with both of whom I discussed the fortunes of the Indian National Army and Subhas Chandra Bose.

ACKNOWLEDGEMENTS

I should like to thank Stan Charles, Mike Hore and the officers of the 5me Régiment d'Infanterie Coloniale who added an indisputably metropolitan flavour to the otherwise provincial air of Saigon. I owe to Stephen Brickley my first glimpse of life in occupied Japan. Translators V made the early days of research into this book – though they may not have realized it at the time – a constant delight: Roger, John, Ken, Jim, Stan, Johnnie, Bev, Sarge, and, *honoris causa*, David Anderson. They and I recall with affection those who initiated us into the awe-inspiring *arcana* of the Japanese language: Frank and Otome Daniels, Shōki Ko, Canon France, Tsubota Sōchō and, of course, General Piggott. I don't know whether he would have liked this book about the Japanese or not, but without him it would never have been written. That remark applies, too, to Richard Storry. Like so many writers on modern Japanese history, I owe him much for his constant and untiring encouragement, selflessly given, and for the opportunity to test out some of the findings of the chapters on Burma and Indo-China in seminars at St Anthony's Oxford, where I was lucky enough to have the late Geoffrey Hudson in my audience to comment on them. If Richard Storry finds any of these pages of interest to him, then this book will have been worth writing.

My thanks go, too, to the Research Fund of the University of Durham and the Japan Foundation for having made it possible for me to visit Japan and South-East Asia. And to the following for permission to quote from books of which they hold the copyright: Mme Yvonne R. de Medeville (Amiral Jean Decoux, *A la barre de l'Indochine*, Plon), Sir Andrew Gilchrist (*Bangkok Top Secret*, Hutchinson), Mrs Theda Maw Sturtevant and Mr William C. Sturtevant (Ba Maw, *Breakthrough in Burma*, Yale University Press). I would like to thank the Japanese authors and publishers of the various books and articles to which specific reference is made in the text, and to acknowledge my indebtedness to these sources even where copyright has lapsed or the publisher has not been traced.

PREFACE

Long before 15 August 1945, the Japanese Government knew that the war which had begun so brilliantly for them was likely to end in the slaughter of millions of their people. Before the atomic bombs were dropped on Hiroshima and Nagasaki, before the Russians invaded Manchuria, American carpet bombing of the Japanese mainland and control of Japan's sea-lanes by Allied planes and submarines had ensured Japan's ultimate defeat. Through all neutral channels, Japanese diplomats put out feelers to sound out the attitudes of the powers ranged against her. Sweden, Switzerland, the Vatican, Portugal and – until the breaking of the pact on 9 August 1945 – Soviet Russia, were all approached. When the end came, and the Emperor of Japan decided by his own intervention in the Supreme War Council to sue for peace, the industrial cities of the homeland were devastated.

But there were still millions of men under arms overseas. Political control of vast areas of the Asian mainland and South-East Asia lay in the hands of the Japanese Army and Navy. Some of these forces had known great defeats. In the Philippines, the Japanese were reduced to marauding guerrilla bands. In the watery labyrinth of the Pacific, garrisons had been by-passed almost everywhere. In Burma they had met the most resounding defeat of the entire war, and were in full retreat. Elsewhere, they had not joined battle. Even in China, where hostilities had begun in 1937, they were still in occupation of the most productive areas. They had tightened their grip on Thailand and French Indo-China, where they finally toppled the French régime on 9 March 1945. They still held Java, Sumatra and countless islands of the Netherlands East Indies. Even when the central authorities in Tokyo announced that they were finally willing to accept the Potsdam Declaration, it was by no means certain that those Japanese armies overseas which had not experienced defeat directly would obey the Imperial decision, even when it was transmitted by Princes of the Blood.

Japanese generals flew to Manila and Rangoon to sue for terms with the Supreme Allied Commanders, Mountbatten for South-East Asia, MacArthur for the Pacific. But in the very precincts of the Imperial Palace itself, when it became known that the Emperor had accepted the Potsdam Declaration, rebellious officers tried to seize the recording of the Imperial surrender broadcast, and assassinated the general officer commanding the Imperial Guards Division in their attempt. The murders and suicides which followed this event showed that the Japanese military would not be easily persuaded to lay down their arms.

Others were involved, too. Not merely the Japanese civilian settlers who had gone out to Manchuria and Korea under army protection to pioneer the 'New Order in East Asia'; but also the leaders of Asian independence movements who had believed Japan's declaration that she came to free them from the colonial powers of Europe. What would become of them and their recently proclaimed independence when the Allied armies came back?

Numerous accounts have been written of the surrender period, of the diplomacy which led up to it, of the dropping of the atomic bombs, of the suicide of War Minister Anami, of the Palace revolt. My purpose in this book is different. I have tried to show the impact of the surrender on the Japanese forces overseas, how the decision was received in their vast but short-lived empire, what tragedies it brought to the Japanese themselves, what problems it created for the returning Allies, what fears arose in the minds of Allied prisoners-of-war as liberation came nearer, and, most of all, what political changes it brought in its wake. For the modern map of Asia derives from those few months, August to October 1945, of the Japanese surrender.

Japan did not simply hand over her conquests. Her claim to be the liberator of the peoples of Asia may have rung hollow in the ears of thousands of Chinese in Malaya and Singapore who had lived under the appalling cruelties of Japan's military police. But we would be foolish to ignore that Japan's Army and Navy *did* contain idealists. There *were* those, in Japan and on the continent of Asia, who sincerely believed that Japan had brought independence to Burma, to Vietnam, and to Indonesia. I have therefore tried to show how the countries which she conquered or liberated – your point of view determines the verb you use – or countries she had forced to collaborate with her, stripped themselves of the Japanese connection and assumed the burden of their independence.

Much of the detailed history of what occurred has remained hidden in Japanese archives or is available only to a Japanese readership, sometimes not in books but in privately printed bulletins of limited circulation. I have not only used these, but have also drawn upon my own recollections of the moods and events of those days. They cover directly what is said in the book about Burma, Thailand, French Indo-China (now Vietnam) and the Indian National Army. I took part personally in a number of surrender negotiations, and later in interrogations of a political or historical nature, in most of the countries of South-East Asia. In doing so I made the acquaintance of highly-placed Japanese civilians and army officers who were involved in some of the incidents which I describe. Some of them I met again in Japan, years later, by which time most of them had been absorbed into civilian life or had begun to serve with the Defence Agency.

I was a witness of the tangled negotiations between French, British, and Vietnamese in Saigon in 1946. In Bangkok, I heard what seemed then to be fantastic rumours of a Japanese colonel hiding in a Thai monastery disguised as a Buddhist monk – rumours which turned out to be sober fact, as my chapter on Thailand shows. I saw the first attempts of Burma's new political leaders to come to terms with the returning British. I was able to explore the ramifications of Subhas Chandra Bose's Indian National Army and to judge its impact on Indian troops and Indian politics. That is why I have wanted not simply to write a political history, but also to convey, through individual narratives, something of the excitement of a moment of great historical change. I have tried to make the new shape of Asia visible through the eyes of the Japanese who took the decisions or suffered from them, and of the new leaders of Asia – who built their own dreams on the ashes of Japan's New Order.

NOTE

*The Japanese order of reading Japanese names
is kept in this book: family name first,
personal name last.*

BOOK ONE

The Japanese Surrender
in South-East Asia

CHAPTER ONE

BURMA

i *The First Parleys in the Sittang Bend**

The day after the Imperial broadcast, Lieutenant Sawayama Yūzō was in the headquarters of Burma Area Army in Moulmein. The Army General Headquarters had fled to Moulmein nearly four months before, when the British came back into Rangoon. The Army commander, General Kimura Hyōtarō, had realized there was no question of his holding any part of Burma other than this south-west corner, Tenasserim, which he had been ordered to build up as a fortress to prevent the British moving into Siam and Northern Malaya. The surrender came before his preparations were put to the test.

Sawayama was a journalist in civilian life, and had worked for the *Asahi Shimbun*. He didn't relish the order he had just received. He was to accompany a staff officer, Lieutenant-Colonel Shōji, to the British lines near the village of Waw as an envoy to negotiate surrender terms. 'You're a newspaper man, Sawayama, aren't you?' Major-General Ishida Jirō, the Army's deputy chief of staff had said. 'Well you're very suitable for the job. It'll make a good story when you get back to Japan.' Hastily borrowing boots, shirt and map case, Sawayama prepared for this unprecedented mission.

Shōji, he discovered, was new to the staff, and had come from the 53rd Division, which had been knocked about very badly in the recent fighting. He really belonged to the 33rd Army staff, which was to stay behind in Burma and organize three divisions (the 18th, 31st,

---

* My source for this episode is my own recollection of the period, and the narrative of one of the Japanese participants, Sawayama Yūzō's 'Hakki wo kakagete' ('Hoisting the white flag'), in *Hiroku Dai Tōa Senshi* (History of the Greater East Asia War), Fuji Shobō, Tokyo, 1953, pp. 367–81.

and 53rd) for its defence, while the main force (the 15th Army, controlling the 15th, 33rd, and 56th Divisions; and the 28th Army controlling the 54th and 55th Divisions) withdrew to Siam and French Indo-China. All these moves were going ahead in great secrecy when the news of the surrender came through, so the headquarters was in chaos. Shōji was trying hard to muster his new-found dignity, though he was red-eyed from lack of sleep. Sawayama found him just a little *too* correct. They were not to go alone. The party was to be five strong. They had an interpreter, a civilian called Saitō who had been managing director of a business concern, the New Asia Trading Company and, like most Japanese civilians in Burma, was conscripted into the army when Rangoon was about to fall. There was a lance-corporal to carry the Japanese flag, and a private who turned out to be the bugler. These last two were lively and quite bucked by the thought of the expedition. The bugler was a little puzzled about his role. 'Mr Sawayama,' he asked the lieutenant, 'what do I play on the bugle?' Sawayama didn't know. No officer from the Military Academy would know. The word *kōfuku* (surrender) did not occur in Japanese Army regulations. 'Go and ask the Colonel,' he answered. Shōji didn't know either, and he moodily ignored the question. So they all set off in a truck, Shōji sitting in front.

As they jogged towards the ferry, Sawayama recalled how it had begun. About half past eleven on the night of 18 August he had been awakened by a soldier. He slept in the wireless room of the intelligence section, and lights were forbidden, as an air-raid precaution. But he didn't even need to make out the soldier who stood in the dark by his pillow, to realize he was excited: he could tell by his breathing. 'Japan has surrendered,' he burst out. 'I mean, there's been a broadcast saying Japan has surrendered. From Australia. The BBC says the same thing.'

He could hear one of the interpreters and a *Nisei* soldier talking in English.* 'Unconditional surrender...except...Imperial...pre...pre...prerogative of Emperor...' Sawayama was wide awake by now. 'No one outside the wireless room is to be told of this. No one.' They woke Major Shōgenji, the head of the intelligence section, and

* *Nisei* are Japanese–Americans of the second generation. Many were caught on holiday in Japan when war broke out, and were conscripted into the Japanese Army. In the USA, hundreds of them served in combat battalions, or as interpreters and translators in the Pacific.

he told Sawayama to go and make a report to headquarters. It was pouring with rain, and Sawayama put on his cape and made his way along the mountain path. He was soaked to the skin in a couple of minutes. Like several Japanese headquarters units, this one had set itself up in a pagoda after the retreat from Rangoon, on the theory that the British, fearing to offend Burmese Buddhist sensibilities, would hesitate to bomb a pagoda. They were disappointed. This particular pagoda had already been the target for two or three bombing raids.

When he got there, a staff officer, Lieutenant-Colonel Takagi, took the report from him and asked him to wait. He was gone about ten minutes. 'I'm sorry you had to come through the rain,' he said. 'You must see your men keep this absolutely secret.' Then, almost casually, 'There will be a truce...however, best say nothing for the time being.' As Sawayama left, Takagi gave him a cake of soap – very scarce at the time, and very precious. The prohibition didn't have much effect. The secret was all over the mountain headquarters the following day. They all knew. They pretended not to, and put on what the Japanese call a *shirankao*, a 'not-know face'. But they knew. They were wondering whether General Kimura would feel compelled to commit suicide in the traditional fashion. The General did not, in the event, read out to his troops the proclamation ending the war. Several men from the intelligence staff heard it in the wireless room on 15 August, and the news spread.

To go north into Tenasserim, you had to cross from Moulmein by ferry to Martaban on the other side of the Salween. The river was in full spate at the end of the monsoon, and Sawayama shuddered as he got into the boat. Even a skilful swimmer wouldn't stand a chance if he fell in at this point. But the crossing was uneventful, and they pushed on to 18th Division headquarters close to the Sittang River. The road, lined with papaya trees, was painfully familiar to Sawayama: he had trodden it four months before, during the tragic retreat from Central Burma. Japanese troops by the roadside called out to them, 'Can we go back to Japan? Will they send us to India? Will they send us to the Siam–Burma Railway?' They had heard rumours of the cruelty meted out to Allied prisoners-of-war. By evening they had reached 18th Division headquarters in the jungle ten miles from the Sittang. They were amazed to see a whole division encamped on a site where no human beings could normally live, in groups twenty to thirty yards apart. They shared the headquarters'

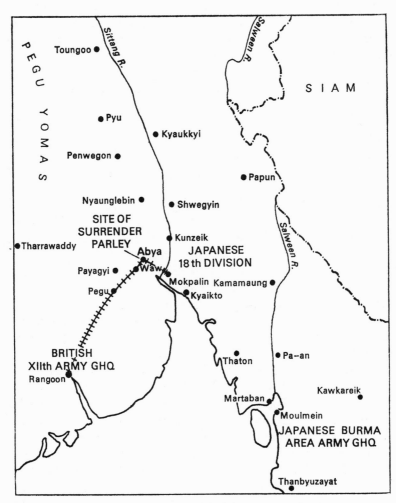

LOWER BURMA

evening meal: soup of processed bean-curd with grass roots and leaves floating in it. Afterwards they went through the parley arrangements by candle-light. A staff officer from the 28th Army would go along with them to discuss with the British what course of action to take with units which refused to believe in the surrender. Some units of 28th Army had been out of touch with headquarters since June.*

The next day they were on the opposite bank of the Sittang. From this point forward they went on foot. The officers left their swords behind in the truck. More than anything else, that act of relinquishment made them aware of their status as envoys suing for peace. After an hour's march, they passed through Waw and came out on the railway track. This was the spot the British had indicated as the rendezvous. They had seen no one the whole time they were marching, not a single Burmese had shown himself. Colonel Shōji brought them to a halt. 'Smarten up your uniforms.' They took off their capes, and the flagbearer unfurled the Rising Sun flag, which was fastened to a young bamboo. The bugler braced himself, and set his bugle at the ready, then paused. 'Colonel, what do I blow?' The same question he'd put the day before. 'Blow what you like!' 'Don't blow the charge though!' added the staff officer from the 28th Army. He seemed to be in a good humour. Nobody laughed.

In front marched the flagbearer and on his left the bugler. Then came Shōji and the officer from the 28th Army. Lastly the interpreter Saitō and Sawayama. 'Forward march!' *Ta Taraaa!* went the bugle and came to an abrupt stop. The group halted. 'Sir, I don't know what to blow!' The bugler sounded as if he was going to burst into tears. 'Well, stop blowing then. You don't need to blow anything at all.' They moved off again, along the railway track.

Then, not very far off, about twenty figures emerged on the track ahead. Three hundred yards away. You couldn't make out their faces through the drizzle, but there seemed to be two at their head, and about a section of men behind, in four ranks. Two hundred yards. One hundred yards. Shōji had given no orders, but the bugler and flagbearer halted. The approaching figures were much clearer now. They wore green shirts, green trousers, and broad-rimmed hats. They were Gurkhas, about the same height as Japanese. An

---

* Sawayama refers to this officer as a 'major from 18th Division'. From recent conversations in Japan, this seems to be a mistake. The officer in question was Lieutenant-Colonel Tsuchiya, a staff officer from 28th Army headquarters.

officer stood with legs apart, in the at-ease position, arms akimbo. 'What's going on?' 'He made some sort of signal,' said the flag-bearer, his voice quivering with nervousness. The officer raised his hand again. It was a sign to come nearer. 'Forward march!' Fifty yards. Thirty yards. Twenty yards. The Japanese were not marching very rhythmically by this time. Ten yards. Then, quite naturally, the march came to a stop. A British officer came one pace forward.

He made a gesture which to Sawayama was characteristic of the white man, index finger raised briefly in the Japanese direction. 'Five paces forward!' The Japanese told themselves they must not flinch, must not avert their gaze. Who was going to speak first?

'Are you General Kimura's envoys?' In a Japanese which was faltering but clear, this phrase came from the British officer standing on the right.

'Yes.' Saitō, the interpreter, hastily came to the front. 'Yes.' Then once again, 'Yes, SIR.'

The tension was dissolved. The Gurkha section broke ranks too, and they scattered to either side of the railway track. Two wagons now appeared. With a gesture, the British officer indicated they were to get into the front wagon. Shōji and the staff officer did so. Sawayama and Saitō took the spare seats. There was room for just five men, and the young lieutenant who had spoken Japanese climbed in with them. The officer who seemed to be in command stood in the wagon behind; they could see him through the celluloid window. It was all rather odd, the Japanese thought. Is this how you treat envoys? They were being excessively cautious. The wagons were pulled by a jeep, the wheels of which had been adapted to run on rails. As the wagons gathered speed, the Japanese saw groups of Gurkhas along the track, with shovels and picks, working on the line. Their faces seemed very strange, as they caught sight of the Japanese, and watched them curiously. Sawayama's experience of the army had been confined to headquarters. It was his first glimpse of the enemy, the British Army.

The young officer smiled and said something. He looked only about twenty-two or twenty-three. Sawayama decided to answer. 'Your Japanese is very good.' 'Well, I can manage a little.' Then, a little self-consciously, 'Did you understand what I said?' Sawayama answered he had understood very well, and there was another smile, of satisfaction this time. They learned that he had been taught Japanese for a year at London University. For one year it was good, there was no doubt about that. He said he knew two thousand Japanese characters, too.

The jeep-train ran for about fifteen minutes and stopped in a small village, with a few houses scattered here and there. This was Abya, where the British brigade had its headquarters. Sawayama had half expected a host of journalists and cameramen to be lying in wait for them, but there was nothing of the kind. 'If I'd been the British,' he thought, 'I'd have mobilized every information unit for miles.' Sawayama's last fear vanished; the whole way from Moulmein he'd anticipated being asked all kinds of hurtful and insulting questions and losing his temper as a result. There were two cameramen, no more, with 16-mm cameras, who took shots of the Japanese as they entered the brigade headquarters. He didn't think they were professionals. They were in uniform, for one thing, and didn't hold their cameras up beside the nose, as professionals would; instead they seemed to hold the camera by their side.

The headquarters was an ordinary Burmese house, and they climbed up to the first floor. Some wooden camp stools were arranged round a rough table. The Japanese sat down along one row of stools, except the bugler and flagbearer, who waited downstairs. Two or three minutes passed, then a tall man came in, lazily, followed by a short, thickset officer, and the young lieutenant who spoke Japanese. The three of them stood in line, motionless, facing the Japanese who stood and then straightened up instinctively. The gaze of the two groups met. The tall man looked fixedly at each one in turn. He was clean-shaven, with a long, oval face, rather sallow in complexion, Sawayama thought, and his eyes gleamed fiercely. They were bloodshot eyes, forbidding, ominous. He sat down calmly, and gestured them to do the same. He was polite; there was nothing domineering about him, no high-handedness.

In a low, slightly hoarse voice, Shōji introduced himself. Then, one by one, the rest of his group. Saitō translated this into English. Saitō sounded a little shriller than usual, but he seemed self-possessed enough. The tall man nodded his head, and said, also in a low voice, that he was Brigadier Smeeton, commanding the 48th Brigade.* He introduced his brigade major. It was the turn of the young English lieutenant to translate. It proved too much for his one year's Japanese. He stumbled at the Japanese for brigadier, became

* So Sawayama remembers it. In fact he was the commander of the 63rd Brigade: both belonged to the 17th Division.

flustered, and began to blush. 'It's in between colonel and major-general,' he said to the Japanese, and his face went red. Far from causing embarrassment, the lieutenant's failure relaxed the atmosphere. Saitō immediately perceived the difficulties of his opposite number. Brigadier Smeeton said he wished to discuss twenty items of agreement which had already been passed over to the Japanese Army. Had they come prepared to do this? The voice cracked out, businesslike, without any striking of attitudes. Ignoring his own interpreter, he attracted Saitō's attention with a glance. Saitō had some fellow-feeling for the young lieutenant's predicament, and hesitated. Also, though Saitō's English seemed to be understood, the brigadier had a fearful accent. In the end Saitō interpreted, and when he couldn't follow, the young lieutenant came to his aid, and corrected his English. The mood grew easier. Shōji settled himself more deeply into the camp stool, and furtively loosened his belt one notch.

The negotiations went smoothly, breaking every now and then for discussions about the meaning of a word, but Saitō became more and more accustomed to the brigadier's speech. The gist of it was that the Japanese Army was to withdraw east of the Sittang, and the British would pull back west of Waw. Both sides agreed to this. But there was a difficulty. Sick and wounded Japanese from the 28th Army were still making their way south after their last defeat. Would they be allowed to reach Japanese rear areas, using the Sittang River? Maps were produced, unit dispositions shown, corrections made on both sides. Within an hour most of the items had been agreed upon. Shōji turned to Sawayama with a smile, and Sawayama felt light-hearted too. Then he remembered how tired he was. His shirt and tunic were soaked, but the heat of the room was making him drowsy. But it would hardly do to fall asleep at this point. He glanced round the room and noticed how quiet it was outside. Then he began to observe the brigadier.

What had at first seemed a sallow complexion was a face tanned brown by the sun. The face was masculine, soldierly, very much out of the common run. Now and then it would twitch nervously, the cheek would show a tic, and the brigadier would tap the table with his pencil tip and spin it round and round with his fingers. He had an odd symbol on his shirt. As he turned to one side for a moment, the Japanese noticed that he wore a big badge with a black cat on his left shoulder. Ah, they had heard of that. That was the famous

'Black Cat' Division, the 17th Division. He and his brigade major began to talk to each other rapidly, the brigadier's face beginning to tic uninterruptedly. Then they came to a stop, and there was dead silence.

This was the difficulty foreseen earlier about the 28th Army. The brigadier wanted it to interrupt its withdrawal and concentrate in a camp the British had ready. But the Burma Area Army had planned to withdraw the 28th Army south towards Moulmein, and diminish further loss of life by providing medical supplies and food. So far Smeeton had been very understanding. Now he became stubborn.

Saitō began to sweat as Shōji enumerated reason after reason why the 28th Army should concentrate under the wing of the Burma Area Army. Sawayama's drowsiness fled. He strained his ears so that he wouldn't miss a single word. The 28th Army, he knew, were shadows of men; they had reached the very limits of exhaustion. They were an army in rags, starving. Surely the British knew this? The war was over now. Was it not the law of humanity to save even one life if that were possible? 'Wait a moment.' Smeeton gave a meaningful glance at his brigade major and the lieutenant and walked out of the room ahead of them. Only the Japanese were left. Nobody spoke. If this particular item fell through, their day's business would not have been a success. Why were the British so obstinately insisting on concentrating the 28th Army in their own area?

They heard footsteps climbing the stairs. Just as they thought Smeeton was about to reappear, a huge aluminium tea-pot came into view, then a brown arm followed it, and the face of a Gurkha soldier. Then came another, this one carrying four big enamel mugs. Hesitant and sheepish, the two Gurkhas arranged the mugs at the end of the table, indicated 'drink' with gestures, then escaped downstairs. A delicious aroma filled the air. It was coffee. Saitō drank his down in one gulp – the mugs held about half a pint. Shōji and the staff officer drank half of theirs, then set them down on the table. Sawayama could see how it had been made. They'd put raw coffee in the pot, with milk, and brought it to the boil. There were grounds on the bottom of his mug, he crushed them with his teeth, and drank. Delicious. The Gurkha soldier came back with a fresh pot, smiling with approval at the Japanese when he felt the empty one. The Japanese could feel the coffee gurgling in their stomachs, and Sawayama pointed to his water-bottle. Saitō grinned and nodded.

Sawayama filled his bottle with the steaming coffee and reached out for Saitō's. Both Shōji and the staff officer stared disapprovingly.

Smeeton returned, sat down again and made a proposition which startled the Japanese. He suggested they went to Rangoon. General Numata Takezō, the Chief of Staff of the Southern Area Army, was due to arrive there from Saigon to discuss negotiations with the British. The 28th Army's problems would no doubt be part of their talks. It was *ultra vires*, as far as he was concerned, to change anything. But they could get a decision in Rangoon. 'I understand your point of view,' he said. 'On the other hand, I cannot ignore my own orders and give in to you just as I please.' Shōji was impressed and thanked him. But the 28th Army's problems might not be grasped by Numata, and the Japanese knew that going to Rangoon would be useless. So Shōji politely refused. They had had orders to go as far as Abya. That was all. Today's main objective had been to organize a local ceasefire. He pointed out to Smeeton that the 28th Army was not fighting, it was merely on the move. Finally the brigadier let them go, leaving this one item unsettled. He praised the courage of the 28th Army's commander, Lieutenant-General Sakurai Shōzō, and smiled. 'I was really surprised at General Sakurai: what a reckless thing to do!'* He also enquired if Sakurai were suffering from malaria.

The staff officer from the 28th Army brought up the question of units which refused to surrender. It appeared a British officer had been captured while trying to make contact with the Japanese, Smeeton said (a reference to Major Turrell of Force 136). His brigade major added that it was desirable to make contact with the unit which held him as soon as possible. The Japanese delegation had heard a rumour that units led by the former Japanese Olympic swimming champion, Kitamura Kusuo, were still holding out in the mountains. Perhaps he had been taken by one of these? The matter would be investigated. The discussion came to an end. It had taken three hours in all. They had put up a good show, Sawayama thought. Shōji and Saitō had done very well. They stood up and saluted. The same wagon they had come in took them back to Waw.

On the way, Sawayama turned to the other two. 'Didn't you get any coffee?' They smiled and tapped their bellies. 'We're full.'

---

* Smeeton was alluding to the last battle in Burma, in which Sakurai had tried to force his way through a British encirclement and lost two thirds of his men doing so. Cf. Louis Allen, *Sittang. The Last Battle*, Macdonald, 1973.

'When did you get it?' 'About twenty minutes after we got to that village.' Then Sawayama understood. Shōji had thought the coffee had been sent in on the brigadier's orders, but in fact the Gurkhas had given the bugler and the flagbearer a drink first, and when they saw how welcome it was had ventured upstairs. Sawayama remembered the kindness as much as the delicious aroma. 'They asked us for our flag,' one of the men said, 'but we couldn't give them our national flag, could we?' 'That's right isn't it, Mr Sawayama?' Before Sawayama had time to say anything Colonel Shōji answered, 'You could have given it to them.' Sawayama turned to look at Saitō. Ideas were already beginning to change.

ii *Ba Maw, Aung San, and Burmese Independence*

The Burmese themselves took no part in all these negotiations. It was their country which had been fought over, their resources which had been destroyed, their people whose lives had been uprooted. Yet they figure in the war narratives as marginal to the main march of armies, as suppliers of guerrilla fighters or labour, as people to be tortured or beaten if they refused information, as villagers whose pathetic wooden huts were ruthlessly burned to the ground if they recouped their losses by raiding the corpses of dead soldiers. Both Japanese and British had devised civil affairs administrations to look after the Burmese population once their armies had conquered and passed on. But under both these administrations the Burmese, like the rest of the peoples of South-East Asia, were developing their own institutions for self-government and, even more important, the determination to be free from outside rule, whether by the East or the West.

The British had occupied Lower Burma and taken Rangoon in 1824. They had completed their conquest by taking Mandalay in 1885 and annexing Upper Burma the following year, though guerrilla resistance lingered on until 1891. It was ruled by the Government of India until the Government of Burma Act (1935) came into force on 1 April 1937, bringing Burma directly under the British Parliament. Its British governor was responsible for defence, finance, foreign affairs, and the excluded areas (i.e. the Shan States, Karenni, the Tribal Areas). A cabinet of ten under a prime minister was responsible to the legislature, consisting of a half-elected, half-nominated

Senate, and a House of Representatives which comprised ninety-two members from territorial constituencies and forty members elected by various community interests. About one third of the male population and one tenth of the female was enfranchised. Maurice Collis cynically describes the role of the British business community in Burma which, in his view, explained the British political presence: 'Their aim... was to buy cheap in Asia and sell dear in Europe... Their prejudices were very marked, their opinions jejune, but they felt themselves to be the most patriotic of men, for their lives were devoted, not like the Indian Civilians, to giving the Burmese a sound administration... but to conducting to London the stream of profits, on which the very existence of England depended.'[1] Collis is speaking of the period before the First World War, but a similar view is implied in a comment made by an American oil-driller to the Burmese politician, Magwe U Pu, during the thirties: 'You will get your independence... when your country ceases to produce a single drop of earth-oil and when there is not a single teak in your forests, and when your paddy fields have become barren. These British have come out to Burma just to make money.'[2] Despairing of shaking off the British grip by constitutional methods, some Burmese leaders began to turn to Japan.

Burma's first Premier under the new 1937 régime was Dr Ba Maw, a European-educated lawyer, 'a man of immense vanity (in the words of one British writer) who looked and behaved like a film star'.[3] Ba Maw had come into prominence as the defence lawyer for Saya San, a leader of the 1930 rebellion against British rule. His party was known as the *Sinyetha* (Proletarian Party) and was based on a group of Buddhist associations, the Young Men's Buddhist Associations, consciously modelled on the YMCA. Another Western model served for the party which rivalled the *Sinyetha* in strength and attraction, the *Dobama Asiayone* (We Burmese), the name of which was directly derived from the name 'Sinn Fein'. The writings of the Sinn Fein leaders were as eagerly studied in the Burmese independence movement as those of Lenin and Sun Yat Sen. The *Dobama Asiayone* appealed chiefly to Burmese youth and students. There had been a student strike at the University of Rangoon in 1936 and a number of young Burmese decided the time had come to apply to themselves the title *Thakin* (Master, sahib) hitherto reserved for Europeans. It was the Thakins who started the initial collaboration with the Japanese. They provided the officer class for the Burma

Independence Army of 1942. As the Anti-Fascist People's Freedom League they ruled Burma after the British finally withdrew in 1947. They still rule Burma, and they provide its main opposition: General Ne Win is an old Thakin, and so is his rival, U Nu, the former Premier now in exile who leads the opposition to him from Siam.*

There was a third party, the *Myochit* (Patriotic Party), led by the ambitious U Saw, a man willing to employ the most atrocious violence to achieve his ends, as the post-war assassination of Aung San and most of his cabinet shows. All these parties, at one time or another, had been sounded out by the Japanese. Ba Maw's family doctor, for instance, was a Japanese who was in touch with the Japanese consul in Rangoon, and also with Japanese naval intelligence.† But it was with the problem of cutting the Burma Road supplying Chiang Kai-shek and the creation of the *Minami Kikan* (Organization South) to do it, that Burmese–Japanese collaboration really began. The *Minami Kikan* was the creation of a Japanese staff colonel, Suzuki Keiji, whose mission was to contact revolutionary groups in Burma and use them to harass traffic moving along the Burma Road into China. Together with the Indo-China route (Haiphong to Yunnan) which was to be otherwise dealt with, the Burma Road was Chiang Kai-shek's main channel of supply from friendly nations for his resistance to the Japanese. If he could not disrupt the traffic, Suzuki was at any rate to keep it under close surveillance. He had already started a Japan–Burma Society in Tokyo to discover sympathizers, and came to Burma in 1940 in the guise of a journalist from the *Yomiuri Shimbun* (a cover which can have fooled no one). Two young Thakins trying to dodge the British police were helped to escape from Rangoon. Later, when they had gone as far as Amoy on the coast of southern China, they were contacted by Japanese emissaries who suggested they make their way to Japan instead of China. Under Suzuki's aegis, these two, Aung San and Bo Yan Aung, collected together a group of Thakins, thirty young Burmese who received Japanese military training on Hainan Island. When the Japanese invaded Burma in 1941, these Thakins accompanied the first columns as guides and interpreters along

* Cf. Bernard Fergusson (Lord Ballantrae), '*Unfinished tragedy of a divided Burma*'. *The Times*, Wed. 2 June 1971, p. 2.

† The Japanese Navy had long considered Burma to be in its province, not the Army's, and one of its agents, Kokubu Shōzō, had lived in Rangoon for many years and made contacts among the Thakins. He was the author of a number of articles on Burma.[4]

rarely used tracks between Siam and Burma. They also acted as a recruiting nucleus for the Burma Independence Army, in the wake of the victorious Japanese.

Unfortunately, the Burma Independence Army was a racialist organization and oppressed the minorities in Burma who were not Burmese, particularly the Karens, whose undying enmity they earned by massacres of Karen communities in the Irrawaddy delta.* The Japanese had to stop the depredations of the Burma Independence Army, and they did so. They reconstituted it as the Burma Defence Army under Aung San, who was made a major-general. The Japanese trained its officers and used the force as an auxiliary in asserting their control over Burma. It is the creation and running of this army that a Japanese historian regards as Japan's incontrovertible contribution to Burma's independence in the post-war world.[6] Its role was, of course, purely political. After the initial raids and skirmishes of 1942, the Burma Independence Army had no external military function at all, and Ba Maw's request that Burmese troops be employed in the later campaigns against the British was simply not taken seriously by the Japanese commander.[7]

After much unwillingness on the part of the Japanese Southern Area Army, Burma achieved independence, under a very firmly held Japanese umbrella, in August 1943. Independence had in fact been proclaimed in the township of Tavoy early in 1942, by members of the Burma Independence Army, with the active cooperation of Suzuki. But Suzuki's quasi-autonomous operations were distrusted by the Japanese 15th Army headquarters, and in the summer of 1942 he was shipped back to Tokyo. This early claim to independence was passed over. The source of opposition to it was not so much General Iida Shōjirō, Commander-in-Chief of the 15th Army, who was very friendly with Ba Maw, as the staff of Terauchi's Southern Area Army, in particular Colonel Ishii Akio, senior staff officer in the General Affairs section. Ishii was all for going warily, since Japanese experience of the Wang Ching-wei Government had shown that

---

* Not only the Thakins, but Ba Maw's government also was racially based. Its slogan was 'Ta-thway, ta-than, ta-meint' 'One blood, one voice, one command' – a sinisterly familiar ring); and Ba Maw, as Naingandaw Adipadi (Head of State) proclaimed to the East Asia Conference in 1943, 'I seem to hear the voice of Asia gathering her children together. It is the voice of our Asiatic blood. This is not the time to think with our minds, this is the time to think with our blood, and it is this thinking with the blood which has brought me all the way from Burma to Japan.'[5]

where the Japanese Army encouraged nationalism on the Asian mainland it proved difficult to control. According to Ishii, Wang's demands on the Japanese, after he had left Chiang Kai-shek's Kuomintang Government in 1940, and set up a collaborationist government in Nanking under the Japanese wing, showed he was no less determined than Chiang himself to preserve the prerogatives of China; there were some Japanese who considered he was Chiang's agent.[8] Besides, the Japanese Army in Burma was still in the midst of complex operations, and any independent government would have to yield to their military requirements. In so far as the Japanese were seen to be imposing these, they would earn the hostility of the population. Ishii's steady and zealous lobbying, not only of Southern Army staff, but also of General Iida and his staff, and the Chief of the General Staff, General Sugiyama, in March 1942, effectively postponed Burmese independence for more than a year.

Less than two years of Japanese-style independence was enough to make Aung San and the Burma Defence Army decide they had better look elsewhere. Once it became clear that the British were coming back in force, and that the Japanese were powerless to prevent them, Aung San changed sides. That he was already dissatisfied with the Japanese in 1943 had been conveyed to the British in India by Major Hugh Seagrim, who was left behind in the Karenni when the British retreated and organized a guerrilla movement there. One of Seagrim's agents, a Karen named San Po Thin, actually dined with Aung San and Bo Ne Win in Rangoon in 1943, and learned from their own lips that they were thinking of organizing an anti-Japanese movement in Burma.[9] In November of the following year, a captured member of the Burma National Army (a later metamorphosis of the Burma Defence Army) was dropped by parachute near Pegu. Through him and other agents the British kept in touch with the dissident Burmese, and news came early in 1945 that on 16 March Aung San intended to commence hostilities against the Japanese.[10] They were going to assemble in Rangoon, ostensibly in preparation for departure to the Irrawaddy front on behalf of the Japanese. They were then simply going to march out of the city and defect to the British.

In the last week of March 1945 Aung San held a press conference in Rangoon. Usually at these conferences, the Burmese served coffee with milk to their Japanese guests, but this time there was nothing, and Aung San appeared not in smart military uniform but in unwashed khaki shirt and a *longyi* (skirt) of coarse material. Some of the correspondents admired this rough and ready appearance as being symbolic of a departure for the front. Others were merely puzzled.[11]

The Burmese Army paraded, then marched out of Rangoon. When it became evident that they were not joining the Japanese forces, the Japanese liaison officer with Aung San, Captain Takahashi, who had also become a close personal friend, left Rangoon on 23 March and went after him. There was no question of bringing him back by force. Takahashi hoped to persuade him to change his mind. He caught up with Aung San in Shwedaung, south of Prome, but it was too late. The Burma National Army came out in open rebellion against the Japanese on 27 March. 'What do you intend to do now?' Takahashi asked Aung San. 'It would have meant the destruction of Burma to go on working with the Japanese,' the young general replied. 'What kind of deal have you made with the British?' Takahashi wanted to know. 'Our deal is total independence for Burma,' was the answer. 'No doubt that is out of the question now. In which case we shall be a self-governing dominion, and we are at present negotiating along those lines. If the British won't grant us one or the other, then we will fight them too. It's important for us to adopt an anti-Japanese posture to show the British we mean business. So we have rebelled against you.'[12]

Aung San still had to make personal contact with the British. It had been arranged through the agents of Force 136 that he should, with Mountbatten's full consent, be offered safe conduct to and from British headquarters, but he hesitated to take advantage of this until 15 May, when he crossed the Irrawaddy at Allanmyo. He turned up at General Slim's headquarters the next day, dressed in the full regalia of a Japanese major-general, complete with sword. There were no recriminations, but Slim told him he could defeat the Japanese without Aung San's help, that there was only one legitimate Burmese government – even though Ba Maw's had been recognized by the Axis powers, and the Vatican – and that was the British Government, acting through the Supreme Allied Commander, South-East Asia. Slim intended to recognize no provisional government; if Aung San joined him it would be as a subordinate commander accepting Slim's orders. Aung San was naturally disappointed at this forthright rejection of all his pretensions, and did not disguise the fact. He demanded to be treated as an Allied commander.

Slim admired him for not being overawed, but pointed out that there were people in British headquarters who held that there was a well substantiated charge of civil murder outstanding against him, so that he was taking a chance in coming to see Slim at all on a purely verbal promise, at second-hand. Aung San answered that it had never occurred to him to doubt the word of a British officer, which put Slim on his side at once. Slim was even more impressed by his frankness when, to Slim's assertion, 'Go on, Aung San, you only come to us because you see we are winning!' Aung San replied, 'It wouldn't be much good coming to you if you weren't, would it?' Slim judged him to be ambitious, but a genuine patriot, and a well-balanced realist. 'The greatest impression he made on me was one of honesty,' he writes. 'He was not free with glib assurances and he hesitated to commit himself, but I had the idea that if he agreed to do something he would keep his word. I could do business with Aung San.'[13]

While Aung San was taking the Burma National Army over to the British, Ba Maw clung to the Japanese to the bitter end, and fled with them to Moulmein just before the British re-entered Rangoon, at the end of April 1945. It was a hair-raising expedition for Ba Maw. His eldest daughter was about to give birth to a child, and the shocks and strains of the journey began to tell on him. Ba Maw had been the first ruler of his own independent country; now he and his family were reduced to living like hunted animals. On the night of 28 April his daughter Tinsa gave birth to her baby. They were driving through the night towards Kyaikto when she felt her first labour pains, and they reached the town just in time for her delivery.[14] The family settled in a house in Mudon, where the British caught up with him. Three days before the Japanese surrender, a British plane circled over the house in leisurely fashion, then flew away. The next afternoon Ba Maw was talking with U Nu in his front room when they heard the sound of a number of aircraft approaching. As they jumped for shelter into a shallow ditch, one of the planes peeled off and dived low over the house, raking it with bullets. Another plane came from another side and did the same thing. They came again and again, until the house walls were torn to pieces and the roof was shattered. After an interval, they returned, and repeated the performance. 'They were making absolutely certain,' writes Ba Maw 'that no one in the house or anywhere near it would remain alive.'[15]

On 14 August the Japanese ambassador, Ishii, called on Ba Maw and told him the war was lost. Two days later Ba Maw left Burma by the Siam–Burma railway. He took two days to reach the Siamese capital, where the Thais impressed him by their carefree unconcern with the political storms which were rocking South-East Asia. He then made for Saigon, where a huge demonstration was in progress, with armed men among the marchers – less emotional than the Burmese, he thought, and more disciplined. The Vietnamese store of will power and endurance looked likely to last. He left his family behind in the peace of a plantation in Cambodia, and on 22 August flew to Taiwan, where his great friend the Indian leader Subhas Chandra Bose had met his death a few days before. He had to be in Japan before 25 August, which was the date by which all Japanese flights had to stop. But he was not to make the journey without danger:

> We flew across a perfectly peaceful sea (*he writes*) and were soon making our way through great masses of white foam like clouds that seemed to fill the whole dazzling sky. I was dead tired and was on the point of falling asleep when I noticed vaguely a large shadow pass over our planes. A few moments later our plane dropped and rolled and a stream of fiery objects streaked past just over it. Someone then shouted out that they were tracers fired at us. By now I was wide awake, but I remained absolutely frozen and convinced that the end had come. All my senses had gone cold and numb. Our plane kept losing height and limping till it got very close to the sea, but when the other plane flew away and the danger was over, it slowly rose again and continued its flight as if nothing had happened.[16]

That night in Taiwan, Ba Maw felt at breaking point. He had left his country, possibly for ever; his family was in Cambodia, and he might never see them again; and his co-fighter for independence from the British, Subhas Chandra Bose, was dead. Small wonder that during the night, after an enjoyable evening, but inwardly convinced that there was nothing left to live for, Ba Maw had a vision of his mother pointing to half past twelve on a large luminous clock. He was sure he was to die the following day at half past twelve.

To avoid American planes which were closing in on Japan, his aircraft the next day hugged the coast of China as it moved north, until it reached Korea. It then swung round towards Japan from the north. Flying across water he fell asleep, and was awakened by his

Japanese companion, Kitazawa, crying out that they were over Japan, safe. He looked at his watch, and saw it was half past twelve. Late that evening Ba Maw landed at a military airfield near Tokyo. He was horrified by the journey into the city. It was a charred and burnt-out waste, with big blocks of buildings standing in isolation here and there, as if to emphasize the desolation of the rest. But the Japanese had not forgotten their courtesies. The Foreign Ministry, on the instructions of Shigemitsu, took charge of him and lodged him in a Buddhist temple in the village of Ishiuchi. The young officers who escorted him there were pleased because he was the only important foreign fugitive not yet in American hands; they meant to keep him that way. From his refuge – with some contempt, and later with deeper understanding – he watched the Japanese conform utterly to the requirements of their conquerors. Then he began to feel, not free and in hiding, but buried. His escorts were sure that if he gave himself up to the Americans he was certain, in the mood of that time, to be executed; but he talked with a Foreign Ministry official and they agreed that he should give himself up to the British. There was a Labour Government in Britain,* he reflected, and his friends were influential in the new régime in Burma. His fate might not be so extreme, after all. One evening he left the temple with a Japanese companion and went to Tokyo by train. The next day he surrendered to Colonel Figgess.†[17] Figgess treated him with great courtesy, but it was inevitable that sooner or later Ba Maw would see the inside of an Allied prison. He was lodged in Sugamo just before the end of 1945. He found the American-run prison clean, with a good library, but very strict rules. His gaolers, he thought, were arrogant, and made him do menial tasks, to which he objected: as Supreme Commander of the Burmese Army, he complained, he was exempt from such duty by the Geneva Convention. They promptly placed him in solitary confinement. Figgess had him released from Sugamo in July 1946. They went to the British Embassy, where the ambassador read out an order from the British Government pardoning Ba Maw for all the offences he had committed by collaborating with the Japanese. On 1 August 1946 he was back in Rangoon, with the family he had thought he would never see again.

* Since 26 July 1945.

† He spells the name Figesse, but it is presumably John Figgess, who was military adviser at the British Embassy in Tokyo at the time.

In the same town of Shwedaung, where he had had his discussion with Takahashi, Aung San sat down to write to Ba Maw.

My dear Adipadigyi (*the name meant 'Leader'*), I am sorry that I was unable to meet you before I came out here as I had promised you. Conditions were such that I had to do things in a hurry. Sometimes I am afraid you might misunderstand me. I shall be coming back to Rangoon and, if conditions do not worsen so unexpectedly, I hope to meet you again. Meantime I wish to send you some report.

As I said in my speech, I would do my best to save the situation. But as you would also understand, these are dark days for us. The Japanese troops are withdrawing to all intents and purposes, and I shall not be surprised if, before monsoon, the war in Burma is over. Anyway I think I don't blame the Japanese too, for from the strategical point of view, if you might understand, this is the only wise and sound course for them to do. Nevertheless, there is still hope for us, I suppose. Of course, we shall have to be prepared to struggle alone for some time. But I have every confidence that our cause will win ultimately. War or no war, peace or no peace, the struggle for our national independence must go on till it ends in victory. And I will do my best. You might understand me now perhaps. But believe me, after some time you will see whether I mean what I say. At present I have to fix up many things because there are so many angles to be straightened. Meantime, I wish you to be prepared for the worst and do whatever possible in your line.

Yours,

Aung San[18]

There was a sentence in the letter which he did not finish. He wrote 'Please tell the Japanese that...' and then crossed it out. Aung San's debt to the Japanese, whom he had abandoned in the hour of their defeat, was very great, and he knew it. He did not want to break his links with them, and they did not disdain to renew theirs with him when Burma had returned to peace. All Burma's political leaders were active again by the end of 1946, when the British Prime Minister, Attlee, invited Aung San to London for talks on Burma's future. In January 1947 Attlee and Aung San signed an agreement which, as interpreted by Aung San, promised Burma 'full independence within one year'. The new government would be the executive council which ruled Burma under a new Governor, Sir Hubert Rance. Of its nine members, six belonged to Aung San's Anti-Fascist People's Freedom League (AFPFL), so it was clear who would wield supreme power in Burma once independence was complete. His meetings with Attlee and other Labour ministers mellowed Aung San and he returned from London far less anti-British than he had been, to face the factious U Saw, the opposition of the Communists and the hostility of the hill peoples. The Communists were in a state of armed rebellion in Central Burma by this time. The Karens felt they had been betrayed by the British, from whom they had expected support for an autonomous Karen state, since they had been staunchly pro-British even in the worst days of the Japanese occupation. The Frontier Areas Committee, which decided the fate of the hill peoples of Burma had, they said, handed them over to the tender mercies of the Burmese.*

Perhaps the AFPFL, under Aung San, might have brought peace as well as independence to Burma. Aung San might have become one of Asia's greatest leaders. We shall never know. On the morning of 19 July 1947 four young toughs in the pay of U Saw, armed with tommy guns, broke into a cabinet meeting and savagely massacred all save three of the ministers present. Aung San was among the dead. The speaker of the Constituent Assembly, Thakin Nu (U Nu), was persuaded to take Aung San's place, and a constitution creating a federal union was approved in September 1947. Burma did not stay inside the British Commonwealth. The Independent Union of Burma at last came into being on 4 January 1948 and was plunged almost at once into the horrors of civil war, with army malcontents, two varieties of Communists, and Karen dissidents all contending for power.

The terror and violence were partly an inheritance of the Japanese period. But the Japanese did not see it that way. They were proud, for one thing, that the Thakins still esteemed them highly. Lieutenant-General Sawamoto Rikichi, who had been the Chief Military Adviser

---

* Burma's final independence from Great Britain became law on 4 January 1948. As part of the discussions leading to independence, negotiations were held with representatives of various border peoples, Shans, Kachins, and Chins at Panglong in the Southern Shan States in February 1947, to which the Karens sent observers. A Frontier Areas Committee enquired into the problems of these minorities in March and April 1947 and decided on the establishment of 'states' for them, within the Union of Burma. This did not, however, give them the independence of the Burmese majority which they sought, because the states had no separate legislatures, and decision-making was still centralized in Rangoon. Cf. Richard Allen, *A Short Introduction to the History and Politics of Southeast Asia*, Oxford UP, New York, 1970, p. 106; and Hugh Tinker, *The Union of Burma*, Oxford UP, 1957, p. 24.

to the Burma National Army, encountered Bo Let Ya, by this time a Brigadier in the Burmese forces under the British, in February 1946. Sawamoto had been imprisoned near Thaton, and was moved later to Ahlone Camp in Rangoon. Going from the camp to British headquarters one day, he came face to face with Bo Let Ya (also known as Thakin Hla Pe), who had been the Burma National Army Chief of Staff until 1945, and was later Deputy Prime Minister of Burma. 'How is Mr Kitajima?' (it was the pseudonym used by Captain Takahashi) asked Bo Let Ya. Takahashi had been taken to India, and repatriated to Japan from there. Bo Let Ya said how glad he was to hear this: Aung San had been anxious over Takahashi's fate, and would be relieved to know he had come to no harm. And when Suzuki Keiji, a major-general by this time, was sent for from Japan and lodged in Rangoon Gaol, Aung San sent Bo Zeya, another of the 'Thirty Comrades' (the Thakins of Hainan Island), to visit him. General Sawamoto was moved to Kokine Camp from Ahlone, and one night in February 1947 a Burmese came over the stockade secretly and reported to him. 'Aung San has sent me to enquire what the Burmese Army can do for Japan,' he said. Sawamoto was touched by Aung San's consideration and told the messenger there were three things. First, to do what he could to see those Japanese still in Burma were sent back to Japan as soon as possible. Second, to free the war crimes suspects held in prison in Rangoon. And third, to make it known abroad that war crimes trials held unilaterally by the victors were unreasonable. The messenger came again five nights later, 'Aung San sympathizes with you,' he said, 'and has already begun to do something about your first two points. But he said that it was not possible to do anything about the third, in the state Burma now finds herself.' The Japanese generals who heard this news were overjoyed. They had not been forgotten. Even Aung San's death did not put a stop to his work for them. They are convinced that it was the Burmese Army's pressure on the British which caused the last Japanese detained in Burma, and the last work parties, to be released and sent home on the *Pagoda Maru*, on 3 August 1947, under Sawamoto's command.[19]

Of all the territories occupied by Japan, one Japanese scholar believes, Burma was the most active politically, and the socialism of the Thakins made its influence revolutionary. They may have been young, opportunistic and weak in political formation, but they were very talented politicians and succeeded in giving an appearance of surface cooperation while extending their organization underground.

Since the Japanese ruled indirectly, the Burmese acquired administrative experience and self-confidence which were invaluable when they had to face the British again. They learned what it was like, even on a small scale, to control the means of physical compulsion through their own armed forces. The original nucleus of the Burma Defence Army under Japanese operational command grew to ten thousand men under arms, and this was a real factor in the background of negotiations with the British after the end of the war. If the various sectors of government are scrutinized for the war period – the protection of life and property, effective policies on commodities, labour, prices, communications, and so on – many of them were undoubted failures. But against this must be set the creation of a body of men able to assume responsibility for central government and the armed forces, mature and experienced enough to take over after the Japanese withdrew.[20]

Perhaps the last word should be Ba Maw's summary:

The case of Japan is indeed tragic. Looking at it historically, no nation has done so much to liberate Asia from white domination, yet no nation has been so misunderstood by the very people whom it had helped either to liberate or to set an example to in many things. Japan was betrayed by her militarists and their racial fantasies. Had her Asian instincts been true, had she only been faithful to the concept of Asia for the Asians that she herself had proclaimed at the beginning of the war, Japan's fate would have been very different. No military defeat could then have robbed her of the trust and gratitude of half of Asia or even more ... Even now, as things actually are, nothing can ever obliterate the role Japan has played in bringing liberation to countless colonial peoples.[21]

CHAPTER TWO

THAILAND (SIAM)

i *Force 136 and the Free Siam Movement*

To make contact with those elements in Siam* thought to be still friendly to the Allies, the British made use of Force 136. This was the name given to the Far Eastern branch of Special Operations Executive, an organization commanded by General Colin Gubbins, the purpose of which was to foster resistance movements in territory occupied by the enemy. Force 136 put out feelers to the Burmese leaders when it became known they were dissatisfied with the reality of the independence which the Japanese had conceded. They also infiltrated men into occupied Malaya. To operate in Siam, a Siam Country Section was formed, staffed by officers who had had wide experience of Siam in peacetime – diplomats, lawyers, businessmen – who spoke Siamese well, and had connections with Siamese ministers.

Two men in Siam held the destiny of their country in their hands. One was the Prime Minister and Commander-in-Chief of the armed forces, Field-Marshal Pibul Songgram, the other his rival, the Finance Minister Nai Pridi Bhanomyong. Siam had been ruled by a council of regency since 1932 when the absolute monarchy was overthrown by a coup d'état led by these two men, one of whom, Pibul, gradually assumed the role of military dictator and brought his country into collaboration with Japan. Tempted by the

---

* On 24 June 1939 the name of the country was changed from Siam to Thailand. The Siamese refer to themselves as '*Thai*' ('free'), and the native name is *Muang Thai* (Land of the Free).[1] The British did not accept the new usage, which was linked, in their view, with Siam's military nationalism and collaboration with Japan. In deference to the victors in South-East Asia the name briefly reverted to 'Siam' on 8 September 1945. 'Thailand' is now the correct usage.

possibility of obtaining *terra irredenta* in French Indo-China, he went
to war with the French in 1941. After a brief and ignominious
campaign – the French land forces were defeated, but they sank a
Siamese warship – both sides accepted Japan's offer of mediation,
which resulted in Siam acquiring what she considered her lost
provinces from Cambodia. The mediation enabled Japan to assume
a dominant position in both countries, and when she invaded
Malaya in December 1941 her forces were based on French Indo-
China and used Siam as a transit and landing point. Siamese coastal
defence forces put up a token resistance for a few hours, and then
surrendered. A cabinet meeting had been called in Bangkok on
7 December 1941 to discuss the crisis. Japan had demanded free
passage across Siamese territory for her troops. By a piece of
calculated discretion, Pibul was absent, and the meeting proved
inconclusive. When he returned he ordered local resistance to the
Japanese to cease, and a fortnight later signed a military alliance
with them.* On 25 January Siam declared war on Britain and the
USA.

Certain Japanese had been in strategic positions in Siamese towns
before the soldiers moved in. In Paknampo it was rumoured that
the headquarters of the Japanese troops were located in an earthen-
ware shop run by a Korean fifth columnist, as a blind, for a year
before the invasion. The main headquarters of the Siamese Army was
in Lopburi and it was not long before the Japanese took over its
buildings. In Bangkok itself they occupied the Chinese Chamber of
Commerce, the main clubs of the Siamese and the foreign business
colony, and the National Stadium. They turned part of Chulalong-
korn University into a barracks, and took over the wharves and
offices of British companies as well as the houses of their employees.
Airfields and railways were commandeered.[3]

Economic pressure followed soon after. A goodwill mission
visited Tokyo under one of Pibul's colleagues from the coup d'état

---

* The British had known this was likely, and Churchill sent a last minute
appeal to Pibul to stand by his proclaimed policy of resistance to aggression
from any quarter. Sir Andrew Gilchrist, a member of the Siam Country Section,
on whose book *Bangkok Top Secret* much of my account is based, writes of this
time, '… everyone knew the British were not the party likely to invade Siam.'[2]
But in fact British military plans for Malaya did include 'Operation Matador', a
pre-emptive strike against points in southern Siam to forestall the Japanese.
It was never carried out, but the British Cabinet were aware of the possibility
of such a move.

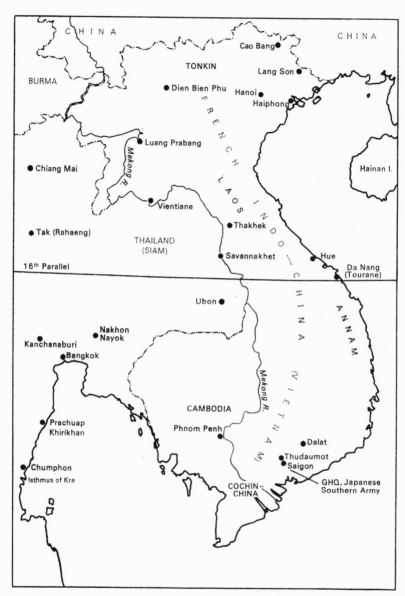

FRENCH INDO-CHINA (VIETNAM)

days, General Phya Bakol. An economic mission left for Tokyo in April 1942, to arrange the sale of rice, rubber, and tin in exchange for goods from Japan which were no longer available from Britain and America. A yen-baht parity agreement was signed on 22 April 1942, though this was hardly of benefit to Siam, as the baht was a more valuable currency on the black market. A return mission under the former Japanese Foreign Minister and Premier, Hirota Kōki, came to Bangkok in July 1942. Japan had in fact little surplus for export to Siam, and the Japanese troops battened like leeches on to Siam's resources, printing Siamese currency themselves when they needed it. On the other hand, Japan helped Siam increase her territory. Besides the territory from French Indo-China, four states were taken from Malaya (Perlis, Kedah, Kelantan, and Trengganu). Their transfer to Siam was made public on 5 July, two days after a meeting between Tōjō and Pibul in Bangkok. Two of the Shan States, Kengtung and Mongpan, were sliced from Burma. The effect of these cessions was to create, in the Indo-China peninsula, a core consisting of a 'Great Thailand', independent in name, but closely bound to Japan.[4]

Pibul knew that his alliance with Japan was disliked by Pridi, and to ensure that Pridi did not intervene against him he removed him from his ministerial post and appointed him Regent, which involved much prestige but little direct political power. The independent-minded Pridi, very much aware of his own dignity, was not to be side-tracked by this appointment. Under Pibul, the Siamese had obediently declared war against Britain and the United States. In theory both countries should have offered a reciprocal declaration. But only Britain did so, and here lies the root of the different approaches made later to the Siamese resistance by Britain and America. The Americans considered Pibul to be acting under constraint. He was not, therefore, the authentic voice of the Siamese people, and they decided not to declare war on Siam. They offered sanctuary to Siamese who would oppose their country's pro-Japanese policy, and the Siamese Minister in Washington, Mon Rajawongse Seni Pramoj, a friend of Pridi, founded a Free Siamese movement in the United States.

There was little concrete evidence available to the Allies about the strength of the movement inside Siam, though in 1943 there were one or two straws in the wind: a man claiming to be an emissary of the movement, Chamkad Balankura, arrived in China in April, having made the journey from northern Siam on foot. He was promptly arrested by the Chinese, who, as usual, made it very difficult for the British and Americans to contact him, though it was learned that he was the bearer of a proposition to bring Pridi out of Siam. Pressure was applied, and they eventually agreed to let Balankura leave for Washington. Before he could make the journey he died of cancer, according to Chinese reports.* Two of Pridi's friends made a similar trek through northern Indo-China and Yunnan in September 1943 and reached Chungking towards the end of that month. Again American and British reactions diverged. The British were disappointed that the Siamese envoys were merely talking politics and evinced few practical suggestions for a military exploitation of the Free Siamese movement. The Americans were prepared to hear what the Siamese had to say and had them sent on to Washington in spite of China's unwillingness to let them go. (China regarded with disfavour any clandestine activities by another power involving Siam.)

It became increasingly evident that the Allies would have to penetrate Siam to provide information for themselves. Under the command of Colin Mackenzie, a civilian who held the rank of Major-General, Force 136 operated against Japanese-held territory in South-East Asia from bases in India and Ceylon, with training schools in a number of places in India. The headquarters of Siam Country Section was in Calcutta, under Major A. C. Pointer. Here a group of Siamese, former university students who had been stranded in England by the declaration of war, and were later commissioned in the British Army, were prepared to infiltrate their country and set up bases for future guerrilla warfare against the Japanese. They were known as 'Whites', and, as native Siamese their use would be conditioned by a pro-Allied and anti-Japanese development on the part of the Siamese Government. In addition to them, Siam Country Section recruited its 'Reds' and 'Blues'. These were young Chinese from Bangkok who were in China at the outbreak of the war and

* Balankura was the bearer of a message from Pridi to Britain and America, which he was supposed to transmit through Mon Seni Pramoj. It claimed that the treaties of friendship between Siam and the USA and Great Britain were still in force, Pibul's declaration of war being considered unconstitutional. Pridi also proposed the setting up of a Free Siamese Government on *Indian* territory, and the exfiltration from Siam of himself and members of the Cabinet and National Assembly.[5] The government was to be financed by the unfreezing of Siamese reserves held in British and American banks.

they were to be used to make contacts with the Chinese business community. In view of the perpetual hostility between Siamese and Chinese, the two groups had to be kept well apart.

The first infiltrations were failures. Some 'Reds' were landed by slow* Catalina flying-boats in the Gulf of Siam but were captured or killed on reaching the shore. Agents parachuted later in the summer of 1944 were captured and held in Bangkok gaol. Then the fortunes of Force 136 improved. The unpopularity of the Japanese occupation led to the overthrow of their ally, the Pibul Government, which was replaced by an administration under Khuang Aphaiwong as Prime Minister. This was in essence a triumph for Pridi's civilian party, and the strange situation developed in which a country allied to Japan was, effectively, run by a pro-Allied government, under the rule of the Regent (Pridi) who was the head of the resistance to the Japanese army of occupation.†

A message smuggled back to Force 136 via Kunming, from one of the 'Whites' held in Bangkok, revealed that although the writer was in gaol, the gaolers and the Bangkok police were friendly, and in contact with Pridi's Free Siamese movement. Soon the leader of the 'Whites' party, Khem, saw Pridi himself and was given back his radio-set to get in touch with Calcutta. From the first contact a regular supply of intelligence came out of Siam to South-East Asia Command (SEAC) headquarters in Kandy. Later still major political figures were flown to Ceylon for discussions with officers from Mountbatten's headquarters. This operation, termed 'Sequence' by Force 136, took place in February 1945. A Catalina picked up the former Siamese Foreign Minister, Nai Direck Jaiyanama, from the Gulf of Siam, off the island of Koh Tao. He was accompanied by General Chatr Naksit, then Chief of Staff and later Commander-in-Chief of the Siamese Army, and Nai Thanat Khoman, a future Foreign Minister. They were safely returned by Catalina, and were back in Bangkok after an absence of only nine days.

A Siam Country Section officer and former diplomat, Andrew Gilchrist, met the group at Trincomalee. It was particularly interesting for him: just before the Japanese invaded Siam, he had been to a cocktail party at Nai Direck's house. 'If the Japanese do invade us,'

---

* Maximum speed was around 110 mph.

† Pridi, who was known to London and Washington by his code-name of 'Ruth', became sole Regent on 24 July 1944, after Prince Aditya Ditabha resigned from the Council of Regents.

the minister had said to Gilchrist, 'I know that people like Nai Pridi and myself will never accept the situation. You may be sure we will work against them. I want you to understand this because you are my friend.'[6] The Siamese had quizzed him about the aid Siam might expect from Great Britain in the event of war. The answer had, inevitably, been a disappointing one. In 1945 Direck talked freely to Gilchrist. Gilchrist was in no way authorized to make any political promises, but Direck hinted that in view of Siamese cooperation in providing the intelligence now coming regularly from Bangkok some favourable consideration might be given by London to a public declaration by the Allies on the future independence of Siam. He was a little taken aback when Gilchrist repeated – as he was bound to – the official British line that Siam had helped Japan invade British territory, had declared war on Great Britain, and was at that very moment in occupation of British territory in Malaya and the Shan States.

Gilchrist was expressing the Foreign Office attitude, which emphasized the difference between the American and British views on Siam. For the British, Siam had become, quite simply, an enemy country. For the Americans, who had not reciprocated Siam's declaration of war, she was an enemy-occupied country. 'Like other countries in like case, "They must work their passage home"', was how a British declaration (proposed but never sent) was worded.[7] A secret letter from the Foreign Secretary, Anthony Eden, to Lord Halifax, the British Ambassador in Washington, explained this case. It is dated 4 September 1944.[8] No less than the USA and China, Great Britain was in favour of a free and independent Siam after the war, Eden wrote. His Majesty's Government did not rate the practical value of resistance inside Siam very highly, and thought it doubtful wisdom to hint to the Siamese that they could have an easy and assured future regardless of their attitude towards the Japanese. 'We feel, in fact, that if resistance is to be encouraged it may well need a spur rather than a sugar-plum.' The US Department of State had expressed disappointment that the Foreign Office had not declared Great Britain had no territorial ambitions at Siam's expense; but, Eden continued, that was already taken for granted in the terms of the Atlantic Charter and the Cairo Declaration. On the other hand, there was no question of Siam retaining the 'ill-gotten gains' she had accepted from Japan at the expense of Burma, Malaya, and French Indo-China. He also hinted that some special security arrangements might have to be adopted, in an international security framework, for the Kra Isthmus.

In an attempt to coordinate US and British policy, Cordell Hull asked Winant, the American Ambassador in London, to tell Eden that he was glad to see their basic objects were the same, and he assured him that the USA supported the return by Siam of territories unlawfully acquired; though he added a rider that this was without prejudice to claims by any nation, including Siam, for boundary adjustments by peaceful processes. But he did not understand what Eden wanted for the Kra Isthmus, and asked for clarification.[9] Through Winant, Eden told him: the role that area had played in the Japanese capture of Singapore and the conquest of Burma – the Japanese had landed there in 1941 – meant that it needed special consideration when future security arrangements for South-East Asia were worked out, in particular for the defence of Singapore.[10]

Eden's caution is adequate explanation for British disapproval of the establishment of a Free Thai government in exile in India; and British political warfare propaganda forbade the use of the term 'Free Thai'.[11] Pridi's efforts to gain support for a Free Thai government met with a polite negative. So, too, but more surprisingly, did another approach he made through Stockholm. The Siamese Minister to Sweden, Arthakitti Bhanomyong, was Pridi's brother. Through American diplomats in Sweden he conveyed to Seni Pramoj in Washington Pridi's request that he (Pramoj) should organize a Free Siamese government in the United States and lead it himself. He was asked to send a representative to Stockholm to discuss this. When State Department officials passed on this message, on 12 December 1944, Seni Pramoj was puzzled.[12] It was not what he had expected, he told them, and was contrary to his principles; nor was it clear why Pridi had made the request. Perhaps, one of the Americans interjected, Pridi was planning to escape from Siam and wanted an organization ready for him if he succeeded. As far as Stockholm was concerned, Seni Pramoj was told, it would be impossible to send a Siamese there without his presence being spotted at once by the enemy. Perhaps an American could go instead, Pramoj wondered; but in the event, nothing was done, and it was decided to go through Arthakitti's message again to weigh its implications.

Three days later, Seni Pramoj got in touch again with Abbot L. Moffatt, chief of the Division of South-West Pacific Affairs in the

State Department. He had given a great deal of thought to the proposal for the Free Thai government and had decided that to go through with it, with himself as head, would be completely illegal. He refused absolutely to take it any further – unless, that is, the message was a hint that the Regent was in a desperate situation under excessive Japanese pressure. Moffatt agreed. Unless there was some compelling reason – and they did not know of one – the establishment of a Free Thai government in America would not help the Siamese and might be embarrassing to the United States.[13]

A few weeks later Moffatt's department prepared a brief on Siam for Roosevelt, who was due to meet Churchill and Stalin at Yalta between 4 and 11 February 1945. Moffatt spelled out the unease which Cordell Hull had merely hinted at in his exchange with Eden:

> Thailand is the one country in South-East Asia which was still independent before the war. We believe that it would be prejudicial to American interests throughout the Far East if, as the outcome of the war in which we will have had the major part in defeating Japanese aggression, Thailand should be deprived of any of its prewar territory or should have its independent status impaired. The history of European pressure on Thailand and of European acquisition of territory in South-East Asia is vivid in Asiatic memories. This government cannot afford to share responsibility in any way for a continuance towards Thailand of prewar imperialism in any guise... It is the view of the Department that an effort should be made to persuade the British to alter their plans so that they are not inconsistent with our own ... Although there are disadvantages from political viewpoints in having American troops, except where militarily essential, participate in the recovery of European colonial areas, there would be an advantage from a political viewpoint in having American troops under independent American command responsible for the liberation of Thailand, rather than in having Thailand occupied as enemy territory by British forces...[14]

Moffatt's suspicions were echoed by those of the US Ambassador to China, Patrick Hurley, who wired to the Secretary of State that the USA should encourage the setting up of a provisional Free Thai government. 'I am not convinced,' he wrote on 2 February 1945, 'by Eden's statement that the British want to see Thailand after the war restored as an independent, free and solid state. I feel that if we do not move forward in this matter the British will succeed in outmanoeuvring us and the Chinese and in gaining some measure of control over Thailand.'[15]

These political speculations were soon – but only briefly – transcended by urgent proposals for a military operation. As a first step towards the recapture of Singapore ('Operation Zipper'), SEAC planned to seize the island of Phuket off the west coast of Siam, almost midway between the southernmost territory in Burma, Victoria Point, and Alor Star in northern Malaya. It was hoped that a force on Phuket would be able to paralyse Japanese communications through the Kra Isthmus and prevent them reinforcing Singapore. Some member of Mountbatten's planning staff, inadequately acquainted with the romanization of Siamese and endowed with an under-subtle sense of humour, christened the operation with the code-name 'Roger', and Siam Country Section was asked to provide intelligence on the Kra Isthmus and examine the possibilities of guerrilla action in support of landings.

The target date for 'Roger' was 15 May 1945, and this made arrangements very tight: it was thought unwise to move agents into southern Siam from the Bangkok area, since this might alert the Japanese and guide them to possible landing points. If parties were to be flown in, on the other hand, it would have to be done before the April moon – 20 April – which left little margin of time for preparations. Siam Country Section managed to infiltrate parties successfully and agents were set up along both east and west coasts of southern Siam, in Prachuab, Chumporn, Bandon, Yala, Takuapa, and Pengnga. In the event, they were not used for the purpose for which they had been intended: in a mood of increased confidence with his own forces, Mountbatten decided to do without a subsidiary operation on Phuket and drive straight for Singapore itself.

Meanwhile another Siam Country Section operation, which had been mounted at roughly the same time, was producing far more astonishing effects. Victor Jaques, a pre-war legal luminary of the Bangkok scene, and by this time a brigadier in the British Army, had arrived in his old haunts by motor launch on 29 April 1945. He returned to Siam Country Section after a week to make his report and promptly went back into Siam as Mountbatten's representative with Pridi until the war came to an end. Jaques was extremely tall – six foot four – and to complicate matters further he insisted he was no spy and would wear his full uniform while in Bangkok. Since it was still a hostile capital, and occupied by a ferocious enemy whose lines of communications it straddled, Jaques's insistence may seem foolhardy. Nonetheless, he rode round Japanese-occupied Bangkok for a period of three and a half months, in British uniform, and in imminent peril of his life.[16] Wireless sets in many parts of the country, operated by Force 136 agents under the protection of Pridi's Siamese movement, kept a constant supply of intelligence on the Japanese forces flowing into Mountbatten's headquarters. It was estimated in Kandy at this time that a rising in Siam would not be required before January 1946. There was no question of telling Pridi that the main British effort would be directed towards Singapore, leaving Siam behind, since that might damage the security of 'Zipper'. On the other hand, the longer the delay in activating the Free Siam movement, the more likely it was that it might be uncovered by the Japanese. It is Gilchrist's view[17] that the Siamese would only put up an effective fight if their movement acted in coordination with, and as auxiliaries of, a large-scale British military operation into Siam;* and 'Zipper' had pre-empted the troops needed for this. If it succeeded, there would be little need to invade Siam. The atom bomb may well have spared us, he affirms, 'The sight of a Siamese shambles ... in which the British and American officers stationed behind the Japanese lines would inevitably have been involved, especially Victor Jaques in his exposed position in Bangkok.'[18]

For, of course, the British were not the only infiltrators. The American OSS (Office of Strategic Services) attempted to move into Siam from China with no success at all, and then began to operate from Ceylon. An OSS party made a blind drop into central Siam and was quickly captured by the Siamese gendarmerie. As luck would have it, they were placed in the same Bangkok gaol which held the Siam Country Section 'Whites', and in a short while they too were passing wireless traffic back to their headquarters on Pridi's behalf. As a result, the OSS managed to infiltrate one of their officers, John D. Wester, into Bangkok. In fact he was operating there before Victor Jaques arrived. Wester was flown in by RAF Catalina, and flown out by the same method when the tension of his position brought about a nervous breakdown.

From Pridi's point of view, the double line out of Bangkok was useful insurance. The Americans were not insisting on the same

* The advance into Siam of 12th Army troops moving from Burma through Karenni and Tenasserim would have been, relatively, a side-show.

conditions as the British, and the Free Thais in America had, possibly with American encouragement, affirmed that there was no question of returning to Burma and Malaya the territory Siam had gained from them. This came to the ears of the British diplomat and scholar, Sir George Sansom, then Minister at the British Embassy in Washington, who lost no time in informing the Foreign Office of what he had heard.[19] J. C. Sterndale-Bennett, the head of the Far Eastern Department of the Foreign Office, had also heard from Sansom that the Free Thais in Washington were speaking of an 'Anglo-American Arbitration Committee' to study the issue of territory seized from the French. Sterndale-Bennett dismissed this as a rather obvious attempt to play off the British against the French.

Towards the end of March 1945 the Americans discussed a possible increase in the help the OSS might give to the Siamese resistance. News had reached the State Department of a secret meeting of the Siamese cabinet which had debated what it should do if the Japanese attempted a *coup de force* as they had done in Indo-China on 9 March. The answer was that they would fight. But Japanese forces were in and around Bangkok in strength, and it was not likely that the Thais would last out for more than a month, if they rose in armed rebellion; unless, that is, the Americans were prepared to drop in anti-tank guns and other equipment.[20] Although it was envisaged that SEAC facilities would be used, there was no question of employing Siam Country Section. As in Burma, after initial requests at local level for cooperation, the OSS was steering clear of involvement with the British Special Operations Executive. This was a specific instruction as far as Burma was concerned, and was taken to apply to Siam too: 'OSS in Burma should do or say nothing,' wrote the acting Secretary of State (Joseph Grew) to the US commissioner in India on 28 April 1945, 'which could be interpreted as political promise and should not under any circumstances become associated in Burmese minds with SOE or any British political propaganda organization.'[21]

While the British and Americans were each preparing their own form of intervention in the affairs of Siam, the Japanese garrison there was beginning to sit up and take notice.

ii *The Metamorphoses of Colonel Tsuji*

Japan's situation in Siam was not unlike that in French Indo-China: she was in military control without having direct rule over the political structure. It was taken for granted that British–Indian forces would invade Siam from Burma in the autumn or winter of 1945, and it seemed probable that the Americans would land in Indo-China after taking the Philippines. Either way, the fairly comfortable situation of the Japanese troops in Siam seemed likely to change. They had constituted a garrison army, busied themselves with building roads into Burma and Malaya, and watching over the security of the lines of communication from those countries into Indo-China. Their general, Lieutenant-General Nakamura, was a very appropriate choice for the command: he had once been GOC of the 5th Division, but what counted more than that was his experience as a general of the *Kempei*, aware of the problems of security and counter-espionage. The Siam–Burma Railway was begun before he took up his command – it started in November 1942 – but he saw it through to completion from Thanbyuzayat in Burma to Non Pladuk in Siam, about fifty miles west of Bangkok, by October 1943, at an immense cost in human life and suffering among the Asian labourers and Allied prisoners-of-war who built it.

The Siamese were not indifferent to the sufferings of the railway workers, and some of them attacked and killed a number of Japanese guards. Southern Army headquarters demanded that the culprits be punished, and ordered the Siamese to pay a fine of 80,000 *bahts* as compensation to the families of the dead Japanese. Nakamura's handling of the affair was skilful. The guilty Siamese were bonzes, Buddhist monks, and there was no law in Siam under which bonzes could be punished for any crime at all.[22] Nakamura accepted this, but insisted that the massive fine be paid. He then promptly wrote to Southern Army to say that he had made over the sum for the maintenance of the families of Siamese soldiers who had died fighting against the Japanese in the first hours of the war. Whether from magnanimity, or a sense of public relations, Field-Marshal Terauchi accepted the *fait accompli*.

Nakamura also supervised the building of a road between Chiangmai and Toungoo in Burma which was completed by May 1944. It was not before time. The success of the D-Day landings in

Normandy made the Japanese in Southern Army reflect that the governments in Siam and Indo-China were likely to look more and more towards an Allied victory and to begin to detach themselves from the Japanese connection. The fall from power of Japan's chief ally in Siam, Pibul, less than two months later, was a straw in the wind. In the winter of 1944, the army of occupation in French Indo-China was reorganized as 38th Army, ready for operations. The same imperative was felt in Siam. The garrison army became 39th Army, the intention being to turn South-East Asia into a fortress area, part of a system which would prevent the Allies from attacking the Chinese mainland, and so helping in the defence of Japan herself. A new Chief of Staff, Major-General Hamada, was appointed in November 1944, and he and Nakamura strengthened military installations in Siam, and intensified counter-intelligence activities against Allied agents who were known to be operating in the country under the protection of highly placed Siamese. In the summer of 1945 they received a new recruit to help them in the task of galvanizing their forces: Colonel Tsuji Masanobu.*

Tsuji was a trouble-shooter with connections at the very top levels of Tokyo military society, who had played a role in every important campaign in the Japanese Army's days of expansion: Nomonhan, Malaya, Guadalcanal, Burma.† He had planned the capture of Singapore, and only a few weeks before his arrival in Bangkok had been wounded on the Burma front, where he was a staff officer of General Honda's 33rd Army. A small two-seater plane had brought him from Moulmein, across the Salween and the mountains on the Siam–Burma border, to Don Muang airfield north of Bangkok. He still bore the outward signs of his wounds; a sling, and a bamboo stick to help him along. A staff officer from the 39th Army, Yano, met him at the airport with a stretcher and took him along to general headquarters.

Tsuji was perplexed about the true nature of his mission with the

* Unless references indicate otherwise, my chief source for this section has been Tsuji's own account, *Senkō sanzenri* (A Three-thousand League Odyssey), Mainichi Shimbunsha, Tokyo, 1950. I have used both the original text and the English translation, *Underground Escape* (An Asian Publication, Robert Booth and Taro Fukuda, Tokyo, 1952) but the latter must be used with caution as the translation is inadequate. For Nakamura's views, I have relied on the official war history volume, *Sittang. Mei-Go Sakusen* (Sittang. The *coup de force* in Indo China), Asagumo Shimbunsha for the Defence Agency, Tokyo, 1969, and Nakamura's manuscript notes in the War History Room, Defence Agency Archives, Tokyo.

† Cf. p. 231.

39th Army. A fortnight before leaving Burma, he had been summoned to Terauchi's Supreme Headquarters in Saigon. He had been
surprised to hear the staff discuss an operation in Siam similar to that
by which the Japanese had taken control of French Indo-China on
9 March 1945. They were thinking of a surprise move to disarm the
Siamese Army and police. This seemed to Tsuji a cowardly proposition, since Siam was a weak country and in alliance with Japan.
Nonetheless, he decided to see how the land lay. When he and Yano
reached headquarters, it was four in the afternoon. He had expected
to find the place a hive of activity; it was nearly empty, all the officers
had gone. Grimly he noted the fact, and drank ice-cold beer and
salted rice cake pretzels with the Chief of Staff, Lieutenant-General
Hamada. The coldness was a luxury, and there was more to come.
Accustomed to jungle tents, he found it difficult to settle down in the
vast double bed in the palatial house which had been allocated to him,
with marble stairways and modern toilet gadgetry.

His unfavourable impression of the life of the Japanese Army of
occupation in Siam was increased the following morning. He noticed
that no officers above the rank of major walked to headquarters.
Worse, most officers used official vehicles for shopping and geisha
parties. He reported to General Nakamura, whom he knew by
reputation from the time the latter had been a *Kempei* general. In fact
Nakamura had been an instructor at the Military Academy when
Tsuji was a cadet. Nakamura rose from his chair, tiny eyes gleaming
in a fat face. 'We're very glad to have you here, Tsuji. We're counting
on you to put things in order for us. How are your wounds?' Tsuji
was still wary. When his appointment to Siam had first been suggested, he had heard that the Army Headquarters had hinted he was
not acceptable. There must have been hostility somewhere high up,
and he mistrusted Nakamura's friendly overtures.

But there were other people who counted as much as Nakamura
in Siam. Ambassador Yamamoto spoke quite frankly:

> I know you've all had a terrible time in Burma, but the situation here
> in Siam is critical too. As far as my own future is concerned, I intend
> to die at my post. You know, Tsuji, I remember something you once
> said in China. 'The only way to get near the Chinese is to trust them
> completely. They'll fool you once, then again, and a third time.
> Never mind,' you said, 'go on trusting them, don't show anger.
> Soon you will be dealing with Chinese who neither fool nor cheat.'
> I feel very much like this about the Siamese. Even if they do turn on

us, I don't feel like playing dirty tricks on them. There is a last gift
we can leave this country, a memory of the trustworthiness of the
Japanese.

Tsuji looked at the elegant, moustached diplomat, with his thin,
carefully combed hair, and his air of determination. If only *he* were in
Nakamura's place, he thought. Here was someone who could be
relied on as a commander even when things were darkest.

Tsuji had more to see. Behind the GOC's residence a small
Shinto shrine had been set up. On the 8th of every month, to com-
memorate the declaration of war, Shinto ceremonies were held at the
shrine, which had been named *Daigi Jinja* (Great Loyalty Shrine).
Civilians representing the Japanese community in Bangkok used to
attend, along with officers from general headquarters. On 8 June
1945 Tsuji went to his first Shinto rite at the shrine. The officers were
lined up along the right side of the compound, the civilians on the
left. Other ranks were outside the compound. There were Shinto
priests among the reserve officers, and they presided over the ceremony. As they began the solemn intonation of their prayers in their
white robes and tall hats, Tsuji noticed a group of girls facing the
officers and making eyes at them. When he got back from the shrine
he asked who they were, and he was told they were waitresses from
the officers' club, whose functions clearly comprehended more than
simply waiting at table, and comfort girls from the officers' brothels.
What on earth were they doing at the shrine, he enquired, and was
told they were there on the commander's orders. Tsuji said nothing,
but at the next monthly ceremony the girls were moved out of
sight.

Tsuji addressed the commanders of the units in the Bangkok area.
While they and their officers were spending their time in entertain-
ment and riotous living, he told them bluntly, an Allied fifth column
was doing its work underground. If the Siamese police and army
rebelled, this would pit 150,000 of them against the ten thousand or
so Japanese troops in the garrison. Since American and British airborne troops could land in the suburbs of Bangkok, it was necessary
to turn the city into a fortress. Grudgingly the orders went out.
Geisha houses were closed, leave was cancelled, officers and men
alike were set to the work of fortification. Garrison barracks were
turned into strongpoints and festooned with barbed wire. Doctors,
nurses, and casualties shared the digging of trenches round their

hospitals as air-raid precautions. Concrete artillery emplacements were built at Don Muang airfield against possible airborne landings. Munitions depots and godowns (warehouses) were surrounded by concrete pill-boxes. This happened throughout Siam. From the divisional headquarters down to the smallest *Kempei* frontier outpost, barbed wire and concrete were used to make fire points and defence perimeters. In the first week of July, Nakamura was constrained to carry out an inspection of what had been done. Tsuji watched with grim pleasure as the commander-in-chief wiped the sweat from his brow, going from one strongpoint to another. In a week he lost all his excess weight.

With the egoism typical of all his accounts of the war in the Far East, Tsuji clearly considered himself the prime mover in all this transformation. In fact, Nakamura himself had set defence plans in motion long before Tsuji arrived. In his diary for the end of April he noted the constant arrival in the Siamese capital of casualties from the Burma front; also the Japanese Government officials and the employees of Japanese firms, with their wives and children, streaming through from Rangoon, either down the Siam–Burma Railway or, more painfully, along the road from Toungoo and Mae Hong Son to Chiengrai. This was one sign among many. If he looked east, it was to a Tokyo which had been bombed in March 1945 and half turned to ashes overnight; the Americans were in Manila, they had begun to land on Okinawa, the Koiso cabinet fell on 7 April. The war was reaching a climax. The skies over Bangkok were a playground for Allied forces, he did not have a single aircraft to send up against them, and his ack-ack could not reach them.

Besides, his function was not merely to strengthen Siam as a garrison. The reason he was there in the first place was twofold: he acted as the supply route to the Burma front, and he was the node of communications between Malaya, Singapore and Southern Army Headquarters in Saigon. His area of command was not confined to Siam, either. The southern part of Tenasserim, in Burma, was his defence responsibility, and in mid-April he flew over it and ordered defences to be constructed at once round Tavoy and Mergui against possible Allied landings. A road was to be built linking Mergui, Tenasserim and Prachuab on the Gulf of Siam. When he heard that Kimura and his staff had fled from Rangoon, he decided to extend his responsibility, and, on his own initiative, without waiting for orders from Saigon, he sent forward the 158th Independent Mixed Brigade, under Colonel Katayama, to the Siam–Burma railhead at Than-byuzayat. Saigon accepted the *fait accompli*, and placed the brigade under Kimura's command in May.

Depots were strengthened in Bampong and Kanchanaburi, and to the north-east fortified encampments were constructed at Nakhon Nayok under the supervision of engineer units of the 4th Division. Anti-tank ditches were dug, signals installations set up, underground oil and ammunition dumps built, and a food depot established at Prachinburi by using water-borne supplies. The Bampong–Kanchanaburi area he considered as his lines-of-communication base for Burma; the area round Nakhon Nayok was a strongpoint for possible future operations inside Siam; the area south-east of Bangkok was his lines-of-communication base as an agent of the Southern Army acting towards Malaya.

Looking ahead, Nakamura saw that communications by land between Singapore and Saigon might well be severed totally by the end of 1945. He would then have to make the army in Siam an autonomous unit, ready to fight to the death on its own. He thought the supply situation was by no means impossible, though there were difficulties. Sugar and tobacco could not be got in Siam, so they would have to be imported. There was also a paper problem. The stocks and installations of the Wang Tzu Paper Manufacturing Company in Singapore were taken over for this purpose and a beginning was made in shifting them to Siam. By the war's end, over seventy per cent of their material had been moved, a big step towards making Nakamura's command self-sufficient in this essential commodity. By and large, clothing was not a great problem, but there was a shortage of shirts, trousers, and mosquito netting. The Japan–Thai Joint Cotton Mills were given the charge of ensuring a supply of cloth, and Nakamura obtained the transfer from Singapore of the Fuji Cotton Company's machinery which had been stockpiled in Singapore en route for Burma.

An order had been issued to build a hundred wooden vessels of 157 tons each. This plan was modified, and the size of the vessels reduced. The Siamese Government received a demand for 95,000 cubic yards of teak to make these boats, and although the Siamese employed delaying tactics, well aware of the direction in which the war was moving, the construction of the boats went ahead. In this, and in the matter of rice, Nakamura had to consider Siam's position as a provider. From the outbreak of war, Siam had been a rice-bowl for Japan, China and Malaya. It had even exported 3,000 tons a month to Burma, and the annual export capacity of Siamese rice had risen from 800,000 tons to 1,100,000 tons. From the beginning of 1945, this dropped spectacularly, and the export capacity was soon down to 300,000 tons. Even so, Nakamura thought he would be able to stock the complete rice requirements of his army and still send every month 10,000 tons to Malaya, 3,000 tons to Burma, and 2,000 tons to Northern Indo-China.

He was more preoccupied with security than supplies. The first question was that of airfields. He had not forgotten that the aircraft in which the Burmese premier, Ba Maw, flew to the Greater East Asia Conference in October 1943 had crashed at Tourane in French Indo-China. The plane had stopped overnight in Saigon and took off for Taiwan the following morning. Ba Maw's own account of what happened next is most vivid:

> ...we noticed that the plane was climbing with difficulty. At the same time a strong pungent smell that reminded me of chlorine filled the plane, and we began to roll and pitch slightly; soon we guessed that we were in for trouble... the plane started to lose altitude near a group of thatch huts, and suddenly it dived down, one of its wings violently struck a tree nearby, which acted like a brake, and the whole plane swung round and crashed right on the huts, with its front portion totally smashed... The huts had saved our lives, but some of them were flattened completely. I found myself surrounded by a mass of twisted metal with one jagged piece in particular pointing straight at my throat...[23]

Ba Maw was shaken but undeterred, and flew on to be in time for the opening of the assembly. En route to the same assembly, the plane of the Siamese delegate, Prince Wan Waithayakon, was delayed for a day by an accident. Incidents of this kind might be a coincidence but Nakamura, with his long experience as a *Kempei* general, thought otherwise. He had to observe the terms of the Japan–Siam alliance, and in conformity with the spirit of this he informed the Siamese Government that the *coup de force* of 9 March in Indo-China was taking place. He invited the Premier, Aphaiwong, and the Minister of Defence, to his official residence at nine in the evening of 9 March. The invitation was left to the last minute, but Nakamura knew that information about the coup was bound to reach the Siamese authorities fairly soon, if only because stragglers from French and Annamite units resisting in Indo-China might attempt to cross the border. The invitation was issued at 7 p.m.

Both ministers arrived promptly at nine (*Nakamura remembers*), and they were ushered into a private room. Here the Chief of Staff, Lieutenant-General Hamada, explained what was happening. The Governor-General of French Indo-China, Decoux, was to receive an ultimatum from the Japanese Ambassador, Matsumoto, at eight o'clock that night; if no appropriate reply was received by ten o'clock, Japan intended to take action. Clashes were likely to occur over the length and breadth of Indo-China, from ten o'clock through to the following morning, and disturbances might occur in those parts of Siam where the Mekong River formed the boundary between the two countries. Defeated French troops might cross the border to take refuge in Siam. He was informing them of all this so that they would know how to assess rumours of all kinds that were bound to originate among the people of the border areas. Japan had not been able to inform them before of her intentions, because of the need for secrecy in the operations. In fact he could not allow them to leave the building, now they knew what was to happen, until ten o'clock. The Siamese ministers expressed their whole-hearted gratitude, and after a few minutes' discussion took their leave at ten o'clock. Signals were despatched to units on the eastern border, and Annamite troops who crossed over from Indo-China were disarmed without incident.[24]

But this apparent openness with the Siamese was, as both sides knew, deceptive. The Japanese were not sure exactly who in the Siamese Government and Army ranks was loyal to them, and the oddest rumours circulated, including one that Field-Marshal Pibul himself was in touch with Mountbatten. But an order issued in January 1945 had already ensured that all Siamese Government ministers were put under surveillance, and the Japanese had drawn up plans for the attack and seizure of those secret airfields whose existence they knew of. There was one about thirty-five miles south-west of Sakhon Nakhorn, which they planned to take by a pincer movement from both north and south should the need arise. The Sakhon Nakhorn area in north-east Siam had been selected for its remoteness. Officials in the area who were considered unfavourable to Pridi were removed and government services were then staffed by his nominees. Similarly the Pha Kradeung Plateau, in the north-east, where a tongue of the Shan States licks down into Siam, had been selected as an arms dump and a possible site for fighter aircraft if Mountbatten decided to move into the Indo-China peninsula through Bangkok instead of re-taking Singapore.

Tsuji made several trips by light aircraft over north-east Siam as he had done over Malaya in the days before Pearl Harbor. He spotted a number of secret air strips. To close in on these airfields, part of the 22nd Division was to move south-west across the Mekong from Thakek in Laos and part of the Bangkok garrison was to be transported by rail to Ubon. Inside Bangkok, the Siamese were to be shown how determined the Japanese were to turn their capital city into a stronghold for a last-ditch battle. Lumphini Park became a forest of barbed wire; the Japanese Embassy, the general headquarters buildings and their shrine, and the 16th Hospital area between the railway and Phyathai Road were fortified and sandbagged. Pillboxes went up at crossroads along the road between Bangkok and Don Muang airport. Nakamura invited Siamese Government officials and high-ranking staff officers to go on a tour of the new installations. The purpose was quite simple: to show them, before they committed themselves to any open collaboration with an anti-Japanese underground, how determined the Japanese were, acting in the spirit of the Japan–Thai alliance, to defend the country. Those who were simply awaiting an opportunity to rebel might well have second thoughts, Nakamura was convinced. The Japanese had placed some of their interpreters in civilian clothes among the guests. They kept their ears open, and reported back later that they had heard young Siamese officers say how well built the fortifications looked: 'We won't be able to do a thing against strongpoints like this.' The demonstration of strength had worked, in Tsuji's view: 'We won at least the fear and respect of the Siamese people.'[25] Complaints which had been made by Southern Army Headquarters about the leakage of information through Siamese defectors to the Allies could now be met. The Japanese positively welcomed the leakage of the information the Allies would be getting at present. But zeal at times overstepped the bounds of discretion.

In mid-July, an urgent message came from Aphaiwong to Nakamura and the Japanese Ambassador, Yamamoto. Both of them thought they were to be quizzed about the vast appropriation for defence works which the Japanese, as the army of occupation, had requested from the Siamese Government. The amount was ten times that budgeted in the previous year. In the oppressive heat, both made their way to the prime minister's house. They were astonished to see that Aphaiwong was pale with anger, his lips tightly compressed, and the veins starting out on his forehead. Unable to contain himself, he burst out that the *Kempei* had a man following him. He had tried to observe the terms of the Japan–Thai alliance, at the risk of being misunderstood by many of the Siamese people. Now what did he find? If the Japanese authorities had no confidence in him, then he would resign at once. He asked them to convey this intention to the Japanese Government.

Nakamura was dismayed. Even though he was a former general in the *Kempei*, he knew that he would be unable to prevent this shadowing of the Thai ministers. The *Kempei* were a law to themselves in the occupied countries of South-East Asia, and since the surrender of Germany in May 1945 they had reported daily to General Headquarters in Bangkok that a group of Siamese police and army officers were in secret contact with the British. They thought the central figure in this affair was Lieutenant-General Adon, the chief of police. Nakamura knew that the *Kempei* could not, in the circumstances, relax their vigilance. On the other hand, he could not afford to come into open conflict with Aphaiwong, whose resignation might upset a delicate balance of power. The commander-in-chief put the issue to his senior staff, and Tsuji at once put forward a typically egoistic solution, which Nakamura accepted. 'Leave it to me,' said Tsuji. 'I'll go to Aphaiwong and publicly apologize on your behalf.' With Colonel Yano, whose special province was Siamese internal affairs, and an interpreter, Tsuji made his way to the prime minister's residence.

Tsuji was amazed that an exalted dignitary could live in such a small house. He also noticed, with some surprise, that there was no sentry, not even a single policeman standing guard. He offered his *meishi* (visiting card) as he went in through the gate. A young man in short sleeves came to the door and Tsuji said they wanted to see the prime minister. 'I am the Prime Minister,' was the answer. Could this skinny unpretentious youth be the premier who had so perturbed the Japanese commander-in-chief? He led Tsuji and his companions into a simple room, decorated by a single oil painting of the young man's father in the uniform of a general. After a brief preamble, Tsuji came to the point.

I have been charged by General Nakamura with protecting Your

Excellency against hostile elements. I am new to Siam and its customs, and I seem to have made a clumsy mistake, but I ask you to believe that what I did was in our mutual interest: I can only apologize to Your Excellency for my lack of care in seeing properly and unobtrusively to Your Excellency's safety. I alone am responsible. Neither the commander-in-chief nor the Japanese ambassador had any knowledge of this. I hope you will forgive me.

'You're very straightforward, Colonel Tsuji,' replied Aphaiwong, 'and in deference to your sincerity, I am prepared to forget what has happened. By the way, how old are you?' It was an odd question, but Tsuji answered: 'Forty-four.' 'Then we are the same age,' said the premier. 'From now on please consider us to be on terms of friendship.' This, at any rate, is how Tsuji reports the conversation. Some days later after an air raid on Bangkok he made his way through the flaming streets to the premier's residence, and he found him supervising firefighters and encouraging the panic-stricken people, oblivious of the falling bombs.

The Japanese began to reorganize their military command structure in Siam. The army was promoted to the status of an Area Army. The 39th Army had come into being as the result of a decision to turn the Siam garrison occupation force into a mobile army ready for battle. In July 1945 this army became the 18th Area Army. To it were added, in the course of the following month, the 15th Army general headquarters from Burma, and what was left of a number of divisions which had been defeated in the Burma campaign: the 15th, 53rd, and 56th. Nakamura remained the Commander-in-Chief. Hamada, on the other hand, though promoted to Lieutenant-General, was made Deputy Chief of Staff, so he was, in function at any rate, being demoted. His successor as the chief of staff was the GOC of the 55th Division who had just left the Burma front after his forces had failed to hold the British thrust south from Toungoo. Tsuji viewed the appointment of Lieutenant-General Hanaya Tadashi with some distaste. Hanaya was a roustabout, a tough, loud and boastful bully, who claimed to have had a large share in starting off the Manchurian Incident when he was a major commanding a special intelligence detachment. In comparison, Hamada was quiet and unimposing, but much respected by Japanese and Siamese alike. His work included the job of military attaché to the Japanese Embassy in Bangkok.

Events took a rapid turn for the worse in the first week of August.

The news of Hiroshima came through to Bangkok. Nobody knew the details of the bombing, but it was evident that the military centre of Hiroshima had been totally destroyed. Three days later a conference of all unit commanders was held at general headquarters in Bangkok and the news of Russia's invasion of Manchuria was announced. If the Siamese were to move against the Japanese occupation, surely now would be the time? The commanders dispersed to their units and ordered their men to prepare for a siege. Scattered billets were suddenly vacated and the troops came in to the fortified positions. Then the blow fell – at least as far as headquarters was concerned – on 12 August. Late that night, the head of the Dōmei News Agency bureau in Bangkok rushed into the General Headquarters building. His services had monitored a foreign news broadcast: 'The Japanese Government is accepting the Potsdam Declaration,' he gasped.[26] It was at once decided that an officer from the 18th Area Army should go to Tokyo to find out what was likely to happen. Inevitably, the task fell to Tsuji, who was stopped in Saigon and coldly informed that the matter was in the hands of the Chief of Staff of Southern Area Army, Lieutenant-General Numata and that he had already nominated Kushida, his chief staff officer, to leave for Tokyo the following day.

Before returning to Bangkok, Tsuji spent an evening talking with an old friend, the *Kempei* Colonel Hayashi Hidezumi. Coldly and factually, they appraised the likely power of the new bomb, and what the best course for their own future would be. That night, Tsuji determined that he would not give himself up to the British when they arrived in Siam. He would disappear from the ranks of the Japanese Army, go underground and, as he put it, 'work for the reconstruction of Japan', though what he actually intended to do, as a deserter, is not clear.

On 15 August, in the basement of General Headquarters in Bangkok, Tsuji stood with the rest of the staff at attention, listening to the halting voice of the Emperor bidding them bear the unbearable, endure the unendurable – the same message that was being heard all over East Asia at that instant. Sobs broke out from the men standing in their rigid ranks. His face wet with tears, Tsuji attended the last conference in Nakamura's room. He felt as if his very bowels were being torn to shreds, but the suffering confirmed him in his decision. He would not only go underground, he would achieve a lasting bond between Japan and Siam through their common faith, Buddhism.

It is difficult to believe that Tsuji was being completely candid when he wrote the chapter in his book which tells of his decision. It was rumoured that Tsuji, when a staff officer of the 33rd Army in North Burma, had had an American flyer executed and had taken part, with other members of the staff, in a cannibal feast, during which parts of the flyer's body had been consumed by the Japanese. Whether he was in fact guilty of the crime or not is difficult to decide, since Japanese atrocities, real as many of them were, tended to create their own legends. It is not referred to in his account of his escape from Siam, but he knew he was wanted by the Allied authorities, and that fact alone provides sufficient reason for his desire to escape, quite apart from any supposed wish for 'the reconstruction of Japan'.

He was not the only officer who had expressed recalcitrance. One high-ranking staff officer burst out in front of Nakamura: 'It's unthinkable for me to hand over this sword at my side. Let us go back to Japan now, as we are, armed and in uniform, let us be disarmed there. If we can't do that I'll hack the enemy to pieces, or cut my own belly open!' Tsuji had no brief for suicide. 'Go ahead,' he told the officer. 'If you don't agree with what His Majesty wishes, then cut your belly open in front of the Loyalty Shrine (*Daigi Jinja*). But we can't have the attitude of the entire army laid down by the emotions of a single individual. Our job is to send back to Japan all the troops under one command.' Lieutenant-General Hamada, who had listened to this impassioned exchange, quietly drew Tsuji aside: 'Tsuji, I have a request to make. It's obvious that Japan is going to suffer for the next ten or twenty years. Why don't you go underground in China, and attempt to open up a new path for the future of Asia there? I have a contact who can help you. He is the chief of a gang of pirates on Taiwan. If you go to Taiwan, I'll give you a letter of introduction.' But that seemed too circuitous to Tsuji: in Siam itself he felt his contact with the Premier, Aphaiwong, and his renewed acquaintance with an old Siamese student of his, Major Att Chalenshilba, seemed more likely to produce results. The major had been a pupil at the Tokyo Military Academy when Tsuji was an instructor on the staff in 1934, and had been of considerable help to him since he arrived in Bangkok. Perhaps there was a final favour he could ask from Att? He was going to need help when the British arrived.

iii *The British Arrive*

The British advance party landed at Don Muang airfield on the morning of 3 September 1945. It was 1,250 strong, and consisted of 7th Division headquarters (Major-General G. Evans) and a number of ancillary units, chief among them being the control staff of No. 5 RAPWI (Recovery of Allied Prisoners of War and Internees). On 5 September Lady Mountbatten herself flew in, accompanied by Major-General Thompson, the SEAC Director of Medical Services. Lady Mountbatten had already taken a special interest in the welfare of prisoners, and there was plenty for her to do in Siam, where they had been employed on that ghastliest of projects, the Siam–Burma Railway.

There were still thousands of British prisoners in Siam, and some had been moved into the recently fortified north-eastern area around Nakhon Nayok. They had travelled two days by train from Kanburi and found that their destination was a piece of virgin jungle ten miles from the nearest village. They finally reached it along a forest track nearly two miles long and only wide enough for them to walk in single file. The first party had to make a road to the camp for those who were to follow, and then carry the building material to the site and erect the camp. There were three hundred of them and their only protection against the monsoon was three old tents. Nevertheless, within a month they had cleared the area, built a road, and put up a number of huts. Parties moved off from Kanburi to Nakhon Nayok throughout the summer. Kanburi was an officers' camp from the beginning of 1945, the reason for the concentration of officers being – the British were convinced of this – that invasion of Siam from Burma was imminent and the Japanese intended to deprive the prisoners of leadership in case they rebelled. The separation from their men had a bad effect on the officers: they lacked the impetus which a duty to their men had given and, as one of them later remembered, they tended 'to become more self-centred, mopish, and introspective'.[27] They noted the increasing number of Japanese fighting troops moving into the camps around them, and the conviction grew that they were going to be massacred if the British moved into Siam in force. The sixth of the parties to go to Nakhon Nayok was ordered to be ready to go on 15 August 1945. There was some difficulty in the move, since the sixth party comprised the entire camp hospital, including many sick. Two days before they were due to leave, one of the Korean camp guards came into a prisoners' hut and told them that he had heard from the Siamese that Japan was suing for an armistice: 'Nippon want peace.' He came back the next night, in tears, and explained that he had heard more news: the Russians had invaded and bombed his own country, Korea. The prisoners were uncertain how to take this, but when the sixth party moved out and volunteers took the very sick on stretchers to the train, they noticed a familiar face among some Siamese who were cycling past. It was a Siamese who had befriended them, and he said as he went by on his bicycle, in Siamese, 'War is over.' The path from the camp gates to the train was five hundred yards long, and he turned and came back past the file of stretcher-bearers: 'The Japanese have surrendered today.'[28]

The prisoners passed the news on at once to the officer in command of the train, Colonel Pargeter. They urged him not to go to Nakhon Nayok, in fact not to go beyond Bangkok. Meanwhile, the volunteers returned to the camp wondering when the camp commandant, Noguchi, who had earned their bitter hatred, would tell them the news or, indeed, if he would do so at all. As it happened, Noguchi was away, and his second-in-command, Matsushita, summoned the senior British officer, Colonel Swinton, at five o'clock in the evening and told him that the war was over; but that they must still regard themselves as his prisoners until British relief arrived. He did not know whether the fighting troops in the area had received the news, but he implored the prisoners not to leave the camp; he did not know how the other Japanese would react.[29]

The prisoners saw the force of this, but they decided some kind of notice should be taken of the day's event. Three flags, the Union Jack, the Stars and Stripes, and the Dutch flag, were hoisted in a matter of minutes. On the following day they decided to send out a party of prisoners, who had learned some Siamese, for food. They called at one of the more imposing houses in the neighbourhood of the camp, and to their astonishment found a British officer and sergeant in full uniform installed there. This was a party of Force 136, who had been training recruits to the Free Siam Movement only ten miles from the camp.

Their nearness was no coincidence. They were in wireless contact with Calcutta, and if conditions in the camp area became dangerous when and if an invasion was mounted, they were to make it possible for the prisoners to escape, by using Siamese guerrillas. Bearing this amazing news with them, the prisoners returned to the camp, where the Japanese guards had clearly decided to accept the situation. They allowed themselves to be disarmed, and the prisoners took over the running of the camp. A few days later, representatives of RAPWI arrived.

In Nakhon Nayok events followed a similar pattern. The prisoners in the camp had even managed to smuggle a wireless set in with them – it had travelled in the personal luggage of the Japanese commandant. As a result, the prisoners heard the news at the same time as the Japanese themselves. Their senior officer, Colonel Philip Toosey, promptly told the commandant that they knew about the surrender and demanded an immediate issue of supplies. He got them, as did those prisoners in other camps who at once began to raid the Japanese godowns and found in them enough food, clothing, and medical supplies to last for months.[30]

They were the lucky ones. Further up the railway line from Kanburi the news travelled slowly. One party of three hundred prisoners at Kinsayok still had not heard what had happened on 19 August when they received orders to move down the line. They were puzzled by the order, and then, as they approached the camp at Kanburi and saw the Allied flags flying over the huts, they realized that the Japanese were no longer in control. They went berserk. They booted the Japanese sentries off the train, brought it to a halt outside the camp, and struggled out of the carriages and into the camp huts. They were in a shocking condition. Their diet up the line had been grass, roots, and insects, and fifteen of them died in the two days after their arrival in Kanburi. For the rest of them the war ended just in time. The medical officer who accompanied them had given them no more than a month to live. But, desperate as was the condition of the Allied prisoners-of-war, it was certainly no worse than that of the thousands of Asian labourers who had worked for the Japanese on the building of the Siam–Burma Railway.

Major Gilchrist, of the Siam Country Section of Force 136, landed in Chumporn (Jumbhorn) on the coast of the Gulf of Siam shortly after the news of the Imperial broadcast. Gilchrist had been involved in planning co-operation between Force 136 and RAPWI, since it was obvious that the Force 136 teams who knew the country were the best people to put RAPWI in touch with prisoner-of-war camps. The Force 136 teams also had constant wireless liaison with India and

Ceylon. In August 1944 there had been one wireless telegraph station operating from inside Siam to the Allies; a year later there were thirty, and each of them was a nucleus for a Siamese resistance network. A dozen RAPWI teams were set up for Siam, and then it was found that the Chumporn area had not been covered. Close to the Kra Isthmus, it was an important point on the railway line between Bangkok and Singapore, and many prisoners were thought to be held there. In the end, Gilchrist obtained RAPWI's consent to go there himself with two young Siamese W-T operators. They landed in the Gulf of Siam by Catalina, and were taken off in a ten-foot lugger by Vic Wemyss, the head of another Force 136 party already established in hiding at Prachuab further up the coast. Wemyss had already been in touch with the Japanese commander in the Prachuab area, and three Siamese fighter planes were put at the disposal of the Chumporn party for the last leg of their journey. On the crater-studded airfield, ten miles from Chumporn, Gilchrist commandeered a Japanese truck. Halfway to Chumporn itself, he passed a Japanese staff car, which pulled up. A staff colonel got out, who spoke English, and told Gilchrist that no one in Chumporn had had any signal from Prachuab, but that his arrival was not entirely unexpected: they had discussed the question of surrender at a staff meeting that morning. 'If you had come yesterday, we would have shot you,' he cheerfully assured Gilchrist.[31]

When Gilchrist came into Chumporn itself, he set about searching for prisoners-of-war. There were no British prisoners at all, but a number of Indian troops were there, who had been left behind when their officers went off to join the Indian National Army. Gilchrist had them put into railway carriages and sent down the line to Penang, in Malaya, which he knew would soon be reoccupied by Mountbatten's forces. And then there were the Asian labourers, from Malaya, Java, Sumatra and other parts of Japan's briefly held Asian empire. Gilchrist visited a Japanese hospital, where the worst cases of sickness were being held. His description of what he found is worth quoting in full.

> It was nothing but a ghastly charnel-house: a series of small rotting huts in heavy jungle with thirty serious cases and a few corpses huddled together on filthy wooden floors. The smell was intolerable; the commonest diseases were tropical ulcers and dysentery – many people had *four* diseases, dysentery, ulcers, beri-beri, and malaria, while scabies, typhoid, pneumonia, syphilis, gonorrhoea, and cancer

were also well represented. The only medicine on view was a kind of weak red disinfectant; no bandages were available and paper dressings, sometimes actually made of what looked like toilet paper, either adhered by themselves or were gummed down round the edges. Food consisted of rice and vegetable soup, in the most meagre quantities. Sanitary arrangements were non-existent, and all the patients were indescribably filthy and verminous.[32]

Gilchrist was puzzled by the Japanese attitude, which seemed to him not one of obstruction but of total incomprehension: 'they could not understand why anyone took so much interest in those miserable creatures'.[33] When Gilchrist summoned the Japanese commander responsible for the area, it was Lieutenant-General Hamada whom he met, the same Hamada whose rectitude Tsuji had so much admired, in contrast with Nakamura's indolence. Gilchrist warned Hamada, whose authority covered the railway units and administration between Prachuab and the frontier with Malaya, that the Japanese command would be held responsible for the condition of the coolies. Hamada protested that lack of medicine and equipment was responsible, but Gilchrist refused to accept this. Even without equipment, it was possible to wash patients and dress their wounds, provide them with mosquito netting, and give them clean water and food. It was not a question of cruelty so much as of inhuman neglect.

He reported what he found, by radio from Chumporn, and passed on a list of the names of the Japanese officers who seemed to be responsible for the area. At the end of August he interviewed Hamada who, through a not very competent interpreter, told Gilchrist what he intended to do. He used a Japanese proverb to do this, and it was several months before Gilchrist realized its true significance. To make doubly sure he had made his meaning clear, Hamada repeated it in a letter: 'The Japanese,' he wrote, 'esteem the carp. When this fish is placed on the chopping block, ready to be cooked, it does not jump and bounce, it stays still and submits to its fate quietly.'[34]

In November 1945 Gilchrist, by this time Deputy Political Adviser to the GOC British troops in Siam, General Evans (now General Sir Geoffrey Evans), asked Evans if he had heard of Hamada. He was told that Hamada had been arrested soon after British troops had entered Bangkok, and had committed *seppuku** because, said Evans,

* The correct term for *hara-kiri*.

he could not face the prospect of being tried as a war criminal. He had written a poem before he killed himself and sent it to Evans, whose Japanese interpreter was tremendously impressed by it, and could not read it without weeping. Evans was merely puzzled by it. He told Gilchrist that all it said was, ' "The evening breeze moves the clouds to the horizon, but the flowers in the garden are fading." Not easy to understand, those Japs, are they?'[35]

iv *Further Metamorphoses of Colonel Tsuji*

In the meantime, Tsuji, whom Hamada had encouraged to go under-ground with the help of Taiwanese pirates, was putting his own plans into execution. First he wanted company. Before the end of the war, to stiffen Japanese resistance, the Southern Area Army had received its quota of *kamikazes*. The term Tsuji used for them – they were not only air force pilots, of course – was 'special assault troops' (*tokkōtai yōin*), and there were about fifty of them in Bangkok, young, fit, and ready for action. Tsuji summoned them and told them of his plan to go underground in Siam, disguised as a Buddhist priest. None of them was over twenty-three, but eight of their number, all second lieutenants and cadets, had been Buddhist priests in civilian life, and all eight volunteered to follow Tsuji. He was deeply impressed by this. The older men had only one thought in their heads, as far as he could see: to return to Japan as quickly as possible. But here were these youngsters prepared to stay behind in Siam for ten, possibly twenty years in the cause of friendship between Siam and Japan. One of the eight was ordered to return to Japan and contact the families of the others to let them know what had hap-pened. He was also told to bring about a reformation of the religious world of Japan. Tsuji's next step was to obtain the assent of the Siamese authorities.

The Japanese Ambassador, Yamamoto, agreed to approach the Siamese Premier and the Minister of Education on Tsuji's behalf. In an inner room at the Thailand Hotel, Tsuji and his seven remaining disciples were vested in their Buddhist robes by the priest Maruyama of the Nichiren sect, who had also been, during the war, a member of the *Hikari Kikan* (the 'Lightning Organization', which had helped to organize rebel Indian troops against the British). Their pictures were taken for identification by the Siamese authorities. They put on the single yellow piece of cloth, four foot by six, which covered the whole body. Underneath they wore, like a skirt, a shorter cloth, three foot by four, held in place by a thin cord. Carrying a *dhuta* bag, Tsuji looked transformed, though he could not imitate the carefree stride of the Siamese priests. On 16 August he changed back into Japanese Army uniform to take formal farewell of the Japanese commander-in-chief, and spent the evening over a *sukiyaki* dinner with General Hamada in the officers' club. The pretty Japanese waitresses, he was told, were prepared for the worst when the Allies landed: each one carried a cyanide phial in her pocket. Hamada gave him the briefest of farewells – '*o buji de*' ('Look after yourself').

After bidding goodbye to his Siamese pupil, Major Att Chalenshilba, Tsuji made his way to the vault inside the Ryab Temple, which had served as an ossuary for the Japanese community in Bangkok for the past fifty years. 'My name is Aoki,' he said to the old priest in charge. 'I beg for your guidance.' The old priest, Chino, was no recluse himself. As a boy he had left Japan and emigrated to northern Australia as a pearl-diver and later worked on rubber plantations in Malaya and as a cabin-boy. He settled in Rangoon, married, and opened a laundry. Under the influence of the priest Fujii, of the Nihon Sanmyōhō Temple, he underwent a religious conversion, threw over his business, and, as Tsuji puts it, dedicated his life to beating the drum. Literally, with an energy befitting a much younger man, Chino beat his drum daily, striding through the streets of Bangkok proclaiming 'Homage to the Sutra of the Lotus of the Wonderful Law' (*Namu Myōhō Renge Kyō*), the rosary phrase used by members of the Nichiren sect. For the past two years he had supervised the Buddhist funerals of Japanese in Bangkok and was a well-known character in the city. He was also shrewd enough to realize that the new arrival, Aoki, and his seven young companions, who had brought enough stocks from army depots to last a whole year – bean curd, rice, dehydrated vegetables, dried fish – were no ordinary bonzes.

The ossuary consisted of two towers, thirty-six feet high and sixteen square feet in area at the base. There was no light or water, and the only drinking water fell from the roof into a trough. When the monsoon was over, the trough dried up, mosquito larvae began to hatch out in it, and they had to buy drinking water. One day, Tsuji, suspicious at the odd smell of the water brought by an itinerant vendor, followed him home, and found him drawing water from a pool in a bomb crater. A dead dog was floating in it...Behind the ossuary was a green stagnant pond which stank, but it was part of Tsuji's training to strip and bathe in this pond every day, after lining up in front of the ossuary with the rest and chanting sutras, to the time of the wooden and metal gongs. Tsuji mastered their texts quicker than he had expected. In a week, he knew by heart the Wisdom Sutra and the Prajna Paramita Sutra, much to the scorn of old Chino, for whom any sutra other than the Lotus Sutra was a waste of time. After the evening meal, a candle was lit, and the monks gathered round it and talked for hours at a time about the future of Japan.

Then came an order that they must all present themselves to be identified at the Religious Bureau in Bangkok on 20 August. Tsuji wondered if he would pass muster: he was more muscular than you would expect a priest to be, and if anyone looked closely the wound on his right arm was still fresh. When he lined up with the other monks at the Bureau, which was close to the Japanese general head-quarters, in a file of a hundred Japanese, he felt sure he would be spotted. His fears increased when he noticed a Japanese in sports shirt and dark glasses staring at him very hard. The man came up to him and dug him hard in the ribs. Tsuji looked closer. It was his old class-mate from the Military Academy, Takeuchi,[36] who had come to Siam several years before, ostensibly with a Japanese business firm but in fact as an undercover intelligence agent. So he too was staying behind in Siam, Tsuji thought. They exchanged glances before Tsuji was summoned to face the head of the Religious Bureau. The head sat in the centre of a room, with assessors on either side. They all turned to look at Tsuji as he came in.

'What sect do you belong to?'

'The Shinshū Sect.'

'How long have you been a priest?'

'In Japan, about twenty years. In Burma, two years. I have just recently arrived in Bangkok and am not yet accustomed to the Siamese way of wearing robes.'

'Do you beat the drums?'

'No, I do not beat the drums. Only the Nichiren Sect does that.'

'What is the meaning of beating drums?'

Tsuji did not know and broke into a cold sweat.

'Ah, it is to . . . it is a charm to frighten away the enemies of the Buddha.'

'For what purposes, and for how long, do you wish to study in Siam?'

'I would like to become a *kusabi* (linchpin) to bind together Japan and Siam for ever in the way of Buddha. I would like to stay for ten years. If you will allow me . . .'

'Good. Study hard, and strive for friendship between Japan and Siam.'

The ordeal was over. Somebody high up, Tsuji felt sure, had put in a good word for him; perhaps the Premier, Aphaiwong?

Tsuji soon began to change his plans. Exasperated by the constant thieving from the ossuary and more and more convinced, that Siamese Buddhism was merely a matter of formal disciplinary rules, he began to think of moving on. Perhaps the answer lay, not in Siam, but China? Now the war was over, he was pretty sure Nationalist China could find some use for experienced Japanese officers. The problem was how to make contact with Chungking? It was no use employing Chinese who had formerly served Japanese intelligence. These men had now gone underground and went in daily fear of their lives from both Siamese and the representatives of Chiang Kai-shek, who were attempting to assert their control over the huge and wealthy Chinese business population of Bangkok. The old temple servant, Lao Tai, provided the answer. He was a Cantonese and did the temple buying through merchants from his native province. Tsuji arranged to sell some spare bedding through him, and as a result got in touch with a Cantonese merchant, Wang Hsiang-cheng, who brought him copies of Chinese newspapers, and the latest gossip. Tsuji was soon able to learn the whereabouts of the Chungking Government's headquarters. It was on Suriwongse Road, and there were three senior Chinese officers in charge, under the command of a lieutenant-general. In preparation for his departure, Tsuji shared out most of his secret service funds, passing 100,000 bahts to another monk, Nagai, who had been a member of the *Hikari Kikan*. Just before the British occupation forces arrived in Bangkok, the Commander-in-Chief, Nakamura, came to the ossuary to pay his last respects to the souls of the war dead. He tried to persuade Tsuji to reconsider his decision and come forward if the British forces wanted him. Tsuji said there were various reasons why he could not comply. The young *kamikazes* who had left the army with him would be dismayed if he returned; so too would those Siamese who had collaborated in hiding him. 'Think of me as one already dead,' he told Nakamura.

Another staff officer came to see him the day before the British came. After they arrived, the Japanese would not be authorized to use their own aircraft and a final plane was to be sent off that day. He could escape to French Indo-China, he was told, but he turned down this last offer too. Then the British arrived. They set up their own general headquarters quite close to the ossuary, and several times a day Tsuji had to pass by British troops who peeped through the hedge to watch old Chino beat his drum. On one occasion Chino beckoned them inside, but they did not accept his invitation. The Siamese police increased their vigilance once the British came in, and plain-clothes detectives kept a twenty-four-hour watch on the temple. One evening, after Tsuji had completed his chanting of the sutra, he noticed someone hiding behind a tree. He went up to the man and in the moonlight made out the muzzle of a pistol pointed directly at him. Tsuji turned and strolled back into the ossuary. They were the only Japanese left free in Bangkok, but the secret police clearly intended to keep them under control. Nonetheless Tsuji soon took another risk. When his friend General Hamada committed suicide, Tsuji had a votive tablet made for him on reading the news in the Chinese press. There were already two tablets receiving special honours in the ossuary, one commemorating Lieutenant-General Shidei, Tsuji's former tutor at the Military Academy, and another for the Indian independence leader, Subhas Chandra Bose, both of whom had crashed to their deaths in Taiwan in mid-August.* Tsuji placed Hamada's tablet beside theirs. A quiet soft-spoken man, who never dodged responsibilities, it is only now he is in his coffin, Tsuji thought bitterly, that his true worth will be acknowledged. Tsuji ran a risk: if the British investigated the ossuary and found the three tablets in a position of honour they might begin to suspect the identity of the priest who had put them there. Tsuji burned them before he left.

The British did begin to push their enquiries a little more closely. Siamese police were sent to the Mahatat Temple where Tsuji's seven young *kamikaze* companions had gone. The questions they were asked and the answers they gave were memorized and written down for Tsuji's benefit, and sent to the ossuary by Siamese messenger.

* Cf. Chapter 5.

Tsuji learned them off by heart so that there should be no discrepancy in their stories. The other priests in the ossuary also had pasts which connected them with Burma, and one of them could not avoid referring to this. The Siamese detective who was putting the questions did not seem to want to take this up, and, when the interrogation was over and Tsuji offered him fruit and cakes, he told them that the investigation was being carried out at the request of the British and was not desired by the Siamese authorities. He hoped they would not bear the Siamese a grudge and said that even though Japan had lost the war the Siamese still had a great regard for them. The Japanese were the second greatest people in the world, he declared. Taken aback at this, Tsuji asked him who were the greatest. 'The Germans,' was the reply. 'Only German-made dyes, used for colouring the robes of priests, do not fade. German razor blades are the sharpest and last longer than any others. The best people I met among the foreigners in Bangkok were the Germans. There were only twenty or thirty of them but they were never arrogant.' Tsuji interpreted these comments as a sign of growing resentment against the British, who had begun to use the green space in front of the royal palace as a landing ground. Whatever the reason, the detective did not press his enquiries and did not search the buildings. When he had finished he knelt before the statue of Buddha and made a ritual hand clap three times. Tsuji breathed a sigh of relief. In the hollow back of that Buddha was concealed his samurai sword.

Two events occurred which strengthened Tsuji's intention to leave Bangkok. On 28 September the Siamese police clashed with the local Chinese community, which had insisted on flying the flag of Nationalist China together with that of Siam. Full-scale street fighting broke out in the city, and lasted for three days. As a reprisal, the Chinese community went on strike. They closed the rice shops, and the fish and vegetable markets. For five days the Siamese market-gardeners and fishermen saw their stocks rot. Food supply in Bangkok came to a rapid halt – a convincing demonstration, thought Tsuji, that the economic life of the capital lay in Chinese hands.

Then, at the end of the month, Japanese NCOs arrived from general headquarters to remove the remains of Japanese troops from the ossuary. This was Tsuji's last chance to contact headquarters. He wrote a final letter to the commander-in-chief, and placed what remained of his secret service funds, 100,000 bahts, in a wooden box which was supposed to carry the ashes of the dead, keeping only 10,000 Chinese yuan and 1,000 bahts for himself. When the Siamese cabinet changed the country's name again, and began calling it 'Siam' instead of 'Thailand' – the name which had become current under the Japanese occupation – Tsuji felt the approach of danger. Perhaps he should transfer to a Siamese monastery? One of his *kamikaze* monks, Kubo, saw the Chief Abbot of the Mahatat Temple to negotiate on his behalf. He returned to Tsuji in great alarm: 'Something terrible has happened. When the Chief Abbot contacted the head of the Siamese Religious Bureau this morning, he was told that all the Japanese priests were going to be placed in detention camps. We are all to be arrested without warning on 29 October!' The same evening he heard from a Japanese officer who came to the ossuary that the British had asked Japanese head-quarters to hand over Tsuji. They were told that he had deserted on 16 August and most likely had taken his own life. The officers came to take away the last remains from the ossuary. There was to be no more contact between it and Japanese headquarters. Tsuji was being abandoned.

Determined not to be taken, he threw himself on the mercy of the Chinese. Accompanied by another monk, who spoke both Siamese and Chinese, he went to the Kuomintang District Office, which had opened up in a block belonging to a Japanese company in Suriwongse Road. The young official he dealt with was a Cantonese, and all Tsuji could manage was a little broken Mandarin, so they conversed on paper in the ideographs they both understood. Tsuji stressed his relations with the Chinese general, Tai Li, and asked to be sent to Chungking to meet Tai Li and Chiang Kai-shek, and so open the way for collaboration between China and the new Japan. He revealed that he was a Japanese officer who had gone underground disguised as a bonze, so if they were unwilling to do this, they might as well arrest him and be done with it.

The Chinese left him, and held a conference which lasted half an hour. Then the Chief Secretary, a Colonel Cheng, entered the room where Tsuji sat. 'All right,' he said, 'We'll do it.' Tsuji returned to the ossuary, said goodbye to the monks who remained, and told them he intended to fake a suicide to cover his escape. The temple gate was closed before ten in the evening, so he must leave before then; and he must somehow evade the Siamese secret police who were watching the temple, and the British sentries who were on guard at their headquarters near by. When it was dark, he turned off the light in his room to make it appear he had gone to bed, lit some incense before a statuette of the Buddha, and placed three suicide notes, together with his watch, wallet, identity card – in the name of the priest Aoki Norinobu – and priest's robes on the desk. He put on the white shirt and trousers of a typical Chinese and slipped out of his room. Standing for a moment in front of the temple, he offered up a brief prayer, then made for the main gate. The main gate to the Ryab Temple, which adjoined the ossuary, had been half destroyed by bombing, and as few worshippers now came to it, it had become a resort for thieves. Tsuji chose a poplar tree to hide behind, and waited for the car the Chinese had promised.

He waited, and nothing came. It would soon be the hour when the thieves began to collect at the spot, so Tsuji decided to move on and wait in a nearby air-raid shelter. He heard a sound in the darkness, and made out the form of a young Siamese, who had been a waiter for the *Kempei* during the war. In broken Japanese the boy whispered, 'Bonze, bonze, you go away?' But the boy was not going to betray him, as Tsuji at first believed. 'Bonze, bonze,' he went on, 'danger, danger, English danger,' and pointed to the street. Tsuji looked through the darkness and could just see the lamplight glinting on a fixed bayonet. It was a helmeted British sentry. Tsuji was sure he would hear the boy, and for a terrifying second was tempted to strangle the youth into silence. Then he felt deeply ashamed. 'I like Japanese. I find *samlo* (rickshaw).' Tsuji let go the boy's hands.

They sat down under the tree. Still no car came. Tsuji had timed the passage of the armoured carriers, mounted with machine guns, which went up and down past the headquarters every thirty minutes. The sentries were changed on the hour. It was already one o'clock in the morning of 29 October. There were almost no passers-by now, save for one or two drunken British soldiers who shouted as they pursued the Siamese girls. The boy pleaded to be released, and swore he would tell no one. Tsuji let him go. Two o'clock. Three. Four. Obviously the boy was not coming back. The sky began to lighten in the east, and small groups of Chinese began to go by in the street outside, carrying bundles of vegetables to market. There was no point in waiting any longer. He picked up his bag, slung his blankets over his shoulder, and passed by the temple gate. The two British sentries were fast asleep, their heads resting on their rifles.

Tsuji coughed, and his footsteps momentarily awoke them. They glanced in his direction, saw a Chinese on his way to work, and went to sleep again. At an intersection, Tsuji called a passing *samlo*: 'Suriwongse Road, ten bahts! and hurry!' It was twice the usual fare.

At a quarter to six, Tsuji entered the Bangkok headquarters of the Kuomintang. They had come for him the night before at nine o'clock, they said, but did not see him. Soon a car was taking him to a hide-out in the suburbs, the house of a rich Chinese merchant, now used by the Chinese underground. Some of them turned up that evening to chat. He was curious to find out how they had got into Siam. They had left Chungking three years previously. Some had entered Siam by submarine or by air from India, others had crossed the Mekong River from Indo-China. The Japanese had caught many of them, but enough had got through to organize the Chinese community on behalf of Chiang Kai-shek. They were all members of General Tai Li's Blue-Shirt Society, and it was this organization which was finally to remove Tsuji from the net the British were slowly drawing round him. He was to go by train to Ubon, make for Vientiane in Laos, then Hanoi, and finally Chungking. The night before he left, in grateful appreciation, he gave the two chief officials presents which he had carried with him throughout the war: a pair of cuff links given him by Prince Mikasa, and a *sake* cup he had received from the Emperor himself.

The young owner of the house, Wu Chien-sheng, turned out to be as adept at clandestine activity as the Blue Shirts. The plan was to take Tsuji to Bangkok Station as a Chinese under escort by the Siamese military police. Wu burgled the house of a military police official, and stole his uniform and identity card. They stuck a photograph of Wu on it, then set off, early in the morning of 1 November 1945. At the station they saw the Siamese police were scrutinizing identity cards and searching luggage under the supervision of British troops. Wu told Tsuji to wait in the car until just before the train left. At five minutes to eight the departure bell rang. Tsuji was given a ticket and made for the turnstile. As the departure time was so close, the scrutiny had stopped, and he hurried through as if he were late for the train. Neither Siamese nor British thought it worthwhile to stop the old Chinese, who was anxiously agitating a newspaper as he leapt for the already moving train. As the train puffed out, Tsuji took a seat near the window and opened his newspaper. 'Japanese priests placed in detention camp!' the headlines proclaimed. He read through the article, which named all the priests at the ossuary. His own alias, Aoki, was missing.

So began the first stage of Tsuji's long odyssey. Five months later, in a plane piloted by an American flyer, he came down on the narrow air strip at Chungking.

v *Finale*

The departure of Tsuji did not mean that Siam's troubles were over, though she was no doubt well rid of her turbulent priest. The British intended to see that she worked her passage home – in the phrase that had won currency in the Foreign Office – after her discreditable alliance with the Japanese; though there were many Englishmen who wondered how it was possible to be so harsh with the Siamese on the one hand and so undemanding with Aung San on the other. In spite of considerable American pressure to relax severity, the British insisted on a form of rice indemnity. One and a half million tons of free rice was demanded as one of the terms of the peace agreement.[37] In the interests of stability, Mountbatten also advised the Siamese to recall their king from Switzerland, whence he arrived early in September. Less than three weeks later, a new Premier was appointed, Prince Seni Pramoj, the former Minister in Washington, and leader of the Free Siamese abroad.

Mountbatten himself was in no doubt of the Siamese desire to resume friendly relations with Britain, and he paid a visit to Bangkok in January 1946 for the peace celebrations, and another in the spring. He found the attitude of the Siamese 'helpful and hospitable'[38] but rice was a stumbling block. The Chinese businessmen who controlled the Siamese rice market did not relish unleashing their stocks *gratis*; and even when a price was put upon their services, it was found to be too low to be successful. They did not view their moral obligations towards starving fellow Asians in quite the spirit Mountbatten and his political adviser, Esler Dening, would have liked.

Later, political troubles developed. Through friends and colleagues like Seni Pramoj, Pridi controlled the government for two years after the Japanese surrender, but his prestige suffered a severe blow when the young King, Ananda, was discovered shot in his bedroom in May 1946 – a mystery which has never been satisfactorily solved.

Pridi resigned the premiership, and in November fled to China, which was soon to be in Communist hands. By the spring of the following year Pibul was in power again, as the result of a military coup.

Then there was the matter of the territories Siam had acquired under Japanese aegis. There was no question of not returning the four northern Malay states to Malaya, in the presence of determined British armed force. But the Siamese resisted as long as possible the retrocession to the French of the Laotian and Cambodian territories which she had occupied since 1941. The French for their part were, understandably, obdurate, and it was only after acquiescing to their demands that Siam was finally, several years after the war had ended, allowed to take her seat in the United Nations.

CHAPTER THREE

THE BIRTH OF INDONESIA

i *The Japanese and Indonesian Independence*

The twin-engined bomber appeared out of the clouds. It came low over Kemayoran airfield, but no one scattered, no one ran for shelter. Instead the crowd assembled at the airfield went mad with joy. The plane came to rest in front of them. The narrow door opened in the side, and a figure dressed in a suit of dazzling pure white stood upright in the opening. 'Long live President Sukarno!' the roar rose from the crowd, 'Long live *merdeka* (freedom)!' They went wild with enthusiasm as the neat figure stepped down, followed by two others. The Japanese Military Governor of Java, Yamamoto Shigeichi, stepped forward with a greeting. Vigorous handshakes were exchanged, and the Japanese, overcome with emotion, began to weep tears of joy. Sukarno came to the dais which had been set up near the airport buildings. He took a grip on his emotions, mounted the dais, and turned to the crowd. 'I told you that Indonesia would be free and independent when the *jagon* (maize) flower blooms. The *jagon* has not yet bloomed, and we have achieved that independence!' The crowd went berserk. Caps were flung in the air, thousands of throats yelled themselves hoarse. Under Japan's aegis, Indonesia was free at last. Colonial rule would never return.

Unknown both to Sukarno and to the screaming crowd, Japan had already accepted the Potsdam Declaration and had surrendered unconditionally. Soon, the new republic would begin to look very fragile indeed. Indonesia had long ago been promised her independence, first by Premier Tōjō and again, in September 1944, by Koiso;

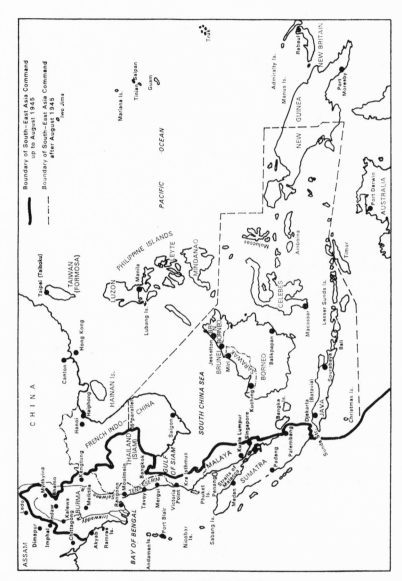

SOUTH-EAST ASIA COMMAND

but Japan's procrastination is understandable. Java was the most populous of Japan's conquests in South-East Asia, and with its tin, rubber and oil, one of the richest. It was to secure the oil fields in the Dutch East Indies that Japan had made war in the first place. Borneo, Sarawak, Java, Sumatra – these places were the target of the drive to the south. The other campaigns – in the Philippines, in Burma, in Malaya, even the capture of Singapore – were all subsidiary to the securing of fuel for Japanese industry which the Indies provided. Having seized them from the Dutch in the lightning campaign of February and March 1942, Japan was loath to release them. So while in Burma and the Philippines puppet governments received their charters of independence, the Indonesians were kept waiting for theirs.

Japan was well aware of the comparison drawn between the various East Asian countries. Koiso had this in mind when his government drew up a draft statement on independence. 'The fact that Burma and the Philippines have already attained independence,' the draft ran, 'is not simply the fulfilment of the traditional desires of the peoples concerned; it is no less than the cornerstone of Greater East Asian co-existence and co-prosperity. The Empire now hopes to give further concrete expression to this national policy and here to make clear its policy of giving full support to the future realization of the independence of Java.'[1] Although formal independence had not yet been granted, nevertheless, as Koiso pointed out, the Japanese had permitted the peoples living under Military Government in Java and elsewhere to participate politically in the direction of their own affairs. The infra-structure of the administration was in fact, as Mohammed Hatta later pointed out, in Indonesian hands: '. . . all posts – with the exception of few at the top – were in our hands'.[2] But Japan did more than train politicians. She organized an Indonesian military force, using some Indonesians who had been NCOs in the pre-war Royal Netherlands Indies Army and others who received their first military instruction at Japanese hands. The Japanese 16th Army, which garrisoned Java, set up an auxiliary 'Corps for the Defence of the Fatherland' (referred to by the Japanese as *Giyūgun*, or 'volunteer force' and by the Indonesians as *Tentara Sukarela Pembela Tanah Air* (Volunteer Army for the Defence of the Homeland), or *Peta* for short.* The *Peta* consisted of thirty-

* There seems to be some discrepancy about the Indonesian description of the *Peta*. According to Pauker, it stands for *Barisan Pembela Tanah Air*;[3] for

five units called *daidan* (battalion), modelled on the Japanese battalion (*daitai*), but with half the strength. Each *Peta* battalion had just over five hundred officers and men, and Japanese officers were attached as instructors. The number of *daidan* were increased during 1944 until they numbered sixty-six in all on Java, with three further *daidan* on Bali. This was not all. The Japanese also recruited close on 25,000 troops in Java and another 2,500 in Timor, called *Hei-ho* (Military Auxiliaries), who acted as labouring auxiliaries to the Japanese forces; and a number of youth organizations, the *Keibōdan* (Defence Corps) and the *Seinendan* (Youth Corps), were formed in 1943, the former to act as auxiliary police, the latter as a kind of 'boy-scout' movement.[5]

When the Japanese invaded the Indies in 1942, the Dutch Governor-General and some of his administrators remained behind and were interned. The Lieutenant Governor-General, Dr H. J. Van Mook, received orders to leave for Australia, where he set up an interim administration in Brisbane. The Japanese at first kept the Dutch system in being, and even retained some Dutch officials for a few months, as they did some Englishmen in their administration of Hong-Kong. These were then replaced by Japanese officials who held the key positions at *Residentie*, or provincial level.[6]

The Japanese formed a Military Government, but made matters needlessly complicated for themselves by dividing it up between army and navy. The 16th Army ran Java, the 25th Army ran Sumatra, while the Navy (2nd Southern Expeditionary Fleet) was responsible for the South-West District Civil Government, including Borneo and the adjoining islands, the Celebes and adjoining islands, and the Lesser Sunda Islands.[7]

It was typical of Japanese Military Government, even when exercised indirectly, that it should attempt to interfere with the most trivial details of the daily lives of those subjected to it. A circular letter on the correct 'spirit and attitude' to be maintained, issued by the Regent of Luwu, Palopo, is instructive on this point. It is dated 27 December 1944 and it inculcates ostentatious industriousness and humourless respect: 'Officials are not allowed to leave their offices without permission from me or from the Japanese who are their superiors. There are many officials who like to walk around when

---

Benda, the full phrase is *Pasoekan soeka-rela oentoek membela Tanah Djawa*, op. cit., p. 252, n. 36; Kahin speaks of *Soekarela Tentara Pembela Tanah Air*.[4]

at work. This I cannot accept.' A particular convention governed greetings: 'During the greeting or when returning a greeting we must not laugh, smoke, etc. but assume an energetic posture. If we encounter a person of higher rank while running, we must at once slow down and then salute. It is forbidden to greet a person while running.' Walking, too: 'We must at all times walk forcefully and courageously; we should look neither right nor left, we should not turn back, and we should not assume an attitude of fatigue... When walking with a superior, we must not stay abreast of him but remain slightly behind him and always walk on his left side.' It was forbidden to sing or whistle in the Regent's offices, to speak in a loud voice, to squat, to sit with crossed legs or even with one's mouth open, 'lest one be considered empty-headed'. Idleness, of course was prohibited: 'When we have no work to do, we must read regulations concerning work.' Cleanliness was next to godliness for women as for men: 'We must bathe every day; female officials must wash their hair at set times and not use coconut oil as hair oil.' And the inevitable injunction concerning the Emperor: 'During every conversation in which the name *"Tennō Heika"* (His Imperial Majesty) occurs, one must stand at attention.'[8]

Javanese nationalism had developed strongly in the period between the wars, in spite of imprisonment or exile inflicted by the Dutch authorities on known nationalists, and by 1939 the various nationalist organizations were federated into the *Gaboengan Politiek Indonesia* (Indonesian Political Union). To convince the Indonesians that they were serious in their talk of independence, the Japanese allowed them to form an association known as the *Poesat Tenaga Rakjat* (Centre of People's Power) in March 1943. Abbreviated to *Poetera* (*Putera*), this association included most of the nationalist bodies on the islands of Java and Madura and was intended to serve as a bridge towards self-government. It was run by a committee of four, who were termed the *Empat Serangkai* (Four-Leaf Clover), all of them tried nationalist revolutionaries. Sukarno was its chairman, an engineering graduate of the Bandung Technical College who had been imprisoned and then exiled by the Dutch for subversive activities in the thirties; its vice-chairman was Mohammed Hatta, leader of the Indonesian Union (*Perhimpoenan Indonesia*, or PI); and the other two members were Ki Hadjar Dewantoro and a Mohammedan leader, Kiaji H. M. Mansur. The *Putera* was all things to all men. To the Japanese it was a means of strengthening their hold on

Java. To the Indonesians, not all of whom were active Japanese sympathizers, it was an instrument in the struggle for independence. It soon became clear to the Japanese that the latter function was predominating, and they dissolved the *Putera* in February 1944.[9] It was replaced by a new organization which they hoped would be under more effective Japanese control, the *Java Hōkōkai* or People's Service Association (in Indonesian: *Perhimpoenan Kebaktian Rakjat*). The Japanese insisted that it should incorporate not merely Javanese, but other elements in the population, Chinese, Arabs, and Eurasians. Sukarno and Hatta continued to be chairman and vice-chairman respectively.

It was to counter-balance this nationalist strength – at least this was the intention – that the Japanese had created in 1943 the Consultative Council of Indonesian Muslims (*Majlis Sjuro Muslimin Indonesia*, abbreviated to *Masjumi*). In spite of peasant rebellions against rice requisitioning in 1944, which led to savage reprisals, the Japanese were determined to use Islam as a means of securing their political base in Indonesia.[10] They encouraged the Islamic movement on Java, declaring they would 'endeavour to protect and advance Muslim religion, together with their religious leaders who are the foremost educators of the people...'[11] Such leaders would have to be 'sufficiently versed in Islamic law and Muslim customs and usages, in addition to showing a clear appreciation of the Dai Nippon Military Government.'[12] Japan was making an attempt to continue her rule by dividing off the secular-based nationalists from the Islamic Masjumi element.* The policy was not unsuccessful, but after Premier Koiso's promise of independence in September 1944 the Masjumi came out firmly on the side of the secular nationalist movement. Their executive met in Djakarta in October and called on all Muslims to prepare for the independence of their country and religion, and – with one eye on the Japanese – to support the Holy War. 'With Nippon we stand,' they concluded, 'with Nippon we fall, in the path of Allah, to destroy a tyrannous enemy.'[13] An even more surprising ally was sought, by some Japanese at least. Rear-Admiral Maeda, commander of Japanese naval forces in Java and Madura, and chief of naval intelligence for Indonesia as a whole, started a school for semi-educated Indonesian youths in October 1944, under the name of *Asrama Indonesia Merdeka* (School for Free Indonesia). The school was in Jakarta, with a branch in

* Cf. Kahin, op. cit., p. 115.

Surabaya. As its head, Maeda selected Wikana, whom he knew to be connected with the underground Communist Party. Wikana was associated with Achmad Subardjo, a former leader of the Indonesian Union in Holland who had spent a year in Moscow in the twenties, and who, by a strange metamorphosis, had become a civilian official in the Japanese naval headquarters.*

Maeda contacted many nationalist leaders, non-Communists included, to lecture to his young men on such topics as politics, sociology, and economics, the purpose being to train them as nationalist leaders. Hatta was willing to do this, as was Sutan Sjahrir, a Dutch-educated left-winger and leader of the anti-Japanese underground since 1943, and a youth group-leader, Mas Sudiro.

The lecturers were given complete freedom to say what they liked, and Maeda did not intervene even when it became obvious they were attacking the Japanese administration, which Sjahrir and Hatta did not hesitate to do when propagating their nationalist ideas. On the other hand, in stressing the study of Communism, Maeda skilfully put before the students the ideal of national independence as linked to a world-wide struggle against capitalist imperialism, in which the enemies were not the Axis powers but the old colonial régimes of Britain and the Netherlands, and their backer, the USA. The school's graduates, in their hundreds, were recruited into an underground nationalist organization led by Subardjo. Views differ on Maeda's motives. Some Indonesians later thought he had simply intended to split and secretly control the Communist underground; others that he was attempting to ensure it would resist American forces, should they invade Java; others again believed that Maeda's leanings towards Marxism were genuine.[15] Tan Malaka, a well-known Communist underground worker who had led a Communist uprising against the Dutch in 1926, was also thought to be working with the Japanese at this period.[16]

While the Japanese in Java were juggling with these various elements of Indonesian political society, and at the same time training Indonesian guerrilla leaders against an Allied landing, events moved fast in the homeland. Between January and July 1945 draft memoranda on Indonesian independence were discussed by the Supreme Council for the Direction of the War, the Greater East Asia Ministry, the Foreign Ministry, and the Southern Army. The Japanese intended to proclaim independence for Java first, and then

* He was chief of its Consulting Office on Political Affairs.[14]

to extend it later to the rest of the Netherlands East Indies.[17] The new nation was, of course, to maintain 'close and inseparable relations with the (Japanese) Empire'.[18] Discussion of these drafts came to a head on 17 July 1945 with a firm decision by the Supreme Council. Its decision No. 27 read: 'In order to aid the successful completion of the Greater East Asia war, the (Japanese) Emperor approves independence for the East Indies at the earliest possible moment, and independence preparations shall be advanced immediately and reinforced.'[19] Independence was to begin in Java, and a Preparatory Committee for Independence was to be set up there.* But the whole of the Dutch East Indies was involved, and the date of independence was to be determined as soon as possible. The sixth and last clause then proceeded to pass the buck. 'The local execution of these measures shall be entrusted completely to the local military authorities.'[20] This did not mean the local military authorities in the Indies themselves. It referred to Field-Marshal Terauchi, Commander-in-Chief of the Southern Army, whose headquarters was in Saigon, in French Indo-China.

Following receipt of an order from Imperial General Headquarters, Terauchi put things into motion. He reported to Tokyo that he envisaged an announcement being made probably at noon on 7 August, establishing the Preparatory Committee for Independence, the date of independence itself being fixed for 7 September. The new country would be expected to declare war on Britain, the Netherlands, and the USA. Japan should recognize it at once, but should postpone appointing an ambassador. The local army commander would act in this role, and a military officer should become minister for Java. The Japanese Empire would retain control of foreign affairs.

Some in Indonesia had begun to fear what they believed Terauchi had in store for them. Thousands of Allied prisoners, British as well as Dutch, had surrendered on Java in 1942 and been held prisoner there. Some had been sent to work on the Siam–Burma Railway, others did forced labour in Java, but in the summer of 1945 they knew that Allied forces were preparing to move into the Indonesian archipelago. The Australians and Americans had landed in Borneo, and took the various oil field areas between February and July. From Rangoon, Mountbatten was preparing to mount Operation Zipper against Malaya and Singapore. Lieutenant-

* Panitya Persiapan Kemerdekaan Indonesia, or PPKI for short.

74

Colonel Laurens van der Post, who had been ordered by Wavell to remain behind in Java in 1942, and had been taken into captivity, received regular intelligence from Chinese friends outside his prison. Through them he learned something of the rising tide of nationalism in Java, and also of what the Japanese were said to be planning for the hundred thousand Europeans held here. Some officers in the camp had managed to construct a secret radio-set, and this provided van der Post with an exact picture of the progress of the war. It also showed him something else which disturbed him profoundly.

He had lived in Japan and knew the Japanese well, and was dismayed that nothing he heard on the set showed 'the slightest hint of what the Japanese would regard as an "honourable" alternative to fighting according to the logic of their spirit, and their sense of history: namely, the annihilation of themselves and of all those of their enemies whom they held as prisoners.'[21] The implications of this were confirmed by news from a Korean informant, a Christian employed by the Japanese. He reported that a new batch of orders had arrived in May 1945 from Terauchi in Saigon. Any notion of defeat or peace by negotiation was rejected. All subordinate commanders were to commit suicide in the traditional Japanese manner to avoid falling into Allied hands. All prisoners, civilians as well as military, were to be concentrated in the central Java plateau at the hill station of Bandoeng, and when the Allies began their final attack on South-East Asia, all prisoners were to be massacred.[22]

So the dropping of the atomic bomb on Hiroshima, which to the rest of the world was the threshold of release from war, was received by van der Post over his secret radio with a mixture of optimism and foreboding. Terauchi and his officers in South-East Asia might take a dreadful revenge for Hiroshima on the prisoners in their hands. On the other hand, it might conceivably make the Japanese feel they had been the target of something so cataclysmic as to be almost supernatural, and so make them able to withdraw from the war without dishonour. Five days later they heard that the Emperor was suing for peace. There were also rumours that Terauchi was going to reject the Imperial command and refuse to surrender. While the Indonesians were preparing for their independence, van der Post and his fellow prisoners were getting ready for a last desperate battle within the walls of their prison camp.

ii *The Proclamation*

Sukarno had already laid down the basis of a new Indonesia in a speech on 1 June, his so-called *Pantja Sila* or five basic principles: nationalism, internationalism, government by consent, social justice, belief in one God.[23] These principles would only be achieved through risk: 'If the people of Indonesia are not united, and are not determined to live or die for freedom, the freedom of Indonesia will never be the possession of the Indonesian people, never until the end of time!' ran his peroration. 'Freedom can only be achieved and owned by a people whose soul is aflame with the determination of *merdeka* (freedom) – freedom or death!'[24] The final Committee for the Preparation of Indonesian Independence was set up for all Indonesia, on Terauchi's authority, on 7 August 1945, with Sukarno as its chairman. It was no longer merely an advisory body. Its twenty-one members, drawn from all over Indonesia, and all well-known nationalists, were to prepare for the transfer to themselves of the authority exercised by the Japanese Army and Navy. On the following day Sukarno flew to Saigon with his colleagues Hatta and Radjiman Wediodiningrat, who was chairman of the Investigating Committee for the Preparation of Independence.*

Sensibly enough, Terauchi was not there. Saigon is intolerable in the humid heat of August, and Southern Army General Headquarters had withdrawn to the hill station of Dalat. There, in the evening of 9 August 1945, Terauchi conceded independence to Indonesia on behalf of Japan. An elaborate ceremony had been arranged on the lawn of Dalat's biggest hotel, on the edge of a lake, under the shade of the palm-trees. The Indonesian delegation had been escorted by a Japanese colonel and a representative of the Foreign Ministry, the Consul Miyoshi. They listened carefully as Terauchi, in his usual high-pitched voice, delivered a congratulatory address to the newborn state. Sukarno spoke in reply, and said he not only rejoiced in independence but took the opportunity to

* In Indonesian *Badan Penjelidik Usaha Persiapan Kemerdekaan Indonesia*, or BPKI for short. Set up by the Japanese in March 1945, this committee's work was concerned only with Java. A separate committee for Sumatra was set up by the Japanese Army on 25 July 1945, but the Navy established no preparatory organization in the Celebes, Borneo, the Moluccas, or the Lesser Sundas, though it allowed a National Party to function there in June. This was suppressed within six weeks.[25]

praise Terauchi's loyalty towards the Emperor. The whole atmosphere was very cordial.[26] Terauchi was celebrating his sixty-sixth birthday, too. But the day was a notable one for two quite different reasons – the Nagasaki bomb and the Russian invasion of Manchuria – neither of which were known to the three Indonesians as they left for Singapore to pay a courtesy visit to General Itagaki on their way home.

Terauchi had told them that independence would be publicly proclaimed on September 7.*

On the evening of their return, Hatta received a visitor. It was Sutan Sjahrir, who was quivering with excitement. Like the Allied prisoners-of-war, Sjahrir had his own secret short-wave receiver, and he had heard the broadcasts which made it clear that Japan was suing for peace. Hatta changed colour, then controlled himself and told Sjahrir, 'If this does happen, we shall go through with our independence in collaboration with Japan, just as we decided.'†

But that collaboration was not entirely dependent on Hatta or his friends. The Japanese commander's consent would be needed, and on 15 August he had other things on his mind. With his staff, he stood solemnly in his headquarters, stiff as a ramrod, listening to the Imperial voice, interrupted by the buzz of atmospherics, surging and dying in echoes like the waves of the sea. They could not make it all out clearly, but there was no doubt about the unconditional surrender. They choked back their sobs of grief, and stood there in an oppressive, leaden silence, until General Nagano, the 16th Army commander, turned on his heel and went into his own room without saying a word. The Military Government Commander, General Yamamoto, who also functioned as Chief of Staff, went to the door and knocked. 'Your Excellency, there are two things you must decide. First, as commander-in-chief of Java, are you going to

---

* Kahin says he promised them Indonesia would be granted independence on 24 August.[27] But Tanaka, whose evidence is nearer the time, is quite specific: '...dokuritsu sengen no hi "kugatsu nanuka" to sadamerareta' ('The day for the proclamation of independence was fixed as "September 7th"').[28]

† The sequence of events in the days immediately preceding and following the Japanese surrender is far from clear. The account I give is based on that of Tanaka Masaaki, a staff member of the Kōa Dōmei (Asia Development Union), No. 5 Bureau, with special responsibility for South-East Asia.[29] Unless references indicate otherwise the narrative in this section is based on his account. It should be compared with the timetable given by J. D. Legge.[30] Legge's account is partly based on an interview with Hatta in 1969, whereas Tanaka's version is nearer to the events.

fight it out to the finish, to the last man? Are you going to continue
a war of resistance to the bitter end? Or are you going to accept the
Imperial order and surrender? Second, what do we do now about
the independence of Indonesia?'[31]

Nagano answered quietly, pausing, as if he found it difficult to
breathe. 'There is no question. Of course we obey superior orders.'
The other problem was not quite so simple. Sukarno and the
Indonesian leaders called on the chief of the General Affairs Department of the Military Government, Major-General Nishimura, to
confirm whether Japan had surrendered or not. They were told he
was in an important meeting, and could not be disturbed. They
were at once to see Rear-Admiral Maeda Minoru.* 'No public
announcement has been made yet,' Maeda told them, 'and when it is,
I'll let you know immediately. Until then, I'd be grateful if you'd all
be very circumspect.'

It was decided to convene the Committee for the Preparation of
Independence at 10 a.m. the following morning, 16 August. The
day was clear, serene, and cloudless. The committee members
arrived one by one and waited. Sukarno and Hatta did not appear.
At eleven o'clock they still had not arrived. By noon the place was
in an uproar. The committee realized that something totally unfore-
seen must have occurred. It had indeed. That morning before dawn,
Sukarno and Hatta had been seized in their homes by young
Indonesian extremists belonging to the youth organization *Angkatan
Muda* (The Young Generation). They were dragged to a truck at pistol
point and driven off. Sukarno's wife and child had been taken too.

This move was not the result of unconsidered violence, nor of
envy of those about to wield power, though it is true that the
Angkatan Muda was not represented on the independence committee.
There was a divergence of policy between leaders like Sukarno and
the young Indonesians, who believed that an independence conceded by the Japanese was useless. If Indonesia was not seen to have
seized power from the Japanese by its own struggles, the Allied
armies would not recognize its independence when they arrived.
They would say the independence was not genuine, that Sukarno
and his colleagues were Japanese puppets, and they would be swept
away. The *Angkatan Muda* plan was to start riots in Jakarta and they
intended to begin at midnight.

* So Tanaka.[32] Benda calls him Maeda Tadashi,[33] and Kahin promotes him
to Vice-Admiral.[34]

In the *Peta* barracks at Rengasdengklok, where they had been taken, Sukarno and Hatta pleaded passionately with Sukarni, the youth movement leader. Though he was head of a youth movement, Sukarni was a force to be reckoned with. He had led youth movements against the Dutch in pre-war days, and during the war had become involved with the Japanese Military Government propaganda department (*Sendenbu*), which made him slightly suspect to some of the other Nationalists.[35] Now he was saying to Sukarno that independence must be proclaimed against the Japanese, not in cooperation with them. He had at his disposal, he claimed, fifteen thousand youths ready to march into Jakarta that night. They were on the outskirts now, waiting for the word to move in.

'If you start riots now and fight the Japanese,' Sukarno told him, 'all our efforts will have been in vain. The independence we have sought will disappear like a bubble on the water. Who will benefit if a struggle breaks out between the Japanese and the Indonesians? The Allies, of course, and our enemy the Dutch. We will provide the troubled waters, they will be the fishermen. It will not be long before they are our masters again. Don't you know that Japan has surrendered unconditionally?' There were tears in his voice as he pleaded; it had an edge of frantic despair.

The Japanese began to be perturbed, too. Subardjo, who was connected with the Sukarni group, decided to consult Maeda. He took Mas Sudiro with him. Maeda was appalled when he learned what had happened. 'We must act at once,' he told Subardjo. 'No waiting for 7 September now. You Indonesians must proclaim your independence immediately. I'll take the responsibility for persuading the Japanese authorities. See that Sukarno and Hatta are safe, and bring them to me as soon as you can.'

Subardjo and Sudiro needed no urging, and went at once to the Rengasdengklok barracks. The place was bristling with arms, and youths from the Volunteer Army crowded threateningly round the two as they approached. By this time Sukarno and Hatta had been talking for hours and had exhausted all their arguments. They had no intention of yielding to Sukarni, but the time was fast approaching when the revolutionary rioters would be unleashed upon the Japanese. Then Subardjo managed to reach Sukarni. He told him what Maeda had promised and he added, 'If he breaks his word, you can shoot me on the spot.'[36] Sukarni and his staff were finally convinced by Subardjo's pleas, but they insisted that they

79

should accompany Sukarno and Hatta to the Japanese admiral's residence. A long procession of cars left Rengasdengklok for Jakarta, while the Japanese attaché Nishijima took some of the youth leaders with him to the medical college in Parapatan where revolutionary headquarters had been set up. They found the young soldiers of the Volunteer Army and the students all ready to attack the broadcasting station and the *Kempei-tai* barracks. They were within a hair's breadth of crisis when Nishijima arrived to talk them out of it.

Maeda's house was set back from Nassau Road, in a grove of trees – it gave the impression of a villa set in the middle of a forest. It was kept under surveillance by *Kempei*, and on its lawns members of the Preparatory Committee for Independence walked anxiously up and down, waiting for the decision then being hammered out in the dining room on the first floor. Japanese Foreign Ministry officials, Nishijima, Yoshizumi, and Miyoshi, were there, and on the Indonesian side Sukarno, Hatta and Subardjo. The Japanese Army representatives had not turned up, though Maeda said he had notified them. The draft declaration of independence was discussed. There was an important question of wording. Was political power to be 'seized' (*dasshu*) or 'transferred' (*ijō*)? The latter was finally chosen, and the final draft declared that 'We the people of Indonesia hereby proclaim the independence of Indonesia. The transfer of power, and the items connected with it, will be effected by peaceful methods within the shortest possible time.' Sukarno and Hatta signed it as representatives of the Indonesian people.

The following day, 17 August, Sukarno read out the declaration of independence at ten in the morning.* Then the national flag was ceremonially raised for the first time. The two colours, red and white, flapped high in the morning breeze. The anthem *Indonesia Raya*, long forbidden by the Dutch, and prohibited for some time by the Japanese too, burst forth from excited throats.

Sukarno made no attempt to wipe away his tears, and told the crowd, in a voice choking with emotion, 'Independence has been proclaimed. But the struggle is not yet over. Far from it. The way ahead is more difficult than the past. We must stake our lives on this declaration of independence. Our national flag has been raised on

* 'Before a crowd of several thousands gathered in front of his house,' writes the Japanese observer, Tanaka;[37] 'To a small group outside of his own house,' writes Kahin;[38] 'A comparatively small crowd...' writes Legge.[39]

high. Promise me you will never let it be taken down!' The crowd roared their approval.

After the enthusiasm and the frenzy, it remained to build the state. The Independence Committee was re-formed into the People's Committee on 18 August and the Constitution of the Republic of Indonesia was adopted. Sukarno was made President of the Republic, and Hatta his Vice-President. On 22 August the formation of a People's Peace Army was proclaimed, and on the 25th the first People's Congress was held. But forming committees was one thing, the possession and control of their own armed forces was another. Here the new republic ran into difficulties. Since the Japanese had surrendered, they had also to be disarmed, which meant that local auxiliary forces had to be disarmed too. The Defence Volunteer Army, or *Peta*, was now about 40,000 strong, and was equipped basically as infantry, with 19,000 rifles and 900 heavy and light machine guns. The Japanese Army in Java and the Lesser Sundas numbered 59,480 men, with 4,984 naval personnel. There were also many thousands of Japanese civilians in Indonesia, the businessmen who had exploited Indonesia's resources on Japan's behalf.* Had the *Peta* shown fight, the Japanese might have found it difficult to disarm them, but in the event the affair went peacefully enough, and was concluded by 19 August.

Four days later, the Japanese commander in Java sent a farewell message to all Indonesians. He made a formal statement that Japan had surrendered, and then thanked the peoples of Indonesia for their friendship and cooperation over a long period of time (it had been about three and a half years). 'We pray,' he concluded, 'that the Indonesian peoples will achieve by peaceful means, the independence they have so long desired.' His next step was to begin the process whereby his own forces would be disarmed. First he determined to concentrate them at key points in Java, leaving behind only the minimal force for maintaining civil order, for which the Japanese were still responsible. Weapons were stored, and the commander is credited with the intention of handing over to the Allies what they

---

* The figures are from Hattori.[40] SEAC's estimates on 15 August 1945 were rather different: Army 38,905, Navy 12,025, Air 4,038, with 6,735 civilians. The map brought by the Japanese delegation to the Rangoon conference on 27 August gives the following figure: 55,565 (total for the 16th Army). Tanaka gives for the 16th Army the ridiculous figure of 15,000 men, with 70,000 civilians.[41] Such discrepancies are common.

required, and returning his troops in safe order to Japan.[42] Then the Allied intervention, which was to alter everything began to take shape.

iii *British and Dutch*

As with French Indo-China, the allocation of the Dutch East Indies to Mountbatten's South-East Asia Command (SEAC) was very recent; in fact the formal transfer took place only on the day Japan surrendered. Before that only Sumatra had been under his command. Throughout the spring and early summer of 1945 Mountbatten had discussed the take-over of the East Indies, which had previously been under MacArthur's South-West Pacific Command. MacArthur wanted his hands free for the assault on the Japanese home islands, and wished to be rid of the responsibility for liberating the Dutch territories. The Dutch themselves were not keen on the transfer. Their interim government in Brisbane had put its military forces at MacArthur's disposal, and Dutch units had been involved in the campaign in Borneo. They claimed that it would be difficult to make a last-minute transfer of their administrative resources from Australia to a command which operated from Ceylon.[43] They also realized that stretching Mountbatten's command as far as the Celebes and including Southern Indo-China in it meant that his resources would be inadequate for reoccupation of Japanese-controlled territories, at any rate in force. And Mountbatten was very short of reliable intelligence on the situation in the Indies. Although van der Post speaks of informing him on the nationalist situation in Java, such information only seems to have percolated through when van der Post himself was released from imprisonment.

The Dutch in Brisbane were confident that as soon as they returned to Indonesia the old rule would be accepted. The Dutch in Holland, who had survived the horrors of the German occupation, needed the return of the Indies to restore their faith in themselves and their economy. Once the machinery of Dutch administration had been installed again, they intended to satisfy the aspirations of various groups in the Indies who wanted a greater autonomy than they had had in pre-war days. In their view the message of Queen Wilhelmina on 6 December 1942 was the framework for these reforms. The ideal was one Dutch Kingdom, united and indivisible, with each part enjoying a wide degree of home rule and liberty. The Dutch were even worse placed to enforce this ideal than the French, who had *some* troops available. Like the French, their shipping was tied up in the Allied Shipping Pool; and the Americans were unwilling to release it to transport the thousands of Dutch prisoners who were held in various parts of Asia by the Japanese, particularly in the Philippines.[44]

To men who believed as they did, Sukarno in particular was anathema, a corrupt traitor who had offered to sell his colleagues in the nationalist movement when the Dutch arrested him before the war, guilty of crimes against his own people by sending them as slaves to work for the Japanese. The Dutch were proud of their achievements in the Indies, and Professor Gerbrandy, their wartime Premier in exile, quotes the British historian Furnivall's comparison between British and Dutch methods of colonization which is so favourable to the Dutch:

> Our officers are magistrates; yours are policemen and welfare officers. Our methods are repressive; yours are preventative. Our procedure is formal and legal; yours informal and personal. Our civil service is an administrative machine; yours is an instrument of order. Our aim is negative – to suppress disorder; yours is positive – to maintain order...[45]

It was the Dutch, Gerbrandy claims, who made the Indies archipelago what it is: 'We fashioned its great and modern architectural structure, we ordered its communications; we gave it a clean bill of health; our technicians worked wonders in every field. We made the Indies.'[46]

'I had been given no hint of the political situation which had arisen in Java,' Mountbatten wrote later.[47] MacArthur's command apparently passed on no intelligence whatever on the state of the Indies. The Brisbane Dutch told Mountbatten on 3 September 1945 that there might be active opposition to the return of the Dutch by the forty-thousand-odd republican troops on Java, but apart from that they gave no warning of the strength of nationalist feeling. On 8 September a small advance party of seven SEAC officers was parachuted into Java – on to Kemayoran airfield – to report on the situation. Against all the evidence, they told Mountbatten that the bulk of the population of Java was indifferent to political movements, that the nationalist movement was the creation of a few intellectuals, and that reoccupation would be simple enough once transport and security problems were overcome.[48]

The first Allied forces to approach Java in strength were on board HMS *Cumberland*, under Rear-Admiral W. R. Patterson, carrying Civil Affairs staff under van der Plas, the Netherlands Indies Civil Affairs Chief Commanding Officer. There was also an American colonel on board, K. K. Kennedy. Later in the year Kennedy reported to Washington that van der Plas had told everyone on board the *Cumberland* that the Javanese would welcome the Dutch back. After one day ashore, van der Plas was obliged to return to the ship for safety. Patterson was in a quandary. He had been told by Mountbatten that British forces should not be used to eliminate freedom movements in the colonial territories of other powers, even when those powers were friends and allies, and even if the movements were of a dubious nature. He had also been told that he should do nothing whatever which might imply recognition of the new Indonesian Republic. 'This meant,' as Donnison rightly points out, 'that he was permitted neither to use the Republic nor to suppress it.'[49] Kennedy went ashore and, he later claimed, was the first to make contact with Sukarno and his associates.*[50] They told him on what terms they would treat with the Allied forces. No political interference was to take place inside Indonesia. The Allies were only to disarm the Japanese and evacuate prisoners-of-war and internees. Lastly, and most difficult, no Dutch elements were to be permitted to land. Kennedy reported to General Christison, who became Commander-in-Chief Allied Forces for the whole of the East Indies at the end of September, and as a result Christison talked to Sukarno. This was a step which the Dutch themselves at first refused to contemplate. Feeling was particularly strong in Holland and was aimed partly at Britain. The Netherlands Government issued an official statement on 1 October 1945 which roundly declared:

The difficulties that have arisen as a consequence (*of limiting the reoccupation to Jakarta and Surabaya*) probably explains the tendency which, according to press reports, exists in certain British circles to recognize the so-called Sukarno government as the *de facto* government and persuade us to have discussions with them.

* This makes it appear as if no mediation took place without American intervention. The British official history points out that Admiral Patterson was in touch with Sukarno through van der Post.[51]

The Netherlands Government cannot do this. Sukarno had allowed himself to be the tool and puppet of the Japanese for which he had received a high Japanese Imperial decoration. This man, with his fascist tendencies, has systematically preached hatred against the Allies... The representatives of the lawful authority cannot sit at the conference table with this man who may have certain demagogic gifts but who has proved to be a mere opportunist in choosing the means to attain his end.

The Netherlands Government felt that everything had been said in Queen Wilhelmina's 1942 speech: '... complete partnership of the Netherlands Indies within the Kingdom of the Netherlands and freedom of conduct regarding their internal affairs. This was the policy and that remains the policy. The government has nothing to add to this.'[52] In the spirit of this decision, the Governor-General of the Netherlands East Indies, Tjarda van Starkenborgh Stachouwer, who had been a prisoner in Japanese-held China throughout the war, refused to make any concessions to the Indonesians, and resigned. Mountbatten tried to persuade Lieutenant-Governor-General H. J. van Mook, who had headed the Netherlands East Indies Government in exile in Brisbane. He was similarly obdurate to start with, but gave way to Mountbatten's pleas and agreed to meet the leaders of the new republic. But the Dutch at home repudiated such an attempt before it even took place, thus sapping van Mook's position as negotiator.[53]

Mountbatten's political adviser, Esler Dening (later Sir Esler Dening, and British Ambassador to Japan), thought the Dutch were making a mistake about Sukarno. He was not a great man, Dening thought, and if he were held responsible for law and order he would rapidly show his incompetence for the task. But the Dutch had singled him out for opposition, and were effectively building him up in the eyes of the Indonesians by making a martyr of him.[54] The American Ambassador at the Hague was Stanley Hornbeck, for many years a China expert in the State Department and resolutely hostile to Japan throughout that time. He went further than Dening into what was happening in South-East Asia, and saw the struggle there as part of a potential alignment of the peoples of the world into two great hostile groups: 'On one hand the "white" peoples of the Occident together with those "coloured" peoples in various parts of the world who remain under their influence and partake of their ways of thinking, and on the other hand those "coloured" peoples who reject or escape from the influence of the "white" and Occidental peoples...' The second category were, he thought, susceptible to the leadership Japan had offered for four decades, had recently attempted to impose, and might be expected to try to exert again.[55] Like Gerbrandy, Hornbeck was sure that, far from abandoning their Indonesia project, the Japanese were furthering it through the new republic: 'More and more, the evidence... indicates that the present situation in the Netherlands East Indies is a product of Japanese inspiration and a projection of the Japanese war effort.'[56]

Hornbeck was, on the whole, thinking along lines contrary to the views of the State Department. Officially, it still held to the Roosevelt doctrine that the United States should not assist the European colonial powers to reassert their rule over their former Asian colonies. This view was shared by the British Labour party, which had come to power in the 1945 elections, and its Secretary of State for War, Jack Lawson, made this view known to the generals in South-East Asia when on tour there in September. On 28 September he was present at a meeting in Singapore which Mountbatten held with Lieutenant-General Christison and the Dutch Civil Affairs Chief, van der Plas. It was the day before Christison left for Jakarta (still called Batavia by the Allied forces), and Lawson impressed on him that his forces were not to be used to help the Dutch establish colonial rule. They were to ensure their own self-defence and maintain law and order. Christison should endeavour to bring together the Dutch and Indonesian leaders.[57]

Nor was the Indian Government enthusiastic about the use of Indian troops to quell Indonesian resistance to the return of the Dutch. The Commander-in-Chief, General Auchinleck, made this point quite clear at an inter-command meeting with Mountbatten. 'There can be no objection,' he said, 'to the employment of Indian troops to deal with any Japanese or disturbances inspired and led by the Japanese in the occupied countries. It is essential however, that Indian troops are not employed against nationalist movements save in the most exceptional circumstances, as such action would have grave political repercussions in India.'[58]

These views soon reached Holland, and the Dutch decided to put pressure on the USA. The Dutch Ambassador in Washington called on the State Department and saw Dean Acheson, the Under-Secretary of State, on 10 October. He said that the Netherlands had foreseen the situation which would arise in the Indies, but could do nothing about it since her resources were tied up by the overall strategy against Japan: everything had been centred on the main attack against the Japanese homeland. Both the nationalist leaders who had risen to eminence, Sukarno and Hatta, were collaborators with the Japanese. They represented Japanese influence intended to keep the Japanese underground alive until the Allied hold upon Japan relaxed. He also went on to say, in an attempt to have the best of both worlds, that they were a foothold of Communism in the Far East. They had both been to Moscow before the war and were, he believed, Communist-inspired. He very much regretted the change of command in the Pacific which transferred the East Indies from the American zone to the British. The British did not have the forces, or apparently the will, to do anything about the Indies or help the Dutch at all. The British were using what forces they had in Burma, Indo-China and Malaya, and the Dutch East Indies were a bad last. The ambassador intimated that the Dutch people felt they had been abandoned by their allies after having behaved well towards them and having sacrificed themselves in the Far East.[59]

The crucial factor in all these events was, of course, the role played by the Japanese Army in disposing of its weapons to the Indonesians. When the Japanese came aboard HMS *Cumberland* in the harbour of Tandjoengpriok (the port of Jakarta) on 15 September, they were told by Admiral Patterson that the Japanese were to maintain the *status quo* until Allied forces were in position, and to see that order was maintained. It would be necessary to use arms to do this, and they must repress any disturbances. Among the delegation of twenty-four staff officers were the Army Chief of Staff, Major-General Yamamoto, and Rear-Admiral Maeda. To Maeda, who had done his best to get the Indonesian revolution off the ground, it was an appalling order. He knew that what Patterson referred to as 'disturbances' was, in effect, the Indonesian independence movement. The Allies were not going to suppress it themselves, but they were going to use the Japanese to do so. His belief was turned to conviction when a further order was issued forbidding popular assemblies and controlling the carrying of weapons and the raising of the new flag.[60]

The Japanese became aware that the Indonesians were watching carefully the stores that were being handed over to the RAPWI organization for the welfare of prisoners and internees, some of whom were now in a very poor state. 'Why does the Japanese Army give to the enemy what it did not give to us, its allies?' the Indonesians asked. 'Do you really mean us to have our independence, or are you going to become a tool of the Dutch, and suppress us?' In theory, of course, the Japanese had no choice. Mountbatten had already sent a message to Field-Marshal Count Terauchi to say that he understood Terauchi to have declared a republic in Indonesia under the nationalist leaders, that such an action was in contravention of the agreement signed in Rangoon by his Chief of Staff, Lieutenant-General Numata, on 27 August, and that he must resume responsibility for civil government in the East Indies.[61]

The difficulties of ensuring that Terauchi's new orders to this effect were obeyed are illustrated by the Square Gambir meeting described by Tanaka Masaaki.[62] The Indonesians began to call at Japanese houses in Jakarta, demanding that the houses themselves be turned over, and that any weapons should be given to them. Small arms and swords were taken from Japanese troops, and when a crowd of tens of thousands assembled in Square Gambir in the centre of Jakarta for a republican meeting they were armed to the teeth with Japanese weapons, their own mountain-knives, and bamboo spears. The Japanese garrison forces, responsible for the maintenance of order, were told by Allied authorities to disperse the crowd. With a crowd armed as this one was, the Japanese knew that a move of determined hostility would be followed by reprisals against the Japanese, civilians as well as armed forces, and they had no intention of being used as cat's paws by the Allies. A staff officer, Miyamoto Shizuo, drove to the square and summed up the situation. Japanese troops could certainly disperse the crowd by firing into it, but that would mean war between Japanese and Indonesians. 'There must be no clash between Indonesia and Japan,' thought Miyamoto. He disregarded Allied orders completely, and took the decision to withdraw Japanese troops at once. This kind of disobedience to Allied orders resulted in the arrest of Major-General Nakamura in Jakarta. He was sent to Singapore for trial by Terauchi's general headquarters.[63]

But the Japanese were under constant pressure to release their weapons to the new republic. Isolated Japanese detachments were attacked; the Indonesians even grew bold enough to assault *Kempeitai* units and take arms from them. Godowns were looted for stores, the telephone exchange and post offices in Surabaya were attacked, women and children were kidnapped as hostages and maltreated. Both sides committed abuses. In some cases, the Dutch and Eurasian civilian internees, who had suffered years of deprivation and humiliation at the hands of the Japanese, left their camps if their homes were reasonably near. Those who remained were under constant harassment by irregular Indonesian forces. On the other hand, Lieutenant-General van Oyen's Dutch and Ambonese troops, who had landed in spite of Indonesian protests, were described as trigger-happy and likely to shoot at anything suspicious. When hunting was poor, an American journalist had said, 'they were not above forcing an Indonesian's house and dragging off, without charges or warrant, some or all of the inhabitants'.[64]

Factions developed within the Japanese Army, as violence and anarchy grew in Indonesia. One faction was for openly disobeying higher orders. There should be mass desertion on behalf of the Indonesians. Japanese troops should take weapons and vehicles and join the forces of the independent republic. They considered that Japan's surrender policy had betrayed the Indonesians, and it was their duty to redeem that betrayal by sacrificing their own lives. Naturally enough, the Indonesians welcomed the desertion of those Japanese with military experience.

iv *What Happened at Surabaya*

Events in Surabaya showed how Indonesian attitudes to the Japanese began to change. Surabaya was the headquarters of the East Java Area under Major-General Iwabe. There were several thousand Japanese Army troops there, and it was also the second fleet base in South-East Asia after Singapore, and as such the headquarters of the 2nd Expeditionary Fleet under Vice-Admiral Shibata, with Rear-Admiral Tanaka Kikumatsu as commander of the land forces at the base. The base itself had eleven torpedo-boats and thirty-four aircraft when war ended, and well over a thousand military civilians were employed there. The local people showed great sympathy for the Japanese when the surrender was announced, but when the Dutch returned to the town from internment in central Java, apparently under the auspices of the Japanese, anti-Japanese feelings began to run high. On 1 October the Indonesians attacked spots where the Japanese garrison was weak, the broadcasting station, the hospital, and the signals station, and seized them by force. Many Japanese units had already left for concentration areas in the hills, leaving behind a small garrison to maintain order. The five or six hundred Japanese troops vainly attempted to do this but they were forbidden to use arms and were in danger of being incarcerated by the Indonesians. Both admirals, Shibata and Tanaka, were anxious to avoid bloodshed, looking ahead to the time when Japan would be able to re-establish friendly relations with a new Indonesia. Orders were therefore issued by the Japanese Navy not to fire, but to use persuasion with the local leaders.

Then the Indonesians began to break the Japanese garrison's control of the town. They cut telephone wires, and contact between army and navy came to a halt. Liaison officers were captured, cars taken from them, fuel depots were invaded by wild crowds brandishing swords and spears, food stores were rifled. By midday the former Indonesian Volunteer Army (*Peta*) units and some *Hei-Ho*, the auxiliaries, with youth groups at their head, had begun to exercise command over the vast crowds which packed the streets, yelling '*Merdeka! Merdeka!*' ('Freedom! Freedom!'). Around nine o'clock in the evening, waving the weapons they had taken from the Japanese elsewhere in the town, they tried to break into the eastern Java headquarters and were prevented by the sentries and NCOs. As Japanese officers ran towards the crowd, flourishing drawn swords, General Iwabe came out on to his balcony and shouted in Indonesian, '*Nante! Nante!*' ('Wait! Wait!'). The officers came to a halt, and the crowd was finally subdued by the garrison. The danger of open hostilities had been averted by a hair's breadth.

The 2nd Expeditionary Fleet headquarters was similarly threatened. A crowd of several thousands surged towards it, headed by tanks. (The Japanese in this area had let the local Indonesian *Peta* division take over its armour.) They broke into the 21st Signals Unit and imprisoned the staff in a small room, thus ensuring that no messages for help would be sent out. They then demanded that all Japanese in the headquarters surrender their arms. Some even managed to break into the commander-in-chief's office and stripped him and his staff of their swords. Here old friendships came into play. Commander Norinaga and Rear-Admiral Mori, the chief of the Navy Works Department, had had dealings with an Indonesian who later became the commander of the Surabaya Defence Force, Colonel Afundeh, and with Munaji, the head of the Public

Relations Section. These latter were persuaded, with some difficulty, to call off the rioters and release the Japanese naval officers who had been on their way back from a conference of naval unit commanders and had been arrested by the crowds.

The rioting continued for two or three days more, led by the provincial governor, Sudirman, and Dr Mostopo. On the third day, the Japanese Army and Navy authorities called a conference with the Indonesians and the unrest momentarily came to an end. The Japanese had not gone unscathed: they had lost the commander of the signals unit and several medical officers and nurses, and about three thousand Japanese had been gaoled. Hospitals, signals installations, supply dumps, all had been seized by the Indonesians, leaving the Japanese with their Army and Navy headquarters, the fleet base, and a garrison battalion.

Then there occurred a strange episode which partly explains why the Indonesians in East Java did so well out of the Japanese disarming. The British official historian Woodburn-Kirby mentions in a footnote that General Christison told him in 1965 that he received an apology from the Dutch Admiral Helfrich for an action taken 'by a comparatively junior Dutch officer who apparently landed on the airfield at Surabaya and took the surrender of the Japanese troops in the town. No official record of such an action has been found, but, as the Japanese laid down their arms, it would partly account for the large number of arms in possession of Indonesian extremists in Surabaya.'[65]

The Japanese have their own version of this episode. They say a Dutch naval commander leading a RAPWI unit in Surabaya was completely taken aback by the violence of the Indonesians, and discussed it with the Japanese area commander, Iwabe. The Dutchman, whose name was Hooyer,* said to Iwabe, 'There is only one way to avoid the spread of this rebellion. That is for you to surrender to me as Allied representative, and hand over all your arms and ammunition. I will deposit them in Indonesian custody, and will obtain Mr Sudirman's solemn oath that they will not be touched.' He gave Iwabe five minutes in which to decide. The Japanese Military Government Commander, Andō, realized that accepting Hooyer's suggestion would let the Japanese off the hook completely,

---

* This is my reading of the Japanese phonetic Hoieru, but given the approximate rendering of European names, and the substitution of R for L, it could equally well be read Hojel.

as far as both sides, Allied and Indonesian, were concerned, and he added his persuasion to that of Iwabe's staff officer, Tanaka. Iwabe finally gave in, and in earnest of his good faith offered Hooyer his sword. That surrender covered not merely Surabaya but the whole of East Java, where about one third of all the arms and ammunition possessed by the 16th Army were stored.

The naval authorities, in the presence of Sudirman, signed the transfer of all arms and military installations over to Afundeh, after which Admiral Tanaka made over the control of the naval dockyard area. They then notified the 16th Army in Jakarta of what they had done. 16th Army headquarters were delighted. The British divisional commander,* on the contrary, was in a blazing fury. 'That is illegal! Cancel the arrangement at once!' he ordered the Japanese. By the terms of the Rangoon agreement, the Dutch officer had, of course, acted *ultra vires*; only the British commander was empowered to make surrender arrangements. Both Iwabe and Yamamoto, the 16th Army Chief of Staff, were arrested and gaoled later for disobeying Allied orders and handing over arms to the Indonesians without notification. They did not mind very much. The handing over of arms to the Indonesian independence movement had been achieved. This was the parting gift of the Japanese Army and Navy to the Indonesian Republic.

So Tanaka's story runs.[67] That there is some truth in it is proved by Christison's memory of such an event. But it seems highly unlikely, on the face of it, that a Dutch naval commander could have thought, at such a time, and given the experience of the previous few weeks, that any promise he extracted from Sudirman – if there *was* such a promise – could ever have been kept.

Even in West Java, where Allied control was much stricter, the Japanese managed to hand over large quantities of arms to the Indonesians. Major-General Mabuchi Itsuo, who was placed in command after the Army Commander-in-Chief, Nagano, and three other

---

* The Japanese use the term *shidanchō*, divisional commander, to refer to this officer, but Major-General Hawthorn, GOC 23rd Division, landed with his main headquarters at Jakarta on 10 October, and Lieutenant-General Mansergh, GOC 5th Division, later in the month. It is possible the Japanese are referring to Lieutenant-General Christison, who was a corps commander (15th Corps) and later GOC, Allied Forces Netherlands East Indies, from 16 October; he had arrived in Jakarta on 29 September to a very rough reception.[66] On the other hand, it is curious that there should be no official British record of such a transaction.

generals had been removed for disobedience to British orders, contrived to collect the arms of Japanese who were sick in hospitals, loaded them into trucks, and had them driven to Cheribon. The arms were thrown into a dry river bed. On the opposite bank, Indonesians were waiting. As soon as the deposit was completed, they swarmed over and collected the lot. In this way, Japanese arms and ammunition throughout Java were made available to the forces, regular and irregular, of the new republic. The Japanese estimate that there was enough ammunition for two divisions, 35,000 assorted rifles, tanks, armoured cars, and about 2,000 smaller vehicles with medium and small calibre guns: about fifty per cent of the Japanese Army stocks on Java. The Navy in Surabaya provided enough arms for 3,000 men.

The Japanese had also given them something else. When the 250,000 Indonesian troops began their struggle against the British and the Dutch, they used tactics which, the Japanese assured them, had been the secret of their initial success against Western forces: attack by night. Mountbatten deployed two British–Indian divisions in Java alone, and some of the forces were cut to pieces. Brigadier Mallaby, of the 49th Brigade, was brutally murdered on the evening of 29 October. He had landed there four days before and managed to negotiate an agreement with Dr Mostopo in Surabaya which at first seemed likely to bring peace to that fire-torn and beleaguered city. It was clear to him that any attempt to unseat the republicans there would be met with fierce resistance. Unfortunately, faulty communications resulted in a British Dakota flying over the city, on orders from General Hawthorn in Jakarta, dropping leaflets stating that British military administration would replace the Indonesian republican authorities there. Mallaby told the Indonesians the leaflets had been dropped without his knowledge, but that he would have to do as they said.[68] This was the cue for the extremists to thrust Mostopo aside and call for armed resistance to the British. It took the 5th Division, under General Mansergh, a month of bitter fighting, throughout November, to occupy Surabaya. It was a city of 750,000 people, and although the British managed to control it until the spring of 1946, when the Dutch arrived to take over it was impossible to prevent Indonesian terrorists infiltrating back into the city. But it was clearly time for the Dutch to go. Sjahrir had formed a cabinet in November 1945, and the new republic, against bitter opposition from the Dutch, gradually won recognition abroad. It took four years of fighting before the Hague Agreement was reached in November 1949, by which the Dutch recognized Indonesian rule over the entire territory formerly called the Netherlands East Indies, with the exception of Western New Guinea.

There can be no doubt that had the Dutch been less intransigent to start with, and better informed about conditions in their former possessions, things might have been easier for both sides. There was, in particular, one moment in mid-September 1945 when Mountbatten advised van der Plas, the Deputy Governor, to treat with Sukarno, and to make known to the population the exact terms of Queen Wilhelmina's 1942 broadcast, which the Japanese occupation had prevented them knowing. The Allied commander, Christison, described the effect of van der Plas's broadcast as 'electrical'.[69] It was the cue for the moderates among the Indonesian leaders to assure van der Plas that they would cooperate with the Allied forces. Without consulting either the Allied Commander-in-Chief, Christison, or van der Plas himself, the Netherlands Government at the Hague promptly disavowed the approach to Sukarno in van der Plas's broadcast. Sukarno's reaction was equally prompt. He told Christison he could not now control the extremist elements, he would oppose any landings by the Dutch, and he would fight the British if they covered the Dutch landings. A great opportunity had been lost.

The resulting bloodshed was made possible by Japanese weapons. But, and it is impossible not to see a certain poetic justice in this, the Japanese themselves suffered as a result. There were many cases of Japanese being ambushed by Indonesians, and of Indonesians rounding up Japanese civilians and massacring them. The Bekasi incident is an example of the first. Over eighty Japanese en route from Jakarta to Bekasi for defence duties were stopped by about six hundred Indonesian youths as they approached the iron bridge near Bekasi. The youths demanded their arms, and one of the Japanese called out 'We are not carrying arms'. The youths made them all stand in a row and searched them. They discovered two officers were carrying pistols. 'Why did you lie?' they yelled angrily. Before the Japanese could explain, 'Finish them off!' came the order, and all eighty were killed with bamboo spears and their bodies thrown under the bridge. Similarly, at Semarang, there were about seventy Japanese staffing an army transport office; they had their women and children with them. On the night of 14 October they were forced to line up in their night attire outside the office gates and were taken to the police station at nearby Baru. There they were searched, beaten, and packed into a cell, like rice in *sushi** as the Japanese phrase goes. They were given no food or drink throughout the night, and no means of relieving themselves. In the midst of the choking tropical heat, the stench in the cell was soon indescribable. They spent a whole day in that cell, and about midnight on 15 October ten extremists armed with pistols and rifles appeared. 'The Japanese must die!' they shouted angrily, and began calling the men out one by one and shooting them then and there. Those who remained in the cell protested, and the Indonesians turned their guns upon them and deluged the cell with rifle fire. Every one of the Japanese died. The story goes that one of them, before he died, wrote on the walls of the cell in his own blood BAHA GIYA INDONESIA MERDEKA (glory to the freedom of Indonesia).[70] These words are, apparently, preserved on the cell wall in remembrance of the friendship between Japan and Indonesia. It is not impossible that a Japanese, about to die, might have foreseen the day when *merdeka* would not lead to massacre and had magnanimously forgiven his murderers; it is also not impossible that in his death throes he might have scrawled the words in bitter, mortal irony. Either way, the conjunction of Japanese death and Indonesian freedom was a reality. The Japanese casualties in Indonesia at the end of the war, about one thousand, were strangely similar to those she suffered when she first invaded Java. The weapons with which Indonesia fought her war of independence against the Dutch from 1945 to 1949 were largely Japanese weapons; Japanese officers and men in the Indonesian forces taught their use, and died fighting in battle beside the Indonesians. It was a fair exchange.

* Rice cakes rolled in seaweed.

CHAPTER FOUR

FRENCH INDO-CHINA

i *The Japanese* coup de force, *9 March 1945*

The country we now know as Vietnam, which has one of the saddest histories of the twentieth century, was a French possession at the time of the Japanese surrender. It consisted of five territories: the colony of Cochin-China in the south, which had been ceded to France in 1862, the chief city of which was Saigon; and four protectorates: Annam, which held the old capital Hue; Cambodia, which had been a powerful kingdom in the Middle Ages; Laos, a mountainous country bordering Siam; and Tonkin in the north-east, bordering China. The population was around twenty-three million. The country produced rubber, maize, anthracite, zinc, and tin, but its main export was rice: before war broke out its annual product for export was 1,500,000 tons. Like the Siamese, the people were Buddhist, though there was a strong Catholic population. The old administrative structure of the country was based on a Chinese pattern with an Emperor ruling through a mandarinate selected by examination. Under French rule, there was a governor-general, who had under him three advisory councils on economics, defence, and general affairs. The state was administered by both French and local officials. Cochin-China was administered directly by the French, under a governor. The protectorates of Laos, Cambodia, and Annam had a system of indirect rule, as had Tonkin, but the French had so diminished the role of the native government that its protectorate status had virtually disappeared. Nationalist movements had grown up in the twenties and thirties and been savagely suppressed. The Annamites had a long cultural tradition of their own, with a very full literature and a history of fighting for independence, particularly against China, their great neighbour to the north.

The defeat of France in 1940 weakened her authority in her overseas possessions, and Japan decided to move in. There was no question of obtaining help from Britain or the United States and so in 1940 the French were compelled, in concession after concession, to give way to Japanese demands for a foothold in the country. On 15 July 1941 Roosevelt's envoy to the Vichy Government (Admiral William D. Leahy) was warned by Admiral Darlan that Japan would shortly occupy bases in Southern Indo-China 'for the purpose of projecting military operations southward'. Leahy telegraphed the news to Washington, and four days later conveyed the American government's reaction. It was a warning, couched in the terms of the crudest power politics. 'It was necessary to say bluntly,' he later wrote, 'that if Japan was the winner, the Japanese would take over French Indo-China: and if the Allies won, we would take it.'[1] The Japanese left the French administrative structure intact, under the Governor-General, Admiral Decoux. They occupied railway centres, port installations, and airfields, their first purpose being to stop the shipping of goods to Chiang Kai-shek through the port of Haiphong (it was a much more important supply route than the Burma Road), their second being to ensure the occupation of bases if they decided to embark on a military operation in the rest of South-East Asia. In fact, torpedo-bombers operating from airfields near Saigon played a crucial role in the outcome of the Malayan campaign: they found and sank the *Prince of Wales* and the *Repulse*. But throughout the rest of the war in the Pacific, as Decoux pointed out, Indo-China remained a tranquil haven in the centre of a storm.[2] It was Decoux's intention that Indo-China should remain in this happy, if slightly less than honourable position, until the Japanese capitulated. By the end of 1944 this desired aim seemed to be in sight. On the other hand, the liberation of France had given an impetus to resistance, and contacts were made with de Gaulle. Decoux was an unqualified supporter of Marshal Pétain, but after September 1944 there could be no pretence that Pétain's writ ran anywhere, let alone in Indo-China. In November 1944 Decoux was instructed by de Gaulle to retain his post. The Japanese were to be deceived into thinking that the French had no immediate intention of acting against them. De Gaulle's original plan had been to reaffirm the French presence in the Far East by despatching forces across the Indian Ocean under General

Blaizot, who was attached to Mountbatten's headquarters in Kandy. Later, when it seemed possible that the Americans might land in South China, or Indo-China, de Gaulle envisaged a French expeditionary force participating in such a campaign. He replaced Blaizot by Leclerc, under whose command were to be placed some of the 2nd Armoured Division under Massu, and two colonial divisions (the 1st and 3rd). But demobilization after the defeat of Germany so reduced the ranks of these divisions that they had to be combined. Besides, there seemed to be no way of transporting them to the Far East. French shipping was under the control of the Allied Shipping Pool and could not be released. The only unit actually present in Mountbatten's command was the 5th Colonial Infantry Regiment, itself only a battalion strong, under Colonel Huard. A Senegalese brigade was awaiting orders in Madagascar.[3]

There were other troops available, but they were in no condition to intervene. These were the remnants of that part of the French garrison (fifty thousand strong) which fought the Japanese in March 1945, and had been compelled to retreat into China under their general, Alessandri. The Japanese *coup de force* was perhaps the crucial event of 1945 for Indo-China. On 9 March, in anticipation of a rising which they thought might accompany an American landing, the Japanese moved against the French administration and the French Army. The plans had been drawn up in great secrecy, so that no false move should warn the French of what was happening: planning staff wrote out the plans and printed orders themselves, and they were conveyed by staff officers only to those of regimental commander rank and above.[4] In January, General Tsuchihashi's 38th Army had organized special units distributed in three areas, North, South, and Central Indo-China, to come into action once the signal was given. They were to collect intelligence on French Army dispositions, track down anti-Japanese propaganda, secure leading personalities round the Emperor of Annam, Bao Dai, and make contacts with the Vietnamese underground independence movement.[5] There were diplomatic manoeuvres, too. At the end of 1944 the old Japanese Ambassador, Yoshizawa, with whom Decoux had for the past three years managed to maintain relations of courtesy, if not cordiality, and who, in Decoux's view, had often acted on behalf of the French to moderate the excessive demands of the Japanese military, was replaced by Matsumoto, who immediately began pressing Decoux to increase occupation expenses levied on the Govern-

ment-General. 110,000,000 piastres per month were required for the
first quarter of 1945, far more than was needed for the upkeep of the
Japanese forces. Decoux refused, and also rejected a Japanese demand
that he should hand over American pilots who had fallen into
French hands while on bombing or reconnaissance missions over
Indo-China.

Before he left, Yoshizawa had confided to a French official that if
the Americans captured Manila – which seemed quite certain then –
the Japanese Government would have to revise its policy towards
Indo-China. Decoux took this warning to heart. He had already
learned that de Gaulle's emissaries were active. A Major de Langlade,
who had been a rubber-planter in Malaya, entered Tonkin clan-
destinely in June 1944 and began to recruit a resistance movement;
and Mordant, who was soon to retire as commander-in-chief of the
French Army in Indo-China, was named by de Gaulle as head of the
resistance. Decoux was only informed of this fact in October 1944.
The following month de Langlade called on him in person. When
Decoux learned what was happening, it became for him the explanation of the anarchy and indiscipline which reigned in the French
armed forces under his control, from the top ranks down.[6] The
situation was even worse in the South, and he decided to leave his
post in Hanoi and establish himself for a while in Saigon where the
French population was, he had heard, in a state of considerable
'fermentation', and on whom he intended to enjoin prudence and
caution. On 5 February 1945 the situation envisaged by old
Yoshizawa arose: Manila fell to the Americans. Eighteen days later
Decoux summed up the situation in a most secret telegram to the
Minister of Colonies in Paris, in which he demanded to be addressed
personally by the Government, and to be kept informed of all
underground activities and plans: lack of prudence in the organization of resistance could be a great hindrance to the unity of Frenchmen in Indo-China and could have grave consequences. Given
Japan's military situation, the eviction of her troops from French
territory was only a question of time. It was therefore in French
interests not to undertake premature moves likely to produce a sharp
Japanese reaction. Indo-China was not, he affirmed, subject to
Japanese military occupation, and French sovereignty was respected.

Decoux had also sent secret and personal instructions to heads of
local administration throughout the country, at the end of January,
telling them to help Allied forces with all the means at their disposal,

if an American landing took place. As he saw it, Indo-China had in fact been in a state of war with Japan since Marshal Pétain had left France (virtually a prisoner of the Germans at Sigmaringen) and the new Metropolitan Government had declared war against Japan; this was certainly the case juridically, though the Japanese had not so far taken any action.[7]

Had he but known it, he was serving the Japanese purpose by going south to Saigon at this juncture. They intended to demand that Decoux place all his armed forces and police under the command of the Japanese, who would also control all internal and external communications. If he accepted, then there would be no need to use force; if he did not, then the Japanese Army would intervene. This was to be what was termed Operation Mei. These demands would have to be put to Decoux and negotiated, and the venue of the negotiations was of considerable importance to Japanese movements. Since Hanoi was the seat of the Government-General, it would be no more than appropriate for any demands by the ambassador to be made there, in which case both ambassador and commander-in-chief would have to go to Hanoi. But at that time the Japanese Army's signals network in Indo-China was based in Saigon, and it would not be easy to maintain from Hanoi the kind of simultaneous contact with all forces that a surprise *coup de force* required. If the disarming of French troops did not go according to plan, and if French troops controlled the Hanoi airfield, then General Tsuchihashi would be trapped in Hanoi and unable to exercise his command. So the Japanese needed a meeting with Decoux in Saigon. They knew that the governor-general customarily spent some time there in spring and autumn, 'to remind the natives of the place who governed them', as the Japanese official history puts it.[8] When Tsuchihashi called on Decoux on 4 February he made it his business to learn at what time the governor-general was likely to be in the South, and was told that if the situation in the North was unchanged he would be in Saigon for about three weeks from the end of February. There would be no need to make any special moves to negotiate in Saigon: negotiations could be carried out there quite naturally, if the governor-general happened to be there.[9]

Decoux came south on 20 February. He was in a state of some perplexity. In contradiction to the secret order he had given to his local authority heads to aid an Allied landing if it took place, de Gaulle had sent him an instruction at the beginning of February to proclaim the neutrality of Indo-China in such an eventuality. As soon as he arrived Matsumoto contacted him. There was a rice agreement between Japan and Indo-China, which was renewed at intervals. Matsumoto sent in a request that an agreement to cover the deliveries for 1945 be signed as soon as possible and suggested 9 March as a convenient date, to which Decoux agreed. In this way, Matsumoto ensured that the governor-general would be in Saigon when the Japanese Army came to the moment of decision. The meeting had been fixed for 7 p.m. Tokyo time (local time 6 p.m.).

Meanwhile Decoux entertained the Japanese in a desperate endeavour to keep relations working smoothly. On 2 March he invited Matsumoto, with Tsuchihashi and his chief of staff, to dinner. Then on 4 March he went to Dalat to visit his wife's grave. The Japanese then had great misgivings about the signature for the rice agreement, but they breathed freely again when he was back in Saigon by the evening of the 7th. On the evening of the 8th Tsuchihashi invited to his residence the Chief of Staff of Southern Army, Lieutenant-General Numata, the Chief of Staff of the 38th Army, Kawamura, the Ambassador Matsumoto, and his Minister Tsukamoto, for a last-minute conference. It was arranged that Matsumoto should withdraw to 38th Army headquarters after negotiations with Decoux were concluded, and the governor-general's reply should be delivered to the ambassador there by ten o'clock in the evening. The address of the headquarters was to be written down and handed to the governor-general (a very odd precaution). If there was a delay in the arrival of the reply, then five-minutes' grace was to be allowed – 'the generosity of the samurai' ('bushi no nasake wo motte').[10] The decision whether or not to accept Decoux's reply would be Tsuchihashi's, thus clearly demonstrating that the diplomats were being contemptuously treated as mere go-betweens for the military.* Lastly it was decided that Numata, Tsukamoto, and all the chief officials at the Embassy should assemble at 38th Army Headquarters at 7.30 in the evening of the 9th.

* Tsuchihashi had already had a furious argument with Matsumoto over the role of the officials attached to the Embassy if the Japanese Army took over from Decoux. The country would then no longer be independent, and the ambassador and his staff would become redundant. Tsuchihashi proposed that Matsumoto should become his 'supreme adviser', which Matsumoto rejected. Pressure was then applied, and Matsumoto finally accepted the situation, his officials becoming shokutaku, civilians attached to the Army.

To keep up appearances of normality on the 9th, Tsuchihashi had invited guests for lunch and dinner. When night fell his house was ablaze with lights, but at 7.15 he slipped out and within five minutes was at his headquarters, impatiently waiting for Matsumoto to arrive.

When Matsumoto had left Decoux, after dinner on the 7th, he had mentioned that he would like a short discussion with him about the occupation expenses after they signed the rice agreement. In the evening of the 9th, in the magnificent palace of the Government-General, Matsumoto's audience with Decoux began shortly after 6.30. He spoke about the situation in Europe, and Decoux agreed with his view that it was serious. Germany would soon be out of the war. Decoux thought Matsumoto seemed nervous and preoccupied, and somewhat incoherent. Suddenly the Japanese shot a question at him: 'Are you in contact with the French Government?' Decoux said he was not, and reminded the ambassador of the powers which the previous French Government had bestowed, intimating that he acted independently of the metropolis. 'My Government is disturbed,' Matsumoto went on, 'by certain declarations made by General de Gaulle concerning Indo-China. He has recently expressed the hope that Indo-China will soon take its place again within the French community. He has also announced that France intends to grant a more liberal régime to the peoples of Indo-China.' Decoux answered that this seemed to be a normal development, but he felt as he did so that Matsumoto was only pursuing the conversation to gain time. The Japanese Ambassador kept looking at his watch, and as soon as the hour of seven drew near, he brought up the question of the war in the Pacific. It was reaching a decisive phase, and the Government in Tokyo was deeply concerned. An American landing might take place at any moment on the coast of Indo-China. Collaboration between Decoux and the Japanese Government would have to become closer.

Then at seven o'clock Matsumoto, in Decoux's words, 'unmasked his batteries'.[11] 'I have received formal and precise instructions from my Government,' he said, 'which deem it necessary to strengthen our mutual defence agreement.' Decoux replied that the agreement had been in force for four years and had never been called upon, and he saw no reason to change it now. 'That is not the view of Imperial General Headquarters,' replied Matsumoto, and produced from his pocket a memorandum which he read to Decoux and then handed over. It was an explicit demand to put the French forces under Japanese command, in preparation for an eventual American landing. The governor-general's affirmative reply was awaited by nine o'clock.*

Given the gravity of the situation, Decoux wanted a witness to what he was going to say. He summoned the Director of Diplomatic Affairs, de Boisanger, and in his presence protested energetically to Matsumoto about the conditions in his document, the character of an ultimatum which it bore, and the unacceptably short period of two hours within which to reply. He could not in any case, he told Matsumoto, make any dispositions about the French forces without first conferring with the French commander-in-chief. 'But you have full powers,' expostulated the ambassador, 'you can therefore give your agreement immediately.' Whatever his powers, Decoux replied, he was bound to consult the commander-in-chief whenever the latter's responsibility was involved. In any case, with or without full powers, he would sign no agreement contrary to his own honour or that of the French forces. Matsumoto began to cavil, in a rather clumsy manner. How unsubtle he was, thought Decoux, how lacking in *nuance* – so unlike his predecessor.

The demand was a natural one in the circumstances, Matsumoto pointed out. The Japanese general staff wanted a single supreme command, the necessity of which had been realized by both sides in both world wars. Decoux retorted that a single command might be obtained by agreement but not by veiled threats, and that such an agreement might possibly be made between allies, which Japan and Indo-China certainly were not.

'If a favourable reply to the points in the memorandum is not received by the Japanese military authorities by 9 o'clock,' Matsumoto told him, 'Japanese troops will be forced to take emergency action. Have you thought of the fate of the 40,000 French people who are in Indo-China?'

'Do you mean that reprisals will be carried out against the French?' Decoux asked. 'In that case, the Japanese Command, and your Government will be entirely responsible in the eyes not only of France and Indo-China, but of the whole world.' Matsumoto did not reply, but handed Decoux a letter of acceptance already made out, lacking only his signature. Decoux spurned it.

* The discrepancy of one hour between French and Japanese accounts is presumably due to the fact that Decoux is using local time,[12] while the Japanese plan was drawn up with Tokyo time in mind.[13]

De Boisanger then intervened, attempting to bridge the gap, and suggested that if the time for a reply were extended some solution might be found. But de Boisanger had realized the memorandum was couched in the terms of an ultimatum, and was trying to gain time himself in order to alert the French military command. He managed to leave the room for a few moments, and sent a warning to the various authorities throughout Southern Indo-China.

Matsumoto indicated that no further delay would be acceptable, but offered to come to the governor-general's palace at nine o'clock for an answer. Decoux told him briefly that he had done everything he could, within the limits of what was possible, to maintain acceptable relations between France and Japan for the past four years; if Japan used force against Indo-China now, she would dishonour herself. The Emperor had given a solemn guarantee that Japan would respect French sovereignty. He drew the interview to a close, assuring Matsumoto that a French officer would bring a reply to the memorandum within the time required. He also asked him to withdraw the Japanese detachment which had just been placed at the gates of the Government-General, on the pretext of ensuring Decoux's safety. Matsumoto left at 8.15, and Decoux at once convened a meeting of his advisers, together with the French Army and Navy chiefs. With their agreement, he composed a note rejecting the Japanese demands, but leaving the door open to further negotiation. The note accepted that the Japanese Army Command should assume entire responsibility for operations in the event of an American landing, but made it clear that Decoux could only come to an agreement about the disposition of French forces after consultation with the French High Command. He assured the Japanese that French forces would commit no hostile act against them, unless the Japanese attacked them first.

The French naval captain Robin, who is described by Decoux as 'Commissioner-General for Franco-Japanese Relations',[14] was to carry Decoux's note to Matsumoto. The Japanese say that Robin did not know where the Japanese headquarters was, and burst into their Public Relations Office demanding a guide to take him there. The headquarters was quite close – as near as an eye to a nose, in the Japanese expression – so he should have been there almost at once, but fifteen minutes went by and still he had not appeared. Meanwhile, at 9.18 p.m. (local time; 10.18 Japanese time), a telephone call came through from the army general headquarters that fighting had already broken out at Hanoi. Tsuchihashi wondered if there had been some mistake, but it was already twenty minutes past the agreed time. Probably some unit had been chafing at the bit, or had anxiously feared an order had not been transmitted – either way, it had decided to act on its own initiative, thinking its honour would be compromised if it delayed. The fact that things had been set in motion at Hanoi would cause no problem if the French rejected the Japanese memorandum; if, on the other hand – it was a thousand to one chance – they accepted the terms, someone might have to accept the responsibility for starting the action. Even though the French envoy would probably show up at any moment, they should not wait for him any longer. This was Tsuchihashi's view at the time, and he called his Chief of Staff, Kawamura, and his chief staff officer in charge of operations, Saeki: 'We shall send out the operation orders now,' he told them. Kawamura attempted to dissuade him: 'The envoy's likely to come at any moment, shouldn't you wait a little longer?' But Tsuchihashi gave the following verbal orders:

i Regrettably, the Governor-General has rejected the Japanese demands.
ii All units are to act at once.

The time was 9.21 and Lieutenant-Colonel Saeki went immediately to the wireless room and ordered the signal to be made continuously: '7. 7. 7'. The transmission ceased at 9.23. At 9.25, Tsuchihashi saw Captain Robin being taken to Matsumoto's room near by. After a few moments he heard Matsumoto shout 'This is clearly a rejection'. By this time the arrow had already left the bow.*

Decoux is probably right when he suggests that whatever reply he had made, the Japanese High Command would not have altered its decision to take over Indo-China.† French garrisons all over the

* The Japanese official history says it is not clear what the contents of the reply brought by Captain Robin from the governor-general were, and quotes Maurice Martin du Gard's La Carte impériale for a summary of its contents. In fact Martin du Gard's version is that given by Decoux, and since the latter figures so largely in the Japanese account, and his memoirs are quoted by at least one author (Ellen Hammer), whose book figures in the notes of the Japanese history, it is surprising that no direct reference to A la Barre de l'Indochine is made. Decoux's reply with the time (9 p.m.) and the date (9 March 1945) is given in his book.

† Imperial General Headquarters had issued an order dated 28 February 1945, to the effect that centres of administrative and military power in Indo-

country were attacked simultaneously, and they soon surrendered, though there was bitter fighting, notably at Lang Son and Dong Dang in the north, where the Japanese massacred the survivors. Decoux was placed under arrest, and the Japanese military police (*Kempei*) began to round up Frenchmen suspected of working for the resistance. They turned the Saigon Chamber of Commerce into a temporary gaol which was, in effect, a torture chamber. Water-torture, fearful beatings, the tearing out of toe-nails, and an almost total lack of medical care – the cumulative effect was horrifying. The *Kempei* did not have many French-speakers, and either used English in their interrogations or employed Annamite interpreters. Either way, the results were not very accurate, and violence became a substitute for intelligence.* There is no doubt that some Frenchmen had been consistently providing intelligence to the US Air Forces which operated from China in bombing raids against installations in Hanoi: wireless communication with the 14th Air Force seems to have been fairly regular. So Japanese suspicions were not unfounded, but their method of verifying them involved the obscene brutality now linked with the name of *Kempei*.

The resistance did not react very sharply. Its chief, the retired

---

China should be taken over. The French military attaché in Chungking had told the Americans that the French Army in Indo-China was being pressed to disband and disarm. This information was given on 2 February 1945, and passed by Wedemeyer to Washington.[15] Paris does not seem to have reacted swiftly either. Colonel Dominique Renucci, the French military attaché in Canberra, had sent a warning of what was likely to happen, on 5 March. His information was derived from MacArthur's cryptographic services.[16] In Indo-China itself, other information was available. A police official, Fleutot, told Bonfils, an administrator, that the Japanese were preparing a coup; Bonfils in turn conveyed this to a number of civil and military authorities in Hanoi. The date was not certain, it was to be either the night 8–9 March, or 9–10. When nothing happened on 8 March, the Hanoi authorities stopped worrying and relaxed precautions. In the far North, at Cao Bang, a French double agent Liong Sui Lan, who was employed in a gambling den, informed the commander of the territory during the night of 5–6 March that the date would be 9 March. Sabattier was in command of the troops in northern Tonkin and took Liong's warning seriously. He gave general alerts on 8 March and left Hanoi at nightfall that day. The troops had been ordered to disperse throughout the area in the case of a general alert, but unfortunately the warning was not received by all units.[17]

* There is a useful account of the Kempeitai arrests and interrogations in Saigon after the *coup de force* in Jacques le Bourgeois; 'Prisonnier des Japonais'; *Revue de Paris*, juillet 1949, pp. 120–42. And cf. Georges Condominas, *L'exotique est quotidien*, Plon, Paris, 1966.

General Mordant, refused at first to believe that a *coup de force* was likely. When he heard firing in the evening of 9 March, he climbed the wall of the citadel in Hanoi, sprained his ankle, and took shelter in the quarters of the chief medical officer, Botreau-Roussel, where the Japanese arrested him on the evening of the 10th. Under Generals Sabattier and Alessandri, some units managed to gain the comparative shelter of Yunnan Province in Southern China. At Dong Dang, near Lang Son, which the French call 'the gates of China', a Japanese unit attacked a French military post at 9.15 in the evening of the 9th, but retreated with heavy losses. On the 10th they brought up ladders and tried again, but with no success, though the French commander was killed. The fort was defended by the 3rd Regiment of Tonkinese *tirailleurs*, and on the third day of the fighting their captain, Anosse, still refused to surrender. On 12 March the Japanese made a mass attack with three thousand men, who swept into the fort when the French and Tonkinese ran out of ammunition. The Japanese brought Anosse before them. A Japanese officer beat him on the nape of the neck with a sword scabbard, and as he fell other officers fired pistols into his body. It was the signal for a general massacre of prisoners, who were tied up and beheaded, including the civilian customs official and two army concubines.[18]

The question naturally arises whether Allied intervention could have helped the beleaguered French. The French Ambassador in Washington, Henri Bonnet, asked the American government to intervene with the combined chiefs of staff to ensure that the French resistance in Indo-China was supported in its operations by the parachuting of arms, medical equipment, quinine, and food. He suggested that the American Air Forces in China were best placed to give such help. The approach was made on 12 March. The following day de Gaulle spoke to the American Ambassador Caffery, in Paris, and told him that the American military authorities in China and the British authorities in Burma had refused to send help to the French, the British having simply followed the American lead. He warned Caffery that if the French public thought the USA was acting against them in Indo-China there would be intense disappointment which might have post-war repercussions in the balance of power between Russia and the United States. 'We do not want to become Communists,' de Gaulle said, 'we do not want to fall into the Russian orbit, but I hope that you do not push us into it.'[19] A week later the French Ambassador Bonnet called at the State Department in Washington and said that the 14th US Air Force, under Major-General Claire Chennault, had planes already loaded in China to take supplies to the French, and asked for this to be authorized immediately.[20] In the end, Admiral Leahy, Roosevelt's Chief of Staff, gave the authorization. Chennault's planes did take in supplies, and strafed Japanese columns which were attacking the five thousand French troops making their way north into Yunnan. The American pilots observed British planes over Indo-China, delivering infantry weapons. This report incensed General Wedemeyer, who believed that British forces should not intervene in Indo-China without permission from Chiang Kai-shek, since it fell in the China Theatre and not in Mountbatten's South-East Asia Command. He also objected to Mountbatten's headquarters organizing clandestine operations into Indo-China, but Mountbatten justified this by claiming a gentleman's agreement with Chiang, a claim that Churchill backed.* It was finally agreed, at the very highest level, between Roosevelt and Churchill, that Mountbatten would operate in areas deemed to be in the China Theatre only after prearrangement with Chiang.[22]

This hesitation and political debate, while men were dying for lack of help, reflects Roosevelt's attitude towards the French in Indo-China. He had already made it clear that nothing was to deflect the main American effort against Japan, and he used this as an argument not to become involved in operations in Indo-China. But de Gaulle was not deceived. Caffery visited de Gaulle on the afternoon of 24 March to introduce Samuel I. Rosenman, Roosevelt's Special Counsel who was then on a mission to Europe. As they took their leave, de Gaulle said to Caffery, 'It seems clear now that your Government does not want to help our troops in Indo-China. Nothing has yet been dropped to them by parachute.' When Caffery spoke of the great distances involved, de Gaulle retorted, 'No that is not the question; the question is one of policy I assume.'[23]

Summing up the operation, the Japanese general Tsuchihashi reflected that its success was due to the poor quality of the French

---

* Some Frenchmen attributed Wedemeyer's hostility to his German antecedents. 'Don't forget I'm a former pupil of the Berlin *Kriegsakademie*,' he is supposed to have said, when asked by the French why he delayed assisting their compatriots in Indo-China. 'I don't give a damn for the French.'[21] On relations between Mountbatten and Wedemeyer, see a top secret memorandum by Roosevelt's naval aide, G. M. Elsey, in *For. Rel. US*, 1945 (Potsdam), I, pp. 915–21.

troops in Indo-China. They were very much a colonial army, and their officers were second-rate material. Their morale was low, and their offensive spirit sluggish.* Even so, he could not understand why they did not react more swiftly. Surely they must have suspected that the Japanese were likely to move against them soon? In which case, why were the troops not stood to, and why was the commander in Hanoi not told of the presentation of the Japanese demands? When authorities like General Delsuc, the commander of the Cochin-China-Cambodia division, were convened by Decoux to discuss the demands, why did they not send out an alert at once? In Tsuchihashi's view Delsuc must be held responsible for this in his own area: even if Decoux had declared it unnecessary, he should have taken it into his own hands to warn his men. That he did not do so is even more inexplicable, in Tsuchihashi's account, because a Japanese airfield company commander had let slip to his local employees – this was at Thudaumot, north of Saigon – on the morning of the 9th that he would be on duty all that night. The employees smelt a rat, and left early to inform the provincial governor, who immediately got in touch with the governor of Cochin-China. At twelve noon, the governor summoned Delsuc, the naval commander and other notables and told them he thought it would be advisable to declare a state of emergency. Whereupon Delsuc said they had put out warnings many times before, and nothing had ever happened. The Japanese Army was probably going on night manoeuvres, nothing more. 'Imagine,' he said, 'if you proclaimed your state of emergency at noon, in the Rue Catinat, which is crammed with shoppers and people in the cafés. The word would be all round Saigon in no time, and you'd cause an immense disturbance.' In face of this opposition, the governor's proposal was dropped. Tsuchihashi learned later that the governor had reported this to Decoux, but he does not know when. On the other hand, if such a meeting had taken place in the morning, and either the governor or Delsuc had, later in the day, attended the discussion on the Japanese memorandum convened by Decoux, would they not have recalled what had been said and warned Decoux? It was lucky for the Japanese that nothing like that seems to have occurred.[25]

* Based on French accounts, the Japanese give the figures of the French troops in Indo-China at the time of the *coup de force* as 15,000, plus 35,000 native troops. The Japanese forces were estimated to be 40,000.[24]

ii *Japan, Ho Chi Minh and an Independent Vietnam*

Severe as they were, the military humiliations inflicted on the French were as nothing compared to the political ones. The Japanese did not only remove the French from the administration and imprison their forces; they encouraged the native population to declare French rule to be at an end. This was not merely a blow against the vanished authority of Vichy. It was an attempt to frustrate further plans already adumbrated by de Gaulle's government in Paris. They prevailed upon the young Emperor of Annam, Bao Dai, to denounce the French protectorate and proclaim the independence of his country under its earlier name, Vietnam, which he did two days after the *coup de force*. Under the Vietnamese scholar, Tran Trong Kim, a nationalist government of middle-class intellectuals was formed, but it proved incapable of fulfilling its most urgent duty, the provision of rice to starving Tonkin. There was plenty in the South, but in Northern Indo-China thousands died of famine in 1945. Bao Dai's writ did not run in the former colony of Cochin-China, or its capital Saigon, which the Japanese had no intention of permitting anyone but themselves to control.* In Cambodia, the Japanese 2nd Division had been ordered to 'protect' the young King Sihanouk, and as a precaution against his attempting to escape from Phnom Penh, the capital was ringed by road-blocks. The divisional commander, General Manaki, ordered all his units to cooperate with the *Kempei* in a search for the King, who had still not made an appearance on 10 March. On the 11th, the King was discovered in a temple in the grounds of the royal palace, disguised as a monk. Manaki at once despatched his Chief of Staff, Colonel Kinoshita, to the palace. With the Japanese consul Takashima acting as his interpreter, Kinoshita explained that the Japanese operation was aimed only at disarming the French, that it had no objectives as far as Cambodia was concerned other than to have the King take over the government. Sihanouk declared his country's independence on 13 March.

The Japanese emissary to Laos did not fare quite so well. Luang Prabang, the capital, is in a mountainous area with poor communications, and the Consul, Watanabe Taemi, did not arrive at the

* They finally ceded it on 16 May, together with the special cities of Haiphong, Hanoi, and Tourane (Bao Dai was also sovereign of Tonkin).[26]

royal palace before 20 March. He reported the events of the past fortnight to the King and was taken aback when Sisavang-Vong flatly refused to believe him. The old king – he was past sixty – did not speak French very well, having learned it at the *École coloniale* in Paris at the turn of the century, and he had suffered a great deal when part of Laos was transferred to Siam as a result of Japan's mediation in the Franco–Siamese war of 1940. But he was a great friend of France, had negotiated a fresh protectorate agreement with Decoux some years before, and had travelled to Hanoi to visit him. However, the arrival in Luang Prabang of two Japanese infantry battalions on 7 April succeeded in convincing him that Watanabe had not lied, and, bowing to the inevitable, he proclaimed the independence of Laos the following day.

Japan had done to the French what she had done to the British three years before. By planting the Japanese flag over Singapore she had brought British rule to an end. There would be an attempt to re-establish the old régime, but the forces Japan had liberated would ensure that it would never succeed in implanting itself again. She had replaced French rule by that of the local monarchies, supported by her Army. But there was another actor in the wings.

Among the various nationalist groups in Indo-China, one had been as hostile to Japanese as to French control: the Communist Party of Indo-China under its leader Nguyen Ai Quoc, later and somewhat better known as Ho Chi Minh. In his youth a seaman and then a dish-washer in London hotels, an accomplished linguist and a puritanically dedicated patriot (that is what the name Ai Quoc means), Ho took part in the Chinese Communist movement in Canton and founded in that city the Revolutionary Youth Association, to work in Indo-China. He was not an enemy of France: in 1920 he had taken part, as a delegate, in the Socialist Congress at Tours and had made an impassioned speech on behalf of his oppressed fellow Vietnamese to the assembled Socialists and Communists of France. His theme was 'Comrades, rescue us!' but he knew that his people would first have to rescue themselves. Conditions were not ripe for Communism in Indo-China. His people were a peasantry, not an industrial proletariat. The country's first step out of the clutches of the French exploiters would have to be political independence under a régime of bourgeois democratic nationalism. Such a programme was likely to win outside support, whereas Communism was not.

For decades he worked in obscurity. The French police savagely repressed nationalist movements in Indo-China in the 1920s and 1930s, and the cells in the offshore island of Poulo Condore, the Pacific equivalent of Devil's Island, were crammed with political prisoners. A number of Vietnamese revolutionary groups met in South China in the spring of 1941, close to the border with Tonkin. A joint anti-French programme was agreed, and a united front formed, called *Vietnam Doc Lap Dong Minh* (League for the Independence of Vietnam), *Viet Minh* in its abbreviated form. In its first manifesto, dated 25 October 1941, the party's aim was said to be 'the union of all anti-Fascist forces in the struggle against French and Japanese colonialism until all Vietnam is liberated'. The inclusion of Japan reflects the fact that for left-wing parties of the thirties and forties Japan was the fascist aggressor against a democratic China, though Japan had already acted as a haven for Vietnamese exiles. Prince Cuong De had been sheltered there, so too had Phan Boi Chau, who had directed, from Japan, an underground revolutionary movement in Indo-China before the First World War.

Ho became the Viet Minh's general secretary. His party existed on Chinese soil, but it could hardly be said to have flourished. It proclaimed its allegiance to the Allied cause against the Japanese, and engaged in espionage in Indo-China. But Chiang Kai-shek mistrusted Ho. He feared the setting up of a Communist stronghold on his Southern frontier, which might match the internal one in Yenan. In 1942 Ho was arrested and imprisoned under conditions of unspeakable hardship for fifteen months. He wrote poems to keep himself sane:

The rice-grain suffers under the pestle: yet admires its whiteness when the ordeal is over.[27]

Partly as a result of a campaign by his fellow exiles, partly as a piece of calculation by the Chinese, who had hoped to use him as a tool for their policies in Indo-China, Ho was released in the spring of 1943. He then turned to the Americans for aid, which was generously given. Ho and his men attacked the Japanese posts near the China–Tonkin border with American logistical support, and were back in Tonkin by October 1944. The Northern provinces were gradually liberated from Japanese control: Cao Bang, Bac Can, Tuyen Quang, and part of Thai Nguyen, Lang Son, and Ha Giang. Ho did not use his entire force for this purpose. Ten thousand men

were trained and held in waiting for the campaign against the
French which was sure to come. They were led by a former Vietnamese history teacher and law graduate, who was bitterly hostile
to the French in a way that Ho was not. His name was Vo Nguyen
Giap and his wife had died in a French prison. With the active
collaboration of the Americans in Kunming and the assistance in
the field of OSS (Office of Strategic Services) units, the Viet Minh
continued its liberation of Northern Tonkin. The French had
mounted a column against them, which was to start out on 12 March
1945. The Japanese *coup de force* put an end to that. A few weeks
before, Ho had a meeting with Colonel Helliwell, area commander
of the OSS in Kunming, in which Helliwell agreed to supply
him with arms, provided he would guarantee they would not
be used against the French, and American officers should be
allowed to operate in areas he controlled.[28] American aid to Ho was
more enthusiastic than this meeting suggests. Officers of the OSS
who had penetrated into Tonkin were photographed in smiling
groups with Ho and Giap in the months which followed.* In the
French view, the activities of the OSS were uniformly hostile to
French interests. On the other hand, at this time, Ho himself was
prepared to meet the representative of the new Paris Government.
Since it was the product of a movement of national resistance, he
may have hoped it would not suppress nationalism in its former
colonies. At any rate, he would see what they had to say. An Annamite
lieutenant called Phac, who escaped from Tonkin with the Alessandri
column, made contacts with the Vietnamese nationalists in Kunming,
and told Sainteny, head of de Gaulle's military mission to Kunming,
that he could arrange a meeting. In the first few days of August 1945
Sainteny met, for the first time, one of Ho's staff, Nguyen Tong Tam,
later to become Vietnamese Foreign Minister. The encounter took
place on the first floor of a little restaurant in a Kunming back alley.

* 'Ho was an awfully sweet guy…If I had to recall one quality of this old
man sitting on his hill in the jungle, it would be his sweetness.' The remark is
that of a US officer quoted by *The Reporter*, 27 January 1945.[29] Cf. also OSS
reports recently released by the Senate Foreign Relations Committee: 'Forget the
communist bogey. VML (the Vietminh League) is not communist, stands for
freedom and reforms from French harshness. If the French go part way with them
they might work with the French.' (Major Allison Thomas, commander of a US
mission, quoted in *The Times*, 26 February 1973.) Major Thomas also reported
Ho objecting to the presence of a French officer in the OSS team, but Thomas
added, 'he will welcome 10 million Americans'. (ibid.)

He struck Sainteny as the perfect type of Vietnamese intellectual. In addition he had 'something frank and manly which is fairly rare in that class of Indo-Chinese'.[30] Nguyen Tong Tam's purpose in meeting Sainteny was to convey to Paris, through him, the strong determination of his compatriots to free themselves from French tutelage, a determination which had been strengthened since the Japanese had dismantled the French administrative machine. Sainteny countered this by saying he had just returned from Paris, and that the Provisional Government of the French Republic had no intention of abandoning a single scrap of its legitimate rights in Indo-China. The most developed colonies would receive a more enlightened treatment than had been accorded them in the past, but these concessions would not be forced from France by violence. France was always prepared to discuss affairs with Indo-Chinese recognized as representing their country. Sainteny was concerned above all to avoid further bloodshed and to keep paths open to the revolutionary parties. For his part, Nguyen Tong Tam did not want to establish his country's independence by a bloody uprising, and he offered Sainteny the possibility of further discussions in Hanoi, where his brother was one of the chiefs of his party, the ultra-nationalist *Viet-Nam Quoc Dong Dang*. He gave him a coded letter which would enable contact to be made.

That interview was the only direct contact made by Sainteny during his stay in Kunming. Other contacts were made through the Americans only. The OSS conveyed to Mission 5 (the code name for Sainteny's mission) a message from the Vietnamese command, then in Tuyen Quang, which the OSS knew under the name of 'The Viet Minh League'. The message contained five requirements which Ho and his colleagues wished to see embodied in any new form of government for Indo-China:

We, the Viet Minh League, ask that the following items be made known to the French and observed in future policy in French Indo-China:

1 That there should be universal suffrage for the election of a Parliament which shall govern the country; that there should be a French governor acting as President until independence be secured; that this President choose a cabinet or group of advisers accepted by Parliament. The precise powers of all these officials can be clarified at some future date.

2   That independence be granted to this country in a minimum of five years and a maximum of ten.

3   That the natural resources of the country shall revert to its inhabitants after equitable compensation to the present holder; that France shall be the beneficiary of economic concessions.

4   That the sale of opium be forbidden.

We hope that these conditions will be deemed acceptable by the French Government.[31]

The tone is democratic, and conciliatory to French interests. The French authorities in Kunming examined the text closely (it was written in English, no doubt at the request of the OSS) and sent a reply, also in English. Sainteny does not give the details of this reply, but says it referred necessarily to decisions which had to be taken in Paris, so it can hardly have been judged a satisfactory answer by the Viet Minh. In the course of the previous month, there had also been military contacts with the Viet Minh guerrillas. The head of the French mission 'Picardie', which had been set up in Tsin-tsi, reported favourably on the units he had met, and had suggested to them the possibility of a conference in Kunming between Sainteny and the Viet Minh leader. On 16 July a mixed Franco-American mission was parachuted into Indo-China to cooperate with the Directing Committee of the Viet Minh. Towards the end of the month another possibility of contact between Sainteny and Ho was offered by Major Gordon, who ran a resistance group in the border area between China and Tonkin. Sainteny understandably refers to him as an American,[32] since he was working for US Navy intelligence, but Gordon was in fact a Canadian, who had been the Haiphong representative of the Texaco Company in pre-war days. There seems little doubt that the Viet Minh leaders would, at that particular time, have welcomed Sainteny's presence, and even had tricolour flags ready to greet him when he arrived. But the monsoon rains put a stop to air communications in the region, and in a matter of days the talk was all of the Japanese surrender.

The surrender caught the Viet Minh short. They had a rudimentary organization in the North of the country, and a military force; but in the South their assets were negligible. Their first task must be to establish themselves in the capital, Hanoi. Ho had already prepared for such a step. On 10 August, anticipating the Japanese surrender, he had convened a meeting of sixty northern delegates of varying political complexion to a meeting in Thai Nguyen province. This resulted in the formation of a National Liberation Committee of Vietnam on the 13th, the purpose of which was to take power before the Allies could prevent it. 'The defeat of the Japanese,' they warned their countrymen in a manifesto, 'does not render us automatically free and independent . . . Let us free ourselves by our own energies . . . Onward under the flag of the Viet Minh.'[33]

There was little opposition in Hanoi itself. Giap's troops moved into the city, where demonstrations in favour of independence were already in progress. In theory, it was ruled by Bao Dai's viceroy, Phan Ke Toai, who did not take long to sum up the situation. He surrendered to Giap, and the Viet Minh took charge of the city. By 20 August, five days after the surrender, Ho controlled the capital of Indo-China.

Then events moved even faster. Under pressure from Hanoi, the Emperor Bao Dai abdicated on 25 August and accepted the post of supreme adviser to the new administration, under the name of Vinh Thuy. A delegation from Hanoi travelled south to Hue and was greeted by frenziedly enthusiastic crowds. Its triumphal procession continued through the towns and villages of Central Annam, where the main question on everyone's lips was 'Who is Ho Chi Minh?' Within a week they were on the border of Cochin-China, at Bien Hoa, where they drove straight for Saigon. They were led to the Governor's palace, where the leader of the delegation, Hoang Quoc Viet, sent a telegram to Ho in Hanoi: IN 21 PROVINCES I HAVE CROSSED POWER IS IN OUR HANDS EVERYTHING GONE SMOOTHLY ALSO THROUGHOUT NAM BO.*

Ho replied briefly: PROCLAMATION INDEPENDENCE 2 SEPTEMBER.[34]

The result might not have been wholly displeasing to President Roosevelt, had he survived to see it. But it was hardly what Britain or France desired for South-East Asia. This divergence of views goes a long way back in the history of the war. In an incredibly offhand way, Roosevelt had offered the country to Chiang Kai-shek at the Cairo conference in November 1943. 'The first thing I asked Chiang was,' he later recalled, '"Do you want Indo-China?"' Chiang politely refused the offer. The inhabitants were not Chinese and would not assimilate to the Chinese, though it is not clear whether or not Roosevelt was aware of this. Both of them agreed it should not be returned to the French.[35] Roosevelt's hostility to the return

* Nam Bo is the Vietnamese name for Cochin-China.

of Indo-China to the French was maintained consistently throughout the war. A month after the talk with Chiang, he sent a memorandum to his Secretary of State, Cordell Hull, suggesting a post-war international trusteeship.*

'France has had the country,' he wrote, 'thirty million inhabitants – for nearly one hundred years, and the people are worse off than they were at the beginning . . . France has milked it dry for one hundred years. The people of Indo-China are entitled to something better than that.'[37] Just over a year later, a week after the Japanese *coup de force*, he was talking to Taussig, the adviser on Caribbean affairs in the State Department, and the conversation turned to the Far East. Roosevelt reaffirmed his intention to see Indo-China taken from the French.

> I asked the president if he had changed his ideas on French Indo-China (*writes Taussig*) . . . He said he had not changed his ideas; that French Indo-China and New Caledonia should be taken from the French and put under a trusteeship. The president hesitated a moment and then said – well, if we can get the proper pledge from France to assume for herself these colonies with the proviso that independence was the ultimate goal. I asked the President if he would settle for self-government. He said no. I asked him if he would settle for dominion status. He said no – it must be independence. He said that is to be the policy and you can quote me in the State Department.[38]

iii *The 16th Parallel Decision*

It is against this background that the decision to split the country in two to deal with the Japanese surrender must be seen; a decision the consequences of which are still with us. It was adumbrated at the Potsdam Conference at a meeting of the Combined Chiefs of Staff on 18 July 1945. No French representatives, of course, were present. The idea of extending Mountbatten's South-East Asia Command had been mooted, and the US Chiefs of Staff, in a paper on 'Control and Command in the War against Japan',[39] commented on a proposal

* Stimson, the US Secretary for War, later hoped that Korea could be put under trusteeship, and feared that British and French refusal to allow Hong-Kong and Indo-China to be put under a trusteeship would make the Russians stand out for solitary control of Korea by themselves.[36]

from their British opposite numbers that Indo-China south of latitude 15° North should be included in his command. They said they had no objection to this from a military point of view, but it was primarily a matter for Chiang Kai-shek to decide. They had already been reminded by Admiral Leahy two days before, when the question of sending two French divisions to participate in the Pacific War was under discussion, and their use in Indo-China was mooted, that that area was held to be under Chiang.[40] A shift of part of the area did not appear practicable until his agreement was obtained. The British Chiefs of Staff submitted a counter-memorandum the following day, 18 July, saying they realized Chiang's agreement would have to be obtained, but they hoped the US Chiefs of Staff would support a recommendation to the President (Truman) and Churchill to press Chiang to give his consent. Such a recommendation should go in the conference's final report.[41]

The memorandum was discussed later the same day, and when General of the Army George C. Marshall, Chief of Staff of the US Army, asked the British Chiefs of Staff for their views on dividing Indo-China into two, the northern part to be left in the China Theatre, admiral Cunningham pointed out that the line of division would depend on contemplated operations through Siam. The American Admiral, King, said that the line of 15° North was an arbitrary division and might be changed to suit operational requirements. The British replied they would have to consider the line before making any firm proposals.[42] Marshall returned to the idea on 24 July 1945 and asked Mountbatten what he thought of using two French divisions (both were composed of white men, he pointed out) for service in Indo-China, and dividing that country along the line of 16° North. Mountbatten replied that he had just heard of the proposition and his first reactions were favourable. He would have liked some latitude in the northern limit of the area in case his operations developed north of 16°, but he did not feel very strongly on the point.* The French, on the other hand, might find the proposition rather less agreeable.

When the Combined Chiefs of Staff approved their statement of 20 July, they included an appendix giving 15° North as the Indo-China division boundary. A corrigendum was circulated by the

* These reactions make Mountbatten's later comment on the division as 'arbitrary' seem a little disingenuous.[43]

secretaries on 7 August substituting a fresh appendix, which gave the line as 16° North. No elucidation of the change is given in the documents.[44] The report of the Combined Chiefs of Staff to Truman and Churchill, dated 24 July 1945, recommended that Mountbatten take over operations in Southern Indo-China on the grounds that they were more closely related to those of South-East Asia Command than to those of the China Theatre. The arrangement that he should control the area south of 16° North meant that General Wedemeyer would still control that part of Indo-China which covered the flank of projected Chinese operations. They added that at a later date it might prove desirable to place all or part of the remainder of Indo-China under Mountbatten. In this way the Combined Chiefs of Staff disposed of territory which did not belong to them. When the upshot of all these deliberations was conveyed to Chiang, he agreed to the dividing line, provided it ran through Siam as well, and allowed him to operate in that country down to 16° North. The reply did not reach Truman until the Potsdam Conference was over and in the drawing up of MacArthur's General Order No. 1 on 2 September 1945 Chiang's rider on Siam was ignored, fortunately for that country.[45]

This addition to Mountbatten's command, agreed upon at Potsdam, made his new task enormous. He now had the whole of the Netherlands East Indies to re-take, whereas previously only Sumatra had been within his province; and Indo-China south of the 16th parallel. His area contained 128,000,000 people, including 122,700 prisoners-of-war and internees who were in desperate need of all kinds of help; and almost three-quarters of a million Japanese troops and civilians (in proportions of 633,000/93,000). These were to be disarmed, concentrated, and repatriated when Japan surrendered. In addition 10,000 Taiwanese and Koreans would have to be returned to their respective countries.

He was not, at first, sure that the Japanese generals in South-East Asia Command would obey his orders, but a meeting in Rangoon with Lieutenant-General Numata, Chief of Staff to Field-Marshal Terauchi, on 27 August 1945, convinced him that he could rely on their capitulation if not on their good will. He at once arranged for token forces from his command to enter Siam and Indo-China. On 3 September an advance party of the 7th Indian Division flew into Bangkok, and prepared the Don Muang airfield as a staging post for the forces going to Saigon. Eleven days later, the 'Supreme

Allied Commander South-East Asia Commission' for the control of Field-Marshal Terauchi's Southern Army headquarters was set up in Saigon under Major-General Douglas Gracey, GOC 20th Indian Division. A brigade of this division had begun its fly-in on 13 September, and along with it Mountbatten established an Air Headquarters, with two RAF tactical squadrons, and a Naval Port Party. Gracey was also to disarm and concentrate all Japanese forces in his area, approximately 60,000 with nearly 2,000 civilians (an undertaking named 'Operation Nipoff' by a wag in Mountbatten's headquarters).* He was to maintain law and order and ensure internal security; and to protect and evacuate Allied prisoners-of-war and civilian internees.

The order had qualifications. He was to occupy no more of Southern Indo-China than was necessary to ensure control over the Japanese Army. The British force was to be withdrawn as soon as its task was done, and the French would then be responsible for all political and administrative key areas.[47]

iv *The British in Vietnam*

The situation did not permit Gracey to keep within the prescribed limits. He arrived to find Saigon in a state of chaos. On the same day that Ho Chi Minh proclaimed the independence of Vietnam in

* As always there was a slight discrepancy in the figures. The Japanese delegates to the Rangoon conference on 27 August brought a map with them showing the troops under the 38th Army as numbering 44,392. SEAC produced their own map of Japanese dispositions on 15 August, derived from Japanese sources, which gave the following figures: Southern Army Headquarters, 38th Army, 21st, 2nd and 55th Divisions, and 34th Independent Mixed Brigade, a total of 43,392 men. They estimated an additional figure of 6,282 for naval forces, 10,686 for air forces, and 1,871 civilians, a total of 62,231. Woodburn-Kirby gives an originally believed figure of 71,000 troops, including 9,000 air force, 5,000 navy, and 17,000 administrative personnel.[46] The figure was found to include the 21st Division, about 13,000 strong, which was in the north, in the Chinese zone; and the 22nd Division, also about 13,000 strong, which had moved to Siam. Some of the 34th Independent Mixed Brigade's 2,300 troops also fell into the Chinese zone, since it was stationed at Tourane (Da Nang), close to the 16th parallel. The crucial figures for Gracey were the 17,000 troops in his immediate area, Saigon–Cholon, made up of Southern Army headquarters (1,500), 38th Army rear headquarters (500), the 2nd Division (8,000), plus 7,700 non-divisional troops. 55th Division headquarters, with one regiment, was in Cambodia, estimated at 1,000 strong.

Hanoi a rising took place in Saigon. Before this, a United National Front party had been created in the South to fill the vacuum left by the Japanese. The Front consisted of Trotskyist, nationalist, and religious groups (*Hoa Hao*, *Cao Dai*), and the Viet Minh, and they organized a celebration of national independence in Saigon on 22 August, when thousands of people marched along the boulevards under banners proclaiming various revolutionary slogans. Anticipating the arrival of Allied forces, the Viet Minh claimed that they should head the United National Front, since they were on good terms with the Allies.[48] If the Front rejected this proposal, it risked having the Allies dismiss its members as puppets of the Japanese. The Viet Minh claim was provisionally accepted. A Committee of the South was then formed to govern Cochin-China. Dominated by Communists, but asserting that it was a democratic and middle-class government, it took over public installations in Saigon without resistance. Not wishing to confront the hostility of the British–Indian forces which were known to be on the way, it tried to repress the natural ebullience of the population in these rather heady days, but on 2 September, in the course of a mass demonstration along the Rue Catinat, the main boulevard of the city, shots were fired, one of which killed a French priest, Father Tricoire, who was standing in front of the cathedral. Four other Frenchmen were killed, and others injured, as were some of the Vietnamese. Looting of French property followed, and many French people were imprisoned (they were released by the Viet Minh police chief within forty-eight hours). The effect of these events on the French population of the city was profound. They had hoped to be delivered from the trauma of 9 March by the Japanese surrender. Instead, as they saw it, one Asiatic oppressor was being substituted for another.

In the next few days, there was an internal power struggle in the United National Front. Trotskyists and nationalists wanted to retain their arms. The Viet Minh considered this would be a foolhardy provocation of the Allied forces, and ousted their opponents from the Front. They got in touch with de Gaulle's commissioner for Southern Indo-China, Henri Cédile, and learned from him what had been proposed by the Provisional Government of the French Republic for the future of Indo-China. Cédile had been parachuted into the Tayninh region and arrived in Saigon, after being taken prisoner by the Japanese, on 22 August. An Indo-Chinese Federation of the five areas of the country (Tonkin, Annam, Cochin-China,

Cambodia, and Laos) had been proposed, in which all offices would be available to all citizens of the country without discrimination. Freedom of worship, freedom of association, and freedom of the press were promised. The Federation would have its own armed forces. This seemed fairly positive, but there was a negative side. The French would retain control of foreign affairs and defence decisions, and French interests would have separate representation in the federal assembly, the chief task of which would be to vote on taxes and approve the budget. Ultimate control was to be vested in a high commissioner (a governor-general under another name) with ministers to advise him. The Association of Indo-Chinese in France had already rejected these proposals as inadequate, and when Cédile saw the Committee of the South on 27 August they politely told him the terms would not do. They already had better than this, and had won their own independence, though that did not necessarily imply a break with France.[49] Besides, the Vietnamese intended the union of the 'three Kys' (i.e. the three parts of Vietnam: Tonkin, Annam, Cochin-China), not the perpetuation of their divisions, even in a federation.

The rejection of the proposals by the Committee of the South and the violence of 2 September seem to have turned Cédile against the new local institutions. He then turned for advice to a group of French planters and lawyers who were hostile to the Annamite population and unimpressed by the views of the new government in Paris. They urged upon him that a hard line was the only answer: 'The Annamites are cowards. As soon as you show that you're firm, and get out the big stick, they'll be out of your way like a flock of sparrows.'[50]

As the forerunner of the new High Commissioner, Admiral Thierry d'Argenlieu, Cédile's function was to restore French sovereignty. He totally lacked the means to do this, but that did not prevent him holding a press conference on 9 September, in which he declared: 'The Viet Minh does not represent popular opinion. It is incapable of maintaining order and putting down looting. First and foremost, order must be established, then we shall set up a government in conformity with the Declaration of March 24.'[51]

Cédile clearly would have liked to use the big stick which had been recommended. But the only big stick at his disposal was General Douglas Gracey. Gracey's troops had arrived in Indo-China expecting trouble, at any rate from the Japanese. After hostilities broke out, one brigadier (Brigadier C. H. B. Rodham of the 100th Indian Infantry Brigade) warned his men that there would be no clear front in their operations: they would be dealing with guerrillas and might find it difficult to distinguish friend from foe. They were to use the same vigilance against ambushes and doubtful friends that was required on the North-West Frontier of India. They were also warned of 'nibbling' at opposition: 'Always use the maximum force available to ensure wiping out any hostiles...If one uses too much no harm is done. If one uses too small a force and it has to be extricated we will suffer casualties and encourage the enemy.'[52] This mood was to develop later, but there is no doubt that Gracey arrived prepared for a situation in which he might have to use force to carry out his mission.

Both American and British writers have been extremely critical of the way Gracey did this.*[53] In fact the situation left Gracey little room for manoeuvre, and it would have been beyond his competence to have treated with the Viet Minh as if they had been recognized by the Allies as the government, or even the future government, of Cochin-China. The Gurkhas of his 20th Indian Division, which had begun to land at Saigon airfield on 11 September, took over the airfield itself, then the powerhouse at Saigon, the police stations, the gaol, the banks, and the Post and Telegraph Offices, relieving the Japanese guards. Owing to bad flying conditions the build-up of Gracey's first brigade, the 80th Indian Infantry Brigade, was very slow, and it was 26 September before it was concentrated in Saigon.

Cédile informed him, on his arrival, of the troubles of 2 September, and of Bao Dai's abdication in favour of the Government of the Republic of Vietnam. The Japanese had done little to maintain law and order, Cédile said. Gracey lost no time in informing Field-Marshal Terauchi that the Japanese forces, which were present in strength throughout the South, were responsible for ensuring the security of life and property in Saigon. He did not, at first, wish to

---

* Ellen Hammer says Gracey was confronted with a political problem 'for which he had neither the background nor the advisors...'[54] and George Rosie speaks of the situation calling for 'tact and real political imagination' whereas Gracey merely acted 'by the book'.[55] Both of them seriously underestimate Gracey's political nous, though Rosie fairly concedes he was far from being a 'Blimp', and was not 'opposed to Asian nationalism as such'; but as an Indian Army officer he was, in the eyes of the Viet Minh, associated with 'a key instrument and symbol of European repression'.[56]

apply firm measures against the Viet Minh, because he knew the Labour Government in London did not wish to become involved in the repression of Asian nationalism. General Sir William Slim, former 14th Army commander, and now (since 16 August) Commander-in-Chief Allied Land Forces South-East Asia, passed through Saigon on 18 September and emphasized to Gracey that he had only one mission in Saigon, and that was to disarm the Japanese. He was not to get involved in the maintenance of order.[57] This was easier said than done. The people of Saigon had celebrated the previous day as Independence Day and there was disorder in the city. The Viet Minh ordered the market to be closed, and French shops to be boycotted. French property was attacked. Gracey believed the Saigon newspapers were partly responsible for stirring up trouble, and on 19 September he prohibited their publication. He also sent a deputation to the Vietnamese authorities demanding that they hand over buildings they had requisitioned, and furnish him with a list of their armed police and the locations of their armed forces. He had drawn up a proclamation that day, and sent it to them, saying he was going to issue it on the 21st. The proclamation prohibited public meetings and the carrying of arms (even sticks). Looters and other wrongdoers would be summarily shot. A curfew was to be strictly enforced between 9.30 p.m. and 5.30 a.m.

Gracey sent a copy of his proclamation to Mountbatten, pointing out that he had been forced to act, since the French on the spot were too weak to do so, and asking the Japanese to round up Annamite forces would have resulted in the Japanese warning wanted Annamites, who would promptly vanish.[58] The proclamation was posted throughout Saigon–Cholon on 21 September.

'Mountbatten was quick to realize,' says the official British history, 'that the action taken was not only courageous but sound...'[59] This may refer to Gracey's occupation of vital installations in Saigon, in which case it is correct; if it refers to Mountbatten's acceptance of Gracey's proclamation, it is very far from the truth. 'While appreciating that the military situation in Saigon was grave,' Mountbatten later wrote in his despatches,

> ...I felt that this proclamation – addressed, as it was, to the whole of Southern FIC (*French Indo-China*) and not merely to the key points – was contrary to the policy of His Majesty's Government; and since proclamations of this nature may well appear to have been initiated by Government policy, I warned Major-General Gracey

that he should take care to confine operations of British/Indian troops to those limited tasks which he had been set.[60]

He told General Leclerc, Commander-in-Chief of French forces in the Far East, who had arrived in Kandy on his way to Indo-China, that Gracey had overstepped his orders and that he was going to disavow him. Slim was in Kandy too, and, after discussing the affair with him and Leclerc, Mountbatten was persuaded to refer to the chiefs of staff the situation that had been produced by Gracey's action.

He telegraphed to them on 24 September that he saw two courses now open to him:

i he could implement the proclamation and retain responsibility for civil and military administration throughout southern French Indo-China, or,

ii he could limit his responsibility solely to the control of the Japanese Supreme Headquarters.[61]

Gracey had acted with courage and determination, he told the chiefs of staff, but his forces were inadequate, the river and the port of Saigon were not yet open, and the small British–Indian force and the French population might have been compromised.

The first course suggested by Mountbatten would imply directly controlling all French forces and civil affairs until Leclerc could take over and would mean the use of British–Indian troops throughout Southern Indo-China. The second would entail senior French authority reaffirming Gracey's proclamation since, in Mountbatten's words, 'it would be dangerous now to revoke it'.[63] Leclerc was not prepared to do this until he had enough force to back him. Mountbatten asked the chiefs of staff for a ruling, stressing that he preferred the second course, as soon as force was available.

The chiefs of staff reacted by changing Mountbatten's instructions. They wired him on 1 October that he was to use British–Indian troops throughout the interior of Southern Indo-China to help the French, 'so long as this does not prejudice (his) prime responsibility for Saigon'.[63] The troops' role was to be preventive, not offensive, but none the less it was clear that the chiefs of staff endorsed Gracey's action.

Meanwhile, events had gone much further than a mere proclamation. Gracey had permitted the French forces in Saigon to carry out their own *coup d'état*. His troops took over the Saigon gaol and freed French paratroops who had been imprisoned by the Vietnamese. At Cédile's request, he allowed the men of the 11th Colonial Infantry Division, who had been under guard in their barracks since 9 March, to be rearmed and to leave the barracks. These French troops, about fifteen hundred of them, were spoiling for a fight, and went out into the streets to throw their weight about against the Annamite population. Before dawn on the 23rd, they occupied the police commissariats, the *Sûreté*, and the *Hotel de Ville*.* Those whom the French historian Devillers terms 'the mediocre elements' in the French population then began to harass the Vietnamese mercilessly.† This can be explained by their fears of a general massacre, but Gracey had no intention of letting the pendulum swing back into violence against the Vietnamese. He ordered the 11th Colonial Infantry Division to return to their barracks and be disarmed. The Japanese command was given full responsibility for maintaining order.

Order was the first casualty of the next phase in Saigon. The electricity generating station was attacked by Vietnamese on 24 September, and dozens of Frenchmen were kidnapped or killed in the port area. The next day, there was a massacre in the Tan Dinh suburb: three hundred French men, women, and children were abducted, of whom half were killed in atrocious circumstances. This happened in the space of two hours, while Japanese sentries stood by, idle and indifferent.[64]

Colonel Peter Dewey of the OSS was driving to the Saigon airfield on 26 September when his jeep was attacked. He realized the Vietnamese had taken him for a Frenchman, and cried out '*Je suis Américain*', but it was too late. His body was removed by the Vietnamese before Allied troops could rescue it.

Gracey again rebuked the Japanese for failing to keep order, and warned Numata, Chief of Staff of Southern Army, that Japanese

---

* Devillers says the decision was Cédile's.[65] Woodburn-Kirby speaks of Gracey 'ordering Cédile' to take over the administration of Saigon.[66]

† 'On the Rue Catinat...the French population went wild; they insulted and attacked any Vietnamese who dared appear on the streets, while French and British soldiers looked on. Correspondents, both French and foreign, who happened to be on the scene, were shocked by the outrages.'[67] The British account agrees that 'the behaviour of the French citizens during the morning of Sunday, 23 September, absolutely ensured that countermeasures would be taken by the Annamites'.[68]

commanders who failed in this task would be treated as war criminals. Numata answered that the Japanese were unwilling to fire on the Vietnamese because they feared reprisals in the future when they would be disarmed themselves. He offered to act as intermediary between the Vietnamese and the British–French forces, pointing out that he had instructed his officers in Hanoi to maintain contact with the Viet Minh government there, in the hope of inaugurating a conference between Japanese, Viet Minh, British, and French.

The political impact of the Labour Government in London now began to be felt. It was hostile to colonial exploitation, and committed to emancipating its own colonies. It had no intention of stifling Asian nationalism by force of arms. This view was transmitted in Singapore on 28 September by the former Durham miners' leader, Jack Lawson, Secretary of State for War. Mountbatten held a conference with Gracey and Cédile, and Lawson made it clear to them that although the British would keep their commitments to France, it was the policy of the British Government not to interfere in the internal affairs of Indo-China but to encourage mutual understanding between rulers and ruled.* Mountbatten reinforced this by pressing Cédile to start negotiations between French and Vietnamese.[69] Cédile answered that he had been attempting to do just that for the past three days.†

When Gracey returned to Saigon, he contacted the Committee of the South and arranged a ceasefire. Within a matter of days it was broken by Vietnamese attacks on British and Indian troops. Mountbatten summoned a conference, this time in Rangoon, which was attended by Gracey and Cédile, and by Leclerc, in his capacity as Supreme Commander of the French forces in the Pacific. While the

---

* On 9 October the British Foreign Secretary, Ernest Bevin, signed an agreement with the French Ambassador to Great Britain, recognizing the French civil administration as the only authority responsible for civil affairs south of the 16th parallel.

† Decoux had attempted to sow mistrust of the British in Cédile's mind. Cédile visited him in the internment camp at Loc Ninh on 31 August, and Decoux hinted at what, in French eyes, might be termed a repetition of the 'Syria syndrome' by the British. 'You no doubt recall the events in Syria?' he asked him referring to the Free French and British invasion of Syria in 1941. 'There too, French units came into the country, arm-in-arm with the British. You know what happened next. The story can begin again.' The reference embarrassed Cédile, who replied that Syria was a different case, since there was no Franco–British competition in the Far East.[70] Devillers speaks of the 'absolute sincerity' of British officialdom in South-East Asia.[71]

conference was in progress, further news came in of attacks on Gracey's forces, and Mountbatten was compelled to order the 20th Division to secure the key points in Cochin-China, while continuing to negotiate. The Vietnamese leaders came to 20th Division headquarters to say they would not oppose British troops, but they *would* resist the French. Gracey refrained from using the French troops, but the Vietnamese did not keep to their assurances: guerrilla warfare began to develop throughout the whole of Southern Indo-China.

It was in this atmosphere that France's two highest officials in Asia came on the scene. Leclerc landed in Saigon on 5 October, and the High Commissioner, Thierry d'Argenlieu, arrived on 30 October. Leclerc had already been present with MacArthur at the Japanese surrender in Tokyo Bay, and at Itagaki's surrender to Mountbatten in Singapore on 18 September. The latter occasion had been memorable for him in more ways than one. Intensely susceptible as far as French military honour was concerned, his touchy temper had been sorely tried. He had not been informed of the Potsdam decision to divide Indo-China before he left Paris, and although his orders contained a reference to a 'high commissioner' he did not know that one had been designated, still less that it was Thierry d'Argenlieu, with whom he was not on the best of terms. Worse still, at the Singapore ceremony he had watched a parade of French sailors from the battleship *Richelieu* and had drily commented to his neighbour, 'Don't you think they're too fat?' Any Frenchman who had not fought alongside de Gaulle was anathema to Leclerc, and when the *Richelieu*'s commander sent a boat for him that evening, commanded merely by a leading seaman, and greeted him without any special honours on deck, Leclerc was furious. He summoned the ship's officers to the ward-room, made them stand to attention, and gave them a terrific dressing-down: 'The Navy has taken no part in the War! This behaviour must cease ... To start with, the *Richelieu* will now come under my command. I'll show you what stuff I'm made of, and how you make war!'[72]

Thierry d'Argenlieu was equally authoritarian and equally sensitive to slights on his authority, but devious in achieving his ends. A Carmelite monk, whose name in religion was Father Louis de la Trinité, he had been called up in 1939, was taken prisoner by the Germans and escaped by fishing-boat from Brittany to join de Gaulle in 1940. Tortuous and given to secret intrigues, he had served under Leclerc in Africa. Now the boot was on the other foot, and Leclerc did not relish the fact. Between the two of them, they had somehow or other to re-establish French sovereignty. Leclerc had remained in Kandy until sufficient French forces were available for him to act effectively in Saigon. With the arrival of elements of the 2nd Armoured Division, and the presence in Saigon River of the chastened *Richelieu*, Leclerc began to take over from Gracey the responsibility for government and for disarming the Japanese. The 20th Indian Division packed its bags in January 1946, and on 1 March, with the approval of the combined chiefs of staff, Indo-China was withdrawn from South-East Asia Command.

v *Return to Hanoi*

In the Red River Delta, and in Hanoi, things were very different. No one, it became clear, ally or enemy, intended to allow the French to return to Tonkin. Jean Sainteny was only allowed to fly into Hanoi in the company of the OSS Major Patti. Pierre Messmer (later Prime Minister of France) was appointed Commissioner of the French Republic and parachuted into Tonkin, where he was captured by the Vietnamese. One of his officers was poisoned.* When Sainteny managed to reach the palace of the Government-General in Hanoi, he became a virtual prisoner, guarded by Japanese sentries, his only contact with the outside world being a radio link with Kunming. He was forced to watch helplessly from the windows when the crowds swarmed past on 2 September joyfully shouting *Doc Lap! Doc Lap!* (Independence! Independence!)

There were worse humiliations to come. In mid-September the Chinese arrived. Their army descended on Tonkin like a plague of locusts. They looted whatever could be moved, and bought up immovable property by manipulating the rate of exchange of the Chinese dollar against the piastre. They lost no opportunity of humiliating the French in the eyes of the local inhabitants: when Sainteny flew back to Hanoi from a trip to Kunming, his bag was flung open on the tarmac of the airfield and its contents strewn on the ground by a Chinese customs official. French troops imprisoned

* Messmer finally reached Hanoi, but was not well enough to act as Commissioner, and handed over his functions to Sainteny. He returned to France soon after.

in the Hanoi Citadel since 9 March were subjected to a search by Chinese soldiers under the watchful eye of a Japanese major. To add insult to injury, the French even had to pay the costs of the Chinese occupation forces, since in theory they were there on behalf of French interests, as the result of an Allied decision. The French flag was forbidden to be flown on buildings and vehicles, and when Sainteny chose to disregard this, a mob tore the pennant off his car in the streets of Hanoi. The Chinese, not the French, took the surrender of the Japanese forces.

Small wonder that Leclerc was impatient to move north of the 16th parallel. But he was shrewd enough to realize that if he entered Tonkin as a combatant, in opposition not merely to General Lu Han and his Chinese but also to the forces of the Vietnamese Republic, he might be militarily successful in taking Hanoi and Haiphong, but he would drive the Vietnamese into permanent opposition in the villages of the Delta and the mountains to the north. A guerrilla war would start in which he would never be victorious, with the twenty thousand men at his disposal. Long and patient negotiations by Sainteny obtained an agreement on 28 February 1946 that the Chinese would withdraw; another agreement with Ho Chi Minh permitted the French to land in Tonkin on 6 March.* Exactly a year after the Japanese *coup de force*, Leclerc began unloading his armour into the port of Haiphong under the thoughtful eyes of Vo Nguyen Giap – who had greeted him earlier as 'Great Frenchman of the Resistance', comparing him, imperturbably, with himself as 'the first resister of Vietnam'. After renewed opposition from the Chinese, Leclerc was in Hanoi nine days later, to the delirious welcome of the thirty thousand French inhabitants, who believed, wrongly, that their long calvary was coming to an end.

Later in the year Ho Chi Minh was to fly to France to ratify new agreements signed with Sainteny. In the changed political atmosphere of 1946, when a third of France's electors were Socialist and another third Communist, he certainly thought that a left-wing Socialist coalition would take power in France and grant him what he wanted. But he reckoned without the French administration on the spot. Even if the Communists had come to power in France, the administration in Indo-China was still staffed by the body of officials who had served Decoux under Vichy. Eighty per cent of Decoux's civil

* Largely with the help of the British secret agent, Colonel Trevor Wilson, who acted as British Consul-General in Hanoi during this period.[73]

servants still remained. Under their influence, Thierry d'Argenlieu was devising the separation of Cochin-China from the rest of Vietnam. By one of the crassest pieces of post-war diplomacy, he took advantage of Ho's absence at the Fontainebleau Conference to declare Cochin-China a 'free republic', in flat contradiction to the 6 March agreement, which stated that 'As far as the reunion of the three *Kys* (countries) is concerned, the French Government binds itself to ratify the decision taken by the populations consulted by referendum.' No such referendum had taken place.

Ho received this news in the aircraft which was taking him to France. His position as negotiator was ruined. 'Don't let me go back empty-handed,' he begged Sainteny, who knew as well as he did that the failure of the negotiations would be the signal for extremists on both sides. Ho himself was termed '*Viet Gian*' (traitor to Vietnam) by Vietnamese workers in Toulon when the news came through. In despair, he told Sainteny and Salan who had come to Hanoi as Leclerc's representative, 'If you make us fight, we will fight. You will kill ten of our men for every one of your own, but in the end it will be you who will give in.'[74]

The breach was consummated by a quarrel over customs dues in the port of Haiphong. The French seized a Chinese ship loaded with contraband. The Vietnamese militia intervened, and shots were exchanged. The French riposted by shelling Haiphong and then occupying it by force. It was an almost deserted city, with six thousand of its inhabitants dead. At the end of 1946 open warfare broke out in the streets of Hanoi, and Sainteny was severely wounded when his car was blown up by a mine. The war between French and Vietnamese, 'the filthy war', as the French called it, was not to end until Giap destroyed the French Army at Dien Bien Phu and brought the French Empire in Indo-China to a close.

CHAPTER FIVE

SUBHAS CHANDRA BOSE
AND THE
INDIAN NATIONAL ARMY

i *Foundation of the Indian National Army*

By and large, British opinion is still uninformed about the activities of the Indian National Army and its leader, Subhas Chandra Bose, though there are signs that more information is becoming available and that historians are beginning to use that information to reassess the political evolution of South-East Asia under Japanese occupation.* Militarily, the Indian National Army was a fiasco. Politically, it became a factor of great importance in India in the days following the Japanese surrender. Some Indians claim it was decisive in influencing the British to concede independence.

Though there were less than a thousand Indians in Japan before the Second World War, some of them were highly incendiary persons. Japan had always been a haven for political refugees from the Asian mainland, and although she had to tread carefully, because of her relations with colonial powers, some of the exiles managed to make

---

* An excellent biography of Bose by Hugh Toye, *The Springing Tiger* (Cassell), was published as long ago as 1957; and a recent study of the war as a whole, by Guy Wint and Peter Calvocoressi, *Total War: Causes and Courses of the Second World War* (Allen Lane, 1972), made the unusual decision to devote an entire chapter to Bose. Otherwise most of the material is either unsubtly hostile, like Sir Francis Tuker's memoirs, *While Memory Serves*; or printed abroad and hence difficult to obtain: K. K. Ghosh, *The Indian National Army*, Meenakshi Prakashan, Meerut, 1969; Joyce C. Lebra, *Jungle Alliance*, Donald Moore, Singapore, 1971; Hayashida Tatsuo, *Higeki no eiyū* (Tragic Hero), Shinjusha, Tokyo, 1968. There is now a flourishing study centre and archive on Bose, headed by his nephew, Dr Sisir K. Bose, in Calcutta. The centre held a symposium on Bose in 1973, and the proceedings, which shed light on a great variety of aspects of Bose's life, should be available in the near future.

contact with important elements in the Japanese political structure. One of them was Rash Behari Bose, a Bengali who had been involved in an attempt to assassinate the Viceroy of India, Lord Hardinge, in 1912. During the First World War, Rash Behari Bose had connived with the German Consul-General in Shanghai to send arms and ammunition to Indian revolutionaries. Exiled in Japan, he became friendly with Toyama Mitsuru, the head of the Amur River Society, who arranged for him to marry a Japanese and settle in Japan, to protect him from the British police. During the twenties and thirties, Rash Behari Bose came out of hiding and began to spread anti-British propaganda from Japan, organizing the Japan branch of the Indian Independence League in 1937. When war seemed imminent in South-East Asia, he realized that it was possible to work for Indian independence by collaborating with Japan and asked the general staff headquarters for their help.

The Chief of the General Staff, General Sugiyama, decided to investigate the possibilities of using the Indian communities in South-East Asia in Japan's military plans, and sent a mission to Bangkok to see what could be done. The selection of Siam was not fortuitous. Not only was it a focal point in the planned strategy against Malaya and Burma, it also had a large Indian community, fifty-five thousand strong, some of whose members, Sikhs mostly, had been involved with the Ghadr party, an anti-British organization which had tried to foment disturbances in India with the help of German arms during the First World War. A Sikh missionary, Giani Pritam Singh, organized a secret movement in Bangkok called the Independent League of India*.

In December 1940 three Indian revolutionaries escaped from prison in Hong-Kong and made their way to Canton, then occupied by the Japanese. They asked the Japanese for political asylum and it was arranged that they should be smuggled into Siam, where they were sheltered by the military attaché, Colonel Tamura, and then handed over to Pritam Singh. In this way, Pritam Singh first came into contact with the Japanese Army authorities.

The contact was used the following year by the mission from Tokyo. This was a small six-man affair but one of the men was of crucial significance for the future of the Indian independence movement. His name was Fujiwara Iwaichi, and he was a major attached

* This movement, a forerunner of the Indian Independence League, constituted a link with previous Indian revolutionary movements.

133

to the 8th Section (propaganda), Second Bureau, of Imperial General Headquarters. Under the civilian alias of Yamashita Hirokazu, Fujiwara stayed at the Thailand Hotel in Bangkok for a short while in October 1941. It was he who had organized the flight of the three Indian refugees from Hong-Kong, and he had been briefly in the Siamese capital in March of that year. He was in charge of the mission, and his job, as specified by Sugiyama in Tokyo on 18 September, was to help the Japanese military attaché in Bangkok develop contacts in Malaya, to work with anti-British movements among the Indians, and also with Malays and Chinese. If war broke out he was to ensure cooperation between the Japanese Army and the peoples of Malaya. He was given five officers and a Hindi-speaking interpreter.

Fujiwara was put in touch with Pritam Singh by Colonel Tamura. They met first in Tamura's quarters and then in the house of an Indian cloth merchant situated over a Japanese pickle factory in a back alley in the city. Pritam Singh told him he had already begun to distribute anti-British propaganda among the Indian troops in Malaya.* He assured Fujiwara that many Indian troops were disaffected and harboured anti-British feelings. This was particularly true of the nationalistic Indian officers. Later, even those who remained loyal to Britain while captives in Japanese hands remembered with bitterness that they had been insulted by the British. They had been forbidden to enter many of the clubs in Malaya. There was even an order issued by the railway authorities that Europeans and Asiatics could not travel together in the same compartment, even though both might hold the same rank and belong to the same unit.[1]

The Japanese played on this resentment and disaffection when they invaded Malaya. Fujiwara was attached to the 25th Army for the campaign and his organization, F Kikan (F Organization), was to act as liaison between the Japanese troops and Indian prisoners-of-war. It was not long before he made a crucial encounter. A unit of Punjabis stationed at Asun near the Siamese border was scattered by the tanks of the Japanese 5th Division as it thrust south from Singora

---

* 'We advise you to follow the Programme of the Indian National Congress,' he had written in a letter dated 8 September 1941, 'under the direct leadership of our great saint Mahatma Gandhi and the programme instructed by our Indian patriots abroad. The programme for you is that you should never obey the orders of your English commanders... and you should never fight Japan, Germany, or any country which is the enemy of the British, because all such countries are our indirect friends... If England loses this war there would be an ample chance for India's freedom.'[2]

on 11 December 1941. The battalion commander, Lieutenant-Colonel Fitzpatrick, with one of his captains, Mohan Singh, retreated south through the driving tropical rain. They took shelter in the village of Kuala Nerang, exhausted and starving, after four nights without sleep. Mohan Singh reconnoitred the village, and learned that the Japanese had already gone far south on the road to Singapore. The Punjabis' retreat was cut, and there seemed no alternative but surrender.

Through the rain they saw two figures approaching, one in Japanese uniform, the other a Sikh. It was Fujiwara and Pritam Singh. The previous day, Pritam Singh had raised the Indian nationalist flag in the Siamese village of Ha'adyai close to the border with Malaya where, as the Japanese official history puts it, 'the first blow for the freedom of the Indian motherland was struck'.[3] He had heard that remnants of the 1/14th Punjab were in the jungle east of Alor Star, in no mood to continue the fight, and he passed the news on to Fujiwara, who promptly made his way to Kuala Nerang. 'You have done everything a soldier's honour requires,' Fujiwara told Fitzpatrick. 'Your men are finished and can never join up with their main party. Your responsibility as a British officer is not to sacrifice them uselessly but to surrender.' The colonel was weak from his wounds, and had expected rough treatment rather than this appeal to his soldierly honour. He accepted Fujiwara's advice.

That surrender set the pattern for F Kikan's intervention in the rest of the Malaya campaign. At every battle, Fujiwara sent his infiltrators through the lines, sapping the will to fight of the half-trained and bewildered Indian troops. The Japanese became used to the sight of Pritam Singh's bearded Indians in jodhpurs riding unarmed round the battlefield, shepherding prisoners back to the local headquarters of the Indian Independence League. Fujiwara was present at the surrender of the British forces in Singapore, and afterwards spoke to a vast assembly of Indian prisoners who had been gathered in Farrer Park. His voice was crisp, eager, determined, with a fanatical edge, the voice of a man utterly convinced of his cause.

Japan is fighting for the liberation of the nations of Asia which have been for so long trodden under the cruel heels of British Imperialism. Japan is the liberator and the friend of Asiatics. Japan wishes to inaugurate a New Order in East Asia. This New Order will take the form of a Co-Prosperity Sphere of East Asia, which will consist of free and equal nations, cooperating with each other for the common good. The independence of India is essential for the independence of Asia and the peace of the world; and it is the duty of Indians to free themselves. Japan is willing to give all-out aid and assistance to Indians in East Asia to achieve their aspirations.[4]

Then Mohan Singh came to the microphone to proclaim that India stood on the threshold of freedom, and the Japanese would help them achieve it. With their help, he was going to form an *Azad Hind Fauj*, an 'Indian National Army'. It had not taken long to convert Mohan Singh to Japan's cause, and some of his fellow officers suspected he had been subverted long before the campaign began. The Indian prisoners were in a desperate situation. The Japanese had separated them from their British officers and put them into camps: they could stay there and rot or join Mohan Singh's force. The speeches had a mixed reception. Some of the Indians, angered or dismayed at being, as it seemed to them, abandoned by their British officers, yelled '*Inqilab zindabad!*' ('Long live the Revolution!'), but many were repelled by the idea of breaking their oath and also by the possibility of having to fight their brother Indians. But enough of them were recruited by Mohan Singh to form the nucleus of an army. Gradually, out of the 65,000 Indian prisoners-of-war in Singapore and Malaya, he enrolled 25,000, and offers from thousands of Indian civilians came in. By August 1942 he had obtained pledges to himself personally of 40,000 men. Some, obviously, hoped for freedom from the camps. Others had given in to the strong-arm persuasion of camp commandants eager to stand well with Mohan Singh. The military detention centre at Bidadari soon became a concentration camp of very unsavoury reputation, where every form of torture was inflicted on those suspected of harbouring pro-British sympathies.

By this time Fujiwara had gone, and his place had been taken by Iwakuro Hideo, a regimental commander in Malaya who had been involved in pre-war diplomatic negotiations with Washington as a Japanese Army spokesman. He was a more important figure than Fujiwara in the Japanese military hierarchy, and the *F Kikan* was expanded into a new organization called the *Hikari Kikan* (Lightning Organization). The conduct of civilian affairs was vested in the Indian Independence League, under Rash Behari Bose, who came from Tokyo. But neither Rash Behari Bose nor Mohan Singh were of sufficient standing to head the entire Indian national movement in South-East Asia. Friction grew between them, and between them and the Japanese, who seemed to think in terms of no more than one Indian National Army division. Japanese behaviour towards the civilian population of Malaya had made Mohan Singh suspect that India, if liberated from the British, would simply become another Manchuria. On 29 December 1942 Iwakuro had him arrested, and as a result the first Indian National Army came to an end.

ii Bose Enters the Scene

A new leader was available. The young politician who had broken with Gandhi's non-violence policy and had been President of Congress was in exile in Germany: Subhas Chandra Bose. After leaving Cambridge, Bose had become General Secretary of the Indian National Congress party in 1927, along with Jawaharlal Nehru. He later became President of the Bengal Provincial Congress Committee, and Mayor of Calcutta. Bose paid several visits to Europe, and was overwhelmed by the attention paid to him by Benito Mussolini, who talked to him knowledgeably of Indian problems, even though Bose was known as a left-wing radical. Bose's hostility to the Axis powers was much diminished by these visits, and after he escaped from British internment (for sedition) in 1941 he made his way back to Europe from India.

Bose never lacked the spirit of adventure. To get out of India he had to escape in disguise from Peshawar to Kabul. He kicked his heels in Kabul until March 1941, and, finally, under the auspices of the Italian Minister, Pietro Quaroni, crossed into the Uzbek Soviet Socialist Republic at Tarmiz, and arrived in Berlin, under the Italian alias of Mazzotta. In Germany, Bose spent some time under the aegis of the ambivalent Adam von Trott zu Solz, attempting to organize Indian prisoners-of-war taken in Africa into an Indian Legion to fight the British. He also came into contact with the Japanese military attaché in Berlin, Colonel Yamamoto. When it became clear that Hitler had no interest whatever in supporting Indian independence, Yamamoto arranged for Bose to return to Asia.*[5] He left Kiel by

* On Bose's two years in Germany cf. Toye, op. cit., and Christopher Sykes, *Troubled Loyalty* (on relations with Adam von Trott zu Solz), Collins, 1968; A. Werth, *Der Tiger Asiens, Subhas Chandra Bose. Ein Leben für die Freiheit des Subkontinents*, Bechtle Verlag, Munich, 1971; and an extract from Erich Wollenberg's 'Hitler, der deutsche Militarismus und der europäische Frieder' (on Mussolini's fascination for Bose) in *Die Zeit*, 19 May 1972.

U-boat in February 1943, and trans-shipped to a Japanese submarine in the Indian Ocean, four hundred miles off Madagascar, on 28 April. The submarine landed him in Sumatra, whence he flew to Tokyo.

Tōjō, the Japanese Premier, gave him at once what the European Axis powers had refused: an open declaration in the Diet that Japan would free India from the British. He added in private that Bose must realize that India would remain under Japanese control for some time after liberation. Bose did not care. He could deal with the Japanese when the time came. The British were the first enemy. Bose did what neither Rash Behari Bose nor Mohan Singh could do. He provided a leadership in one person of the military and civilian elements in the Free Indian movement. From Tokyo he went to Malaya, and in July 1943 was made President of the Indian Independence League, and in the following month commander-in-chief of a reorganized Indian National Army. To keep relations sweet, the Japanese replaced Iwakuro as head of the *Hikari Kikan* with Bose's friend from Berlin, Yamamoto. In a brief space of time, Bose, or *Netaji* (Leader) as his followers called him, was the chief non-Japanese political figure in occupied Asia. He was the only one who did not operate on his own national territory, but he insisted fiercely that the Indian National Army should be an independent force, and demanded that the Japanese recognize him as head of the Provisional Government of Free India (*Arzi Hukumat-e-Azad-Hind*) in October 1943. The Japanese convened a Greater East Asia Conference in Tokyo in November, and Bose brought off a great personal success.

Militarily, the story was less brilliant. The Japanese did not really relish creating a large, independent Indian Army. In their drive against British territory they wanted small units of interpreters, guides, agents, and saboteurs, and the Indian National Army (INA) carried out these roles with some success. A Japanese account of the battle of the 'Admin Box' in the Arakan in February 1944 describes how an INA major, Misra, subverted a unit of the Gwalior Lancers in the front line and helped the Japanese break through and surround the headquarters of a British division.[5] But in the main attack on Imphal, which was the central battle of 1944, the INA troops were ill-supplied with food and weapons, and, contrary to their expectations, they found that their brother sepoys in the British–Indian Army did not rush into their arms. They were regarded as renegades, and this, with the collapse of the Japanese supply system, sapped the

INA morale. They withdrew with the Japanese to the Irrawaddy, where desertions to the British began to multiply. When the British 14th Army broke through the Japanese defence line all along the Irrawaddy, the Indian National Army simply disintegrated as a coherent force.

Bose and his Provisional Government left Rangoon when the Japanese general headquarters in Burma retreated from it in April 1945, with the single difference that Bose himself, at one stage of the journey, refused motor transport and insisted on sharing the hardships of the march with his men. He had wanted to stay on in Rangoon to fight to the end, but was persuaded that it would be better to make for Bangkok and continue the struggle from there. His women's unit (The Rani of Jhansi Regiment) left in a convoy of lorries and cars on 24 April. Before he left Rangoon Bose seems to have been more concerned than the Burmese Premier, Ba Maw, about the fate of the Burmese capital. It would be open to looting and pillage, he knew, and he was responsible for the Indian civilians left behind. So he instructed Major-General Loganathan to remain in Rangoon in command of five thousand INA troops until the victorious British arrived to reinstall their administration.

During the retreat, Bose seemed to bear a charmed life. He sat calmly smoking as the British planes swooped down on his little group, and emerged unhurt when his car skidded into an eight-foot ditch on the road to Waw, on the west bank of the Sittang. There was no bridge at Waw, and the Japanese allotted one of their ferries to Bose's party. General Isoda, Yamamoto's successor as head of the *Hikari Kikan*, suggested to Bose that he cross first, but Bose insisted on letting the women's unit precede them. 'Go to hell!' he told Isoda. 'I will not cross over till all the girls have gone across first.'[6] They found a place where the river was only six foot deep, and the girls were ordered by their commander, Janaki Thevers, to swim across, which they did. After two more days on foot, Janaki Thevers asked Bose to remove his heavy boots and let her wash his socks. She was shocked to see that his feet were a mass of blisters, but he refused a car when the march resumed, took the head of the column and covered fifteen miles with them during the night. He must have been sorely tried, for he let slip his contempt for Ba Maw, who had left his own capital to the British – the same Ba Maw for whom he had expressed great admiration during the Greater East Asia Conference of 1943. Isoda came up from Moulmein with lorries for Bose and his staff and the Rani of Jhansi women: the men were to follow on foot. In a rage Bose turned on Isoda: 'Do you think I am Ba Maw of Burma that I will leave my men and run for safety? I have told you time and time again that I will not go unless my men have gone on ahead.'[7] The party at last reached the temporary safety of Moulmein on 1 May 1945, and then moved into Siam.

iii *The Death of Bose*

Bose continued to broadcast radio propaganda into India during the summer, and moved to Singapore to do so. But it was clear that Japan's hold on South-East Asia had a limited future, and his Chief of Staff, Bhonsle, urged him to move to the Supreme Headquarters of the Japanese Southern Army in Saigon, a less vulnerable spot than Singapore. But Bose had more ambitious ideas. He had already thought about leading an invasion of India from the north, and had sounded out the Japanese about the possibility of being smuggled into Uzbekistan. If they helped him, he could reach Soviet Russia through Manchuria. When he received official confirmation of the Japanese surrender on 16 August, Bose went at once to the Southern Army commander, Field-Marshal Terauchi, and asked for a plane to take him to Russia. Terauchi wired to Tokyo and the reply came back that Bose was not to go. But Terauchi was a proconsul in his own domain, and he saw no point in forbidding Bose to continue his struggle against the British. On his own responsibility, he told Bose he could take a plane which would fly him to Dairen, in Manchuria, via Taiwan. Once he was in Dairen, he could make his own arrangements with the Russians. They were now at war with Japan, so there was no question of the Japanese negotiating a passage through Russian territory.

At four o'clock in the afternoon of 17 August 1945 a Japanese medium bomber* took off from the airfield at Saigon. It had to run the entire length of the runway to take off, because it was overloaded, so at Tourane (Da Nang), the next landing field, all the ammunition and twelve machine guns were off-loaded. In this way the plane's weight was reduced by thirteen hundred pounds. Bose had hoped to

* 'Sally' type 97, Mk II; max. load 22,000 lb; max. range 1,960 miles; crew of seven. The narrative from this point is derived from Hayashida Tatsuo, *Higeki no eiyū*.

take with him a small entourage, but in the event only his aide, Colonel Habibur Rehman, was able to accompany him. The rest were to follow by other routes, for the plane carried Japanese passengers too: Lieutenant-General Shidei, the Chief of Staff of Burma Area Army, Lieutenant-Colonel Sakai, Lieutenant-Colonel Nononaki, Major Kōno, Major Takahashi, Captain Arai, plus the crew: the pilot, Major Takizawa, the co-pilot W. O. Aoyanagi, Sergeant-Major Okitani, and the wireless operator, Tominaga, a total of twelve. The normal complement was seven.

Bose and the rest of the party spent the night at Tourane and set out again at 5 a.m. on 18 August. Before the plane reached Taihoku (now Taipei), the capital of Taiwan, a wireless message came through: the Red Army had already occupied Ryōjun (Port Arthur) and it was feared it would soon be in Dairen (Dalny). It was vital that Bose should be able to land in Japanese-occupied territory in Manchuria, so it became necessary to reach Dairen as quickly as possible. The weather was fine, and the plane landed safely at Matsuyama airfield, where a tent had been erected for the benefit of the Imperial Princes who were to pass through Taihoku bearing the surrender order. The army authorities on Formosa (Taiwan) were in a state of deep despair at the news of the surrender. Many officers were counselling a war of resistance to the end, others were discussing whether to commit suicide. Normally, when a visiting dignitary stopped over at Taihoku, the Commander-in-Chief who was also the governor-general, or his chief of staff, would be at the airfield to welcome the visitor. When Bose arrived there was no one to greet him, and he was met with an air of cold indifference on the part of the officials. While Bose and the Japanese rested in the tent, taking a light meal of sandwiches and bananas, maintenance was carried out on the engine, and its fuel was replenished. Major Kōno reported that the starboard engine had been behaving oddly, and Major Takizawa carried out an engine test twice, to ensure that nothing was wrong. The passengers then took their seats again, en route for Dairen.

The plane began to move along the runway, which was 950 yards long. Normally, when a heavy bomber takes off, the tail is off the ground halfway along the runway, but this time the plane had gone three quarters of its run before the tail lifted. When it finally rose into the air, there was a terrific explosion, the plane swerved to port, and a propeller and engine blew off. The plane hit the ground about twenty yards from the edge of the airfield and burst into flames. Shidei and the pilot were killed instantly.

Nononaki was in the gunner's seat, and was thrown to the ground, almost unhurt; he managed to escape behind a stone wall. Sakai, Takahashi, and Arai were knocked unconscious by the impact, but came to very soon and sprinted out of the plane. Kōno was almost in the middle of the plane, and when the crash came a fuel tank landed between him and Bose. He could not see Bose, but saw Shidei, dead in front of him with a fractured skull, Takizawa, whose face had been pierced by the joystick, and Aoyanagi, who was bleeding from a chest injury. Kōno broke through the windscreen and jumped out. He was splashed with petrol, and he felt that his hands, legs, and forehead were burned. He rolled on the ground to put the flames out.

'I heard Nononaki's voice calling me,' he remembered later. 'Then suddenly a big man, stark naked, burst from the flames. He was completely naked except for a pair of boots, and bleeding. He seemed to stand in front of the blazing plane, like the Niō.'* It was the last time Nononaki saw Bose. By the time he reached hospital, he was blind.

Habibur Rehman's account of what happened is somewhat different. When the plane crashed, he bellowed to Bose, 'Get out from the front. There is no exit from the back.' Bose turned towards the front which was all split open, and already ablaze, and ran into the midst of the flames. Rehman ran after him and made him take off his burning clothes, all except the trousers. He then made Bose lie down, noticing a deep gash about four inches long on the left side of his head, from which blood was welling out. His forehead was scorched, and his hair shrivelled. Rehman's hands were covered in blisters, so that he could do little to staunch Bose's bleeding, and when Rehman looked down at his own legs, he saw his right thigh was badly cut. Bose said to him, in Hindustani, 'Has my skin gone?' Rehman tried to encourage him, but Bose said, 'I'm done for, I think.' 'God will have mercy on us,' Rehman answered. 'You'll be all right.'

'I don't think so,' Bose said. 'When you go back to your country, say this to our people. Tell them I went on fighting to the end. Tell

* The Niō are common symbols in Japanese art. They are huge figures of gods, half naked, who usually stand as temple guardians on either side of temple doors or altars.

them to go on fighting...I believe India will soon be free. Nobody can hold India captive now...'

Then help came, and Bose was moved to the Nanmon Branch army hospital in Taihoku. He asked for the others to be treated first, but Captain Yoshimi, the medical officer, dealt with Bose first when he saw how hideous his burns were. Yoshimi knew Bose would not last until morning, but to ease his pain had him coated with zinc ointment and wrapped in bandages, and administered several injections to stimulate heart action. He was given a transfusion of blood donated by the Japanese soldiers in the hospital. A civilian, Nakamura Hisaichi, who had interpreted for Bose twice in the past when he had stopped at Taihoku, was summoned to the hospital.

Bose spoke about four times after he was told an interpreter had arrived. Yoshimi told Nakamura to note Bose's last will and testament, but Bose didn't take this in and Nakamura asked if there was anything in particular he required. Bose answered that he wanted his followers to be greeted on his behalf when they reached Taiwan. He asked how General Shidei was, and then complained of blood going to his head, and asked for it to be treated. Then he said he wanted to sleep. His English was precise, but mixed with Hindustani. All this time, Bose was suffering intense pain, but never mentioned it. His endurance and cold calm deeply impressed the Japanese who were standing round him, the more so since there was a Japanese officer in another corner of the small ward, in unbearable pain, screaming that death was preferable to his agony. About eight in the evening Bose died. He was forty-eight.

Captain Yoshimi made out the death certificate, writing 'Chandra Bose' (this was how the Japanese always referred to him) in Japanese *katakana* syllabary and naming third-degree burns as the cause of death. Present at Bose's death bed were Captain Yoshimi and another doctor, Tsurumi, Bose's aide Habibur Rehman, Nakamura, two nurses, a medical orderly and a military policeman (*Kempei*), eight people in all. Habibur Rehman fell on his knees beside his leader's bed, and prayed for five minutes. Then he walked slowly over to his own bed and lay down. The Japanese were weeping.

The death was reported at once to the Taiwan Army general headquarters and a staff officer, Major Nagatomo, was despatched to the hospital. He offered up a prayer over the body, and posted sentries to guard it. An order came next day (19 August) from Imperial General Headquarters in Tokyo to send Bose's body by plane to the

Japanese capital. Then the order was countermanded: the body was to be cremated in Taihoku (the coffin was too big for a small aircraft, and in the intense August heat it was necessary to act quickly). This was duly done on 20 August, in the presence of Rehman, Nagatomo, and the interpreter Nakamura. Some of Bose's bones were taken to the Nishi Honganji Temple, where prayers were said for him. Others were placed in a small box, which was wrapped in white cloth, taken by Rehman, and later brought by Hayashida Tatsuo, a 2nd lieutenant in the Japanese Army, to the Renkōji Temple, in Suginami Ward, Tokyo, where they remain to this day.

It is hardly necessary to say that thousands of his supporters refused to believe Bose was dead. His brother, Suresh Chandra Bose, and many more, were convinced the crash had been staged, and that Bose was alive in the Soviet Union. The legend was so persistent that the Indian Government sent an enquiry mission to Japan in 1956 to ascertain the facts. The mission included one of Bose's divisional commanders, Shah Nawaz Khan, and his brother Suresh, who stuck to his disbelief even though the other members were convinced by the evidence of the sixty-seven witnesses they called.* They also expressed indignation at the lack of a cordial reception for Bose at the airfield. It was noted that the Japanese Army did not carry out an enquiry into the cause of the accident, so there was no evidence on the condition of the aircraft or its maintenance record. There were certainly more people on board than there should have been, and their extra luggage made the plane overweight. There were other contributory factors: Matsuyama airfield is narrow, a tall chimney belonging to a nearby brick works soars into the sky close by, and this makes take-off difficult. Because the journey from Tourane had been uneventful, the misbehaviour of the starboard engine was not as thoroughly checked as it might have been. This was also, in part, because Bose was eager to press on to Dairen before the Russians took the city. The pilot did not know Matsuyama well,

---

* At the time of the crash the British too had their suspicions that it had been fixed, and that Bose was alive. 'I wonder,' wrote Wavell, Viceroy of India in 1945, 'if the Japanese announcement of Subhas Chandra Bose's death in an air-crash is true, I suspect it very much, it is just what would be given out if he meant to go underground. My first reaction when I heard it was to tell PSV (*Private Secretary to the Viceroy*) to ask SEAC (*South-East Asia Command*) to make most careful enquiries into the story as soon as they could. If it is true, it will be a great relief. His disposal would have presented a most difficult problem.'[8]

and as the plane ran a longer distance than normal before take-off it had to climb sharply; as a result there was excess pressure on the engines and propellers.

iv *The Delhi Trials*

With its leader dead, its army scattered, and its chief ally in the ruins of her own defeat, it looked as if the cause of Indian liberation by military means was at an end. Then, very oddly, in the depths of its defeat, the Indian National Army began to be effective. The Government of India decided to put on trial leading INA officers, and those who had ill-treated their fellow prisoners to compel them to join. But by the time these men had been brought back to India to face trial, the Indian people, impatiently waiting for the British to leave, had begun to sympathize with the INA, and the Congress Party saw that the trials could become a weapon against British rule. The inept choice of venue for the trials helped: they were to be held in the Red Fort at Delhi, the symbol of Mogul glory, and the very spot where, Bose had proclaimed, his triumphant army would parade in a free India.[9]

The first three officers to stand trial were Shah Nawaz Khan, commander of the second INA division, P. K. Sahgal, commander of the 5th Guerrilla Regiment, and G. S. Dhillon: with comprehensive symbolism, a Muslim, a Hindu, and a Sikh. The charges were waging war against the King-Emperor and abetting murder (specifically, permitting an execution ordered by higher authority). Congress opened a fund for their defence, and India's greatest forensic talent was hired on their behalf, including Bhulabhai Desai, Congress leader in the Central Legislative Assembly, with Nehru himself donning the legal robes he had not worn for thirty years. Nehru was acting as a politician, not as a lawyer: he knew perfectly well that cruelties had been perpetrated against those Indians in Malaya who had refused to join the INA, but he maintained that the motives of Bose's men were his own. Feeling against the accused ran high among British officers of the Indian Army, who felt that a sacrosanct principle of loyalty would be sabotaged if the INA were to be allowed to go scot-free. When he was interrogated at British headquarters in Pegu, after surrendering, Shah Nawaz was told by an infuriated British officer, 'I hope they shoot you!'[10] Major-General F. S. Tuker,

GOC Eastern Command, who seems to have developed a hatred for Hindus and a corresponding affection for Muslims, described Bose as a 'plump Bengali Brahmin of over-weening personal ambition' and demanded condign punishment for the INA.[11] A more moderate view was put by the Viceroy, Field-Marshal Lord Wavell, to the Associated Chambers of Commerce on 10 December 1945, just over a week before the trials came to an end.

> Whatever your political views, if you cannot acclaim the man who prefers his honour to his ease, who remains steadfast in adversity to his pledged faith, then you have a poor notion of the character which is required to build up a nation. I say to you that amongst all the exploits of the last five or six years for which the world rightly extols the Indian soldier, the endurance of those men in captivity and hardship stands as high as any. As a proof of what they endured as the price of their loyalty to their ideals of a soldier's duty, I will tell you this: the 45,000 Indian prisoners-of-war who stood firm are estimated to have lost about 11,000 or one quarter of their numbers, from disease, starvation and murder; the twenty thousand who went over to our enemy's side lost only 1,500.[12]

Wavell was speaking with the future of India in mind; but India was in no mood to hear words derived from the Imperial past. Demonstrations were staged all over India on behalf of the INA and under the pressure of public opinion a compromise was reached whereby the accused were found guilty, but had their sentence of transportation for life suspended. They were cashiered, because the Commander-in-Chief, Field-Marshal Sir Claude Auchinleck, whose duty it was to confirm the sentences, emphasized that it was 'in all circumstances a most serious crime for an officer or soldier to throw off his allegiance and wage war against the State'.[13] Auchinleck was more far seeing than the British officers who felt he had condoned a betrayal. He sensed better than they did the mood of the Indian officers and viceroy's commissioned officers who were the backbone of the army. If that army was to be maintained in its integrity after the British left, the feelings of nationalism which he deemed natural to any Indian should not be pointlessly wounded. British officers in the past had, he felt, been summarily and contemptuously dismissive of the ideal of 'Indianization'. To formation commanders who had criticized his policy of leniency as destructive of morale he wrote a very interesting and perceptive letter.

The loyalty of the Indian Army, he told them, went most naturally to a regiment and its officers rather than to the Government and the King-Emperor. They had a trust in their officers which was child-like, and the fall of Hong-Kong, Singapore, and Rangoon must have seemed like the end of their world.

It is quite wrong (*he continued*) to adopt the attitude that because these men had taken service in a British controlled Indian army, there-fore their loyalties must be the same as those of British soldiers ... they had no real loyalty or patriotism towards Britain as Britain, not as we understand loyalty ... There is little doubt that 'Indianization' was at its inception looked on as a political expedient which was bound to fail militarily. There is no doubt also that many senior British officers believed and even hoped that it would fail ... The policy of segregation of Indian officers into separate units, the dif-ferential treatment in respect of pay and terms of service as compared with the British officer, and the prejudice and lack of manners of some – by no means all – British officers and their wives, all went to produce a very deep and bitter feeling of racial discrimination in the mind of the Indian officers, who were naturally Nationalists, keen to see India standing on her own legs and not to be ruled from Whitehall for ever. It is no use shutting one's eyes to the fact that any Indian officer worth his salt is a Nationalist, though this does not mean that he is necessarily anti-British. If he is anti-British this is as often as not due to his faulty handling and treatment by his British officer comrades.[14]

These were harsh words to address to men who had led one of the finest armies in India's history to victory over Germans, Italians, and Japanese, and who had established deep bonds of leadership and affection with their men. They found Auchinleck's views hard to take. From almost anyone else they would have been insufferable. But they were written by a man who was perhaps more deeply in-volved with the Indian Army than any of them in terms of service, love, and devotion, and who, in the same letter, had not hesitated to criticize those Indian officers he was defending for being in many instances 'false to their trust', in using their influence to suborn their own men under Japanese encouragement.*

* No one was more aware of the political issues of the INA trials than Auchinleck, but he never ceased to point out the dangers to a future India of espousing the cause of the INA. 'Failure to his allegiance,' he wrote to Wavell on 22 January 1946, 'is a crime which cannot be condoned in a soldier, in any

One of the most learned of Indian historians has written that 'but for the INA Britain would not have granted independence to India in 1947'.[15] I do not think this is true, and I do not think the Congress Party thought it was true at the time. But the INA trials were a very useful means of rousing nationalist feeling, and in this way they no doubt helped along the British departure. The Congress Party deliberately adopted the INA cause in spite of its ambiguous past: its aim of liberating India by military force was not easy to reconcile with a policy of non-violence, and its alliance with a fascist power had – initially – alienated Nehru's sympathies.

The major Congress figures, by this time, did not really doubt that Britain was determined to quit India. Sardar Patel was convinced the British had become reconciled to the inevitable: 'It was no use flogging a dead horse,' he thought, 'and, instead of fighting the British, the time had come to help them roll up their bedding and depart.'[17] A Labour Government was in power in Britain, and it was committed to bringing the British Raj to an end. But it was possible to be doubtful about its timing. The INA trials could therefore be used to focus irritation, to speed up withdrawal, and, in doing so, to emphasize the non-communal and secular basis of the INA, which it shared with Congress. In the terms of a communiqué issued by the headquarters of the Indian Independence League in 1943, the Indian National Army was organized along national lines, and 'All distinctions of class, caste, creed, and religion have been abolished'. The INA turned out to have a propaganda value for a free India far greater than its military value had ever been, or was ever likely to be. Though the espousal of its cause by those who were to control the future armed forces of a free India had obvious dangers, as Wavell foresaw, and as Nehru tacitly admitted. In 1948 Nehru promised pensions to members of the INA when they fell due, but added, 'They would not be reinstated in the Army since there had been a long break in their service, and since, moreover, it would psychologically affect the present Army at a time when the latter has been exposed to considerable strain.'[18]

Mohan Singh was not brought to trial, but he was present in the

circumstances by any Government.' (Connell, *Auchinleck*, p. 812.) In his memorandum for Indian Army commanding officers in February 1946 he repeated this: 'It was essential to establish the principle that falseness to his allegiance is a crime which cannot be countenanced in any officer under whatever Government he may be serving.'[16]

Red Fort as a witness. And he had a most moving encounter there, for Japanese witnesses were summoned too. Tōjō, Sugiyama, Shigemitsu, the Navy Minister Shimada, Field-Marshal Terauchi and the former Commander-in-Chief of Burma Area Army, General Kawabe, were all named, but they were already held in Tokyo as suspects by the International Military Tribunal for the Far East. Others were available, lower down in the hierarchy. One of these was Fujiwara, who was in hospital with malaria, in Fukuoka, when news of the surrender came. He was pretty sure both British and Dutch authorities would pursue him for the part he had played in the subversion of their overseas empires; and he was determined not to be taken. He kept potassium cyanide by him, just in case. But when the summons came, it was not the one he expected. In the company of Ambassador Sawada and the former Vice-Minister for Foreign Affairs, Mr Matsumoto, he was to attend the INA trials in Delhi. On the army side, besides himself, the witnesses included the senior staff officer of Burma Area Army, Major-General Katakura. They were lodged in a barbed-wire enclosure inside the Red Fort, where they met other Japanese officers, including the last head of the *Hikari Kikan*, General Isoda. Fujiwara was delighted to meet once again his old INA companions, who greeted him with cries of '*Jai Hind!*'* When he expressed fears about the outcome of the trial, Dhillon told him not to worry: 'India will gain independence within a year. If they punish any one of us, no Englishman will leave India alive.'[19]

Perhaps the most dramatic encounter was that with Mohan Singh. He had heard from a British major that Mohan Singh was to be sent from Singapore, and one day in December 1945 he heard his name called, across a barbed wire fence. Had the barbed wire not been there Fujiwara would have embraced him, he was so delighted. It was nearly four years since their momentous first meeting in the jungles of Malaya. Both had seen the rise of their hopes, and then their shattering fall. The military campaign had ended in disaster at Imphal; but the political war against England was turning into a splendid victory. Mohan Singh had no bitterness over his arrest by the Japanese Army. When Fujiwara said he thought the British were likely to accuse him (Fujiwara) of war crimes, Mohan Singh hotly denied that they could prosecute him, and said that whatever happened the Indians he had helped would do their utmost for him.

The Japanese witnesses appeared at the trial on 10 November.

* 'Victory to India!'

They had been somewhat perplexed what the tenor of their evidence should be. The prosecution was following two lines: the charge of treason and acting under enemy command, and the charges of abetment to murder, which were not in themselves related to the question of allegiance. The prosecution also maintained that, in spite of the INA's claim to be an independent body, acting under the Government of Free India, its war operations were in fact carried out under Japanese command. It hardly needs to be emphasized that the Japanese did not wish to prejudice the defendants' case in any way, since this would be helping their enemies against their friends. They therefore laid stress upon Bose's complete independence of character. It was pointed that a minister was attached by the Japanese to the Provisional Government of Free India, on Bose's insistence. This was Mr Hachiya Teruo, who gave evidence. Despite his lack of regular diplomatic credentials, the very fact that Hachiya dealt with diplomatic affairs in relation to Bose was enough to prove, in international law, that diplomatic relations existed between Japan and Free India as between two independent states, not as between empire and satellite. This was argued by Mr Sawada Renzō, Vice-Minister for Foreign Affairs and formerly Minister to Burma. In this way the Japanese helped to destroy the prosecution case that the Provisional Government was merely a puppet, or a legal fiction.

From the military standpoint, Katakura emphasized that Bose's objective was not cooperation with the Japanese, but the independence of India. Cooperation was merely a means. The independence of India, on the other hand, was not part of Japan's war plans, though it was part of the general liberation of Greater East Asia. The Imphal campaign illustrated the difference in aims between Free India and Japan. For the Japanese, the campaign was in defence of Burma. For the INA, it was part of the struggle for Indian independence.

Furthermore the authority of Bose over the INA officers was absolute, and the INA had an independent policy and military law. From all these points of view, the Indian National Army was an organization more independent of the Japanese than the armies of Manchuria, Burma, and Wang Ching-wei's China. This evidence, cumulatively, tended to show the juridical independence of the *Arzi Hukumat-e-Azad-Hind* and its army, and so reduced the weight which the prosecution could attach to its treason charges.

v *The Fate of Fujiwara**

On 14 January 1946 Fujiwara left Delhi for Singapore. He was now convinced that his own trial for war crimes was near, though in his view he had committed none. But he did not realize that an encounter was awaiting him that would be perhaps even more memorable than that with Mohan Singh. The reason the British wanted him in Singapore was indeed connected with war crimes. A massacre of overseas Chinese had taken place in Singapore when it had been under the control of General Yamashita's 25th Army. None of that army staff was now available in South-East Asia. Yamashita himself was on trial in the Philippines, and Tsuji Masanobu, who had done the planning for the capture of Singapore, was reputed to be in hiding in Siam. Fujiwara was the other name on the British list. They did not seem to realize, he wrote later, that he had been on Terauchi's Southern Army staff, not Yamashita's, and had merely been attached to 25th Army for the Malaya operations. Such chain-of-command niceties were not, in fact, foremost in the mind of the British authorities, who put him in Changi gaol in Singapore.

He was constantly interrogated on the background of the Japanese intelligence organizations in Malaya until he received, one day, a summons of a different kind. Dressed just as he was in shirt and shorts, he was told to present himself at the front gate of the prison, where two plain-clothes detectives were waiting for him. Without a word, they clipped handcuffs on his wrists, pushed him into a car, and drove off into Singapore City. Fujiwara was full of foreboding. Had the British decided to dispose of him without going into the lengthy business of a trial? What exactly was he supposed to be guilty of?

The car drove at full speed through the streets making for the city centre. 'Where are you taking me?' he asked the detectives, but they did not answer. Finally the car pulled up before the entrance to an old building facing the harbour. As Fujiwara climbed out he saw it was the police headquarters. The detectives took him inside, and pushed him into a room on the first floor, after roughly unlocking his handcuffs. He was still not fully recovered from malaria, had

* Unless otherwise indicated, the descriptions and quotations in this section are based on the author's personal recollections and on Fujiwara's account, *F Kikan* ('F Organization'), Hara Shobō, Tokyo, 1966.

had nothing to drink since early morning, and he was feeling pretty weak. There was an old battered sofa in the room, so he lay down and within seconds was fast asleep.

He was noisily awakened, told to get up, and taken to another room. It was a large room, with a U-shaped table in the middle, with ten men seated round it. They stared at him, and Fujiwara realized with a sinking heart that another formal interrogation was about to begin. Another attempt to shuffle on to him responsibility for a crime he had not committed, he thought. Then his eyes fell on the officer in the centre seat, a British colonel with clipped moustache, dressed in punctiliously correct uniform. The colonel gazed fixedly at Fujiwara, a cold smile on his lips. He addressed him in Japanese, couched in brusque, discourteous phrasing: *'Fujiwara! Ore wo oboete iru ka?'* ('Fujiwara! Do you remember me?').

At that instant Fujiwara recalled with a blinding clarity his first meeting with this colonel. It was at the Ford factory in Singapore, on 15 February 1942, nearly four years before. Fujiwara had accompanied General Yamashita and his interpreter, Colonel Sugita, to the parley with the British party, including Lieutenant-General Percival, which had come to negotiate the surrender of the city. It had been the culminating point of a breathlessly brilliant campaign for the Japanese, and a moment of unparalleled despair and desolation for the British. It was one of the most bitter defeats in the whole history of the British Army. The interpreter on the British side was a young staff major, Cyril Wild. The Japanese had photographed the group of four British officers as they approached the rendezvous, one carrying a white flag, another the Union Jack, with Percival slightly in front, walking with Brigadier Newbigging. Photographs of the party carrying their flags of defeat were printed in the Japanese press and flashed round the world. Japanese war artists drew the scene of the parley, and their drawings were reprinted in their tens of thousands for the little diaries Japanese troops carried with them all over East Asia.

It was a moment of great humiliation for Wild, and was to be followed by many others. As a Japanese-speaking officer, he went with the British prisoners-of-war who were sent from Singapore to build the Siam–Burma Railway in August 1942. He visited several camps along the track, and it seemed to him the Japanese deliberately placed the prisoners in situations which led to diseases of epidemic proportions. In addition to the casualties among the prisoners, he estimated that a hundred thousand Asian labourers died, and his testimony was crucial in the Tokyo trials. By a cruel trick of fate, Wild was killed in an air crash when returning from Tokyo after giving his testimony. It was he who had saved the British flag when the Japanese searched for it in 1942, and who kept it hidden until it could be flown again in Singapore in 1945. As a foretaste of revenge, Wild was present when Itagaki surrendered to Mountbatten in the Municipal Buildings on 12 September 1945, and he also interrogated Yamashita in Manila. In his assignment to track down Japanese war criminals, it must have been some satisfaction to him to confront Fujiwara and to emphasize, in the contrast between his power and Fujiwara's present dilapidation, that the wheel had come full circle.

Fujiwara certainly felt this as he faced Wild across the U-shaped table. The reason he had not recognized him at first was that in 1942 Wild had been clean-shaven. But Fujiwara remembered the fear Wild's name now evoked among the Japanese detainees in Changi gaol. 'Yes, I remember you,' he answered. With a brief nod, Wild indicated he was to sit down. Then began a detailed interrogation on F Kikan, and the point gradually emerged. There *was* a war crimes connection. Just after the fall of Singapore, F Kikan had been given the task of collecting materials on political crimes committed under the British régime. The investigation was carried out in this police station by one of Fujiwara's subordinates, Lieutenant Komemura, and two Singapore detectives were said to have died under interrogation. Fujiwara claimed to have no knowledge of such an incident and affirmed that he would have known of it, since the relations between F Kikan members were very close. It was more like a family than a military unit. He was told to give Komemura's duties, personal history, description and present whereabouts, and those of F Kikan men working under him. Fujiwara replied that F Kikan was dissolved in May 1942, and his contact with Lieutenant Komemura had then ceased. He had no idea where he was. He might have been killed in battle. In any case all F Kikan's movements were carried out under his, Fujiwara's, orders, and he alone was responsible. He also suspected that there had been a case of mistaken identity, since Wild referred to a woman typist and armed soldiers accompanying Komemura; whereas no women were employed by F Kikan, and its members went about unarmed.

Fujiwara felt that he was locked with Wild in a battle for his life, when suddenly Wild glanced to left and right along the table, stood up and left the room. Fujiwara had hardly noticed the passage of time. They were breaking for lunch. A detective took him to the back garden of the building. He was very faint by this time. No food or drink was given him – at least not officially. But a Malay police-man, who lived on the premises with his wife, waited until the detective had disappeared and then brought along a heaped plate of steaming hot curry and rice and a cup of water. He was to drink and eat quickly before the *orang puteh* (Englishman) came back. Fujiwara expressed his gratitude till the tears came, and it was more than gratitude for the food. The policeman knew something about *F Kikan*, and Fujiwara interpreted the gift of food as a recognition of the deep sympathy for Japan still felt by the peoples of Asia, which the English would never understand. This was why the British were using war crimes in their propaganda. It was to sever the bond that linked Japan with the Asians she had liberated.

Then the interrogation team reassembled. 'You have answered our questions from the start, this morning, very capably,' said Colonel Wild, 'but I must tell you that in my opinion *F Kikan* was an organization of thieves and murderers.' Unable to bear this accusation, Fujiwara stood up and began to reply, but Wild cut him short with 'Have you forgotten your position as a prisoner?' Fujiwara realized his reaction was inexpedient, but he replied that he had endured Wild's questions for several hours and had answered truthfully. Why should such a recklessly provocative accusation be brought now? Wild then accused him of employing Malay brigands in the Japanese service. This was true, Fujiwara admitted, but they were bandits under the British administration, not as far as the Japanese were concerned. Wild stood up to go, but Fujiwara wanted to say something else.

Colonel Wild! Wait, there is something I should like you to hear! Both of us, as soldiers, fought as our country ordered us. Victory and defeat are the luck of war. Your countrymen are a civilized people, proud of their gentlemanly code, so are mine proud of their warrior code (*bushidō*). I and my men fought with that warrior's code in our hearts. When my organization took over the police offices, just after Singapore fell, I looked after them with the most scrupulous care, your countrymen know that. I deeply regret that you should choose to insult a staff officer of the Japanese Army. I am sorry that the gentlemanly code of England should lead to an unreasonable trial

and the ill-treatment I have endured at Changi gaol. Release me at
once!

It was impossible to guess whether this impassioned plea made any
impact on Colonel Wild. He looked at Fujiwara with the same cold
smile, stood up, and left the room without a word.

On the way back to Changi, though, Fujiwara noticed that the
detectives' attitude had changed. This time they spoke to him and he
learned that one of them had a friend to whom Fujiwara had shown
consideration after the 1942 surrender. They gave him cigarettes in
the car, and, when they saw he was giddy from lack of food, took
him to a Chinese restaurant in a *kampong* (village) before returning
him to Changi. He was touched by this, but it did not prevent him
reflecting bitterly: although he had been able to look after himself,
there must have been many Japanese soldiers who had been caught –
perhaps under pressure by these very detectives? – in the trap of a
long interrogation such as he had undergone, and who had signed
statements in English which they did not understand.

Fujiwara's imprisonment was not, in any event, to last much
longer. In November 1946 he was transferred to Kuala Lumpur, in
handcuffs again, under the supervision of Gurkha guards. The gaol
held three hundred criminals and seventy Japanese suspects, including *Kempei*. After further detailed interrogation, Fujiwara left for
Japan and landed at Sasebo on 2 June 1947. Before he left Changi,
he had written some essays on the Japanese in East Asia for his
captors, and his view of Bose is contained in them.

He had a zealous fighting spirit (*Fujiwara wrote*) though in outward
appearance he was very gentle. His earnest and precise mind, his
vigorous actions, and his initiative, together with his love for the
masses without any discrimination between classes, won for him
respect which later became reverence, from all those who came into
contact with him... When contacting the Japanese, his motto was
'Freedom and Equality', and when and if there was any fear of
oppression, or of the Japanese taking advantage of him, he was quick
to refuse, however slight the matter may have been.

As a leader of the Army, he became the fountain of spiritual
strength and was the pivot of the INA organization. However, the
standard of his operational tactics was, it must be said with regret,
low. He was inclined to be unrealistic. For instance, without being
familiar with the actual fighting power of the INA, he was always

demanding it be employed in a separate and decisive operation on the Imphal front and, in July 1944, when the tide of battle had turned and the Japanese Army had retreated, he urged that although the Japanese might retreat the INA should continue to confront the Allies until their aim was attained. He was temperamental and had strong likes and dislikes. It is also said of him that his stubbornness made him adhere strongly to his arguments on matters of slight moment. This is so, and it cannot be said he possessed much magnanimity or very much tolerance for the opinion of others.[20]

These words were written when Fujiwara was very close to the events on which they are based. He was also a prisoner of the British and still unsure how they would treat him. Whatever the reason, this account of Bose has more nuance than the later evocation of him which Fujiwara wrote in his preface to an Indian scholar's work in 1969, by which time the myth had grown stronger than the personality.

Has there been a man (*Fujiwara asked rhetorically*) who in coming into contact with *Netaji* did not sense him as a rare incarnate of justice, bravery, sacrifice and wisdom?... With his appearance of dignity, magnetic personality having elements of mysticism and spiritualism in it, unfathomable yet realistic words and deeds and unshakable confidence in the cause, *Netaji* was sure to make one feel the air of a revolutionary atmosphere. To many of us, Subhas Chandra Bose symbolized the Indian Revolution.[21]

Consistency, we know, is the prerogative of small minds, and few would grudge the revised version. But whatever history's final verdict on Subhas Chandra Bose, there is no doubt that independent India owes a great debt to Major Fujiwara.

BOOK TWO

The Japanese Surrender
in East Asia

CHAPTER ONE

KOREA

i *The Americans and Korean Independence*

'The Koreans hate the Japanese more than any other people on earth.' There was no doubt strong justification for Syngman Rhee's outburst to President Roosevelt. The Koreans had, in his view, been the first victims of Japan's policy of establishing herself on the mainland of East Asia. Japan had always seen the stability of Korea as the key to peace in the Far East,[1] and Japanese statesmen concluded that this stability could be achieved only by annexation. They established a protectorate over Korea in 1905. On 18 November of that year the King of Korea was forced to yield to Japanese pressures, his country's foreign relations were taken over by the Japanese, and Korean nationals abroad came under the jurisdiction of Japanese diplomatic officials. Humiliated by what he had done, the King attempted to rid his country of Japanese control by rousing the powers on his behalf, and sent a secret mission to the Second Hague Conference in 1907. The Japanese reacted quickly when they found out, and the King was forced to abdicate. Japan's resident-general in Korea, who had previously been an adviser, now ran the country's administration, and founded the Oriental Colonization Company in 1907 to exploit Korean resources. In May 1910 the Japanese war minister, Terauchi, was appointed resident-general, and placed Korea firmly under the role of the Japanese gendarmerie. By August of that year he had concluded a treaty of annexation with the Korean Government, transferring its sovereignty to the Japanese Emperor. So Korea, one of the oldest nations of the east, the very bridge across which Japan herself had received the early impact of the great civilization of China, became part of the Japanese Empire.[2]

In the thirty-five years which followed the annexation, Korean nationalists did what they could to free their country from Japanese rule. Some organized nationalist groups and assemblies, others perpetrated terrorist attacks on the Japanese. The Japanese hit back: after the Tokyo earthquake of 1923, thousands of Koreans resident in Japan were brutally attacked or killed by Japanese, who made them scapegoats for the disaster. There were anti-Japanese outbreaks in Korea in 1929 and 1930, and when the Japanese decided to stage a demonstration to celebrate their successes in China, a young Korean, Yun Bong Kil, threw a bomb on to the speakers' platform. The general in command of troops in China, Shirakawa, was killed, Admiral Nomura lost an eye, and Shigemitsu, who later became foreign minister, lost a leg.

Repression on the one hand, terrorism on the other: it was the classic colonialist situation. Korean exiles in the USA and China were divided on the policy of terrorism, and the cabinet of the 'Korean provisional government', which functioned in Chungking during the thirties under the aegis of Chiang Kai-shek, was on several occasions harangued by Syngman Rhee, the greatest of Korean exiles abroad, to put a stop to the bomb-throwings. They would not win Korea's independence, he told them, and merely added force to Japanese propaganda. Pearl Harbor provided him with the opportunity he needed. Promptly he put at the service of the Allies the armed forces of Korea in China, and persuaded the Prime Minister in exile, Kim Koo, to cable the US government and propose the recognition of the Korean Republican Government in China as the legitimate government of the Korean people.

The State Department acted coolly and carefully. Stanley Hornbeck, the chief of the Office of Far Eastern Affairs, treated Syngman Rhee as a private individual, and held out no hope of official recognition. The War Department's reaction was a little more promising. Koreans in China had declared war on Japan, and hoped their men would qualify for Lend-lease aid: there were thirty thousand of them, and so far they had had to manage with whatever equipment could be spared by Chiang Kai-shek. Hornbeck's coolness was comprehensible enough in the early days of 1941 when America was trying to keep the peace with one hand and push Japan into war with the other. It was less comprehensible once America was at war, but Rhee found it hard to wring from the State Department any kind of official recognition of his government. His friends on the Korean–American

Council addressed a long letter to Roosevelt advocating the use of psychological warfare against the thousands of Koreans conscripted into the Japanese forces, or used as labour by the Japanese. Who are better able, they concluded, 'to refute Japan's claims of establishing a new order in Asia than that new order's first victims, the Korean people'?[3]

But Rhee was not the only Korean voice in the United States, nor were the Koreans in Nationalist China the only organized body of Korean exiles. There was a sizeable Korean community in Siberia, and a number of Korean Communists and Communist sympathizers opposed Syngman Rhee and the 'Korean provisional government' in Chungking. One claimant for the attention of the State Department, Kilsoo Haan, declared that Rhee had lost contact with the Korean people, whereas he, Haan, represented 300,000 of those who did menial jobs in Japan, and was therefore in a position to get access to important Japanese buildings. Both the State and War Departments were impressed by data shipped out of Korea by Haan, and late in 1942 Syngman Rhee was told bluntly by Stanley Hornbeck that he was not known inside Korea and that the 'Korean provisional government' was self-constituted and represented no more than a limited group of exiles.[4] The State Department held this view firmly and consistently. Writing to Rhee in June 1945, the acting director of the Office of Far Eastern Affairs, Frank P. Lockhart, did not mince his words:

> The 'Korean Provisional Government' has never had administrative authority over any part of Korea nor can it be considered representative of the Korean people of today. Its following even among exile Koreans is limited. It is the policy of this Government in dealing with groups such as the 'Korean Provisional Government' to avoid taking action which might, when the victory of the United Nations is achieved, tend to compromise the right of the Korean people to choose the ultimate form and personnel of the Government which they may wish to establish.[5]

The declaration of the three powers at the Cairo conference had adumbrated Korean independence. Mindful of the enslavement of the people of Korea, as they declared themselves to be, they were determined 'that in due course Korea shall become free and independent'. Rhee was puzzled by the phrase 'in due course' and wrote to Roosevelt and the State Department for clarification. No answer was forthcoming, but the Assistant Secretary of State, Archibald McLeish, announced in a radio broadcast in 1945 that Korea would be independent in due course 'which *presumably* means as soon as they are in a position to govern themselves'.[6] 'We desire,' noted Rhee tartly to Frank Lockhart, 'to know more definitely than presumably.'[7] But there is no indication that the State Department offered him any more comfort in 1945 than it had three years before.

American opinion was not, in fact, quite sure of its direction over Korea. The matter had been discussed with the Russians at the Yalta Conference in February 1945, and rumours from that conference had convinced Syngman Rhee that the Americans had signed a secret agreement with Stalin which would effectively mean that Korea would 'remain in orbit of Russian influence until after the end of Japanese war'.[8] Roosevelt's view was, as far as the Secretary of War, Henry Stimson, remembered it after the president's death, 'that there should be an international trusteeship of Korea, pending such time as the Koreans are prepared to govern themselves'.[9] It was not difficult to imagine that the Russians, taking part in such international trusteeship, would use the powerful presence of Russian-trained Korean troops to ensure that ultimately a régime favourable to themselves would be established throughout the peninsula. Indeed, as part of her offensive against the Kwantung Army, Russia mounted an invasion of northern Korea by land and sea before the Japanese capitulation and sent her forces southward as far as they could go before the surrender protocol limited their advance. As it happened, a limit had been agreed upon beforehand.

ii *The 38th Parallel*

When it became clear that the Japanese were going to accept the Potsdam surrender terms the American base nearest to Korea was Okinawa, whereas the Russian forces were at Seishin (Chongjin) on the north-east coast of Korea and in a position to bring pressure to bear on the whole country in a matter of days.[10]

To avoid clashes with Russian forces operating in the same zones once Russia entered the war against Japan, an operational limit for American air and naval forces in the Pacific had already been discussed at Potsdam, where a compromise was reached on a parabola linking La Perouse Strait (between Hokkaido and Karafuto) and

North Hamgyung Province in Korea. Morita, the Japanese historian of the end of the war in Korea, believes that this line was for naval and air operations.[11] But it is clear that the line is not the same for air and naval boundaries, and the full US boundary propositions show that the 38th parallel is quite clearly referred to there as a *naval* boundary:

> United States naval surface forces will operate without restriction in the Seas of Okhotsk and Japan. United States submarine forces will operate without restriction in the Seas of Okhotsk and Japan, south and east of a line established by connecting the following points: Coast of Korea at latitude 38° north, then to latitude 40° north longitude 135° east, thence to latitude 45° 45' north longitude 140° east, thence along the parallel of latitude 45° 45' north.[12]

On 26 July 1945 the Russian Chief of Staff, General Antonov, gave an answer to the US boundary propositions and stated that:

> Separate zones of naval and air operations are to be set up for the United States and the USSR in the Sea of Japan. The boundary between these zones will be along the lines connecting Cape Boltina on the coast of Korea to point 40° north 135° east to point 45° 45' north 140° east, thence along the parallel 45° 45' north to the line connecting Cape Crillon (Kondo) (on the southern tip of southern Sakhalin) with Cape Soya Missaki (Soyasaki) (on the northern tip of Hokkaido).[13]

The extension of this principle to a *land* boundary is attributed by Morita to a plan which had been drawn up by the Americans to make the operational limit between Soviet and American forces a line close to the 38th parallel. He cites Lieutenant-General Hull, who represented the American Army in the discussion of this plan, as his authority for this. Hull also stated that no agreement with the Soviet side was reached.[14] Morita's book came out in 1964, and his two sources are dated respectively 1953 (Feis) and 1961 (Appleman). Since then, the relevant volume of *Foreign Relations of the United States* has provided extra information not available to him.[15] It prints a reply dated 12 July 1950 by Dean Rusk, at the time Assistant Secretary of State for Far Eastern Affairs, to an enquiry on the 38th parallel decision made by G. Bernard Noble, chief of the Division of Historical Policy Research.[16]

Rusk recalls that the suddenness of the Japanese surrender forced consideration of emergency orders to MacArthur and negotiations with other governments involved. Meetings to consider these were held from 10 to 15 August between representatives of the State Department (Dunn), the Army (McCloy), and the Navy (Bard). On the night of 10/11 August a meeting was held in McCloy's office in the Pentagon which lasted all night, the topic being the practical details of the Japanese surrender. Byrnes, the Secretary of State, had let it be known that he thought the US forces should receive the surrender as far north as was practicable. The army noted that US forces would not be available in strength and it would not be easy to go very far north before Soviet troops entered the northern areas of Korea. If the US forces overreached themselves, the Soviets would not accept their proposition. Rusk was then a colonel on the general staff of the War Department, and McCloy turned to him and Colonel Bonesteel, another staff officer, suggesting they retire to another room and devise some proposal which would harmonize Byrnes's political aims with the practical limitations envisaged by the army. Rusk and Bonesteel returned to McCloy's room with the suggestion that, even though US troops might find it unrealistic, the 38th parallel should be selected as the dividing line between Soviet and US operations in Korea, because that would ensure that the capital of the country remained in the area for which American troops would be responsible. The army accepted this recommendation, and the line became official US policy. Rusk himself was surprised the Russians accepted it, because he had thought they would insist on the Americans remaining further south, in view of the relative military positions of the two armies in Korea. So was born the fateful line of the 38th parallel.

The plan to go to the 38th parallel was sanctioned by President Truman and forwarded to General MacArthur in Manila, with copies to the Heads of State of Great Britain, Soviet Russia, and China. Stalin made no objection to it, even though the Soviet military position in Korea was more advantageous than the American. On the face of it, this seems odd, but several explanations have been suggested. Stalin might have wanted to make a strong bid for participation in the occupation of Japan, and therefore was prepared to give way on what was a less important issue, the occupation of Korea. Alternatively, expecting a strong resistance in Manchuria by the Kwantung Army, he may not have judged the occupation of Korea to be a simple task.[17]

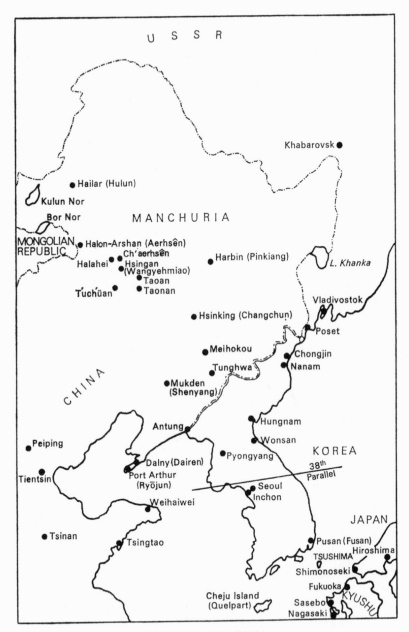

MANCHURIA AND KOREA

The major instrument of surrender to the Allied powers was, of course, General Order No. 1 which was to be issued by Japanese Imperial General Headquarters to all Japanese units, at the direction of the Supreme Commander for the Allied Powers, General MacArthur, in its revised form dated 11 August. Items *b* and *f* of its first paragraph dealt with Korea:

> b. The senior Japanese commanders and all ground, sea, air and auxiliary forces within Manchuria, Korea north of 38° north latitude and Karafuto shall surrender to the Commander-in-Chief of Soviet Forces in the Far East.
> f. The senior Japanese commanders and all ground, sea, air and auxiliary forces in Korea south of 38° north latitude shall surrender to the Commanding General, US Expeditionary Forces in Korea.[18]*

This was issued on 2 September 1945, but General MacArthur had in fact handed it over previously to the Japanese plenipotentiary, General Kawabe Torashirō, who had come to Manila to receive instructions on the arrangements for the surrender in Tokyo Bay. Kawabe received it on 20 August and returned to Tokyo with it the following day. On 22 August the vice-minister for foreign affairs sent a telegram to Endō, the Chief Civil Administrator of the Government-General in Korea:

> Anticipate disarmament of Japanese Army by Soviet Russia north of 38 parallel by US Army south of 38 parallel.

The immediate consequences of this were that when agreements were being reached on disarmament between the Japanese Commander-in-Chief of the 34th Army, Kuchifuchi, and the Soviet commander in Yenchi (Manchuria), it was made clear that the disarmament limit was the 38th parallel, and on 26 August, when the People's Political Committee was set up in Pyongan-namdo, the Russian Commander-in-Chief in North Korea, General Chistiakov, declared that 'the 38th parallel is only a line of demarcation between the US Army and the Soviet Army and has no political significance'.[20]

---

* *f* later became *e*, and 'Commander-in-Chief, US Army Forces in the Pacific' was substituted for the reference to a US Expeditionary Force.[19]

On 27 August the Japanese Military Area Command in Korea (Chōsen Gunkanku Shireibu) proclaimed that:

the end of hostilities in the northern half of Korea, based on agreement between the Kwantung Army and the Soviet Commander-in-Chief, is being negotiated at a local level in Nanam, Hamgyung, Wonsan, Pyongyang, etc. In Hamgyung-pukto and Hamgyung-namdo the Soviet forces are in occupation and will deal with matters their own way. On the Pyongyang and Hwanghae-do areas, negotiations are at present under way in Pyongyang. Negotiations on southern Korea are being carried out by the Supreme Commander, Allied Powers.

The chief of the general staff announced on 28 August that 'negotiators of local ceasefire for units in Korea south of the 38th parallel and the GOC Korean Military District have been decided by the GOC 24th Army'.[21] Hodge was commanding officer of the 24th Army Corps. In this way, the Korean people heard for the first time that their country was divided into two by the 38th parallel.

iii *South Korea: The Americans Move In*

It seems to have been originally planned that Lieutenant-General Wedemeyer, from the China–Burma–India Theatre of operations, a man with considerable experience of dealing with the military-cum-political problems arising from the situation in China, and with some general knowledge of East Asia, should be nominated to command the American occupation of Korea. This decision was altered on 23 August, and the 24th Army Corps commander on Okinawa, Lieutenant-General John R. Hodge, replaced him. The political situation was far from clear, and no orders had been forthcoming to clarify it. The American consul at Manila, Alexis Johnson, had been seconded to the Office of the Political Adviser in Japan at Yokohama and he conferred there with Hodge and the 24th Corps Military Government Officer, Brigadier-General Charles Harris, on 25 August. It transpired that no directive from the Joint Chiefs of Staff had yet been received by Hodge, who therefore intended to apply the directive for Japan *mutatis mutandis* to Korea when he arrived there. In other words, as MacArthur was acting through the Emperor and the existing Japanese political framework, Hodge intended to act through the Japanese Governor-General of Korea – General Abe Nobuyuki, who had once been Premier of Japan – and his Japanese staff, under the overall direction of an American military governor.

Johnson told Hodge that he thought the policy undesirable. He was right, of course. The Koreans would naturally find intolerable the continuance in office of the very régime which had oppressed them for decades and from which the US Army was supposed to be liberating them.

The Japanese themselves had already anticipated the ending of their sovereignty, and a meeting of the Japanese Government on 24 August declared that until the signing of a peace treaty determining the question of independence, the sovereignty of Japan over Korea, which was about to be occupied by foreign armies, must be considered in abeyance.[22] A telegram was sent to the Chief Civil Administrator (Seimu Sōkan) to that effect on the 26th, and this was followed on the 29th by another authorizing the Japanese authorities in Korea to prepare installations for the American occupation forces. All mines were to be swept in a ten-mile channel leading to Inchon Bay (Chemulpo), all shipping was to cease in that area, and anti-aircraft installations were to stop functioning. The Japanese 17th Area Army made wireless contact with US 24th Corps on 31 August, and through an interpreter, Oda Yasuma, and a leader-writer from the *Seoul Press*, Miyanaga Akiyoshi, the Americans passed on their requirements.

On 3 September, Hodge's forces left Okinawa, and on the 5th twenty-four minesweepers approached Inchon. Twelve of them made for Inchon harbour, and landing preparations for the main force were got under way. The Japanese Government was instructed to have the Seoul airfield ready for the 6th, to lay on a work force of 5,000 men for Inchon port duties, and to have available close to the harbour a supply depot able to hold 75,000 barrels of oil. Hotels and apartments were to be found for ten general headquarters officers, and the same for 400 officers of 24th Corps. Barracks were to be got ready for 25,000 men, and a hospital area with 2,000 beds – allowing 100 square feet per bed – dining halls, cold storage depots, etc.[23]

The American advance party arrived by plane on 6 September at the Kimpo airfield. Eighteen aircraft had set off from Okinawa, but adverse winds and rainstorms had scattered them and only three planes made it to the landing ground. One of them contained

Brigadier-General Harris and thirty-one men. Harris had been in touch with missionaries in pre-war Korea who had tipped him off that there was a very good English speaker in the Government-General, Oda Yasuma. To the interpreter who accompanied him in the car to the Chōsen Hotel he said, 'I want to meet Mr Oda, the interpreter.' His companion turned out to be no other than Oda himself, who was amazed that the Americans should know about him before they landed. Harris quickly established a liaison committee with the Government-General and the Japanese Army general head-quarters, and told them to get the Government-General buildings ready to be taken over, together with the Chōsen Hotel, and Hantō (Peninsula) Hotel, and the Mitsui buildings. Japanese troops in Inchon were ordered to withdraw to the suburbs, and those in Seoul were given until twelve o'clock on the 9th to move out. Exceptions were made for *Kempei* and units which were considered necessary for security purposes.

This is where the Americans began to go seriously wrong. Harris had a meeting with the Chief Civil Administrator, Endō, and told him that the administration of Korea was to be carried on in the buildings used at present, with the same personnel and the same functions and installations. 'Is it your intention,' Endō politely asked, 'to establish military government in Korea?', to which Harris replied in the negative: the Americans intended to act through the Govern-ment-General. Endō asked for this to be put in writing, but Harris demurred, saying he could only convey an interpretation of his com-mander's intentions, since his own work was merely one of prepara-tion. Nor could he tell Endō how long the administration system envisaged was likely to last, since that depended on the decision of the Supreme Commander, Allied Powers. The discussion went on well into the afternoon, and Endō took the opportunity to point out that the Government-General was concerned about shortages of food, salt, fuel, transport, and electric power, and about the problems created by the refugees from the fighting in the North and in Manchuria.*

Hodge and Harris were clearly expecting the local Japanese administration to continue to act on behalf of the occupying powers. However, later incidents made it clear that international opinion was not likely to countenance the continuation of Japanese rule in Korea,

* From notes made at the time by Yamana, bureau head in the General Affairs Secretariat.[24]

under whatever auspices it remained. Hodge himself arrived off Inchon, under the umbrella of Admiral Kinkaid's 7th Fleet, on 7 September. On the 8th pilots and interpreters were taken aboard Hodge's 25-vessel flotilla, and at 10 a.m. that day the Vice-Chief of Staff, Kubo, boarded the American flagship and made contact with the staff of the 24th Corps. At 1 p.m. on the 8th, the Americans began landing operations at Getsubi Island, and at 1.30 Hodge was welcomed by all the departmental officials of the Government-General (less the bureau chiefs for education and law) under Endō's shepherding hand, together with the Chief of Staff, Ihara, and garrison staff officers.

Two hundred Japanese had already been conscripted to clean up the island and another five hundred had been drafted to carry the Americans' luggage. The Japanese police had strictly forbidden anyone else to show themselves on the streets that day, apart from doctors, midwives, and postmen. Those who had to be out must obtain written authorization from the police chief. But there were many Koreans who wanted to greet the Americans and they collected at the dockside. At 2 p.m. in Miyamachi Avenue a crowd of Koreans bearing the Red Flag attempted to break into the restricted area, and at the crossroads of Miyamachi and Honmachi they clashed with the special police unit which had been laid on for the occasion by the Japanese. The Japanese opened fire and two men who belonged to the Koreans' own police unit, the *Hōantai*, or Unit for the Preservation of Public Order, fell dead. Many other Koreans were wounded, some seriously. In order to disperse the crowd, the Japanese police fired into the air, and accidentally shot and killed the Japanese head of the Hirokane Ear, Nose, and Throat Hospital, Mr Hirokane Torao. A nurse was severely wounded. When the funeral was held for the two Korean police, the Catholic cathedral in Inchon was crowded, and the Koreans took advantage of the occasion to organize a huge demonstration, several thousand strong, against the Japanese authorities. In addition, the Americans were requested to put on trial the Japanese police who had fired on the Korean crowd. On 13 September, the Japanese police chief, Kano, and the men who had fired were summoned to the shrine office of the former Inchon Shrine and tried. They said in their defence that on the day of the incident the order to restrict movement was based on American Army orders, and that the area in which the incident took place was within the zone of restricted movement. The American tribunal hearing the case approved the submission and declared the Japanese police had acted with complete legality.

The Koreans complained bitterly that the incident occurred in the first place because the Japanese police refused to accept the Korean *Hōantai*'s cooperation in policing activities and had ignored them. They demanded a re-trial, but the Americans told them that no one other than the police was to engage in policing activity, and turned the request down flat. Five days later, President Truman's declaration to the Korean people was issued. It must have fallen on somewhat unreceptive ears:

> The surrender of the Japanese forces in Seoul, ancient capital, heralds the liberation of a freedom loving and heroic people . . . The American people rejoice in the liberation of Korea as the Tae-gook-kee, the ancient flag of Korea, waves again in the Land of the Morning Calm.[25]

The Americans got a very bad press, naturally enough, over this unfortunate affair, both in Korea and at home in the United States. This in turn exacerbated relations between the occupying forces and their own journalists, who were roundly suspected by General Hodge of being left-wing radicals. H. Merrell Benninghoff, the political adviser in Korea, wrote in strong terms to the Secretary of State from Seoul on 15 September:

> The newspaper correspondents covering Korea as a group have behaved badly. They arrived by air after our landing; most of them from Japan with no knowledge of the local situation and without orientation took advantage of the American uniform to run rampant over the area, committing acts of personal misbehaviour. There is reason to believe that by open sympathies with Korean radicals some of them have incited Korean group leaders to greater efforts at agitation for overthrow of everything and to have the Koreans take over all functions immediately. Before they got any glimmer of conditions as they existed, they were highly critical of all policies of the nation, of General Headquarters and of this headquarters relating to the occupation.[26]

Hodge had written to MacArthur about the American press correspondents in much the same vein. 'Most of the undesirable juvenile minded ones have moved on to more exciting fields of endeavour,' he wrote on 24 September. 'Those remaining are more thoughtful

and more mindful of their responsibilities as American citizens.'
None the less he wanted them muzzled: 'There is still a tendency for
them to send in Russian stories which, if published, may jeopardize
the American mission here. It is believed USAFPac (United States
Army Forces, Pacific Theatre) censors here should be warned by
your headquarters to suppress all such as are considered dangerous.'[27]
It is clear from a later letter to the Secretary of State by Hodge's
political adviser, Langdon, who had succeeded Benninghoff on 10
October, that criticisms of the military government's treatment of
Koreans had hit hard.

> As for favouring plutocracy in and excluding popular leftwingers from
> Military Government (*Langdon wrote*), it is quite probable that at the
> beginning we may have picked out a disproportionate number of rich
> and conservative persons. But how were we to know who was who
> among this unfamiliar people? For practical purposes we had to hire
> persons who spoke English, and it so happened that these persons
> and their friends came largely from moneyed classes because English
> had been a luxury among Koreans. But Military Government long
> ago realized the unrepresentative nature of its Korean structure and is
> fast broadening the social base of that structure . . . I am not writing to
> defend our commanders here. They need no defence. But this cap-
> tious press they have had may have left you and the President under
> the impression that the United States is represented here by men of
> few parts, colonial-minded and contemptuous of the Koreans. This
> is not the case at all.[28]

iv *Occupational Hazards*

No doubt the correspondents had no knowledge of the local situation, but in this they seem to have been no worse equipped than 24th
Army Corps. General Hodge had received no briefing, writes one
American biographer of Syngman Rhee, 'was accompanied by no
experts, and had no officers who understood the Korean language or
knew Korean history, customs or psychology'.[29] The omission was
hardly pardonable in an organization like the American Army which
had an adequate supply of American citizens of Korean ancestry in
its service, just as it had had enough second-generation Japanese,
Nisei, to act as interpreters and translators in Japan. Hodge's lack of
briefing was a reflection not so much on the US Army as on the inter-

national situation at the time. No one knew precisely what was to become of Korea, other than that some vague plan to put it under international trusteeship had been put forward. A four-power trusteeship had been agreed between Stalin and Harry Hopkins in a conversation in May 1945. The following month T. V. Soong gave his consent on behalf of China, and the British Embassy in Washington was informed orally by the State Department of what was planned. The official British view was that anything which would secure adequate government for Korea and prevent it becoming a focus of international friction would be acceptable, and the only question was whether trusteeship would work.[30] The head of the Far Eastern Department of the Foreign Office suggested to the US Ambassador in London, Winant, that it might in practice be preferable to set up an independent Korean government, supply it with foreign advisers, and then see that those advisers retained the actual power to govern, under some supreme adviser responsible to the UN.[31]

The British view was a standard colonialist one, and there is no doubt that the Koreans themselves, whatever their political complexion, interpreted trusteeship as colonialism and would have none of it.

After one month's observation in liberated Korea (*wrote the acting political adviser, William R. Langdon, to the Secretary of State*) and with background of earlier service in Korea, I am unable to fit trusteeship to actual conditions here or to be persuaded of its suitability from moral and practical standpoints, and, therefore, believe we should drop it. It is thought wrong because the Korean people have always been a distinct nation except for 35 years of Jap rule and have high literacy, cultural and living standards judged by Asiatic and Middle Eastern standards. It is thought unpractical because it certainly will not be accepted by the Koreans and perhaps will have to be maintained by force ... Military Government came as a surprise and disappointment. However, all classes of Koreans look upon us as deliverers and for that reason and because they have abiding trust in the United States work very amicably with Military Government. But the Department's recent press release concerning trusteeship for Korea, connoting that Koreans would continue to be somebody's wards after MG, agitate (*sic*) all literate elements beyond anything since the surrender. The fact seems to be that all Koreans want their country to themselves in their lifetime and will not have any form of tutelage to attain an alien standard of nationhood. In the Korean people are certain bad traits that cannot be overcome except by actual experience of their evil consequences: Division, obsequiousness, inordinate self seeking, strong sectional rivalries and intolerance of opposition.[32]

Langdon concluded that US caution over association with the 'Korean provisional government' established in China under Kim Koo should be relaxed, that Kim Koo's 'government' had no rival as first government of liberated Korea, and was regarded as quasi-legitimate by all elements and parties; if the Russians would not allow persons in their zone to join a governing commission under Kim Koo, then the plan should be carried out for Korea south of the 38th parallel. In this way, the line began to harden.

In contrast with the Koreans, whom he believed to be 'most narrow, selfish and confused in their political thought',[33] Hodge found the Japanese very cooperative. He met the President, Hodzumi, and two Vice-Presidents, Kubota and Watanabe, of the Seoul Japanese Aid Society on 17 October 1945 and told them so. Hodzumi thanked him for the Americans' helpful attitude in difficult circumstances, when the Japanese had been forced to help themselves by founding their Aid Societies. They kept a record of this conversation.

Hodge: I've come to Korea to carry out the surrender orders. I have no intention of punishing non-combatants. I have no intention of inflicting cruelty on ordinary people. The war is over, and I am only enforcing the surrender orders. We must help the Japanese people to democratize themselves.

Kubota: Firstly, those Japanese who do not need to stay in Korea will return to Japan, but there are various problems in this connection. Secondly, there are special people who are to stay and cooperate with the Japanese Army. Will they return, or not? Thirdly, what sort of guidance can we give to our people, whether they return to Japan or not?

Hodge: I have been giving great thought to this problem and I've still not solved it. Japanese are still needed here, that is an undeniable fact. They have an important part to play in the economic recovery of Korea, and we know this. But my problem is, if I have them remain behind, there is a fear they will be ill-treated by the Koreans. I have discussed this point with General MacArthur and I have so far received no directive whether I am to evacuate *all* Japanese or leave some behind.

I'd like to say though, that those who are not needed now and those who have no definite occupation, I'd like to send them back as soon as I can. Japanese troops will probably return next week, and when that is over, the Japanese civilians can return in order without any unfortunate incidents. They should come to Seoul from the interior and be returned to Japan from there. We can move, I think, some seven or eight thousand people in a day. If we do that, the return should be completed by the end of the year. I would like to make that clear. Those Japanese without any definite job, and those people who don't need to stay, I'd like them to get back quickly. Certain categories, like railway staff and broadcasting technicians, must stay and instruct the Koreans until they can work things themselves.

Hodzumi: As you say, those who have no definite job must return as quickly as possible. The cold weather has already arrived, and everyone is in a hurry to get back. We will cooperate with the Military Government in organizing this return. In the meanwhile, shortages are occurring of food, fuel and medical supplies, and we would like to help in this direction.

Hodge: Yes, I know. As far as the coal shortage is concerned, we should be receiving a fair amount from Japan very soon. As far as medicines are concerned, the Military Government is concerned too, and three ships are on their way to Korea with medical supplies. We intend to see these are distributed on a purely humanitarian basis, without distinction between Japanese or Koreans. Pneumonia will be a problem as the cold gets worse, and we have to have injections and drugs for this. I know the Japanese Aid Society has done magnificent work, and I'd like to thank you for what you've done.

Hodzumi: This does not concern us directly, but there is something else we would like to say, and we'd like to take this opportunity of saying it. There are many Japanese north of the 38th parallel. If they are simply left as they are, with the arrival of the cold season, we are very anxious about what will happen to them. We should be happy to do anything we could for them, if Your Excellency would help us in this matter, from a humanitarian point of view.

Hodge: I know what is happening, and I would like to help. But my information is that conditions north of the 38th parallel have recently begun to improve, and some measures have already been taken. I can make no promises, but I will do what I can to help. The Japanese in the north are being transported by ship from northern ports, by the Soviet Army. There are Japanese in China too, and General MacArthur is very concerned. Whether north or south, I don't want women and children and old people to have to suffer. War is an unpleasant thing, and it seems the aftermath of war is too, as you all know. We must all help each other.

As far as Japanese property is concerned, it's not clear what is to happen. It'll first be decided when we know what the Peace Conference does about indemnities. As far as that goes, the Koreans may take reprisals, as a people, but we will do our level best to prevent this.

But Hodge knew that behaviour on the Japanese side was far from perfect, and he added a word of warning.

Hodge: I'd like to add that I'll have no mercy at all on anyone who breaks the law. In any country, there are men whose judgement is mistaken, or who act in obedience to other men's mistaken judgements. But there are certain groups of Japanese who are creating problems in Korea. I want you to tell me whenever you hear about treacherous and secret activities of this kind, which threaten our work. If any hindrance arises, from Japanese sources, it will be unfortunate for the entire Japanese community here. It will arouse the Koreans, and it would be most unfortunate for the Japanese here as a whole if an incident occurred which made the Americans confront the Japanese with fixed bayonets.

Hodzumi: We will cooperate to the utmost in the preservation of order. We are very grateful to you for listening to us for so long.

Hodge: I think this long conversation has been very profitable. I know what first-rate people the Japanese can be. I hope you will cooperate with me from now on.[34]

Hodzumi had carefully glossed over Hodge's reference to treacherous elements, but he and the others inferred that he was talking about trouble with the *Kempei.* Young members of this powerful secret military police organization, most of them about twenty years old, had taken the surrender very badly, and unlike the rest of the Japanese in Korea, who were concerned to get back to Japan, some of the

Kempei had formed themselves into an organization called the Takuma Organization, the purpose of which was to act as a focus of unrest against the Military Government. At the end of September, a few weeks before Hodge met the Japanese Aid Society, the police station at Todaimon in Seoul, which the *Kempei* used, had been searched and found to contain a small arsenal. Two machine guns, sixteen pistols, two boxes of grenades, other ammunition and assorted short and long swords were discovered. Forty-four men were arrested by the American counter-intelligence authorities, and a *Kempei* sergeant-major, Tsuchii, and six others were given five-year sentences at a court-martial in November.[35]

Then there was the opium case. When the war ended, the government-general was in the midst of despatching eight tons of opium, in 756 boxes, to the Ministry of Public Welfare, and the *Kempei*, with the acquiescence of the head of the Regional Financial Bureau, Mizuta, was in charge of the transportation. When the American forces arrived, and the *Kempei* had to withdraw, Japanese civilians were requested to hand over the opium to them. The Americans confiscated the opium, found that a number of boxes were missing, and as a result of investigations into the Korea Military Area Command and the Korea *Kempei*, Captain Noda Takehiko, of the *Kempei* Special Service Branch, was sentenced to two years' imprisonment, which he served in Sugamo Prison in Tokyo. A Japanese civilian, Kimura Kiyoshi, was given a three-year sentence. Officials of the Government-General's Regional Financial Bureau and the Monopoly Office were arrested and freed after fifteen days, and Mizuta's affairs were investigated.

Seoul seemed to attract Japanese criminals. Sagoya Yoshiaki, who had assassinated Prime Minister Hamaguchi in 1930, and been paroled in 1940, was tried in December 1945 for possession of arms and opium and given three years' imprisonment. Officials of the Government-General sentenced by American court-martial included a secretary, Harada, the head of the Direct Tax Division in Kyongsang-namdo, Ishimura, the head of the Finance Bureau from the same province, Abe, the manager of the Fusan branch of the Imperial Bank (Teikoku Ginkō) and Yamazaki, the Mokpo police chief. For some Japanese, clearly, the temptations of colonialism had been too great.[36]

It was with shock and horror that the Koreans realized that the US occupation forces were prepared to act through the Japanese

Government-General. By 24 September 1945 Hodge had also realized that this would not do, and that, whatever the manpower difficulties, US Military Government would have to be set up throughout South Korea.

It appears at this time (*he wrote to MacArthur in Tokyo*), that the 'Military Government' in Korea will, for the time being, have to be complete and entire except for minor functions. As we get into the structure of what was the Government here, we find that the frame-work was built primarily for Japanese control and exploitation of a subject people and most of it is unsuitable for democratic rule... As we are able to increase our Military Government personnel and increase our occupation to include all the southern provinces, it is hoped that a clear picture may unfold.[37]

In the same letter Hodge told MacArthur that he would start moving the Japanese forces to Japan as rapidly as the port of Fusan could process them, and as soon as his 40th Division had set up control of that port. Though there is evidence that Hodge regarded the Japanese as an element of stability in a chaotic situation, his then political adviser, Benninghoff, interpreted him rightly as saying that stable conditions could not be established in Korea until the Japanese Army had been repatriated. It could not be demobilized in Korea, and it could not be effectively controlled unless put into concentration camps; and that would create new problems for the US forces, which would then be responsible for feeding and housing the Japanese troops. It was, therefore, in the American interests to assemble and repatriate the Japanese as soon as possible. Rail facilities were limited, and if coal could not be obtained soon in sufficient quantities, Hodge reported, the railways would be forced to suspend action south of 38°.[38] Two days later, his political adviser was able to report to the Secretary of State that an agreement had been reached with MacArthur's General Headquarters to the effect that the Japanese Government was to be instructed to send seventy thousand tons of Kyushu coal every month to Fusan until coal could be obtained from North Korea in the usual way.[39]

But the problems of establishing a stable Korean government in Korea were only part of what confronted the US occupation forces. They were primarily concerned, at the beginning, with their reason for being in Korea in the first place, which was to disarm and re-patriate the Japanese. This task was complicated by the fact that in

Korea, as distinct from any other area from which repatriation had to be carried out, there were significant numbers of Japanese who had settled in the country and who effectively controlled the Korean economy and administration. At the time of the annexation, in 1910, the population of Korea was around 13,000,000.*

In the early post-1945 period the population, including the artificial increase represented by the return of Koreans from service with the Japanese in Japan, China, and the Southern Regions, was 29,000,000. This population was largely without men experienced in government or business, as posts in these fields had been held mainly by Japanese. At the end of the war there were about 6,000,000 Japanese in South Korea, soldiers and civilians. The population of South Korea by the end of August 1946 was 19,369,270.

As soon as Brigadier-General Harris arrived, on 6 September 1945, the Japanese Army's negotiating committee saw him and were told, 'Repatriation of the Japanese Army will be carried out by the Americans.' On 9 September the chief of staff, Ihara, was told by the US chief of staff: 'In areas which have not been occupied by the US

---

* The following figures give some idea of the increase in the Japanese population up to 1944:

Year	Japanese Population in Korea
1876	54
1907	98,001
1914	291,217
1926	442,326
1941	717,011
1944	712,583

But these figures do not tell the whole story. If the proportions spread among the various trades and professions are shown, for the year 1942, the picture looks something like this:

Trade/profession %

	Japanese in Korea	Koreans
Agriculture	3·9	68·1
Fisheries	1·2	2·0
Mining	3·1	2·1
Industry	18·7	4·6
Commerce	18·2	6·9
Transport	7·2	1·4
Public Corporation	39·5	3·9
Others	4·3	8·9
No occupation	3·9	2·1

(Based on Morita, p. 12)

forces, 25 % of troops may remain under arms; all other weapons and material are to be moved to a point designated by the US Army to await transfer.' Seven places were named as points where liaison teams of Japanese and Americans were to act under the command of an officer.[40]

At first it appeared there could be no question of an immediate return, given the acute food shortage in Japan which was likely to occupy all available shipping for months to come. The troops were therefore ordered to assemble on Quelpart Island for the winter. The 96th Division had collected enough food and stores on Quelpart to last, it was estimated, until the early summer of 1946.

The Allies were concerned to see that the Japanese did not denude of cash and property the countries they had occupied and put limits to what Japanese returning to Japan could take back home. In pursuance of this policy, by a decree of 13 October 1945 from the Japanese Treasury (Ōkurashō) to heads of transport offices, Japanese civilians and gunzoku (civilians attached to the Japanese Army) at ports of embarkation were allowed to retain 1,000 yen in Bank of Japan notes, or Bank of Korea, Bank of Taiwan, or Bank of Manchukuo currency; officers (including cadets) were allowed 500 yen; NCOs and men 200 yen. Exchange bureaux were set up in ports of embarkation only, and exchange was carried out by the local branch of the Bank of Japan or its representative, taking the Japanese yen at par.

Valuables could be taken back, within limits. The restriction was that an individual could retain only what he could carry himself at any one time.[41]

176,241 men were repatriated from South Korea between 27 September and 28 December, not including the Japanese troops who were refugees from North Korea.

v *The Russians in North Korea*

The Russians had a far less difficult task in North Korea. They came in as a combatant military force engaged in a victorious campaign with no obligation to retain the governmental structure. They handed over political and administrative authority to the Korean People's Committee and arrested Japanese political and legal officials and police staff. In every province police chiefs, heads of bureaux of internal affairs and treasury officials were detained. Police officials were treated by the Soviets as prisoners-of-war and were put into camps like soldiers.

Their treatment of Japanese troops was quite different from the treatment given by the Americans and British. They had no intention of working through the Japanese command. For one thing, the command itself had lost a great deal of its past effectiveness. At the end of hostilities, the Japanese had separated from their units all Koreans and those who had been conscripted in Korea. Many units had been broken up by mass desertions before the Soviet forces disarmed them. Discipline had relaxed, and in some cases as much as half the unit deserted (the 261st Infantry Regiment, for instance). After disarming the Japanese, the Russians separated the field officers and above from the junior officers, NCOs and men. The Japanese Army organization was dissolved. The men were then drawn up into battalion-type formations about a thousand strong, and officers were put in charge of these freshly formed units. About 34,000 men were assembled in the Japanese barracks at Sangori, near Pyongyang. They were a mixture of all sorts of troops: the 137th Division, the Pyongyang District Unit, No. 5 Naval Supply Depot, air force units, Kwantung Army supply units, and oddments which had retreated into North Korea from Hsinking and the Tunghua area in Manchuria. Others were quartered in the nearby town of Bijindo (about 2,500 men). There was space enough there, but the barracks at Sangori were overflowing, and stables and tents had to be used to hold the Japanese troops. Rations were severely cut. Two meals a day was the issue, and the second meal generally consisted only of dried fish.

The terror inspired by the Soviet advance served the Russian purpose very well. Refugees from Manchuria filled the southbound trains into Korea as soon as the invasion of Manchuria began. Thousands of these refugees were collected in the main Korean cities, and many managed to reach the port of Fusan and cross to Japan before movement across the Tsushima Straits ceased. This mass exodus left the Russians' hands free. They liberated the Korean political prisoners and set up local Soviets. They turned factories into camps for the Japanese troops, and used reformatories and the camps from which Australian and British troops had been liberated for the same purpose. In all, there were about 76,000 Japanese in the Soviet zone, troops, police, and Government-General officials.

The camps were ringed round with barbed wire and placed under strict guard. There was little work to do inside the camps themselves, other than collecting fuel and cooking, but the troops were used on outside work, in docks, factories, and railways, and airfield maintenance.

But this was merely an interlude. From the end of September 1945 the Japanese troops were transferred to the Soviet Union. Up to January 1946 about twenty-five battalions had been despatched from Sangori and Bijindo into Manchuria, to the Hsingan and Yenchi areas – about 25,300 men in all. Others (about 53,000 men) were sent by sea to Nakhodka and Vladivostok between the autumn of 1945 and the summer of 1946. The police and government officials, apart from those accused of crimes against the Korean population, were concentrated in Yenchi, in Manchuria.

Then the Russians began to move equipment. There was not the same wholesale looting that had occurred in Manchuria, because the Russians did not wish unduly to antagonize the North Korean population. They did move electrical equipment and water wheels from the Supung Dam, using three thousand troops as forced labour from October until December 1945. The dams on the Yalu provided not only North Korea, but also the South, with most of its electric power, and the Americans were duly perturbed about the seizure. The people themselves also reacted against the looting. The head of one People's Committee broke out in angry protest when a factory was stripped of its equipment. 'If you move any more stuff from here, kill me first!'[42]

There was some raping and some killing when the Russian troops first moved in, but by the beginning of 1946 relations had improved to a certain extent between the Russians and those Japanese who had been left behind in North Korea. One Japanese girl even married a Red Army lieutenant. But the reports which panic-stricken and terrified refugees made in Seoul were transmitted to Tokyo, and the Japanese, though overcome by their own miseries, attempted to do something to alleviate the lot of their fellow countrymen in Russian hands. It is interesting to see how diplomatic activity still carried on. General Abe, the Japanese Governor-General of Korea, sent a telegram to the Foreign Minister Shigemitsu on 28 August, urging him to obtain permission for the Japanese to keep their weapons in areas where they were unprotected. The Japanese Foreign Ministry also received a telegram on 29 August 1945 from the Chief Civil

Administrator in Korea asking it to request the liberation of government officials who had been arrested and begging that something be done for the protection of Japanese property. On 1 September the Foreign Ministry decided to approach the Swedes to act on their behalf. As a neutral, Sweden had acted during the war as a 'protecting power' for Allied interests in Japan. The Swedish minister in Tokyo was therefore asked to intervene with the Soviet Government, since communications with the Soviet Army authorities in Pyongyang were non-existent. Similarly, Okamoto, the Japanese minister in Sweden, who had played a role in peace negotiations earlier, sought an interview with the Swedish deputy foreign minister and asked him to use the Swedish minister in Moscow to bring the Japanese request to the notice of local army commanders in North Korea.

It was a very roundabout way, and the approach received short shrift from the Russians. 'Japan has surrendered,' the people's commissar Lozovsky told the Swedish minister. 'There is no precedent in international law for a defeated country requesting protection from a protecting power. But the matter is being studied by experts, so please wait a few more days.'[43] Finally on 8 September a reply came: 'Since Japan surrendered, her international position has completely changed. The responsibility for protection now rests with the Supreme Commander, Allied Powers (SCAP) in Japan.' The Swedish Government therefore notified its minister in Japan that it considered its duties as a protecting power to be ended.

So the Japanese tried an approach through SCAP the following day. Figures of Japanese detained in areas under Soviet control were submitted, not merely for North Korea, but for all the areas in which the Japanese had surrendered to the Russian forces:

Area	Military	Civilian	Total
North Korea	271,000	500,000	771,000
Manchuria	703,000	1,500,000	2,200,000
Karafuto	19,000	430,000	450,000
Kuriles	53,000	———	60,000 (*sic*)

Even if the figure for Korea includes troops fleeing from Manchuria, it seems inflated, and there is a clear discrepancy in the figures for the Kuriles, but that there were close on three million Japanese in Soviet hands in September 1945 seems likely enough. SCAP replied on 17 September that improved relations with North Korea and the reopening of a direct rail connection with Fusan was a matter for Soviet jurisdiction.

Having drawn a blank there, the Japanese tried another tack. The matter was becoming more urgent. As summer gave way to autumn conditions in the camps began to deteriorate, and the autumn in North Korea is cold. Shigemitsu decided to contact the Swiss. Kase, the Japanese minister in Switzerland, received a telegram from Tokyo on 10 September asking him to seek help from the International Red Cross in connection with the situation in Manchuria and North Korea. Shigemitsu asked for a Red Cross representative to visit these areas, and at the same time wired Okamoto in Sweden that SCAP considered it was not in a position to control the situation in North Korea and Manchuria. The Swedish Counsellor of Embassy in Japan, Erikson, had made an approach to the Soviet Ambassador, Jacob Malik, who had rejected it, saying it was *ultra vires*. Junod, the International Red Cross representative in Japan, had also been contacted, but he had been forced to admit that relations with the Soviet Union were far from harmonious and it was not likely they would listen to him. Because of the fruitlessness of these various approaches, Shigemitsu asked Okamoto to suggest to the Swedish Government that they should continue to act as protecting power, from the humanitarian point of view. Until a peace treaty was concluded and normal diplomatic and consular relations resumed, Shigemitsu was convinced that the belligerents would accept as necessary the exercise of protective powers by a third power. As a practical necessity, the Japanese would have to seek an acquiescence from the Soviet Government in the extension of Sweden's protecting powers to areas newly under Soviet rule: Manchuria, North Korea, Karafuto, and the Kuriles. Okamoto was asked to urge the Swedish Government to put this to the Soviet Union.

Okamoto did so, and was told by the Swedes on 12 September that the Soviet Government refused to accept the approach and that it was difficult to do anything. The next day, Kase saw the deputy head of the Red Cross in Geneva and explained the Korean and Manchurian situation to him. 'I would like to help,' the Red Cross official replied, 'but relations between the Red Cross and the Soviet Union are non-existent. Direct contact with the Russians is impossible, even in Europe. You would do better to get the British or the Americans to make a move. I have instructed Junod, our representative in Tokyo to get in touch with SCAP.'[44] Junod accordingly left Tokyo for Seoul on 6 October, hoping to enter North Korea. But no permission from the Russians was forthcoming so he was reduced to observing the condition of refugees coming from the Soviet zone and reporting on their requirements. On 17 October he returned to Japan.

Another move was made through SCAP on 12 October. Kodama, the president of the Central Liaison Bureau, heard that five Soviet staff officers from Pyongyang were in Seoul, and he at once sent a letter to the SCAP Chief of Staff, Lieutenant-General Sutherland, asking him to forward to the Soviet officers a memorandum urging the evacuation of Japanese from North Korea and the improvement of their conditions, both there and in other Soviet-occupied zones. The memorandum offered relief funds from the Japanese Government, and made the usual request that Japanese civil officials should be released from detention.[45]

In addition to these diplomatic negotiations, the Foreign Ministry sent Kameyama Ichiji, a former counsellor at the Japanese Embassy in Moscow, to Pyongyang to negotiate directly with the Soviet Army on the evacuation of the Japanese. Kameyama obtained permission from Allied Powers General Headquarters and left Tokyo by air on 7 September, reaching Seoul two days later. On 11 September he managed to secure an interview with Polianski, the Soviet Consul-General in South Korea. When Kameyama asked him to intervene on his behalf to enable him to visit Pyongyang, the Consul-General replied that he was sending his Vice-Consul, Konstantinoff, to Pyongyang that very day, and he would contact the Soviet commander-in-chief. He therefore asked Kameyama to wait until the vice-consul returned. Kameyama duly waited, and then on 17 September he went to see the consul-general again. The result was negative. 'My powers are limited to South Korea,' the Consul-General told him. 'It would be pointless for me to introduce you to the Soviet commander-in-chief. The Americans are sending a special train to Pyongyang tomorrow, and the vice-consul will be travelling on it for official discussions. Why don't you use that train?' Then Kameyama received a message from SCAP General Headquarters in Tokyo to say that the US Army authorities in Seoul were negotiating with the Soviet Army commander-in-chief in Pyongyang about sending him into North Korea, so he let the train go and waited in Seoul instead.

The Soviet reply to SCAP was blunt: 'We do not recognize the need for official visits of this kind.' The Americans passed this on to the Japanese Government on 6 October, so Kameyama abandoned his plan of entering North Korea and returned to Japan with Endō, the Chief Civil Administrator.

To support the diplomatic pressure, the Japanese House of Representatives formed a Committee for Aid Towards Overseas Japanese to formulate policy on helping Japanese stranded by the end of the war in various parts of Asia. On 13 September it urged the government to appeal to world public opinion, on humanitarian grounds, to bring to an end 'illegal Soviet Army activities' in Manchuria and Korea, and to do its utmost 'to feed and clothe our compatriots, the soldiers in Manchuria'.[46] But Japan had no standing in world opinion at that time, as far as humanitarian appeals were concerned. They had as little effect as the diplomatic approaches. The Soviet Union rejected every overture, whether made by the Japanese themselves or by the Americans on their behalf. 'This headquarters,' wrote Hodge to MacArthur on 12 October 1945, 'has been rebuffed in all its efforts to reach any kind of understanding on any subject.'[47] Hodge was half-minded to withdraw the favourable conditions under which the Soviet Consul-General maintained his establishment in Seoul (special food supply trains to the north, air transportation to Tokyo, etc.). Hodge's grievances were aired in Moscow. Three weeks later, Byrnes, the Secretary of State, wired to the US Ambassador in Moscow, Averell Harriman, that while Hodge had full authority to negotiate local military problems with the Russians, he had found that the Soviet commander was not so authorized. 'Consequently, the 38 degree parallel has become in reality a closed border with result that Korean national life has been greatly disrupted.'[48]

Byrnes received a message from Tokyo on 12 November on the Korean situation, which mentioned that American officers had gone to Pyongyang on 1 November for coal and chlorine. They had returned empty-handed 'except for coal for the Soviet Consulate'.[49] While in the North, the Americans had observed what was happening, and the impression was far from favourable. The Russians were evidently preparing for a long stay: high-ranking officers' wives were arriving and houses being remodelled for them. Troops were moving south through Pyongyang just as dismantled machinery was moving north. Relations with the local Korean population appeared reserved but stories of Russian excesses had diminished. Soviet morale was high, and the Russians appeared to be living well. They now called their civil administration 'the provisional government'.[50]

The Americans were not faring so well in their zone as far as Korean public opinion was concerned. In a message which MacArthur transmitted to the joint chiefs of staff in Tokyo on 16 December 1945,[51] Hodge made a *mise au point* which was both lucid and forthright. The dual occupation and the break at the 38th parallel was imposing an impossible condition on the occupation. In South Korea the United States was being blamed for the partition, and the word 'pro-American' now sounded in Korean ears as offensive as 'pro-Japanese' or 'national traitor'. The Koreans wanted their independence more than anything else, and they wanted it now. The lack of settled conditions proved fertile ground for communism. The Koreans in the South thought themselves worse off than those in the North because in their view the Russians didn't interfere with politics, and the Koreans 'are the most politically minded people I have ever seen'.[52] If trusteeship were imposed, he believed the Koreans would 'actually and physically revolt'. The Russians had sealed the border, but the seal permitted a daily flow of over five thousand Japanese and Korean refugees, all destitute, which indicated they were letting undesirables through. He summed up his solution: removal of the 38° barrier; the public announcement that trusteeship was to be abandoned, and the promise of independence fulfilled; the complete separation of Korea from Japan in the minds of the public and official bodies. He concluded by advocating a simultaneous, complete withdrawal of both Russian and US forces, leaving Korea to its own devices and 'an inevitable internal upheaval for its self purification'.[53]

Hodge was right about trusteeship. In December the Foreign Ministers of the Soviet Union, the United States, and Great Britain met in Moscow. They decided that a provisional democratic government should be set up in Korea to liquidate the effects of Japanese rule. A joint commission would be established, consisting of representatives from the American and Russian occupation forces, to work with the democratic parties in Korea to formulate proposals for a government, which would then be submitted to Russia, Great Britain, the USA, and China for approval. Korean democratic organizations, the provisional government, and the joint commission would then work together to achieve Korean independence, and while they did so the country would be placed under a four-power trusteeship for a period of five years.

The agreement, which was dated 27 December 1945, caused a

furore in the Korean press in the American zone. It was referred to as a 'second Munich'.[54] Koreans demonstrated in the streets and refused to work in American Military Government offices; shops and offices closed down in protest. American propaganda organs did their best to counter the impression given that the United States was solely responsible for the hated trusteeship clause, but a Russian press release had beaten them to it.[55] Kim Koo, the nominal head of the 'Korean Provisional Government' sent a protest to the Head of State of each of the four powers protesting that the trusteeship clause went against the desires of the Korean people and against the principle of national self-determination. If it were applied, it would eventually destroy peace in the Far East.[56] Kim Koo organized an anti-trusteeship committee, and it became noticeable that it was the right-wing groups which supported his protest. The Communist Party and groups in sympathy with it came out for the Moscow agreement on 3 January 1946. When left-wing leaders were invited to participate in an anti-trusteeship coalition in an Emergency National Assembly in February 1946 they refused. The Assembly proceeded to elect former exiles as officers. Syngman Rhee became president, Kim Koo vice-president. The Americans attempted to wean the Assembly away from its anti-trusteeship policy by forming a Representative Democratic Council a few weeks later, of which Syngman Rhee became chairman. The Americans then found themselves in the position of having cultivated the support of the most conservative elements in Korean society, who were, in any case, hostile to the policy the Americans were pledged to support.[57] The American historian Borton defends the trusteeship agreement on the ground that the Soviets occupied half Korea, and the agreement would make the eventual withdrawal of forces from both sides possible. But Borton was an official of the State Department at the time (chief of the North-East Asia Affairs Division) and was arguing as late as April 1947 that a trusteeship for Korea could be very different from the strict control by the US alone which had been worked out for one of the former Japanese-mandated islands. In the view of one of Rhee's American biographers, Borton was attempting to use Rhee's hostility as a scapegoat for the failure of a policy which was bound to fail, because it was detested by the Koreans themselves.[58]

The joint commission met several times in the first half of 1946, but failed to reach agreement on the kind of provisional government Korea needed (or they required). The separation of the country hardened until it became absolute, with a Soviet-dominated Communist dictatorship under Kim Il-sung in the North, and a highly polarized right-left conflict in the South, both elements of which, though hostile to each other, loathed the American military occupation which made the exercise of their new democracy possible. The South, far more than the North, had to deal with the massive population exchange which the end of the war had brought about. The Americans repatriated two thirds of the Japanese forces in South Korea (nearly 100,000 men) by the end of October 1945. They sent another 80,000 across within the next few weeks, and most of the 750,000 Japanese civilians, among whom were important officials in Korean industry and trade. SCAP published figures on 1 July 1949 showing that 594,812 Japanese had been evacuated from South Korea, and 322,645 from North Korea, of whom 293,968 had been withdrawn through the South.[59] By April 1946 only the Japanese Aid Societies (*Nihonjin Sewakai*), those Japanese undergoing a prison sentence, and Japanese married to Koreans, remained behind.

But Koreans returned from parts of Asia to which they had gone under the aegis of the Japanese armies. 1,500,000 came back from Japan itself, and 150,000 from China, and Korean refugees from the North – giving the lie to favourable reports of the Russian occupation – numbered 838,263. By the end of August 1946 the population of South Korea was over 19,000,000. Small wonder that there was bitter resentment against the Americans for insisting that clause 4 of General Order No. 1, declaring that the rights of property should be respected, included Japanese property. Hodge made this clear to the Government-General on 11 September, and Arnold said the same to the head of the Japanese Aid Society in Seoul on 16 September.[60] This decision meant that Koreans were not allowed simply to take over Japanese installations and property. When they protested, Arnold told them, 'This is Korean property, but we are protecting it from damage, and it will be transferred to Korea before long.' Special procedures were laid down for the buying and selling of Japanese property (on 25 September 1945);[61] all Japanese military and naval installations became the property of the USA and all dealings in them were forbidden.[62] Later in 1945 the disposal of property without previous authorization was forbidden by the occupation forces. These various regulations irritated the Koreans, particularly those who had become owners of Japanese houses. There were 35,000 of these in Seoul alone, and the Koreans who had acquired them found that they had to pay the price to the Military Government, which was the lawful owner of the property. None of this helped Hodge's public relations.

Not all Japanese were repatriated, of course. Both zones continued to hold on to a number of technicians. They were reasonably well paid in North Korea, where their monthly salary was 4,500 to 6,000 yen, at a time when the chairman of the North Korean Provisional People's Committee himself was receiving 4,000 yen a month, and bureau chiefs 1,500 yen.[63] On the other hand their families in Japan wanted them back, and a complaint was made at a Geneva prisoner-of-war conference in September 1953 that North Korea still held 2,061 Japanese. Even by the end of 1963 there were still over 400, in spite of pleas throughout the 1950s by the Japanese Red Cross to the Korean Red Cross for details of missing people. South Korea still held 330 Japanese in 1960. Of course, some must have become the casualties of later events. When the Korean War broke out in July 1950 negotiations were still going on in the South about Japanese held in the North. On 30 July 1950 the Americans bombed Pyongyang, where some Japanese were held in the city gaol. Harmless visitors also ran appalling risks at that time. Just before hostilities broke out, employees of a Japanese firm, Katō & Company, had gone to South Korea at the request of the Ministry of International Trade and Industry (*Tsūsanshō*) to discuss the export of rice. Among them were two officials of the firm, Kimura Sengō and Hatada Yoshio, who were left behind in Seoul. When the North Korean forces entered the southern capital they were arrested. A French journalist belonging to the Agence France-Presse, M. Chanteloup, was arrested at the same time, and gave an account of what occurred.

On the evening of 13 July (1950), Mr Kimura joined the group which was being taken from Seoul into North Korea. Another Japanese, Mr Hatada, taller and tougher-looking than Mr Kimura, climbed into the wagon just before we started. We formed a little group of foreigners in one corner of the wagon, four Frenchmen, a German, a man who was half-Japanese and half-English, and the two Japanese. In the station at Pyongyang, the two Japanese were separated from the rest of us. I don't know what happened to our Japanese friends after that. [64]

Nor does anyone else. M. Chanteloup was taken to Mampo, and in the spring of 1953 he was sent home via Manchuria and Soviet

Russia, but the fate of the two Japanese is still unknown. There were no Japanese in North Korean hands when the colonel in command of the American forces entered Pyongyang later and freed political prisoners. Apart from Koreans, there was only a single Dutchman in the gaol.[65]

Many of the Japanese troops who were removed from Korea into camps in Manchuria or the Soviet Union also failed to return. 66,000 Japanese in North Korea were sent to Russia. They were the victims of curious blandishments, in some cases. Fishermen were recruited to go on fishing expeditions, under the promise that they would be in southern Karafuto where the population was ninety-five per cent Japanese, and that they would be shipped to Japan when the fishing season was over. It later turned out that the destination was not Karafuto, but Kamchatka. Morita's account of their life in Kamchatka is by no means all gloomy; dances were organized for them, films were shown, and they could listen to the wireless quite freely, though they could not receive Japanese stations and so had no news from home.[66] Most of them had returned to Japan via Korea by the end of 1949, save for half a dozen or so whose families were notified, by 1961, that they had married Russian women and were living peacefully in Pechagorsk.

Others were told, as they boarded ships in North Korean harbours, that they were making for Japan. Colonel Ōgi's experience is typical. He was in the 34th Army, and when the news came that they were to leave their camp for the port of Hungnam they did not know what to believe. It was the end of October 1945 and the Russian officer who accompanied them said the ship would go north through the Sea of Japan to avoid mines. They would make for the Tsugaru Straits, then go down the Pacific coast of Japan to Tokyo Bay. Before embarking, all the officers' swords were wrapped in a bundle and loaded on board, then, just before the ship left, the interpreter, Matsumura, heard one of the political commissars say, 'As soon as they are embarked, the Japanese troops are transferred to the control of Soviet Ministry of the Interior.' There was a Japanese staff officer, Kobayashi close by, sheltering from the icy wind in the lee of a vast mountain of luggage, and Matsumura told him what he had heard. Kobayashi thought it odd, since if they were being returned to Japan they would be under the Foreign Ministry. When he conferred with others on board, the true meaning was not long in striking them: they were for a Siberian tour this time.

Halfway through the night of 28 October they left the harbour, and when the sun began to appear it was slightly aft, and to starboard. On the afternoon of the 30th, an island came into view on the starboard side, ahead of the ship. 'That's Sado,' someone said (an island just off the west coast of Japan). When they heard that, some of the men thought they had in fact reached Japan, and began to weep. But as they approached the shore, it was not Sado, but the island at the entrance to the Bay of Vladivostok. The ship stopped at the harbour mouth and made frequent signals to shore. A boat came up, passed on orders, and returned. The ship moved out of the harbour mouth and turned south. In the afternoon of 31 October they entered the harbour of Poset, in the Maritime Province of Siberia.[67]

In their Siberian exile, many thousands of Japanese paid dearly for the domination their country had exercised over Korea in the previous three and a half decades. And its liberators, having sliced the country in two, faced each other with growing suspicion over the line of partition they had created. From being a mathematical concept, that line became a grim political reality, and the two opposing régimes which had been planted in North and South were, within five years, at war.

CHAPTER TWO

MANCHURIA

i *Forces in Presence*

The Allies estimated Japan's total ground forces in the summer of 1945 at around 4,500,000 men, together with puppet forces, of vastly inferior military value, of another 1,500,000.[1] These figures included 650,000 men in Manchuria, 225,000 in Korea, and 325,000 in north China. At the meeting in Potsdam on 24 July 1945 which received these estimates, the Russian Chief of Staff, General Antonov, claimed that the Japanese in Manchuria had thirty divisions (including twenty infantry divisions and two tank divisions) together with twenty divisions of local Manchurian troops, making a total of fifty divisions on what would be the Russian front when she entered the war in the Far East.

In reply, General Marshall, the US Chief of Staff, noted that Japanese forces had been concentrating upon Japan itself. Kyushu had been reinforced against the possibility of an American landing. Two divisions from Manchuria had gone there. Two divisions had been moved out of Korea back to Japan. Japanese troops which had concentrated in the Kuriles as the result of a deception by the US forces had begun to move out, and a division of these troops had recently been identified in Kyushu. Antonov pointed out that the Russian front in the Far East would be at the end of a single railway line, which forbade a rapid build-up. It was vital to prevent the Japanese reinforcing their Manchurian front from China. It was estimated that they could bring ten divisions from China and seven from Japan. Marshall answered that mining by B-29s and American submarine action had reduced Japanese communications with the mainland through Korea, so there was little likelihood of any Japanese troop movements between Japan and Manchuria. Japan's operational shipping had been reduced from seven or eight million tons at the time of Pearl Harbor to about 1,250,000 tons. Air attacks on rail communications in China, and harassment by Chinese guerrillas, would prevent more than a trickle of troops from China reaching Manchuria.

While they were conferring, Japanese intelligence was gauging the strength of the Russians against Manchuria. From observation points constituted by the Japanese consulates at Chita and along the Trans-Siberian Railway, the Japanese knew that troops were being despatched from the European front at the rate of twenty trains a day. They estimated the number of Soviet troops in the Far East to be 1,600,000 men, 6,500 planes, and 4,500 armoured vehicles.[2] Both armies in the Far East had been subjected to similar pressures. The Soviet forces had sent some of their best divisions to Europe after the German onslaught of June 1941. By the end of 1942, only 750,000 men remained, and this figure remained static until the end of 1944. Then a build-up began, and during the spring and summer of 1945 the Russians transferred nearly forty divisions to the Far East until they were more than 1,500,000 strong, eighty divisions spread over three fronts with around 5,000 tanks and nearly 5,000 combat aircraft.[3]

To the outside world, the Soviets inflated the strength of the Japanese Kwantung Army, for obvious reasons. It had made its presence felt in occasional frontier skirmishes with the Russians for many years, and in some large-scale battles; 178 Soviet vessels had been detained in Asian waters since 1941, although there had been a moratorium on actions hostile to the USSR until late in 1944. But the Kwantung Army had been bled white to reinforce other fronts under assault from the Americans. Eleven divisions had left it at the beginning of 1945 for the Southern Regions, a twelfth had gone to China, a thirteenth to reinforce Taiwan. The Japanese desperately tried to maintain a façade of military power in Manchuria by retaining cadres of these divisions to form new ones with locally raised troops, but these ill-trained units had few weapons and were no substitute for the trained fighting men who had vanished southwards. They were paper divisions, and their ability to deceive the Soviet intelligence services would probably be limited. As late as 1 July 1945 the Kwantung Army had only eleven divisions. By

9 August 1945, it numbered twenty-one divisions and eleven brigades. Eight of the divisions and seven of the brigades were only activated ten days before the Russian invasion. In fact the Japanese did with the Kwantung Army precisely what the British did with the supposedly impregnable fortress of Singapore in the decades before the war: they attempted to put off a potential enemy with a myth. Once the aggressor became sufficiently determined, the myth collapsed.

But it was not only men that had left Manchuria. Support units had gone, and great quantities of material. It has been calculated that 30,000 tons of ammunition was shipped out of Manchuria to Japan in the summer of 1945 for the defence of the homeland – one third of the total stocks held by the Kwantung Army.[4] When it came to the test, the Japanese in Manchuria were outnumbered in terms of men and material of every category. The Russians put 1,500,000 men in the field, the Japanese just over a million. The Russians had five times as much artillery (26,000 guns to the Japanese 5,360), five times as many tanks (5,500 to the Japanese 1,155), and more than twice the aircraft (3,900 to Japan's 1,800). In contrast with the Russo-Japanese war of 1904, there were no naval battles, and there is little doubt that if there had been the Russians' superiority would have been quickly demonstrated: their Pacific fleet contained two Kirov class cruisers, eleven destroyers, nineteen destroyer escorts, seventy-eight submarines and over two hundred motor torpedo-boats. This fleet had 1,549 aircraft at its disposal, to which the Japanese Navy could oppose the derisory figure of 170 planes. In fact, given the Japanese withdrawal from the periphery, the number of aircraft actually in contact with the Russians in the northern seas was far less. In southern Karafuto, Japanese aircraft played no part at all in the fighting, and in the Kuriles only seven aircraft were available. They gave a good account of themselves, but in an extended conflict could have counted for almost nothing.

The Russian strategic plan was fairly commonplace. They intended to strike from the Far Eastern front, which they divided into two operational zones, the first under Marshal Meretskov, and the second under General Purkayev; and from the Trans-Baikal front under Marshal Malinovsky. Operations on these fronts were to cut northern and eastern Manchuria into fragments, while further south other units would cross Inner Mongolia and make for Peking and the sea. A new high command to control the whole offensive was devised under Marshal Vasilevsky, the former Chief of the Soviet General Staff.

Malinovsky had at his disposal half the Soviet Union's military strength in the Far East, totalling six field armies. He had also the most formidable logistic tasks. His Trans-Baikal group had to move from Mongolia over the Gobi Desert and to cross the Hsingan mountain range. The Japanese did not expect to be spared a Russian offensive from this quarter, but they never anticipated that the Russians would send such massive numbers over such terrain. In this assessment of the difficulties of terrain, they made the same mistake as the British had made in Malaya.

ii *The Russians Enter Manchuria*

The Commander-in-Chief of the Kwantung Army was Yamada Otozō. On the afternoon of 14 August General Yamada learned from the Manchurian Communications Company that it seemed likely the war would end, and that an important announcement was to be made at noon precisely on the 15th. This came as no surprise. On 9 August it had been his duty to visit the palace, in the city of Hsinking, of the Chief Executive of Japan's puppet state of Manchukuo, Henry Pu Yi, to report that the Soviet Union had declared war on Japan. The short, thin, elderly general had visited Pu Yi before, and usually spoke to him rather slowly and solemnly. On 9 August, however, Yamada was excited and nervous. As he gave a garbled account of the Russian incursions into Manchuria, and reassured Pu Yi that the Japanese were confident of victory, the air-raid warning sounded and the whole party retired to the cellars. They sat there listening to Russian bombs exploding, and Yamada took the hint. No further references to a Japanese victory were made once the all-clear sounded.

The next day, 10 August, Yamada came back to the palace with his Chief of Staff, Lieutenant-General Hata Hikosaburō, to inform the chief executive that the Japanese Army was going to withdraw to positions prepared in the mountains in the south of Manchuria, to form a redoubt on the border with Korea. The capital was to be moved to Tunghua. This did not suit Henry Pu Yi at all. He had a large household and vast property, and it would be impossible without notice to shift enough of it to establish himself at Tunghua. Two days more, he told Yamada, who agreed, with some reluctance.

Yoshioka Yasunori, the Japanese lieutenant-general who acted as attaché to the Manchukuo Imperial Household, and who was at the same time a senior staff officer of the Kwantung Army, hinted that Pu Yi would be unwise to delay. 'If your Majesty does not go,' he warned him, 'you will be the first one to be murdered by Soviet troops.' Pu Yi took the hint, and left Hsinking by train in the evening of 11 August.

On 12 August General Yamada was in the new temporary capital of Tunghua, and returned to Hsinking two days later. In the general headquarters of the Kwantung Army at noon on the following day he listened to the Imperial broadcast. But the broadcast did not deal with details and they had received no orders from Imperial General Headquarters. A staff discussion was therefore opened on the 16th to decide the fate of the Kwantung Army. This was, in fact, the last Kwantung Army conference and closed its history once and for all.

Many people were present at the conference, and many agreed that whatever happened they must leave behind in the hearts of the Japanese people a spark of the will to national reconstruction, by undertaking a war of resistance to the last man. Colonel Kusachi, the Senior Operations Staff Officer, put forward the view that since the order putting an end to the war had been issued, there was no possible course but to obey it. As far as the reconstruction of Japan was concerned, they should await later plans. Discussion of these two views went on into the night, until Lieutenant-General Hata, who was in tears by this time, declared to the assembled staff officers that no course other than that of loyalty to the Imperial command was open to them as soldiers of Japan. Those who refused to obey were traitors and rebels. Those who advocated a war of resistance to the bitter end should start by beheading those who proclaimed obedience to the Emperor. Let them try. Yamada added his own personal decision: as commander-in-chief of the Kwantung Army, he had determined to do his utmost to end the war, and he accepted the Imperial command.

At Imperial General Headquarters in Tokyo it was by no means certain that the proud and quasi-autonomous Kwantung Army would acquiesce in the surrender. As with the two other major areas of conflict, South-East Asia and the Chinese mainland, a prince of the Imperial Household was despatched from Tokyo to transmit the Imperial command in person. On 17 August Prince Takeda arrived in Hsinking as the Emperor's representative. His aircraft was escorted by four fighter planes of the 2nd Air Army under the command of Captain Kamada. Soviet aircraft were lined up on the airfield when Kamada and his fellow pilots were getting ready to return to Japan, and the latter, fearing that the Russians would take them over, blew up their own planes. The Kwantung Army received orders from Imperial General Headquarters on 16 August to cease hostile action and to negotiate local truces with the Soviet forces with a view to handing over arms.

In Hsinking on 18 August, to ensure that his orders were correctly transmitted to subordinate formations, General Yamada convened the chiefs of staff of the 1st and 3rd Area Armies, the 4th Army, and the 2nd Air Army. The Imperial decree was conveyed to them, and also the Kwantung Army's own orders for cessation of hostilities and the handing over of arms.

The truce negotiations with the Russians were carried out through the Soviet consul-general in Harbin. The Kwantung Army chief of staff was flown by Soviet aircraft to the Soviet Far Eastern headquarters in Jaliho on 19 August. There he negotiated terms with Marshal Vasilevsky, the Russian Commander-in-Chief in the Far East, on the maintenance of public order in Manchuria, the disarmament of Japanese troops, and the protection of Japanese nationals.

In the battle zones, where there was considerable confusion, the transmission of the Kwantung Army's order to cease fire and disarm was difficult and uncertain. Until the end of August, it was necessary to send out peace envoys to various units to ensure that the orders were transmitted and obeyed. The Japanese were hampered in this by the Russians themselves, who clamped down completely on the freedom of movement of the Japanese headquarters at a very early stage, as well as destroying or looting Japanese communications equipment and signal stores. As a result, the Kwantung Army found it was impossible to carry out disarmament in an orderly fashion. They could not concentrate their units or successfully exercise command over them. The Soviet forces refused to allow the Japanese to control battlefield areas, and the collection of dead and investigation of casualties missing was rendered impossible.

On 19 August Soviet envoys (colonels and below from the Trans-Baikal Area Army headquarters) arrived at the airfield at Hsinking and ordered those Japanese units which were stationed at Hsinking to be concentrated in the southern outskirts of the city, where they would be disarmed. Signals traffic was strictly forbidden. Because of this prohibition, the power of the Kwantung Army headquarters came to an abrupt end. The General Headquarters building itself was occupied by the Russian Army on 22 August and the personnel were transferred to the Japanese naval attaché's residence. They were permitted wireless contact with Tokyo from there.

The officers and men of the Kwantung Army were in a state of total shock as a result of the surrender. Nothing like it had occurred since the Japanese Army had been founded. Many of them chose to commit suicide. Lieutenant-General Nakamura, GOC 112th Division, and Colonel Yasugi, his chief of staff, took this path. So did the commander of the heavy artillery regiment at Tungning, Colonel Watanabe, and Wakamatsu, the commander of the 3rd Mobile Regiment. There were others who had no intention of surrendering, but for whom suicide was a futile gesture. They opted for escape, and considerable numbers deserted their units.

The slow reaction to the Imperial command on the part of General Yamada and the Kwantung Army staff served the Russians well. As the Japanese did nothing concrete to conform to the Imperial command to surrender – at any rate before the arrival of Prince Takeda – the Russians, to whose clear advantage it was to press on into Manchuria as far as they could before the ceasefire, hastily formed a number of airborne units from their engineer brigades and, together with a spearhead of hardened paratroops, dropped them into the cities of Mukden, Hsinking, Harbin, Kirin, and Port Arthur. Long before the main Soviet forces could reach these cities, the Russian paratroops had seized their airfields and communications centres. The main forces did not take long to arrive. The tank forces from the Trans-Baikal front, which had made the epic crossing of the Gobi Desert and the Hsingan mountain range, ran out of petrol, but the Russians promptly had the force refuelled from the air and got it on the move again. By 20 August it had reached Mukden, and two days later was in Port Arthur. It was a place with historic associations for a Russian army. Stalin unhesitatingly espoused the Czarist past in the declaration he made to the Russian people on the end of the campaign against Japan. But more than sentiment was involved. The secret protocol to the Yalta Conference Proceedings of 11 February 1945 spelled out the conditions under which Stalin was prepared to enter the war against Japan on the side of the Allies. The *status quo* in Outer Mongolia was to be preserved, i.e. its status as a country independent of China, and it was to be run as a Communist state. Those rights taken from Russia by Japan after her victory in 1905 were to be restored, i.e. southern Sakhalin and the adjacent islands were to be given to Russia, together with the Kurile Islands, the Port of Dairen was to be internationalized, and Port Arthur leased to the Russians as a base for their fleet. Since some of the territory involved in this secret deal belonged to China, Chiang Kai-shek's agreement had to be obtained before it was fully valid, but the way in which the secret protocol was phrased made it clear that Roosevelt and Churchill intended to see that Chiang did not make any difficulties. 'The heads of the three Great Powers have agreed,' it ran, 'that these claims of the Soviet Union shall be unquestionably fulfilled after Japan has been defeated.'

Russia's war booty was enormous, too. The surrender of the Kwantung Army placed in her hands a vast labour force of nearly 600,000 men, nearly all of whom were shipped off to the Soviet Union or Outer Mongolia to undertake forced labour. Repatriation did not begin until 1947. Over a period of two years 513,139 of the 594,000 prisoners the Russians had taken were returned to Japan. The material acquired was very great: nearly 1,000 planes, over 300 tanks, thousands of guns, and 300,000 rifles.* The Japanese were stated to have lost 80,000 dead, as against Russian losses of 8,000 dead and 22,000 wounded.

But military losses are only half the story. Manchuria had been settled for many years by Japanese colonists, and these civilians, who had relied utterly on the Kwantung Army, were now left defenceless in the face of the Soviet troops and the people of Manchuria, who turned on them and harassed them remorselessly. It is impossible to give a detailed account of all the Japanese colonists who died in their thousands in the summer of 1945. The story of the annihilation of the settlers of Halahei is typical of them all.

---

* Werth[5] notes a discrepancy between the figures issued at the time by a Sovinformbureau statement dated 12 September and those printed in the official Soviet war history.[6]

	Planes	Tanks	Field guns and mortars	Machine-guns	Rifles
September 1945	925	369	2,566	4,836	300,000
1961	861	600	3,704	13,000	—

The 1961 figures are said to be for the Trans-Baikal and 1st Far Eastern front alone.

iii *The Annihilation of the Settlers of Halahei*

As in the days when the Buddhist monasteries cooperated with the Tokugawa Shogunate and provided a means of thought control over the Japanese people by allowing religious registration to act as a national census, so a number of religious groups in the Japan of the 1930s allowed themselves to be manipulated by the militarist government in its plans to set up a Greater East Asia Co-prosperity Sphere.

Japan needed colonists for the vast areas of Manchuria that were offered for exploitation. Not only were Manchuria's mineral resources to be exploited as never before, but there were in addition areas of country bordering on the wild deserts of Mongolia which could, with difficulty, be cultivated. This seemed to offer some relief to Japan's pressing population problems, and groups of colonists left Japan for Manchuria. Many of them belonged to religious groups derived from Shinto sects or offshoots of the main Buddhist sects, some of them of the faith-healing variety which exerted such a powerful appeal in the devastation of post-war Japan.[7]

One of these sects was the *Ōmoto-kyō* (Religion of the Great Fundamentals), which had been formed in the nineteenth century on the basis of divine oracles supposedly transmitted to a peasant woman, Deguchi Nao, gifted with shamanistic powers. Her son-in-law, Deguchi Onisaburō, preached a mixed doctrine of anti-capitalism, anti-armaments, and anti-war, immediately after the First World War, and attracted a considerable following among the peasantry and among government officials and army officers. Deguchi was arrested in 1921 and his headquarters near Kyoto was destroyed on the grounds that he might start a rebellion against the Imperial throne.

Deguchi seems to have learned his lesson. Some years later his *Ōmoto-kyō* began to advocate cooperation with other religions of Asia, particularly Taoist and Lamaist bodies in China. Japanese militarists saw the obvious advantages of having a religious method of penetration into China and offered it their support. Deguchi repaid this by promptly becoming as chauvinistic as they were themselves and changing the name of his sect to *Kōdō-Ōmoto* (Great Fundamentals of the Imperial Way). Some Buddhists adopted a similar name for a militaristic type of Buddhism which could serve the state: they called it *Kōdō Bukkyō* (Buddhism of the Imperial Way).

There was already ample basis for a faith of this kind in the teachings of the thirteenth-century Buddhist monk Nichiren, whose aim was the regeneration of Japan as the great land of Buddhism, based on the reading of the Lotus Sutra, or Hokkekyō. Nichiren's teaching was simple and militant; it had attracted warriors in medieval Japan just as it attracted twentieth-century nationalists.

One of the modern sects which followed Nichiren was the *Butsuryū-Kō* (The Buddha-exalting Association) founded in 1857, a faith-healing cult which had a great attraction for the poor and outcasts of society. This sect claimed a membership of half a million in the 1930s, and although it had no priesthood or temples of its own, it was affiliated to the Nichiren sect and employed the Nichiren *nembutsu* or incantation: *Namu Myōhō Renge-kyō* (Homage to the Sutra of the Lotus of the Wonderful Law). It was the perfect religion for settlers in a new land, simple in its demands and promising good here and now, not merely in a future state.

One village founded by members of the sect was Halahei, on the railway line between Hsingan and Arshan in western Manchuria. It was built as a frontier outpost, a group of hamlets set among villages of the Manchurian population, with its own Japanese school. To the west the Gobi Desert stretched for hundreds of miles into Mongolia.

By the summer of 1945, the tiny administrative body of the settlers' corps – the *Kaitaku-dan*, as they were called – was in no doubt that if war ever came to their remote little colony, they would be on their own.* They had overheard staff officers of the Kwantung Army roundly declare that there could be no question of defending each and every frontier zone, and they knew this made good sense: if the Soviet armies invaded Manchuria, the Kwantung Army would fall back into Central Manchuria behind the natural defence barrier of the great Hsingan mountain range, until the enemy was fully extended, and defeat them in the Central Manchurian plain, if they ever managed to cross the desert and the passes through the Hsingan.

There were no Japanese Army units in Halahei itself. About thirty

* My account is based on the narrative of one of the few survivors, Mr Iijima Shirō, head of the Honjō Village.[8] Iijima's wife and two children were killed by native villagers. He escaped, and returned to Japan in 1946, where he married the widow of another settler who had also lost her family at the time of the Russian invasion.

miles away in Hsingan there was a *Kempei* detachment and a detachment of the intelligence organization that the Japanese euphemistically termed 'Special Duties' (*'Tokumu Kikan'*). Otherwise Halahei's defence consisted of Mongol troops of the Manchukuo National Army. If war came, Soviet tanks were three hours away.

The settlement learned of the Soviet declaration of war on the morning of 10 August. The following day, before dawn, they heard the sound of big guns to the west, in the area of Wuyukou. Later a Soviet aircraft flew over, turned once or twice in the sky above them,

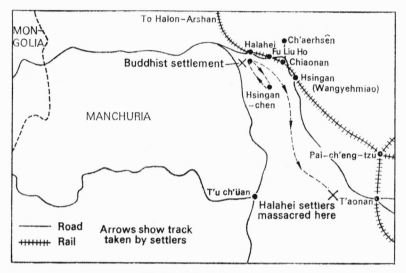

NORTH-WEST MANCHURIA

and then made for Hsingan (later Wangyehmiao). The settlers, who had not been too disturbed by the first news, since they had great confidence in the Kwantung Army, now began to feel tense and ill at ease, as the sound of guns moved nearer. They had no telephone communication with any other settlement or army unit, and the only source of news was the train which passed through daily; but no train had come through since the previous day.

Just before noon, an engine whistle drew Kakubo Akira out of the settlement office close to the Halahei railway station. The train was coming in from Halon-Arshan, and to Kakubo's amazement it was crawling with people – even the engine was covered with them. He could obtain no coherent account of what was happening from the people hanging on, and the train did not stop, but merely slackened speed as it passed through the station, then sped on.

But they were not left entirely without news. Before the train gathered speed, an auxiliary police lieutenant, Satō, whom Kakubo recognized as a police officer from Hsingan-chen, got down from the engine and came over to him. 'What are you taking your time for, Kakubo? The Soviet Army will be here by this afternoon. This is the last train from Arshan. The families or army units on the frontier are all moving south. There's danger if you stay here, get moving. Go to Hsingan-chen, the police detachment there'll take care of you.' Kakubo went on horseback to the settlement head-quarters, and passed on his news. The settlement leader and deputy leader, together with the head of the primary school, assembled the staff and discussed what was to be done. There didn't seem to be much alternative. If the army had left the frontier posts, and the Russians were on their way, then the settlers should make for Hsingan-chen and the protection of the Japanese police.

There were eight villages in the settlement, and the order to move was distributed on foot or on horseback in the morning of 12 August. 'The Russians are coming! Everyone must evacuate! Take only what you can carry in a rucksack, and assemble at Yamato Village!' It was not easy to bid farewell to the pathetic few goods and chattels assembled in half a lifetime of work, and it was evening before the people began to stream out from their villages carrying children on their backs, with their possessions in rucksacks or cloth bundles. The roll-call revealed how few really fit men were left. Only 120 adult males (i.e. between fifteen and fifty-five) were present. Of the 630 people, the rest were women, children, and old men. The procession formed up and began to march off. The deputy head of Mizuta Village returned for something he had left behind and never appeared again. But they could not wait for ever, and only heard later that he had been beaten to death by rebel Koreans. The long snake-like line of refugees moved off, with the old and sick in wagons, in the direction of Hsingan-chen, sixteen miles to the south.

Not a single star showed in the sky, and heavy rain clouds were gathering as Mr Hashimoto Kenzō of Sakurada Village led them all in intoning the prayer *Namu Myōhō Renge-kyō*. They were all followers of the Lotus Sutra, attached to the Jōsen Temple in Azabu, in Tokyo, and they recited the Nichiren prayer together as they said goodbye to their village. The Sutra scroll was placed in the special portable tabernacle (*Gohonzon*). Mr Shiraishi, the primary school headmaster, carried it on his back and went to the front of the column. The women and children were in the centre, and the van and rear were reinforced by men armed with old rifles from the Russo-Japanese war. Those who had no guns carried staves and knives, because the mood of the Manchu villages through which they had to pass was by no means certain. The men had on their dirty khaki working clothes, and the women open-necked shirts and *mompe*, the baggy trousers worn by Japanese working women.

In the darkness the sound of scuffing shoes mingled with the screech of wheels and the cries of children asking for milk, and of mothers scolding them. The rain began to pour, the wind lashed it across them, and their plodding movement gradually turned the dark Mongolian plain into a sea of mud. On and on they went, unaware that their mother country, nearly two thousand miles away, had just climbed the scaffold of unconditional surrender.

They finally reached Hsingan-chen at noon on 13 August, only to find the police station empty. The Manchu villagers laughed derisively at their plight, as they sat by the roadside and attempted to dry their rain-sodden clothing. The women lit fires and prepared food. Everyone ate ravenously, for they had had nothing since they set out. When they had finished, they looked across at the staff, who were talking among themselves. Their anguish showed plainly on their faces. Abandoned by the army and the police, what lay ahead of them now? Even as they sat and ate, members of the column had been attacked by Manchus until young Japanese with rifles had driven them off. Mr Shiraishi stood up.

'We have been completely abandoned by the army and the police. As the staff of the settlement, we cannot have any confidence now in guiding you to a safe place. The alternatives seem to be to push on merely to escape the Russians, without knowing where we're going; or to commit suicide. We think you should discuss these alternatives frankly!'

There were plenty who saw the virtue of suicide. When they left Japan, they had resolved to become part of the new Manchuria. If they died there, they would become part of it for ever. They opted for returning to the settlement headquarters and committing suicide in front of the temple they had built. But this view was not unanimous. Mr Tsuchiya Wataru and Mr Sasaki Junichi from Hachijō Village said that it was hateful to throw life away in that fashion. 'As long as life goes on, we can do something which will serve our country in some way. We are sorry, but we will have to leave you.' Tsuchiya's group was about twenty people strong, and they left the main body and set off eastwards. The rest determined to return to Halahei.

When they approached the settlement, it was evident that all was not well. The settlement headquarters had already been set on fire by bandits, and houses had been looted. They were too tired to worry about this, and went to sleep in one of the neighbouring hamlets. The following morning they gathered before the house of the village head and agreed to commit suicide round the *Gohonzon*. The taking of the decision brought an extraordinary atmosphere of peace. They began to arrange their effects, to wash their clothes in order to die in more suitable garments than those they wore. They intoned the *Daimoku*, the rosary-like phrase *Namu Myōhō Renge-kyō* with its hypnotic repetition. The intoning went on as the settlers gathered round the temple for their collective suicide.

At that moment one of the young men who had been posted as sentries on the hillside came running into the village. The Manchus had told him that the Japanese Army was engaged in a fierce battle with the Russians near Hsingan. The news changed the situation totally: if the Japanese Army was indeed so close, some hope was left, and suicide was not the inevitable course it had seemed. Shiraishi conferred with other members of the settlement staff, and they decided to change the plan and to set out again towards Hsingan.

The change was too much for some of them. As the staff went round assembling the settlers from their homes, they had no reply from Mr Matsuzaki. When they broke in, they found his wife and eldest daughter lying strangled on the floor, and Matsuzaki himself about to strangle his younger daughter. They flew at him, but he got up and cut his throat with a short sword. In five or six other houses the reaction, though less violent, was not dissimilar. They could hear the intoning of the *Daimoku* and when they called out 'Hey there, inside! Assembly!' an old man came out. 'We've had enough walking backwards and forwards across Manchuria. Why should we die in the middle of some barren desert? If we are going to die, it may as well be in the house we have known. Please leave without us!'

In theory, if they moved along the line of the railway, a day would be enough to reach Hsingan; but to do this would be to risk attracting the attention of the Russians, so the settlers took a zigzag path, which increased the time involved. It also made them vulnerable to the attacks of bandits, often on horseback, who began to harass the column. They would wait until fatigue caused a gap in the line of marchers and then swoop down, firing rifles, killing indiscriminately. The settlers grew hardened to leaving their wounded behind, and to the realization that the women and children who were captured would be massacred out of hand. They lost all feeling of compassion and simply pressed on in the panic desire to escape the Soviet invasion. The strong men in the vanguard disregarded the old people who could not walk and were faint with hunger and fatigue, and the women who collapsed by the roadside and wept as the column left them behind. As it happened, their haste led them too far. They came into a Manchu village where the inhabitants treated them well and offered them cooked rice. Shiraishi asked the way to Hsingan. The Manchus looked surprised. 'You're a long way past Hsingan,' was the answer, 'and the streets of Hsingan now are full of Soviet tanks.' The Japanese Army, it was reported, was in Pai-ch'eng-tzu. The column crawled on.

From this time onward, the number of those who died or went mad steadily increased. They would fall out of the column foaming at the mouth, or smiling and cackling to themselves. The babies could not even cry, they were so hungry, their mothers' milk flowed no longer, and they put their thin fingers into their mouths and died. More than half of the children died on this march. The nights were cold, particularly in contrast with the intense midday heat, and as they lay on the grass to snatch some sleep, the nervous expectation of an enemy attack would keep them awake. Mothers put their arms round their children to warm them, and stared at the moon with hollow eyes, unable to sleep. Throughout the night the column was a palpitation of sound on the open moor, the groaning of the wounded, the sobbing of the women, and the endless monotony of the *Daimoku* recited in pathetic faith through the hours of darkness.

Ten days after Japan surrendered, though none of the column was aware of this, they came upon a small flock of sheep grazing. One of the two Manchu shepherds ran off as they came near. Understandably, for the settlers were wild with hunger. As Shiraishi asked the remaining shepherd the way to Pai-ch'eng-tzu, the rest tore into the flock with bayonets, and ate the living flesh greedily. Suddenly a cry went up: 'Soviet troops!'

A troop of Soviet cavalry, with rifles slung across their backs, was approaching. The settlers fled, leaving behind the wagon in which the old people and the wounded had been carried. The Soviet troops came nearer. One of the men in the column raised his rifle and fired. The shot hit a Russian cavalryman who fell from his horse. The rest rode off at once. For another hour the settlers walked on, in a column which was by now over half a mile long, lacking all semblance of order. Then they saw thick smoke rising from the moor behind. They thought at once it was a Soviet armoured column speeding towards them. 'Tanks! Tanks!' they cried out in terror. It was less formidable in the event, but no less terrifying in its result. Truck-loads of infantry came up to them, led by an armoured car.

Without warning the armoured car's machine gun ripped into the column, at least ten of whom fell as they sprinted away. When the sound of firing died away, a dozen soldiers climbed down from the trucks, one of them smaller than the rest. The Japanese settlers realized it was a woman, carrying a 'mandoline' or automatic rifle. The Russians opened up on the settlers, who were still lying prostrate. A boy got up and ran towards them, hurling himself at the trousers of one of the Russians, crying out 'Soldiers, forgive us, forgive us', but he was sent flying and smacked across the face with a rifle butt. To complete their task, the soldiers went round the bodies, bayoneting the adults, beating in the heads of the children with rifle butts. Iijima remembers the woman soldier very well. She was a big-bottomed woman, he recalls, with the same uniform as the men and long boots. She kicked the dead bodies, and laughed. If she noticed anyone still breathing, she turned her 'mandoline' towards them and fired a burst.

After a while the Russians left. The children who were still alive plucked and tugged unbelievingly at the blood-soaked corpses of their mothers. One of the older boys attempted to save the portable tabernacle which his brother had been carrying. He found his brother lying face upwards still holding a sword, his head split open and the brains bulging out. As he reached forward to take the *Gohonzon*, he heard the truck returning, and in a panic smeared himself with blood from his brother's face. He lay face downward. Five men got down from the truck and began to wander among the corpses. They picked up the children who were still breathing and slung them into the truck. Most of the children were in pain, all were frightened and weeping. One of the Russians blew a whistle and the truck moved off. As it gathered speed, the children turned to look at the heap of corpses, and the grass covered with blood and spilled intestines. 'Daddy!' they called out, 'Mummy! *Sayonara! Sayonara!*' ('Goodbye! Goodbye!').

Mr Takeyama was amazed to find himself still alive in the heap of corpses. He had been lying on the grass covered with the blood of his dead son and daughter, and then one of the Russian soldiers must have seen him move. He came over and thrust at him with the bayonet. Takeyama was saved by the blood of his children. It made the skin of his neck slippery and the bayonet went to one side and merely passed through the skin. He saw the truck leave with the Japanese children, and heard their voices crying '*Sayonara*' as they were borne away westward.

When it was dark, he began to go round the bodies, to see who had been killed. Halfway through his task, he noticed that one of them was still moving: it was a neighbour, Mrs Hagiwara, who came towards him. 'You're still alive, Takeyama-san, oh, that's good, that's good! I was just going to walk away from here, there's nothing more we can do, but I feel better now that someone is with me.' She moved away from the heap of corpses, and Takeyama followed some way behind. It was eight o'clock on the evening of 25 August.

Three days and nights later, without food or water, the two of them dragged themselves over the plain towards what looked like a black pool shimmering in the distance. They hastened towards it, Mrs Hagiwara helping herself along with the help of a wooden sword. They were appalled when they reached it. It was no pool, but merely row upon row of the corpses they had left behind. In the pain of their wounds, and crazed by starvation and thirst, they had come full circle. Almost all the corpses had been stripped by bandits or Manchu villagers, and as they looked they saw why they had imagined they saw a pool: the blue-green bodies were moving and swelling up, bubbling with worms.

Mr Takeyama began to recite the *Daimoku*, in memory of the dead, as he stood in that place of annihilation of the settlers of Halahei. A red flower whose name he did not know blew here and there round the pool of dead. Then he and Mrs Hagiwara turned away, across the great Mongolian plain, continuing to recite the *Daimoku: Namu Myōhō Renge-kyō . . . Namu Myōhō Renge-kyō . . . Namu Myōhō Renge-kyō . . .*

iv *The Fate of Henry Pu Yi*

Linked with the fate of the Japanese Army in Manchuria was that of the Head of State who was its creation and its puppet: the last of the Manchu Emperors, Hsüan-t'ung, later and better known as Henry Pu Yi, whose life spans every vicissitude of modern Chinese history.

In an age of great peril for monarchies, and of endless tergiversations, Henry Pu Yi none the less outstrips most candidates for the title of Vicar of Bray of Asian politics. The number of his metamorphoses is extensive: tenth and last Emperor of the Ch'ing Dynasty, political exile, Imperial puppet of the Japanese Army, Soviet captive, and finally Communist Chinese showpiece as plain Henry Pu Yi, citizen of the Chinese People's Republic. Henry reigned for four years as Emperor until 1912, when Sun Yat Sen's revolutionary movement overthrew the Ch'ing Dynasty and ushered in the Chinese republic. Henry was six years old when he was forced to abdicate the Imperial throne. By a somewhat curious arrangement, he was permitted by the new republican government to live on in Peking and was brought up surrounded by the now empty symbols of Manchu power, under the care of a young Scots civil servant and scholar, Sir Reginald Johnston. Johnston was very much taken with his own position, and had four red tablets attached to the gate of his house, listing his functions and honours: 'Companion of the Yu Ching Palace; Privileged to be Carried in a Sedan Chair with Two Bearers; Awarded the Hat Button and Robes of the First Rank; Endowed with the Right to Wear a Sable Jacket.' His aim was quite simple: he was going to turn Henry Pu Yi into an English gentleman. Once, when Henry was fifteen years old, he sent one of his eunuchs from the palace to buy him a suit of clothes. When he put them on they were much too big, and when Johnston saw him wearing them he burst into a fit of rage. 'A person who wears a ready-made suit bought in a shop is not a gentleman!' he expostulated. The name Henry was Johnston's idea too, selected from a list of names used by English monarchs.

This life of complex but pointless ceremonial came to an end in 1924. The republic of Sun Yat Sen had turned into a battleground for opposing warlords, one of whom occupied Peking, arrested the president of China and dissolved the Chinese parliament. Pu Yi found his residence an embarrassment, and asked to be sheltered in the foreign legations. There had been a brief attempt to restore Imperial rule in 1917, and Pu Yi was well aware that as long as he was alive his existence was a threat to a republican government. Johnston tried to arrange for the British Legation to receive him, but before this was done the Japanese had stepped in and offered him hospitality, which he promptly seized upon. He later moved to Tientsin, and accepted at the hands of the Japanese the headship of their new state of Manchukuo in 1932. The separation of this state from the rest of China was merely a preliminary step by staff officers of the Kwantung Army in the conquest of the whole of China, and Pu Yi was prepared to accept Japan's leadership in an attempt to renew Chinese political life, though the arrogance of the Japanese he dealt with – Doihara, Itagaki – filled him with anger.

Pu Yi became 'Chief Executive' of the new state of Manchukuo when on 28 February 1932 the All-Manchurian Assembly passed a resolution declaring the independence of this north-east corner of China. It was in theory the road to recovery of the full Imperial title; but he soon became aware that the Japanese were offering him a not very elegant façade of administrative power. Real power, he found out, was in the hands of the Director of the General Affairs Administration Bureau of the Kwantung Army. He and his Prime Minister were Chief Executive and Prime Minister in name only, the Council of State likewise. The whole thing was an elaborate political hoax.

For Henry's capital, the Japanese picked on the town of Chang-chun, the junction of the Chinese Eastern Railway and the South Manchurian Railway. The town was renamed 'Hsinking', or 'new capital'. A staff officer of the Kwantung Army, Lieutenant-Colonel (later Lieutenant-General) Yoshioka, formerly an instructor at the Military Academy in Japan, was deputed to 'advise' Pu Yi, though it soon became evident that his real role was to communicate to the young ex-Emperor the will of the Kwantung Army. 'The tours of inspection I made,' Pu Yi recalls, 'the visitors I received, the protocol I observed, my admonitions to my subjects, the toasts I proposed, and even my nods and smiles, were all under Yoshioka's direction. He decided whom I should and should not see, the meetings I should attend, the speeches I delivered – everything!'

It was Yoshioka who wrote Pu Yi's exhortation to the Manchurian provincial governors, to support Japan's holy war when Japan

invaded China in July 1937. It was likewise Yoshioka who wrote
the speech in which Pu Yi, at the time of Pearl Harbor, expressed
his wish to live or die with Japan and to smash the power of Britain
and America. Curiously enough, communication between the two
men, on a personal level, was in English. Yoshioka knew a little
Chinese, and would on occasion paint calligraphic pictures, asking Henry to contribute his share of ideograms, but he only
spoke Chinese haltingly, so English became their conversational
medium.

Henry's lack of real power was compensated for by his vigilance
in kitchen rule. He oversaw the kitchen accounts to ensure that the
Imperial Household was not being swindled, he sent agents to spy on
the cooks when they went to the market, and had his staff beaten and
tortured. Not only his staff, but even his relatives who happened to
displease him. He was superstitious, terrified of illness, and convinced
that the Japanese had poisoned one of his wives to make him take a
Japanese wife instead. Peter Fleming, then acting as correspondent
for *The Times*, found that interviewing Pu Yi consisted of listening
to a single phrase, repeated through an interpreter, in answer to every
single question. The phrase was '*Wangtao*' ('The Imperial Way') – if
this were accepted as the basis of life, then all questions would be
answered. Fleming saw the reality of the situation, in which this
'most romantic of the rulers of this world'[9] found himself:

> Disinherited from an Empire, he now finds himself the nominal head
> of a new state which once formed part of that Empire. He is the
> figurehead, owing his position to an alien and – for most of his
> fellow-countrymen – a hated race. All round him they were busy
> working out the destinies of his people, little brown men in khaki,
> little brown men in frock coats, very serious, very methodical, very
> energetic. Officially their actions are an expression of his will, officially
> he is the master. But actually he is at best no more than a privileged
> spectator... What does he feel, as he watches them at work? What
> does he feel, as he signs state papers on the dotted line and lays
> foundation stones and speaks by rote on great occasions?...[10]

Pu Yi's autobiography supplies the answers to these questions: he
alternated between moods of suspicion of all and sundry, and out-
bursts of rage at his own impotence, alleviated by his feeling that,
whatever the impression created by the high-handedness of the
Kwantung Army, there was an understanding between himself and

the Japanese Imperial House which promised a shining future for East Asia. In 1935 he made a state visit to Japan and was greeted at Yokohama by a flight of a hundred aeroplanes in the harbour. Hirohito came to the station at Tokyo to greet him personally, they inspected troops together and joined in a ceremony at the Meiji Shrine. His reception by the Imperial Household went to his head, and he returned to Manchukuo telling himself that his status there was exactly like Hirohito's in Japan. Only a month later, his nomination of his Minister of Civil Affairs, Tsang Shih-yi, as successor to the premier who wished to retire, was turned down flat by General Minami, then Commander-in-Chief of the Kwantung Army. They had chosen their own man, the Minister of Defence, Chang Ching-hui, and that was that. Some of the Japanese called him 'Your Majesty', but it was not army policy to do so. The normal term used was 'Your Excellency', as if to underline the fact that he was not carrying on the Imperial tradition.

Henry's attachment to the Japanese Imperial Household was strengthened by another visit made in 1940. That year was the 2600th anniversary of the founding of the Japanese Empire, one of particular solemnity. Symbolically, this visit subordinated the Chinese Imperial tradition to the Japanese Imperial system in no uncertain terms. He visited the great shrine of Ise, and was persuaded to bring back to Manchuria the Shinto shrine system, emphasizing allegiance to the Japanese Emperor as the heir and descendant of the Sun God. The treasures which are symbolic of Shinto worship, the mirror and the sword, were given to him by the Japanese Emperor, and on his return to Hsinking he had a 'National Foundation Shrine' built next to the palace, altered the religious laws in Manchuria and set up Shinto festivals. Other shrines were dotted over the rest of Manchuria, and a 'Bureau of Worship' established. Once a fortnight, Henry would accompany the Kwantung Army commander-in-chief to the National Foundation Shrine and make offerings in the Japanese manner.

Several years later, Henry Pu Yi was a witness at the Tokyo war crimes trials. 'When I returned from Japan with the "Shinto treasures",' he told the tribunal, 'my family wept... It was the greatest disgrace of my life.' (*'Kono koto wa watashi no isshō no naka ni oite mottomo ōki na chijoku da to omotte iru'*).[11] As an English historian, Richard Storry, has pointed out[12] scepticism was justified when Pu Yi's autobiography appeared.[13] Recalling the eight-day trial, and naïvely pleased with the fact that this was the longest period of time a witness had appeared before the tribunal, Pu Yi added,

> Today I have considerable regrets about my testimony. My difficulty was that I was in constant fear of eventual punishment in China for what I might say.
>
> Even though I did mention some of the facts regarding Japanese behaviour, I also covered up a lot of things owing to my fear and my sense of pride. I therefore did not expose everything concerning the conversation between the Japanese imperialists and myself which had commenced long before the 18 September incident. After all, what had happened after the incident was clearly the result of prior long-term connections between ourselves and the Japanese. But in order to safeguard my own position, I only spoke of how I was compelled to behave as I did and how I suffered at the hands of the Japanese.[14]

That he was aware of the pain his statement on the Shinto treasures must have caused the Japanese is made clear in the same book:

> On several occasions during the trial, I became excited and once spoke most impulsively about being forced to worship the ancestral Shinto Gods of Japan in Manchukuo. A Japanese attorney rebutted me with the remark that the way I attacked the Japanese Emperor's ancestors seemed quite incompatible with my own Oriental traditions of virtue. 'I never compelled them to treat my own ancestors as if they were theirs,' I shouted back.
>
> My reply caused laughter in the courtroom. But even so I still felt angry and thus when I came to the death of my wife Tan Yu-ling (*he had suspected the Japanese of poisoning her*), I turned my suspicions into established facts. 'Even she was murdered by the Japanese,' I said.[15]

Pu Yi's testimony at the Tokyo trials cannot be taken entirely at its face value. He was at the time a prisoner of the Russians and due to be returned to them once his evidence was concluded. But whatever his motives for speaking as he did, there is no doubt that the Japanese listening to him were shocked and dismayed at his reference to the Shinto treasures. From the Japanese point of view, the gift of the Imperial treasures from the hands of the Japanese Emperor himself was the supreme honour. No symbolism could be more direct. No other country, whatever its role in Japan's plans for Asia, had been invited to share in such a direct way in Japan's national being. That sharing was implicit in the gift. The acceptance of the treasures and the building of Shinto shrines in Manchuria to house them was an earnest not merely of a transient political union but of a religious act, in which the last Manchu Emperor expressed a form of allegiance to the Japanese Empire in terms of its mythological roots, the Sun Goddess Amaterasu Ōmikami. 'Whoever looks upon the mirror, looks on me,' the Sun Goddess had said to her grandson Ninigi-no-mikoto, handing over the sacred mirror. This legend was amplified by the transmission of the treasures to Pu Yi. It bound him to the Japanese past.

No wonder that his family wept when he returned to Hsinking. It must have seemed to them that the representative of the Middle Kingdom, the land of the Confucian ethic and the mystical Tao, was, in the person of its last emperor, betraying itself into the hands of a chauvinist animism of a grossly unsophisticated kind. Whatever may have been its values for a simple agricultural people in their early struggles with an ungrateful earth, Shinto had been transformed into a militaristic nationalist cult under the government of the Emperor Meiji.

The harsh reality of war ultimately penetrated even the thick screen of sycophancy and bullying aggression imposed on Pu Yi by the Kwantung Army. He was shocked when the former victor of Singapore, General Yamashita, came to bid him farewell in the summer of 1945. Henry remembered how proud and arrogant Yamashita had been when he arrived in Manchukuo to take over the military command, fresh from his triumph in Malaya. Now, about to return to South-East Asia to take up a combat command once more, he wept openly as he took his leave. 'This is the last time I shall see Your Excellency,' he wept, 'I shall never come back again.' The impression made by Yamashita's conviction was reinforced when Pu Yi watched the young *kamikaze* pilots and suicide tank-destroyers leave for the front. As he read out the farewell speech of good wishes which Yoshioka had drafted for him, he could see the coming defeat of Japan in the ash-grey colour of their faces, and the tears which rolled down their cheeks. He feared for himself. However much he hated the Japanese dominance over him and the new state, Japan's fall would bring him down too.

When the Soviet invasion of Manchuria started on 9 August 1945, the commander-in-chief of the Kwantung Army and his chief of staff came to the palace to report the Soviet declaration of war. Henry Pu

Yi was, naturally enough, shocked into a state of alarm by the Soviet invasion. He began to sleep in his daytime clothes, ready to decamp at a moment's notice, decreed martial law in the palace, and never went anywhere without a pistol in his pocket.

On 10 August Yamada and his chief of staff came to the palace again. There was no confidence in victory now. The Japanese Army was going to withdraw to a previously planned redoubt in southern Manchuria, and he was to move to Tunghua. But there could be no surer way of alienating a ruler from his people than for the ruler to leave the capital and avoid the dangers of war. This view was urged upon him by his Premier, Chang Ching-hui, who said there was no question of Henry leaving Hsinking, even though the city was in an uproar with the preparations being made for street fighting. In spite of Chang's protests, the Japanese Army's insistence prevailed, and Henry decided he would have to move to Tunghua.

Tojima, his Japanese escort, waited for him in the palace, in the room next to the Emperor's. He was impatient, because he knew how little time there was to transfer the whole apparatus of government to Tunghua. Suddenly, he noticed that the light had gone out in Henry's room. Tojima had a premonition that something dreadful was about to take place, but he remained silent and did not dare to knock on the door. Finally, he ventured to call out, 'It will soon be time to leave', and a long sobbing sound came from the room. When he heard Tojima call out, Pu Yi switched on the light again and told him to come in. 'We must take the mirror,' he said.

The mirror was brought into Pu Yi's living quarters from the National Foundation Shrine close by. It was wrapped in yellow and white silk. Tojima went back to Pu Yi's room, and heard him whispering, 'I want to go to Japan. Japan is the only place I can live.'[16] With great reverence Tojima put the mirror, wrapped as it was, in a bag. It was very heavy, and his hands trembled with the weight, and also with the thought of what he was carrying. Yoshioka insisted that if anyone passed by the sacred vessels they were to be compelled to make a ninety-degree bow. Hashimoto Toranosuke, who was both a Kwantung Army staff officer and the President of the Bureau of Worship, took the bundle, and carried it to the first car which was waiting outside the palace. Henry got into the second. As he left the palace grounds, he turned to look through the rear window. The National Foundation Shrine was already in flames.[17]

What happened to the sacred treasures is far from clear. There should have been three: a sacred jewel, a sword, and a mirror. Henry never received the jewel, he said in his Tokyo testimony, and when asked why simply replied 'I don't know.' Documents written by members of the Aisin-Gioro, his family clan, who were prisoners with him in Communist China, and wrote their own accounts of their impressions of him, show that the treasures must have been transferred from the car at Hsinking to the train, because they recalled Pu Yi on the way to Talitzu walking up and down in his compartment and giving a ninety-degree bow to the treasures and to the picture of the Japanese Emperor's mother which he had brought with him.[18]

The historian Umemoto says the mirror was in Tojima's possession in September 1945. Tojima was in a prisoner-of-war camp in Mamling (Hsinking) and died on his return to Japan in 1947. Since the future of the Japanese Emperor and the Imperial system was not clear at that time, Umemoto supposes that Tojima buried the sacred treasures to prevent them being profaned.[19]

The original plan had been to travel via Mukden, but to avoid air raids the train was re-routed through Kirin and Meihokou. Japanese military vehicles were everywhere, and at Meihokou the commander-in-chief came aboard. The Japanese Army was winning, he told Pu Yi, any number of Russian tanks and aircraft had been destroyed. To give this the lie, Pu Yi had merely to look into the station at Kirin to see the Japanese civilian refugees, women and children, begging to be allowed to board the train, screaming and shouting as it drew out. On 13 August the train reached Talitzu, a mining town in the mountains. Two days later, Yoshioka broke the news of the surrender to him. 'The American Government,' he added, 'has given guarantees for the safety and position of Your Majesty.' Both he and Pu Yi went down on their knees to thank heaven for protecting the Japanese Imperial crown. Then Yoshioka told Pu Yi that the Kwantung Army had been in touch with Tokyo about his future, and that it had been decided to send him to Japan.

He was not, it appeared, to be accompanied by his Prime Minister, Chang Ching-hui, or the Director of the General Affairs Bureau of the Manchurian State Council, Takebe Rokuzō, who was a Japanese. They were to return to Hsinking, to make contact with whoever was to set up the future régime in Manchuria. As soon as Chang had returned to the capital without his Imperial master he got in touch with Chiang Kai-shek by radio. He proclaimed that he had set up a

Committee for the Preservation of Public Order, and that he would receive the troops of the Kuomintang. Chang's intentions were clear enough to Pu Yi when he reflected on them later: he must have hoped he would be accepted as a representative of Chiang Kai-shek's Republic of China in time to have a new official status with which to greet the advancing Soviet armies. They were not impressed. When they reached Hsinking they bundled Chang and the rest of his ministers into an aircraft and flew them off to Siberia.

The day after the Japanese surrender, Yoshioka told Pu Yi that transport had been arranged for the next day. The first stage would be in a small aircraft, so Pu Yi chose his companions with care: his brother, two brothers-in-law, three nephews, a doctor, and a body servant. One of his wives wept as she asked him what would happen to her. He assured her that she would reach Japan too, by train and boat if necessary – they would be united again in three days at the most.

The plane took off, and landed at Mukden at eleven o'clock on the morning of 17 August. Pu Yi and his entourage got out and walked to the airport buildings. They sat down to wait for the larger aircraft that was supposed to take them to Japan. As they waited, they heard the sound not of one, but of many aircraft approaching the field. Soviet planes swooped down on Mukden, and Soviet troops poured out of them, sub-machine guns at the ready. In a matter of minutes, the airport – and Pu Yi with it – was in their hands.* The following day he was put on board a Soviet plane and flown to the town of Chita in Siberia, there to begin an exile of five years before he was handed over to the Chinese Communists, for endless sessions of brainwashing, and a final existence as a citizen of the People's Republic.

---

* Pu Yi's abdication, and the dissolution of the state of Manchukuo, were proclaimed on 18 August 1945 in Talitzu, according to Umemoto, who puts Pu Yi's arrival at Mukden in the evening of 19 August.[20]

Hattori says that it was the wish of the Japanese Emperor that Henry Pu Yi should return to Japan, and Umezu, the Chief of Staff, arranged that he should fly via Mukden. He was taken by Soviet airborne troops while stopping at Mukden airfield on 16 August.[21]

A different timetable again is given in H. L. Boorman, et al., *Biographical Dictionary of Republican China*, Vol. III, Columbia University Press, 1970.

CHAPTER THREE

CHINA

i *Peace Feelers between Chungking and Tokyo*

In July 1945 Major-General Imai Takeo, Deputy Chief of Staff of the Japanese Expeditionary Force in China, paid a visit to the enemy. This was less abnormal than it might seem. The Japanese invasion of China had been brutal, China's economy had been ruined, and her citizens massacred, but the Japanese never despaired of making significant sections of Chinese political opinion acquiesce in what they were doing. In their view, they were rousing China from the lethal slumber into which she had fallen in the nineteenth century, a slumber which had enabled the Western powers to exploit her. Only the Japanese had had the strength to resist Europe, and if they could unite with China, then Asia as a whole would be able to stand against the oppressors from the West. In spite of the savagery of Japan's military methods of achieving this union, neither side, therefore, wished to close the door completely on the other; though the Japanese Prime Minister, Prince Konoye Fumimaro, came very near to that when he announced in January 1938 that he would end all contact with Chiang Kai-shek's Nationalist Government and attempt to establish a new régime in China which would treat with Japan. Bleak as this policy of 'not recognizing Chiang as an equal protagonist' (*'aite ni sezu'*) may have seemed, it did have a positive result: the President of the Executive Yuan* of Chiang's Nationalist Government, and Chiang's chief rival within the Kuomintang, went over to the Japanese. Wang Ching-wei's motives are still a matter for debate among historians,[1] but, to prevent the total devastation of

* Roughly equivalent to Prime Minister.

China, he had formed in 1940 a reorganized national government in Nanking. Backed by the prestige of his years as an intimate friend of China's great revolutionary leader, Sun Yat Sen, Wang was an *aite* (protagonist) the Japanese could deal with. In fact they had dealings not only with him, but also with Chiang and any number of his generals, throughout the period of hostilities. They formed a number of secret organizations, or *kikan*, the sole purpose of which was to set up liaison with elements in Chiang's capital, Chungking, or Wang's capital, Nanking, which would cooperate with the Japanese and bring the China Incident to an end.

There were many such contacts, and many go-betweens. There is, for instance, the case of General Lung Yun, the Governor of Yunnan Province, who was in correspondence with the Japanese throughout the war. Lung Yun was a Lolo tribesman, a typical Chinese warlord of the old-fashioned variety, who was loyal to Chiang Kai-shek, but on his own terms,[2] since in Yunnan he sat astride Chiang's lines of communication with the outside world.* The immense American effort to build the Ledo Road in order to bring war supplies into China finally culminated in the vast convoy carrying 105-mm and 75-mm guns into the city of Kunming on 4 February 1945, and Lung Yun was there to greet them, in an atmosphere of wild cheering and exploding fireworks. That same night Lung Yun gave a banquet for the American engineers. The occasion was graced by the American opera star, Lily Pons, and her husband, the musician André Kostelanetz. They might have been a little perturbed had they known that their Chinese host was in regular correspondence with General Okamura Yasuji, the Japanese Commander-in-Chief.[3] Lung Yun's adaptability was considerable. He later became a member of the Revolutionary Military Committee of the People's Republic of China and vice-chairman of its National Defence Committee.[4] The Communists finally got rid of him in 1958. He died in 1962.[5]

One intermediary between the Japanese and Chinese was Dr John Leighton Stuart, later US Ambassador to China. Stuart was president

---

* 'His relations with Chiang Kai-shek were such' writes Barbara Tuchman, 'that on an occasion of political crisis when Lung Yun was needed in Chungking, he did not go until Madame (Chiang) had arrived in Yunnanfu to remain as a hostage during his absence.' (Barbara W. Tuchman, *Sand Against the Wind. Stilwell and the American Experience in China*, Macmillan, London, 1970, p. 316.) For a very idiosyncratic view of what life was like for Americans in the guerrilla zones, cf. C. Rand, 'That was the war. Rip Van Winkle and Fu Manchu.' *The New Yorker*, 19 April 1947, pp. 62–9.

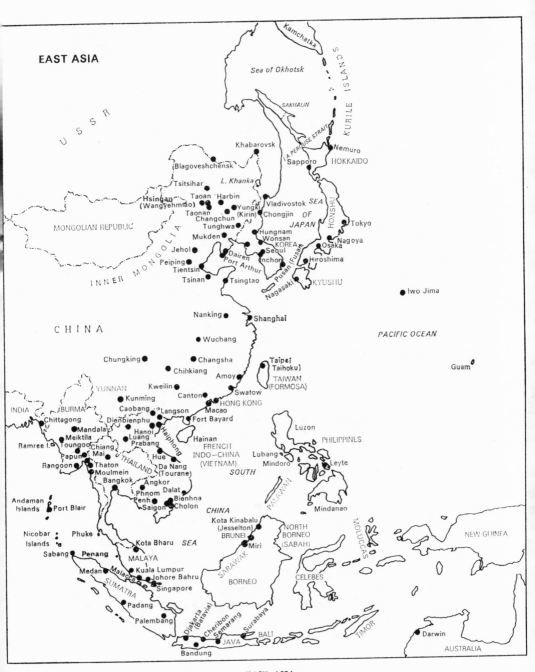

EAST ASIA

of the Yenching University in Peking, and had spent most of his life in China, where his parents were missionaries. On one occasion he acted as go-between for groups of influential Japanese and Chiang Kai-shek. He was on terms of close personal friendship with Chiang and also with President Roosevelt, and he had a great friend in Peking who was an acquaintance of the Japanese Prince Higashikuni.[6] In 1938, Stuart had travelled from Peking to Hankow, at that time the seat of Chiang's government, with the authorization of the Japanese Army in China, to sound out Chiang on the terms upon which he would make peace. Both the American Ambassador to China, Johnson, and the Secretary of State, Cordell Hull, were anxious that Stuart's mission should be seen as a private one. Cordell Hull wired to Johnson that he was to let it be known in Chinese Government circles that Stuart's mediation in no way involved the approval of the US government. Not that Stuart need have worried on that score. He had sufficient authority to bypass the State Department by writing directly to the President. As far as the Japanese were concerned, he was on friendly terms with General Tada, of the Japanese North China Army; and in 1941 he had conversations in Peking with Counsellor Tsuchida of the Japanese Embassy, and General Morioka, of the Asia Affairs Board, both of whom were anxious that approaches be made to Chiang Kai-shek. In February 1941 Stuart was approached by Lieutenant-General Itagaki Seishirō, then chief of staff of the Japanese Army in Central China, who had just attended a military conference in Nanking. Eighteen Japanese commanders in China had been at that conference, he said, and they had declared unanimously that they wanted to end the conflict and recognize Chiang, even if that implied withdrawing all Japanese troops south of the Great Wall. Itagaki also suggested that the Japanese would accept American mediation for this purpose, and told Stuart that one of the commanders at the conference was about to leave for Tokyo to put forward the views of the army in China.

Lockhart, the US Consul-General in Shanghai, who forwarded Stuart's views to the State Department, added that an American missionary in Nanking, Dr M. S. Bateson, had heard from Japanese sources views which tended to confirm what Stuart had said. Stuart was approached by Tsuchida a few months later (April 1941) as he was going to Chungking, and asked if America would mediate between Japan and China. Stuart replied that America would only do so if requested by both parties, and that China would only discuss peace if Japan would withdraw her troops. The initiative lay squarely with Japan. Though his opinion was, like that of certain highly placed Chinese in the summer of 1941, that Japan might sue for peace within a year, Stuart emphasized the 'value of courteous firmness and resoluteness in dealing with Japanese'.*

There can be little doubt that some of Stuart's contacts were even more highly placed than officers like Tada and Itagaki. And he reported them even when his own interpretations of their trends meant adopting a harsher view than his role as mediator might have implied. Within days of a Japanese Imperial conference on the situation in China held in September 1941, Stuart was informed that the discussion favoured 'opposing arrogant American interference and maintaining traditional honour at any cost'.† He even quoted to Butrick in some detail the views of Hiranuma,‡ who had loudly proclaimed that the bravery of Japanese troops had been proved in the four years of war with China and that the navy would be equally courageous if called upon to act in the Pacific. When one general asked him what his solution of the China Incident would be, Hiranuma was said to have replied, 'End the war in China as soon as possible.' After which there was a confused silence and the Emperor closed the conference.

When war against the United States broke out in December 1941, Dr Stuart, like other American nationals in Peking, was interned by the Japanese. He was the subject of a vigorous complaint made through the protecting power (Switzerland) that he had been prevented from corresponding with his relatives;[7] but no further reference is made to peace manoeuvres through him in the American documents. On the other hand, the Japanese Foreign Ministry volume on the end of the war, *Shūsen shiroku*, notes briefly that Prince Higashikuni had thought of using Dr Stuart:

A certain acquaintance of mine in Peking knew the head of the Yenching University at that time, a Dr Stuart, the US Ambassador in China (*a reference to the time of writing*)... Stuart was a Harvard alumnus and friendly with President Roosevelt and very much in the confidence of Chiang Kai-shek over a long period... I supported this

* Butrick, Counsellor of Embassy in China, Peking, to Hull, 21 August 1941 in *For. Rel. US*, 1941, IV, p. 390.
† Butrick in Peking to Hull, 19 September 1941, ibid., p. 462.
‡ Japanese Home Minister and formerly Prime Minister.

very much and encouraged it, speaking to Koiso, the Prime Minister, to obtain concrete results from it . . . the Prime Minister signified his agreement but . . . in the meanwhile the Cabinet resigned *en masse* and the problem was not raised again.[8]

Leighton Stuart's efforts on behalf of Chiang Kai-shek, culminating in the period when he was US Ambassador to China, earned him the hostility of Mao Tse-tung, who described him as a 'symbol of the complete defeat of the US policy of aggression'. The envoy of a United States which had determined to turn China into a US colony, Leighton Stuart stayed long enough in China, Mao declared, to see the total defeat of that policy. When he saw the victorious Communist forces marching into Nanking, 'he was left out in the cold, "standing all alone, body and shadow comforting each other". There was nothing more for him to do, and he had to take to the road, his briefcase under his arm.'[9]

The former Japanese Foreign Minister, Tōgō, also had ideas for using Stuart as a go-between. After the collapse of Germany he discussed peace possibilities with the War Minister, General Anami, for whom the prime issue was China, and who hoped to bring about a separate peace with Chungking by withdrawing Japanese troops from South China and ending hostilities there. They both agreed it would be difficult to do this through the Nanking Government, and Tōgō declared there was no possibility of severing China's connections with America; but there was no objection to the army attempting a ceasefire on a local regional basis.

Two Japanese, Nakayama Masaru and Wakabayashi, suggested to Tōgō in July 1945 that Stuart might be used in an attempt to conclude peace between Japan and China. Counsellor Kawagoe, Under-Secretary Tajiri (who had already been involved, with Foreign Minister Matsuoka, in approaches to Chiang through intermediaries in Hong Kong in 1940) and the Bureau Chief Sugiwara were deputed by Tōgō to study this question. Tōgō then discussed it with General Anami, and Umezu, Chief of the General Staff. They decided it was worth going ahead with the project, and Kawai, a counsellor from the Greater East Asia Ministry, was sent to North China as a matter of great urgency.

As with so many of these China peace ventures, the end of the war came without any news being received from Kawai. Not that it would have made much difference. When Kawai returned to Japan, he reported that once in Peking he had found that Japanese Army authorities in China lacked any keenness to go ahead with his mission, and so the opportunity was lost.[10]

A group round Prince Konoye made a similar attempt. A number of influential Japanese, who called themselves the '1945 Club' ('*Itsuyukai*') worked for peace between Japan and China from 1941 to 1945. Their choice of title was apparently meant to suggest that peace would be achieved by 1945, but their efforts seem to have made no progress at all towards that aim.[11] Konoye's young brother, Baron Miyakawa, left Japan secretly for Shanghai in September 1944, supposedly at the behest of the Emperor himself, to begin manoeuvres for peace. He contacted Mr Ho Shih-chen, who ran the International Affairs Institute in Shanghai. Ho had been principal of Shanghai Independent Academy and though he appeared to have become a political colleague of Wang Ching-wei, the institute was in fact a front organization for a Chungking intelligence service. Through Ho, Miyakawa conveyed the Emperor's wishes to Chungking, and made several journeys between Japan and China in March 1945, but nothing seems to have been achieved by them.[12]

Colonel (later Major-General) Imai Takeo acted as intermediary between Prince Konoye and Wang Ching-wei when Wang defected from the Kuomintang Government and came over to the Japanese, travelling via Hanoi in French Indo-China. The basis of the peace negotiations was Konoye's statement of his 'three principles', given in a press conference in Tokyo on 22 December 1938, once Imai had told him Wang was prepared to collaborate. The three principles were neighbourly friendliness, a common front against Communism, and economic cooperation. The statement had been agreed with Wang beforehand, and he was to use it as evidence to his colleagues in China that Japan had undergone a change of heart since the invasion of China and was genuinely prepared to talk peace. Konoye failed to go any further than vague generalities, and refused to commit himself to anything like a withdrawal of Japanese troops from China south of the Great Wall, without which peace was impossible.[13] It soon became evident that Wang was far from being an easily pliable collaborator and was going to be a thorn in the flesh of the Japanese. But Imai was not committed to working through Wang alone. He mounted what was termed the *Kiri Kōsaku* (Operation Paulownia)* to explore the possibilities of a direct approach to

* A not unusual type of Japanese code-name.

Chungking. Even when Wang Ching-wei formed his new government in March 1940, the Japanese refrained from recognizing it immediately, so as not to hamper such possible contacts with Chiang Kai-shek.

Operation Paulownia began in November 1939. A Japanese colonel, Suzuki, on an intelligence mission in Hong-Kong, met a man who claimed to have the highest contacts in Nationalist China. He said he was Sung Tzu-liang, the youngest brother of T. V. Soong and Madame Chiang Kai-shek. Madame Chiang's sister was married to H. H. Kung and lived in Hong-Kong, and whenever Madame Chiang visited the city for medical treatment there were family get-togethers in the Kung house. The possibility of using such a gathering was dangled before Suzuki, and he contacted Imai. Disguised as a Japanese civilian, Mr Satō of the South Manchuria Railway, Imai came to Hong-Kong in February 1940. He was never really certain that the person he talked to, sometimes in Hong-Kong, sometimes in Macao, *was* Sung Tzu-liang, but some of the others who attended the conversations were definitely genuine Chungking officials: they included General Chao-lin and the Chief Secretary to the National Defence Council, Chang Yu-san. After every meeting, the Japanese learned, the little group of Chinese conferred together by themselves and sent off a plane to Chungking with a report on the latest state of play.

Through Operation Paulownia the Japanese learned what Chiang felt about the Japanese dealings with his rival Wang. He was never going to treat with Wang. And if Japan wanted peace, there was no question of her keeping her troops in North China. Nor could there be any recognition of Japan's puppet régime in Manchukuo, or at any rate Chiang was not prepared to broach that problem yet. But so eager was Japan to reach a solid conclusion with him that the Japanese Army insisted on a postponement of the inauguration of the rival régime in Nanking until they had Chiang's answer about recognition. No reply came, and the inauguration finally took place. The Japanese continued with their efforts throughout 1940, and they even got as far as discussing a ceasefire between both sides in August. A meeting between Chiang and General Itagaki was to take place at Changsha. But Chiang insisted that Japan should not continue to urge upon him the recognition of Manchukuo; such a recognition might precipitate China into civil war. Itagaki was adamant on this point, and saw no point in talking to Chiang. They intended to hold on to Manchukuo, and that meant insisting on its recognition.

In September 1940 the Japanese decided to bring Operation Paulownia to an end. It seems that the person who claimed to be Sung Tzu-liang was in fact simply a Chinese who looked like him. The Japanese who acted as interpreter for Operation Paulownia, Sakata Masamori, spotted him in a Shanghai prison camp in 1945. His real name was Tseng Kuang, and he was a member of the *Fuhsing She*, or 'Blue Shirts', the Kuomintang's secret right-wing organization. He had worked under the orders of General Tai Li, the head of Chiang's secret service.* Imai later learned that Chiang and Tai Li had countenanced the talks, and had great hopes from them, but Chiang decided to withdraw when word of what was going on leaked to the public.[14]

The Japanese did not limit their China peace activities entirely to Wang or Chiang Kai-shek. In April 1945 it was decided in Tokyo to make a tentative approach to the Chinese Communists. This was not in order to make peace in China itself, but to strengthen Japan's hand in dealing with Soviet Russia. Assuming links existed between the Chinese Communists and the Russians, and wishing to use the Russians as mediators in ending the war, it seemed logical for the Japanese Imperial General Headquarters to explore the possibilities of courting Mao Tse-tung. If they were successful, it would also ensure that the Russians did not enter the war against them on the side of the Allies. The theory failed to convince the Japanese Army leaders in China, and the plan was not proceeded with,[15] though agents were sent into Central and North China with instructions to make for Yenan.[16] It is hardly surprising that the army in China was unwilling to cooperate in this venture. Okamura Yasuji, the Commander-in-Chief, who succeeded Hata Shunroku, was uncompromisingly anti-Communist and later figured in Mao Tse-tung's list of war criminals issued in Yenan in August 1945. He became Chiang Kai-shek's 'secret military adviser' after the surrender, according to the editor of Mao's works, and planned the Kuomintang's attacks on Communist areas.[17] In gratitude, Chiang lifted war crimes charges from him in January 1949 and he was able to return to Japan.

* This was a network of agents said to be a hundred thousand strong, known under the euphemism of 'Chinese Central Investigation and Statistics Bureau'.

ii *The Miao Pin Project*

Dissension among the Japanese leaders also brought to an end the Miao Pin project. Miao Pin had been a political bureau chief of China's National Revolutionary Army at the time of the Kuomintang's Northern Expedition (1926) and was later appointed to the party's central executive committee. He was given the post of head of the People's Political Office in Kiangsu Province, but was expelled for corruption by the provincial governor, Chen Kuo-fu. Fearing investigation by the C.C. Society,* Miao Pin escaped to Japan. Once Japan and China were at war, Miao Pin worked for Wang Ching-wei and held various offices in the Nanking Government, becoming deputy head of the Legislative Yuan and then of the Examination Yuan. But he was never trusted by his colleagues, who regarded him as unprincipled. He began to find his situation unsatisfactory, and decided to leave Nanking for Shanghai, where he secretly made contact with Chungking, voicing his criticisms of the Nanking régime and hinting at the desirability of establishing direct peace between Japan and China. He had already made contact with the Japanese, and had met Colonel Imai in June 1939.[18] But Miao's real role was reserved for the later war years.

In 1944, after the destruction of the Saipan garrison, the Japanese cabinet resigned and Tōjō's ministry was replaced by one headed by the retired general Koiso Kuniaki. Koiso was obsessed by the idea of a separate peace with Chiang Kai-shek, and the 'Chungking project', which was to achieve this, was set up by the Supreme Council for the Direction of the War. Miao Pin became the centre of this project. He had come to Koiso's notice through Ogata Taketora, the chief of the Premier's intelligence bureau, who had been introduced to Miao by an *Asahi Shimbun* journalist, Tamura Masaku.[19] Miao submitted to Koiso a plan for negotiations between China and Japan, in which he claimed that Chiang's real attitude to Japan had been misunderstood. He did not desire Japan's total defeat, because that would leave China open to Communist subversion on the one hand and fragmentation between Britain and the USA on the other. If a means could be found of saving China's 'face', there was a hope of achieving peace before Japan's situation became utterly hopeless.

* One of Chiang Kai-shek's intelligence organizations, which was founded by Chen Li-Fu and Chen Kuo-fu, and fathered Tai Li's 'Statistics Bureau'.

Koiso was very taken by this memorandum and decided to summon Miao to Tokyo to discuss an approach to Chiang through him. His cabinet colleagues were decidedly cool, so the invitation was informal. Koiso had already been warned by Imai that Miao Pin was unreliable.[20] Imai had returned to Japan with ambassador Tani Masano in December 1944 and discussed Miao with Koiso at that time, but Koiso was determined to go ahead with his scheme. The Foreign Minister, Shigemitsu, was outspokenly hostile. Any liaison with the Chungking Government, he declared, must be achieved on the basis of agreement with Wang Ching-wei whose fate was inextricably linked with that of Japan. But Koiso knew some Chinese history and had his own views on China. He thought China could not be governed as one whole. Japan's role was to divide China into a number of governable areas. These views were put forward in a December meeting of the Supreme Council for the Direction of the War, and hotly opposed by Shigemitsu and the deputy chief of staff.[21]

Undaunted, Koiso despatched an old friend of his, the reserve colonel, Yamagata, who had been his contemporary at the Military Academy, to see that Miao came to Tokyo. Miao Pin arrived on 16 March 1945, and put a set of propositions to Ogata. He had obtained the consent of Chiang to the propositions, he said. They were as follows:

> The Japanese Government should immediately dissolve the Nanking Government and set up Chiang's secret representatives in Nanking in their place, since they represented the choice of the people of China. If this were agreed, a proclamation would be issued announcing the return to Nanking of the Kuomintang Government. For their part, the Japanese would withdraw their troops and announce the end of hostilities.

Koiso thought the plan workable, and put it to the Supreme Council on 21 March 1945. Opposition in the Council was forceful. What would happen, Koiso was asked, if the Nanking Government were dissolved, and then negotiations with Chiang proved fruitless? It would clearly be impossible to revert to the original situation. This meant entrusting the fate of the Japanese Army in China, ultimately, to the judgement of Miao Pin. Neither Army, Navy nor Foreign Minister was prepared to do this.

It may seem curious that Koiso should have pursued his policy in the teeth of such powerful opposition. But one must realize that he was not the only highly placed person in Tokyo who believed that negotiations through Miao Pin were a perfectly feasible way of achieving peace with the Chungking Government. The Emperor's uncle, Prince Higashikuni, was in favour of peace with China, but extremely cautious about the Miao Pin project – until he met him. Afterwards, his views changed. Miao Pin had made it known on the night of his arrival in Tokyo that he wished to see Higashikuni, so the prince agreed that he should visit him the following day. Before Miao could put any views to him, Higashikuni cut in with a question. There were three things he wanted to know.

Miao Pin: What kind of things?

Higashikuni: First, in Chungking do they or do they not accept the Emperor of Japan?*

Miao Pin: Yes, they do.

Higashikuni: Second, why should they make peace with Japan?

Miao Pin: China has never hoped for the destruction of Japan. Even for China's own defence, the existence of Japan is essential. We want Japan to make peace with America before she is ruined. Japan is China's bulwark, and if peace can be achieved now, it will be possible to prevent an invasion by Soviet Russia.

Higashikuni: You were invited by Premier Koiso, why did you wish to see me first?

Miao Pin: There is no one in Japan in whom I can have confidence. If I look for someone to trust, there is only the Emperor. But it is impossible for me to meet him directly, so I thought I would try and transmit my views without interference, through Your Imperial Highness.[22]

Unlike Colonel Imai and Foreign Minister Shigemitsu, Higashikuni formed a very favourable impression of Miao Pin. He did not strike him as the kind of man who delighted in devious methods, but as someone you could meet and discuss things with quite frankly.†

* Not, of course, as a ruler of China. Higashikuni used the verb *mitomeru* (to recognize, acknowledge, accept), and he was presumably doing what many peace negotiators did: ensuring that the conditions for peace included maintaining the Emperor on the Japanese throne.

† There is a discrepancy in the dates of the meetings. Higashikuni gives the impression that Miao Pin saw him first, before he met Koiso, but his memoirs

However much he may have regretted it later, Higashikuni acted on his impressions at the time. That same evening, he told Koiso that he would cooperate totally with the Miao Pin project. He could not do anything directly, but would apply pressure from the wings. He called together Sugiyama, the Army Minister, and Umezu, the Chief of the General Staff. Sugiyama grunted an assent, though Higashikuni had to work hard to force it from him. Umezu concurred. It was understood between the three of them that when Koiso raised the matter in the Supreme Council, the two would back him. In fact, both of them must have had second thoughts.* No support was forthcoming in the council for Koiso's suggestions, and Shigemitsu made a long speech, backing it with quotations from a telegram sent by Tani, the Japanese Ambassador in Nanking, which destroyed Miao Pin's credibility as a person authorized to speak for the views of those in authority in China. The real basis of Shigemitsu's approach was partly irritation at the bypassing of conventional diplomatic channels by people who were, he felt, less aware than his staff of the true conditions inside China, and less sceptical of scoundrels. He was also eager to make it clear that, whatever the dangers in which Japan found herself, she should not proceed to a solution of her problems other than by open-handed and frank negotiations; whereas Miao Pin represented a furtive, back-alley approach which he deplored.[24]

Undeterred by his defeat in the Supreme Council, the Prime Minister saw the Emperor on 2 April 1945, and explained that he had a peace project which he wished to further, through Miao Pin. The Emperor had known for some time that Miao Pin was engaged in negotiations with the Japanese. Colonel Tsuji Masanobu had already reported to him in February 1944 on feelers that he had put out to Chiang Kai-shek, on behalf of the Emperor's brother, Prince Mikasa. Nothing had come of these overtures, but it was as a result of contact with Tsuji that Miao decided to see Prince Higashikuni in Tokyo more than a year later.[25] The Emperor decided to ask for

make the date of their meeting 27 March, whereas Imai speaks of Miao Pin meeting Koiso on 18 March and Koiso presenting a plan to the Supreme Council, based on this meeting, on 21 March. It is not unlikely that the Prince has made a slip of ten days in the date, since 16 March is given by Imai as the date on which Miao Pin reached Tokyo. This would make 17 March the date of the Higashikuni interview, and 18 March the day he met Koiso.

* Sugiyama's notes at the time are purely factual: a *curriculum vitae* of Miao Pin. No analysis of his own views.[23]

advice. Even though the next day was an important festival, *Jimmu Tennō Sai* (Festival of the Emperor Jimmu), and a holiday, the Emperor convened the Army, Navy, and Foreign Ministers at the palace. He perceived immediately that they were in complete opposition to Koiso's project, and when he saw Koiso the next day he upbraided him for proceeding with a plan which had no backing from his colleagues, and told him to send Miao Pin back to China at once.[26]

Much of the documentation on Miao Pin is from sources connected with Shigemitsu and the Japanese Foreign Ministry who were resolutely opposed to his intervention, so it is not surprising that Koiso appears to have no case at all. But he was no fool. He had intended to bypass Miao Pin if necessary, and to send Ogata to Chungking once an opening was made. On the other hand, the Emperor's open and scornful rejection of his plan filled him with despair. On 4 April he resigned.*

A worse fate awaited Miao Pin. After the war he was arrested by the very people he had claimed to represent, the Kuomintang. In the spring of 1946, Colonel Tsuji Masanobu had escaped from the British and reached his goal, Nationalist China, and was installed in Chungking.† He opened his newspaper on 22 May and learned to his horror that his old comrade in the East Asia Association, Miao Pin, with whom he had collaborated years before to bring about peace with Chiang Kai-shek, had been shot the previous day. Miao Pin was the first of a long list of collaborators to be tried and shot. He pleaded in the courtroom at Suchow that he had acted behind the scenes in an effort to bring Japan and China together. He referred to his interview with Prince Higashikuni and cited telegrams and letters from General Tai Li. But the president of the court was in no mood to listen to extenuating circumstances of what he firmly believed was treason, and curtly told Miao Pin, 'This is not a lecture hall. It is a court-room'. He then sentenced him to death, and the sentence was carried out within a week. As Tsuji saw it, Miao Pin

---

* The Emperor's *homme de confiance*, the Marquis Kido, entrusted with the task of selecting a new candidate for the post of prime minister, picked on Admiral Suzuki. It may perhaps be inferred that Kido thought the time was ripe for getting rid of Koiso and used the Miao Pin fiasco to do this. This is hinted at by Ishiwara Sōtarō: '... *kore wa Kido no yatta koto desu. Kido no saku desu.*' ('This was something Kido fixed. It was Kido's plan.')[27] This was said in reference to the Emperor's scornful rebuke to Koiso.

† See Book One, Chapter 2, Thailand (Siam).

was sacrificed to the Kuomintang desire to bow to Communist demands for the execution of 'collaborators', though the Communists did not scruple to make use of former collaborators in their own liberated areas. As some compensation for his life of conspiracy and furtive betrayals, Miao Pin went to his death with magnificent courage. Death had turned him, he wrote in the last line of a farewell poem, into 'a god of peace' ('*Ssu tso ho p'ing shên*').[28]

iii *General Imai and the Chihkiang Surrender Parley**

One by one the lines to China were put out, and one by one cut away. But Imai Takeo still had his contact in the town of Chou Hsia K'ou, the Deputy Commander-in-Chief of the 10th War Area (Anhwei-Kiangsu), General Ho Chu-kuo. The journey to see him was circuitous. American planes had to be avoided, and Japanese aircraft in the flight from Nanking to Hsuchang in Honan Province were forced to use the intervals between raids. The end of the journey was made by truck and on foot. Imai had changed into the clothes of an ordinary Chinese traveller, which was just as well, because when he arrived he found the place in an uproar. It was the anniversary day of the Marco Polo Bridge incident, and the streets were full of anti-Japanese leaflets and propaganda sheets.

Like many Chinese generals, Ho Chu-kuo was a graduate of the Japanese Military Academy, and he and Imai spent a day and night talking over the prospects of peace in China. He told Imai what the Generalissimo was thinking: there was no question of Japan being completely powerless in the post-war period; both China and Japan were needed as elements of stability in East Asia. If Japan ended the war now, while she still had power in reserve, and used China as an intermediary in negotiations with the USA and Britain, China would help. Japan's emperor system would be preserved.

It was the kind of line that many contacts from Chungking were putting out, and it was not unfamiliar to Imai. But he returned at once to Nanking and reported to the GOC, General Okamura, what were the real feelings of China's political leaders. The report was telegraphed to Imperial General Headquarters, and a detailed

* Unless references indicate otherwise, my source for this section is Imai's narrative '*Shina hakengun no kōfuku*'[29] ('The surrender of the Expeditionary Force in China'), in *Jitsuroku Taiheiyō Sensō*, vol. vii.

written account followed it. There was no reply. Remembering the situation later from a post-war vantage point, Imai observed bitterly that the central authorities in Tokyo seemed to despair of making contact with Chiang Kai-shek as a channel to Britain and the United States. Instead they spent all their efforts coaxing the Soviet Union to act for them, and fatally revealed their own weaknesses as they did so. Perhaps they were sceptical of the good will General Okamura might bring to the task of negotiating. When the end of the war was proclaimed, he was one of those overseas commanders who told Tokyo, in anguish, that he wanted to fight on. The knowledge that such men were in command overseas was one of the reasons why the Army Minister, General Anami, and (in earlier discussions) Umezu, Chief of the General Staff, and Toyoda, Chief of the Naval General Staff, had resisted the peace faction in the Foreign Ministry. They were being asked to surrender to an enemy against whom they had not been given the chance to measure themselves. Anami – and many others – thought that the army in Japan would do more than give a good account of itself on the shores of Kyushu or Tokyo Bay; it might also inflict such casualties upon an American invading force that the Allies would be compelled to reconsider their policy of finishing the war by an occupation of the Japanese home islands.

There were parts of the Japanese Empire, like Burma and the Philippines, where the Japanese had been resoundingly defeated. There were others – Malaya, Siam, Indo-China, and the East Indies – where their forces were still intact. In China itself, the *fons et origo* of Japan's war with the Western powers, the Japanese had gone over to the offensive in late 1944 to seize American air bases in the south, an offensive which had largely achieved its objectives.

The commander of this Japanese Army in China could hardly believe his ears when his staff reported to him the news about the acceptance of the Potsdam Declaration which their monitoring services had picked up. On 14 August he addressed a passionate protest in the form of a telegram to the chief of staff in Tokyo, with a copy to all overseas army commanders. They were to resist the call to peace and fight on.

> In order to preserve our national polity (*the telegram ran*), which has existed for three thousand years, since the founding of our country, and will last for ages eternal, the entire Japanese people has been transformed into a bullet of flame. They are advancing along the road which leads to the destruction of an arrogant enemy, and they are

present on Imperial soil with a strength of seven million men. On the continent of Asia the China Expeditionary Force still marches forward in good heart towards the completion of its task. In the battles that lie ahead we are confident that we shall, without fail, find life in the midst of death.

The humiliating peace terms which have been reported by foreign broadcasts are tantamount to liquidating the Japanese Empire which is now shining in all its glory, and no subject of the Empire can on any account submit to them; it is, without question, absolutely impossible for the China Expeditionary Force to carry them out. At this fateful moment of our Empire's history, our innermost thoughts must reach out to the Emperor to be heard, and we offer our respectful prayer that he will proclaim an Imperial Rescript to prosecute the war to a final conclusion.[30]

The telegram was despatched at 8.25 on the evening of 14 August and by midnight it was in the hands of the chief of staff.

Okamura's protest arrived too late to change Japan's course; it was pointed out to him that military obedience required conformity to the surrender rescript. Had he decided to start an autonomous resistance to it, he would have found his Chinese base, the city of Nanking, erupting beneath him. Wild rumours of an impending Japanese surrender, fed by clandestine listeners to Allied radio broadcasts, were spreading throughout the city. Some of Chiang Kai-shek's agents in the city jumped the gun: a certain Chou Hao set up a forward headquarters of the Chungking Army in the Central Chupei Bank and hung a huge banner outside it: 'Long live Generalissimo Chiang Kai-shek!' The puppet Nanking Government must have known its days were numbered, but it was not prepared to give up without a fight, and riots broke out between the secret agents of Chiang, who now came out into the open, and the supporters of Ch'ên Kung-po, Wang Ching-wei's friend and successor. Ch'ên had been a founding member of the Chinese Communist Party in 1921, and defected from the Kuomintang to join the Japanese puppet government in the summer of 1939. Although he succeeded Wang, the real power in the Nanking Government when the Japanese surrendered was in the hands of the mayor of Shanghai, Chou Fo-hai. Like Ch'ên an early member of the Chinese Communist Party after his education in Japan at the Kyoto Imperial University, Chou Fo-hai later left the party, joined the Kuomintang, and became an instructor at the Whampoa Military

Academy. Of all those who defected to the Nanking Government, Chou Fo-hai was the closest to those in power at Chungking. He was not only a personal friend of Chiang Kai-shek, he had also been intimately connected with General Tai Li and the 'Blue Shirt' organization. Because of these relationships, some Japanese suspected that Chou had never really severed his ties with the Kuomintang. They were right: since 1942, if not earlier, Chou had supplied information to Chungking through a network of couriers, and operated two secret radio stations, one working to General Tai Li, another to General Ku Chu-t'ung. Chou was so confident of the security of his position in Nanking that he actually mentioned these radio-sets to the Japanese later, and said that he was running them to worm information out of Chungking.[31]

Both these collaborators with the Japanese were now at risk. Supporters of the Nanking régime began to defect to Chungking on all sides. The head of the Navy Department, Jen Yuan-tao, working with Chou Hao, set up another forward headquarters for Chungking in the city of Suchow. Only the cadets of the Nanking Military School remained faithful to Ch'ên Kung-po. They dug trenches and put up barricades to defend the régime, some of them uncomfortably near Luchia Road where Imai's house was. This area became the focal point of battles between the Chiang Kai-shek and Ch'ên Kung-po factions, and the Japanese found it too dangerous to go out into the city at night. Japanese headquarters, which was still responsible for the maintenance of civil order in Nanking, told Chou Fo-hai to arrest Chou Hao and put a stop to the riots. Until a formal reoccupation of the city by Chungking forces took place, the Japanese threatened punitive measures against any Chinese who subverted their authority, or that of the Nanking régime. They disarmed Chou Hao and freed the Chinese he had arrested.

Both Chou Hao and Jen Yuan-tao were disavowed by Chiang Kai-shek's representatives when Imai negotiated with them later. But in mid-August they appeared to have enough authority in Nanking to enter banks and exact contributions from merchants. Within three days, Imai was told by Japanese businessmen, Chou and his associates had cleared several million dollars.

While these troubles were breaking out in the city, Ch'ên Chün, head of the Nanking Ministry of the Interior, in the clear expectation of imminent death, spent his time putting his diary in order. Like many such diaries of the time, it is a justification of his collaborationist policy. A graduate of Japan's Meiji University, Ch'ên had once run Chiang Kai-shek's police school and officers' academy and had set up a Japanese-style training in them to replace the hitherto current Soviet style. Ch'ên Chün could not endure the thought of being tried by his political enemy Chiang Kai-shek, and took poison. Ch'ên Kung-po, on the other hand, fled from Nanking once it was clear that the Japanese were not likely to be able to protect him in China much longer. He managed to reach Japan, and went into hiding in Kyoto. Two months later he was sent back to Nanking for trial. He was sentenced to death on 5 April 1946 and, like Miao Pin, met his death in front of a firing squad.[32]

Contact between Nanking and Chungking had been maintained – avoiding the watchful eyes of the Japanese police – by a private telegraph company in Nanking. This now came out into the open, and it was used to arrange an exact time and date for the formal surrender negotiations. On 21 August, at noon exactly (Japanese time; 10 a.m. Chungking time), a Japanese aircraft flew over Changteh, in Honan Province, where it made a rendezvous with six American fighter aircraft (P45s). The contrast, to the passengers in the Japanese plane, was striking. Their transport aircraft had been specially selected for flights by the commander-in-chief, but long use had given it a seedy appearance, bullet traces were evident on the fuselage, and it seemed slow and stolid. The American escorts which accompanied the Japanese envoys to Chihkiang, one and a half hours away, were fast and manoeuvrable. When Imai looked down, the airfield at Chihkiang looked like a tiny saucer among the mountains. There appeared to be only a single runway. But when they came lower they could see hundreds of aircraft which had been concealed from view; and as planes were continually landing and taking off in spite of a thick mist, the Japanese were very impressed by the Americans' airfield discipline and organization. As the plane taxied to a stop, hundreds of Americans and Chinese surged forward, cameras in their hands. The Japanese were searched by two Chinese Army majors and then climbed into a couple of jeeps with a jeep before and behind as a guard. They were driven to an army barracks where a new carpet had been laid and beds and fresh bedding provided. Imai judged that a whole battalion of military police must have been standing on guard.

They were allowed to rest for a while, and at four o'clock they were taken to the surrender site, about two and a half miles away, passing under a number of triumphal arches which had been decked with the flags of the USA, Great Britain, Soviet Russia, and China. The conference room was in the centre of another barracks, and crowds of Chinese and American troops had gathered to watch the Japanese go by. When they entered the conference room, they saw two tables laid out facing each other. At one of these sat Lieutenant-General Hsiao I-su, the Chinese Army's General Affairs Chief of Staff, in the centre; on either side of him were the Deputy Chief of Staff, Lieutenant-General Lêng Hsin, and the American Chief of Staff in the China war areas, Brigadier-General Butler, and their interpreter, Colonel Wang Wu.

Imai took his seat facing them at the other table with his interpreter and staff officers. He kept his sword. Around the two tables were scores of journalists from all over the world, military and government officials. It was a real piece of showmanship, thought Imai. The conference went on for an hour and whatever was said was interpreted into three languages: Japanese, Chinese, English. First, General Hsiao introduced himself with his name and rank, and then presented his staff. Then he asked Imai for Okamura's warrant of authority. Imai was not the bearer of any order from Imperial General Headquarters and the Japanese had come, as they thought, to a meeting before a truce, so he had brought no warrant. The entire assembly seemed very perturbed when this was revealed, but Imai passed over a copy of the order he had received from Okamura, and Hsiao said he would accept it as a substitute. The Japanese were then handed four memoranda in which General Okamura was directed to surrender the Japanese Army in the China war areas, Taiwan and French Indo-China north of latitude 16°. His troops were to surrender to forces under the command of Generalissimo Chiang Kai-shek and his Commander-in-Chief, Ho Ying-chin. Imai pointed out that the Japanese command zones did not correspond to the surrender zones laid down by the Allies, and that General Okamura was not at present in command of the Japanese in Indo-China or in Taiwan. But he was responsible for those in the China war areas, and Imai agreed to pass on the orders for a ceasefire in those areas. He also gave details of airfields close to Nanking and Shanghai.

Brigadier-General Butler then intervened to say the US Army demanded to know the situation of US prisoners-of-war and said there was anger in the USA over ill-treatment they had received. A

Chinese major-general, Niu Hsien-ming, then handed over a further five memoranda, two of which, Imai replied, were outside the scope of his authority. One of them said: 'A representative of the Japanese Army at present in conference in Manila is reported to have said that internal order in China is not being maintained, because of discord between the Nationalists and the Communist Party. This is an insult to the Chinese nation, and must not occur again.' Imai said he did not know whether or not the representative at Manila had said this, but in any case it had no connection with the China Expeditionary Force. The other one declared: 'There is a prospect of a war of resistance starting in the Japanese Army which may not assent to a truce. An investigation is demanded into this question, and movements shall cease immediately.' Imai rejected this memorandum, pointing out that the Japanese had come to discuss terms before any order had been received from the Generalissimo, even if there *was* still a will to resist. The Chinese seemed to accept this, and arranged that a special envoy should return with the delegation and negotiate directly with General Okamura.

On 23 August, Imai had an interview with General Ho Ying-chin himself, and was thanked for his efforts. The same day he left Chihkiang and returned to Nanking, accompanied by a high-ranking Chinese air force officer and a staff officer, the advance party of the surrender negotiators. By nine at night they were landing at the Ta Hsiao airfield in Nanking.

Imai chatted for a while with his pilot, Major Matsubara. He had noticed that while everyone else at the conference had eaten voraciously – and the tables, though primitive, had been laden – Matsubara had barely touched his food. Imai asked him why.

The fact is, General (*he answered heavily*), I'm already forty-three, which is three years over the statutory period for a pilot – and I've reached the highest seniority a pilot can reach. The war's over now, this may be the last time I'll ever fly a plane. It sticks in my gut that my last flight should be such a miserable occasion. And the plane itself!

On the airfield at Chihkiang, they kept picking off the roundels as souvenirs, as if it wasn't scruffy enough already. I noticed the Americans were surprised we left it out in all weathers, and started it by swinging the propeller. We were lucky not to have fog in Chihkiang when we set off, otherwise we'd have had to postpone the flight. Whereas they can fly in any weather, in fog, at night, in any conditions

– it shamed me as a pilot to see them making comparisons. That's why I couldn't eat.

As the delegate of a defeated nation, Imai had naturally had uncomfortable feelings, but they were nothing to do with wounded professional pride. Something even deeper was involved. The two Chinese majors attached to them in the barracks had been known to him. One had been a journalist, and Imai had known him for eight years. The other was a graduate of the Japanese Military Academy. So was the interpreter, Colonel Wang Wu. In fact Imai had been the examining officer there when Wang Wu had passed in. And Major-General Niu's father and Imai had been close friends. Later in Nanking, when the full Chinese delegation arrived in September, the two majors wore badges of much higher rank, one a major-general, the other staff-colonel. They had put on insignia of a lower rank while in Chihkiang. Why was this?

Imai discovered why; it was to avoid an appearance of overawing the Japanese by a show of rank. He also discovered that General Hsiao I-su had originally arranged for the talks to take place at a round table and had prepared the conference room accordingly. His motive was simple; the Japanese were to be treated as equals, and it was to be an equal exchange of views. Just before the conference began, the Americans approached Hsiao and told him that the round table should be removed and replaced by two long tables, arranged so as to confront each other in a formal debating style. The Chinese officers who were graduates of the Japanese Military Academy were annoyed at the American lack of understanding of what was a procedure of politeness between fellow-orientals. After the conference was over they talked with the Japanese delegates about Japan, with great pleasure. There had been a great military defeat, but Japan was the country where they had spent part of their youth. The Japanese understood the Chinese attitude and appreciated it. They were in the depths of despair, in enemy territory at a moment of surrender; and then suddenly they felt the warmth of this neighbourly feeling.

The day after his return, 24 August, Imai went to visit the President, Ch'ên Kung-po. The official residence was newly opened, an elegant building with an enormous front garden, surrounded by woods. Wang Ching-wei had died when it was half finished, so Ch'ên was its first resident. When Imai arrived, Ch'ên had some of

his advisers with him, and Imai had the impression that his arrival
had interrupted a secret conversation. He told Ch'ên about the
Chihkiang conference, thanked him for his cooperation with Japan,
and told him how sorry he was that Japan's defeat would have
repercussions on those who had worked with her. Ch'ên was
unmoved. 'Don't worry about me,' he said. 'From the time I
volunteered to join the revolution, I have always been balanced on
the dividing-line between life and death. I don't think the present
time is a particularly special situation.' He said he was grateful to
Imai for his friendship and clasped his hand firmly. 'If I stay in
Nanking as things are,' he went on, 'it's going to cause difficulties
when the Chungking authorities move in. I think I should leave for
Japan.'

There was a problem here, Imai realized. Ch'ên intended to leave
the following day, 25 August. That day Lieutenant-General Lêng
Hsin was due to arrive in Nanking on behalf of the Chungking
surrender delegation; and noon of that day had been fixed as the
time-limit beyond which Japanese aircraft would not be allowed to
circulate freely. Ch'ên would somehow have to reach Japan that
morning. Imai detached Captain Ogawa of the Military Affairs
Advisory Bureau to act as escort and went to the airfield to see
Ch'ên off. There were seven passengers in all, Ch'ên himself,
Madame Ch'ên, the head of the Industrial Bureau Ch'ên Chün-hui,
the propaganda chief Lin Pai-sheng, the Inspector-General of the
Finance Bureau Ho Ping-yin, the head of the private secretariat
Chou Lung-hsiang, and a secretary Madame Mo Kuo-k'ang. Normally the departure of a head of state would have been attended with
considerable ceremony, but Ch'ên had no wish to draw attention to
himself. The only Japanese officer from the army general headquarters who assisted him was a staff officer, Ogasawara. The plane
left Nanking before dawn.

The idea was to make Japan in a single hop, but through shortage
of fuel the plane could not reach Tokyo and was forced to land in a
little airfield in the mountains, Yonago in Tottori Prefecture. They
were within an hour of the total prohibition of flights when the
Japanese Government finally took charge of them and found them a
residence in Kyoto. Just before his plane took off from the airfield
at Nanking, Ch'ên handed to Ogasawara a document, written in
pencil and addressed to Chiang Kai-shek. He asked Ogasawara to
give it to Ho Ying-chin, with the request that it be forwarded to the

Generalissimo. He wanted Chiang to know that he had not flown to Japan to avoid punishment, and that he would return when asked.*

He *was* asked. A message came on 20 September from Ho Ying-chin to say that he should return to China. On 3 October the group from Nanking, with the exception of Madame Ch'ên, was met by a Chinese plane which they boarded, Regulus-fashion, for the journey to China and a tribunal. Before his departure Ch'ên had a two-hour-long conversation on 1 October with the former premier, Prince Konoye. Konoye was visiting Kyoto for a Buddhist ceremony in memory of his dead mother. It must have been a curious conversation, between two men who had been, with diminishing degrees of effectiveness, leaders of two great countries of Asia. One of them was soon to die by his own hand, the other to be executed by political enemies. Ch'ên was very brave in the courtroom. In the gaol at Suchow he had written a defence, several thousand words long, of the eight years of his stewardship, and of the policy of his friend Wang Ching-wei. When the president of the court handed down the death sentence, Ch'ên gave a slight smile and thanked him for allowing him to voice his opinions. With great composure, he said that he had no intention whatever of appealing against the sentence.

The month of September 1945 was a time of triumph for the Kuomintang Government; though the triumph was short lived. On the 6th – it was a glorious day – Ho Ying-chin descended upon Nanking in a cloud of fighter aircraft, and made his entry into the city. Three days later, he took the formal surrender of all the Japanese forces in China. The site had been carefully chosen: it was the auditorium of the Central Military Academy at Whampoa, of which Chiang Kai-shek had been the first president in 1924. He was accompanied by the Commander-in-Chief of the Chinese Navy, Admiral Chen Shao-kuan, and a galaxy of high-ranking generals. In the visitors' gallery were officers of the Allied armies and senior Chinese Government officials. On the Japanese side, accompanying General Okamura, was the Commander-in-Chief of the China Area Fleet, Vice-Admiral Fukuda Ryōzō, with representatives from the Japanese armies in Taiwan and Indo-China.

They surrendered to Ho all their land and sea forces in China (excluding Manchuria), in Taiwan, and in Indo-China north of the

* Some accounts say the letter was never delivered. Cf. G. E. Bunker, *The Peace Conspiracy. Wang Ching-wei and the China War, 1937–1941*, Harvard UP, 1972.

16th parallel, a total of 1,313,240 men.*[33] At least, that was the theory. But they had reckoned without a very important figure, who intended to have his say.

iv *Mao Tse-tung and Chiang Kai-shek*

The surrender of Japan was only one stage in the conflict that was being waged in China. Although the Potsdam conference had declared that all Japanese forces in China were to surrender to Chiang Kai-shek, the head of the National Government of China, the Communists had no intention of allowing the Kuomintang troops to march into areas they held and to seize weapons which might make all the difference between victory and defeat in the months – or years – ahead.

In a speech delivered to cadres in Yenan two days before the surrender was officially announced, Mao Tse-tung unambiguously attributed Japan's final defeat to the intervention of the Soviet Union: 'The decisive factor for Japan's surrender is the entry of the Soviet Union into the war. A million Red Army troops are entering China's North-east; their force is irresistible.'[34]

Nor had the Kuomintang forces done much to resist Japanese aggression in the previous eight years. During what Mao termed 'the War of Resistance', the credit for keeping the Japanese in check belonged to the Communist forces, who had liberated vast tracts of territory and pinned down the bulk of the invading armies and their puppet troops. He did not want civil war, Mao went on, but it was clear Chiang Kai-shek did, in order to re-establish the old rule of

* There is some discrepancy with the figures provided later by the official (Nationalist) Chinese war historians:

	Japanese	Koreans	Taiwanese
Forces	1,240,471	14,428	44,118
Civilians	779,874	50,935	
	2,020,345	65,363	44,118

Of this total of 2,129,826, by 20 April 1946, 1,464,303 men had been moved to the ports. The shipment of the remainder (665,523 men) was not completed until the end of June. The Chinese were responsible for internal transportation, the Americans for shipping, and 85 LSTs, one Liberty ship, and some Japanese vessels were used. Hsu Long-hsuen, Chang Ming-kai, *History of the Sino-Japanese War*, Chung Wu Publ. Co., Taipei, Taiwan, 1971, p. 571.

landlords and bourgeoisie. In which case, Mao's policy was to retaliate. Chiang had said (1 March 1945) that the Communist Party could only participate in a Chinese government if it gave up its army, but Mao had no intention of doing this. He derived his mandate from the people.

Likewise there was no question of allowing Chiang to pluck the fruits of the victory over the Japanese: 'To whom should the fruits of victory in the War of Resistance belong? It is very obvious. Take a peach tree for example. When the tree yields peaches they are the fruits of victory. Who is entitled to pick the peaches? Ask who planted and watered the tree.'[35] Chiang would grab a lot of big peaches, Mao realized: Shanghai, Nanking, Hangchow and other cities would fall into his hands, because his alliance with the US imperialists had ensured that they would. But the Communist armies, based on the rural areas which they held securely, would contest the medium-sized and small towns. The Communists were sure they could hold the rural areas and many towns in Hopei, Chahar, Jehol, Shansi, Shantung, and the northern part of Kiangsu. By linking big and small towns in a single area, and making contacts between such areas, Mao hoped to set up from three to six revolutionary bases. In terms of physical strength, they had a million troops and two million people's militia already in the liberated areas. In terms of spiritual strength, the political consciousness of the Chinese people was much further advanced than it was in the 1930s.

The only resources Chiang had were US aid and the Japanese. Colonel David D. Barrett, the head of the US Army observer group with the Communists at Yenan, said to Mao in 1944 that he should heed the advice of Patrick Hurley, the US Ambassador to Chungking, and send Communist officials to join the Kuomintang Government. Mao refused, on the grounds that such participation would hinder his freedom of action. Barrett replied that if he refused, the Americans would back Chiang Kai-shek.

If you Americans, sated with bread and sleep (*Mao answered*), want to...back Chiang Kai-shek, that's your business, and I won't interfere. What we have now is millet plus rifles, what you have is bread plus cannon. If you like to back Chiang Kai-shek, back him, back him as long as you want. But remember one thing. To whom does China belong? China definitely does not belong to Chiang Kai-shek, China belongs to the Chinese people. The day will surely come when you will find it impossible to back him any longer.[36]

He was not deceived into thinking that the atom bomb had made Japan surrender: 'If atom bombs could decide the war, then why was it necessary to ask the Soviet Union to send her troops? Why didn't Japan surrender when the two atom bombs were dropped on her and why did she surrender as soon as the Soviet Union sent her troops?'[37]

There were some Communists who believed the atom bomb was all powerful, but they were mistaken: 'These comrades show even less judgement than a British peer. There is a certain British peer called Lord Mountbatten. He said the worst possible mistake is to think that the atom bomb can decide the war.'[38] Bourgeois schools had indoctrinated these comrades, who were more backward than Mountbatten, into believing that weapons decide everything.

Communist actions had already anticipated Mao's speech. On 10 August 1945 the Communist Commander-in-Chief, Chu Teh, sent an order from his Yenan headquarters to all forces in the liberated areas:

Japan has announced her unconditional surrender (*the order ran*) and the Allies will meet to discuss measures for accepting the surrender on the basis of the Potsdam Declaration. I hereby issue the following order to all our armed forces in the Liberated Areas:

1 In accordance with the provisions of the Potsdam Declaration, any anti-Japanese armed forces in the Liberated Areas may serve notice on enemy troops and headquarters in cities and towns or along communications lines in the vicinity, requiring them to hand over all their arms to our fighting forces within a given time; when they have handed over their arms, our forces will protect their lives in accordance with our regulations on the lenient treatment of prisoners-of-war.

2 Any anti-Japanese armed forces in the Liberated Areas may serve notice on all the puppet troops and puppet government organs in the vicinity, requiring them to come over with their troops to our side before the signing of the surrender by the Japanese invaders and to wait for reorganisation and disbandment; those who fail to comply within the time allowed shall hand over all their arms.

3 All anti-Japanese forces in the Liberated Areas should resolutely wipe out all those enemy and armed puppet forces which refuse to surrender and hand over their arms.

4 Our armed forces have full authority to send their units to take over and occupy any city, town or communication line held by the enemy and the puppets, to set up military control, to maintain

order and to appoint commissioners to take charge of all administrative matters there; in case of any act of sabotage or resistance,
the culprits shall be punished as traitors.[39]

The second paragraph of Chu Teh's order is interesting. In spite of
the third paragraph's menacing tone, the Communists showed
themselves to be considerably more lenient towards the troops and
officials of the Nanking puppet government. A lack of tact towards
the puppet troops lost the Nationalists many valuable forces, in the
view of one military critic. Resentful of harsh treatment at Nationalist
hands, many of the puppet troops, taking their equipment with
them, fled to the Communists, who welcomed them with open arms.
One American observer, Colonel R. B. Rigg, estimated that at least
75,000 such troops went over to the Communists in Manchuria
between 1945 and 1946.[40]

Chu Teh's general order was followed, the next day (11 August),
by six detailed orders describing action to be taken by various
named forces in particular liberated areas. Mao Tse-tung and Chu
Teh claimed they were acting in accordance with the provisions of
the Potsdam Declaration, conveniently .passing over what that
conference had specified about the authorities to whom the Japanese
were to surrender.

The Kuomintang Central Executive Committee reacted at once,
describing Chu Teh's order as 'a presumptuous and illegal act'. Mao
replied that Chu Teh's order was precisely the resolute fulfilment of
the provision in paragraph 2 of the Potsdam Declaration, 'prosecute
the war against Japan until she ceases to resist'.[41] Chiang Kai-shek
wanted to ensure he had Japanese arms so that, with a merger
between his government and the Nanking puppet government, he
would be able to pursue his policy of anti-communism. 'To speak
plainly,' Mao added, 'in China only the anti-Japanese armed forces
of the Liberated Areas have the right to accept the surrender of the
enemy and puppet troops.'[42] Spelling it out for the world at large,
Mao went on:

We declare to all our fellow countrymen and to the people of the
whole world: the Supreme Command in Chungking cannot represent
the Chinese people and the Chinese armed forces which have really
fought Japan; the Chinese people demand the right of the anti-
Japanese armed forces of China's Liberated Areas under Commander-
in-Chief Chu Teh to send their representative directly in order to

participate in the acceptance of Japan's surrender and in the military control over Japan by the four Allied Powers and also to participate in the future peace conference.[43]

Chu Teh's order was in open defiance of the National Government of China, telegraphed Patrick Hurley, the US Ambassador in Chungking, on 12 August. Japan should be required to surrender all Japanese arms in China, including those in the hands of the puppet troops, to the National Government of China; the terms of surrender should include penal sanctions against Japan 'for any attempt to arm belligerent forces within China against the National Government.'[44]

The Communists were quick to act as well. They controlled the north bank of the Yangtse opposite Nanking, and a few hours after the Imperial broadcast at noon on 15 August a shabby-looking figure, wearing filthy clothes, and looking for all the world like a coolie, suddenly presented himself at the gates of the General Headquarters of the China Expeditionary Force. To the sentry who challenged him he answered, with great authority, that he was Chang Keh, an envoy from the New 4th Army. He demanded an interview with General Okamura, and when asked the purpose of his visit, he presented a document requiring the General Headquarters to hand over the arms of the forces under its command.

Okamura had no intention of arming the Communists, and he replied that he was to treat only with the army of the Kuomintang Government. He had no authority to negotiate with any representative of the New 4th Army. The Communist envoy was far from being a coolie. He was the same Chang Keh who had acted many years before as secretary to the Soviet Army adviser to China, Michael Borodin. Chang Keh made further approaches, and was most pertinacious, but Okamura stood firm.[45]

It might be thought that Japan profited from releasing arms to indigenous political movements in South-East Asia, but there was little temptation for her to arm the Chinese Communists; particularly since there were those in the Japanese Command in China, including Okamura himself, who were convinced they could come to an agreement with Chiang Kai-shek.

Chu Teh, for his part, intended that the US government should be fully informed of the Chinese Communist view of the situation and sent Hurley a long message for onward transmission to his government. This was forwarded on 17 August, and claimed, *inter alia*, that the Chinese Communists had liberated nearly a million square kilometres of territory and more than a hundred million people from the Japanese; that it was their troops and not those of the Kuomintang which had opposed 69 per cent of the total Japanese troops in China – excluding Manchuria – and 95 per cent of the puppet forces. The majority of the Kuomintang troops had been withdrawn to the rear to prepare for civil war. On this basis, Chu Teh insisted that his forces should be able to accept Japanese surrenders and should participate in the peace conference. He ended with a plea to America to stop supporting Chiang:

> For the sake of reducing civil war in China, the Government of the United States of America is requested to stop immediately Lend-Lease to the Kuomintang Government,* acting in the common interest of both the Chinese and American (*sic*). If the Kuomintang Government launches a nationwide civil war against the Chinese people, the danger of such a civil war has now become extremely grave, the American Government is requested not to help the Kuomintang Government.[46]

In a message drafted by J. C. Dunn, the Assistant Secretary of State, the State–War–Navy Coordinating Committee replied to Chu Teh on 22 August, rejecting his demands, and insisting that Chiang had been designated by Potsdam to accept the Japanese surrender in China. The message was to be sent over the name of General Albert Wedemeyer, in his joint capacity as commander of American forces in China and chief of staff to the Commander-in-Chief of the Chinese Army.[47]

The US government attempted to persuade the Soviet Union and Great Britain to support a statement backing Chiang Kai-shek. Great Britain agreed, with some slight changes in the wording to safeguard her interests in Hong-Kong; but the publication of the text of the Sino-Soviet treaties, signed at Moscow on 14 August, made a separate declaration by the Soviet Union superfluous, and in the event the statement was not proceeded with; especially since General MacArthur's General Order No. 1 made Chiang's position crystal-clear (at least in theory):

* Hurley had already informed Chiang that all Lend-lease would end with the surrender of Japan (Telegram to Secretary of State, 11 August 1945, *For. Rel. US* 1945, VII, p. 530).

The senior Japanese commanders and all ground, sea, air, and auxiliary forces within China (excluding Manchuria), Formosa and French Indo-China North of 16 degrees North latitude, shall surrender to Generalissimo Chiang Kai-shek.[48]

The practical details of the Kuomintang–Communist conflict over the Japanese surrender are revealed in a report from General Wedemeyer in Chungking to General Marshall on 19 August 1945. Wedemeyer felt that stopping help to Chiang would be equivalent to actively aiding the Communist cause. Key points were surrounded by organized Chinese Communist troops. If Chiang's men were not flown in – and that meant flown in by the Americans – then the Communists would occupy such areas, or at any rate prevent the Kuomintang forces from doing so. Within a few days, he added, two US sponsored armies were to be flown into the Nanking–Shanghai area, to open the port of Shanghai as soon as possible. Once sea communications through Shanghai were established, movement of troops by air and land throughout China would be expedited. He estimated the strength of the Communist forces in the areas as between fifty and eighty thousand. If the central government forces met opposition from the Communists in securing Shanghai – and American 'liaison personnel' were to support them in securing their base in order to deal with the Japanese surrender – then American forces would be 'inadvertently' helping the central government to subdue Communist forces. This kind of situation might well be repeated elsewhere.

The reason it *was* repeated elsewhere, not always successfully, is given by Liu in his *Military History of Modern China*. After the Japanese surrender, the central government's military policy reflected a suspicion not merely of the Communists – which was well founded – but of any armies which were not under the immediate control of the central authorities. As one means of parrying the declared Communist intention to receive the Japanese surrender, two of Chiang's generals, Li Tsung-jen and Pai Chung-hai, proposed that those Kuomintang armies nearest to the North China front should be sent to North China to stabilize the confused situation. Instead of doing this, Chiang had other units airlifted to North China, from points as far distant from it as Burma and Indo-China, or had them shipped by sea after a long delay. This delay gave the Communists a considerable advantage: they had an early start in setting up their own control of the area. Chiang had delayed precisely because he felt he could trust the units from Burma and Indo-China; they had been trained under his central command.[49]

Of course Mao was right in suspecting that Chiang would use the Japanese surrender for his own ends. The Japanese were helping the Kuomintang against the Communists, either by supplying military advisers* or by allowing whole units to serve under Chinese orders. Most Japanese troops in China were repatriated fairly quickly, but there were exceptions. The Japanese could always claim that they were merely maintaining order. The Communists' attempt to seize the Shantung-Hopei region was defeated by collaboration between Nationalist troops and Japanese and puppet troops, according to the American ambassador. Their move northward from that area towards Peking and Tientsin was also hindered by the Japanese, who controlled the lines of communication. In October 1945 the American consul in Tientsin reported that American marines in his area depended almost entirely on puppet government troops and the Japanese to keep order in the towns. Later still, in November, General Wedemeyer said it was impossible to disarm the Japanese because they were guarding vital lines of communication against the Communists. The Shansi warlord Yen Hsi-shan, a graduate of the Japanese Military Academy, who intended to keep both Nationalists and Communists out of his bailiwick once the war was over, employed Japanese advisers to help him. An industrialization programme was started in the province with the help of technical advisers from the Japanese company Sansei Sangyō Kabushiki Kaisha (Shansi Industrial Company). Its president turned out to be a former Kwantung Army colonel, Kōmoto Daisaku, who in 1928 had engineered the assassination of Marshal Chang Tso-lin.† Yen's son-in-law, General Wang Ching-kuo, negotiated an agreement with the commander of the 114th Division, Major-General Miura Saburō: he would not disarm the Japanese troops provided that they cooperated against the Communists.

The arrangement seemed to work very well. In the spring of 1946 Yen would inspect his troops accompanied by a Japanese general, still in full Imperial Japanese Army regalia, and the assembled soldiers

---

* This explains Colonel Tsuji's assurance that an experienced staff officer like himself would be acceptable to Chungking cf. Siam chapter.

† The assassination was intended to provoke hostilities between Chinese and Japanese forces, enabling the latter to advance beyond the Railway Zone which they then held in Manchuria.

customarily gave voice not only with 'Long Live the Republic of China' but also 'Long Live the Empire of Japan'. Eighteen months after Okamura's surrender of his troops, American observers in Taiyuan noticed that the streets of the city were still crowded with Japanese soldiers. They wore Chinese uniform now, but they were still commanded by their own officers. Yen Hsi-shan fought against the Communists in Shansi for four years. He was finally overcome in April 1949, and Japanese troops were among the very last to die for this cause. The Japanese general, Imamura Hōsaku, who was in supreme command of these troops, took poison rather than surrender himself to the Communists. Rather more resilient, Yen declared his readiness to do the same, but finally opted for retreat with Chiang Kai-shek to Taiwan, where he died in 1960.[50]

Shansi held out for years, but in Manchuria the case was hopeless from the start. One of the ablest Communist generals, Lin Piao, entered Manchuria, then under Russian occupation, with unarmed Communist troops from Shantung and North China, about 100,000 in all. There had been close on 600,000 Japanese troops in Manchuria, and the booty was considerable. The Communists were the richer by 300,000 rifles, 138,000 machine guns and 2,700 field artillery pieces.[51] Soldiers of the Manchurian puppet forces were released from captivity by the Russians and took service with Lin Piao, whose strength increased by colossal proportions: he managed to raise eight columns, seven cavalry divisions, one artillery division and three independent divisions.

v *The Surrender in Hong-Kong*

While Chiang exerted himself on the southern periphery of China, he was losing the real core of China's future, the north and the industrial areas of Manchuria. He had Kuomintang forces in Burma long after the Burmese had asked them to leave; Lu Han, his governor of Yunnan, had replaced the Japanese in northern Indo-China and was systematically looting that rich province while its former French owners stood agonizedly and impotently by; and Chiang was insisting that he or his delegates should take the surrender of the Japanese forces in Hong-Kong, in opposition to the British who were equally determined that he should not. He was so remote from practical realities as to suggest that British forces should return merely to the *island* of Hong-Kong, and that Rear-Admiral Harcourt, who was to take in British naval units to free the colony from the Japanese, should act as his delegate, since he, Chiang, was Supreme Commander of the China Theatre of which, geographically speaking, Hong-Kong was part.

He had on his side the US ambassador to China, who had received oral instructions from President Roosevelt, on his appointment to Chungking, to ensure that China's future was not harmed by returning European imperialist interests. The British attitude was that although General Order No. 1 prescribed the surrender of Japanese forces 'within China' to the Supreme Commander of the China Theatre, they refused to accept that the phrase 'within China' included Hong-Kong. Three days after the Japanese surrender, the British Prime Minister Attlee wired to President Truman that a British naval force was on its way to release Hong-Kong from the Japanese occupation. Since Japanese commanders on the spot might regard Hong-Kong as being 'within China', he requested Truman to instruct MacArthur to ensure that the Japanese local commanders surrendered to the commander of the British naval force when it arrived. It was the British view that, irrespective of the confines of an operational theatre, a sovereign power should resume its authority over occupied territory and accept the Japanese surrender there, if it had sufficient forces available.[52]

The British official history gives the quite erroneous impression that Chiang Kai-shek ultimately conceded the point.[53] 'After some negotiation,' it states, 'Chiang Kai-shek agreed on the 27th to Rear-Admiral C. H. J. Harcourt (Flag Officer 11th Aircraft Carrier Squadron, British Pacific Fleet) accepting the surrender of the Japanese forces in Hong-Kong on behalf of both the British Government and himself as Supreme Commander, China Theatre.'[54]

Truman had instructed Hurley to tell Chiang that the US government had no objection to the surrender of Hong-Kong to a British officer provided military coordination was effected with China. This emphasis on the Hong-Kong surrender as a purely military operation conflicted totally with what Chiang required. He wanted to create the impression that the British were returning only with the authorization of the President of the Chinese Republic. Chiang notified Truman on 23 August that he had told the British that he agreed to delegate his authority to a British commander, and that he was designating a Chinese and an American to participate in the surrender ceremony. These were difficult concessions, he added, but he made them in the desire to cooperate with the United States in every way possible.[55] Truman thanked him, but four days later Hurley was writing again to the State Department to say that the British had sent Chiang a verbal communication through their ambassador in Chungking that they regretted they were unable to accept Chiang's suggestion that the British commander would be acting as his delegate. Chiang told the ambassador he could not subscribe to the position the British had taken up. It was not his intention to send Chinese troops into Hong-Kong, he simply wished to fulfil his duties as Supreme Commander of the China Theatre.[56] Trying to make the best of a *fait accompli*, he affirmed that since the British Government had nominated Rear-Admiral Harcourt to accept the Japanese surrender, he did in fact delegate his authority to him, as from 27 August.

The British in Hong-Kong had in fact done a little anticipating on their own. Mr F. C. Gimson, who was Colonial Secretary in Hong-Kong at the time of the Japanese invasion, had been interned with 2,500 European civilians in Stanley Camp.* During the years of internment, Gimson had organized committees of officials to be ready to take over the administration again one day. When rumours began to circulate round Hong-Kong that the Japanese were about to surrender, Gimson approached the camp commandant and asked to be told the truth. On 16 August he was told that the Emperor had been pleased to accept the Potsdam terms, but the Japanese protested when Gimson ordered out of the camp those officials whom he thought essential to the administration of Hong-Kong. This protest, as the historian of British military administration in the Far East points out, was 'brushed aside as an impertinence',[57] and an emergency administration was set up.

There had been some looting, though not on the scale on which it took place in Rangoon and Singapore, between the surrender and the arrival of the first Allied troops. Nevertheless some of Gimson's emergency provisions strike one as somewhat bizarre. He had little in the way of a police force, though there were around 250 British members of the pre-war force in Stanley Camp. To increase the

---

* Not immediately, but in March 1942. The Japanese had at first retained Gimson in office, together with the attorney-general, the head of the Sanitation Department, and employees of the Hong-Kong and Shanghai Bank, to work under their direction. Some civilians were kept at work for the Japanese until their internment in July 1942.[58]

number of law-enforcers, a group of seven hundred Chinese gang-sters were given police duties on the old and hallowed principle of 'set a thief to catch a thief'. These gangsters had run gambling dens under the Japanese administration but Gimson put a stop to that. He paid them as policemen instead, and gave them a guarantee that when the British Administration resumed its full peacetime authority they would be allowed to make themselves scarce without interference.[59]

The reoccupation of Hong-Kong took place on 30 August with very few incidents. British aircraft attacked three Japanese suicide boats which were seen moving out of a bay on Lamma Island, and then bombed every other boat lying in the bay, presumably *pour encourager les autres*. The few snipers in the town were soon disposed of; but there were cases of groups of Chinese attacking Japanese. On 1 September Admiral Harcourt proclaimed a military administration, Mr Gimson being appointed Lieutenant-Governor. The town wore an air of seediness and neglect after the years of military occupation, and in Mountbatten's view starvation was imminent. The colony did not form part of his command, but he was responsible for its equip-ment and food supplies, and for providing ground and air forces for its protection; so he ordered a rice ship, which had been loading up at Rangoon at the time of the Japanese surrender, to leave for Hong-Kong at once.[60]

There were certainly shortages of food and fuel, but the situation was not serious. On 16 September 1945 the Japanese forces officially surrendered, under Major-General Okada and Vice-Admiral Fujita. The ceremony took place at Government House and Admiral Bruce Fraser, the Commander-in-Chief of the British Pacific Fleet, who had arrived in his flagship, the *Duke of York*, two days before, looked on as the Japanese handed their swords to Harcourt.

As Hong-Kong rapidly came back to life – civil government was re-established on 1 May 1946 – the Chinese mainland began to move towards civil war. Chiang's American chief of staff had begged Washington to move seven American divisions into Manchuria to prevent the Communists getting a foothold there once the Russians withdrew; but his request was not granted. He did, however, manage to have Nationalist troops airlifted to Shanghai, Peking, and Nanking, which for a time consolidated the Kuomintang control of these crucial areas.

An effort to stave off civil war was made by Chiang in late August 1945. He invited Mao Tse-tung to come to Chungking on 28

August, accompanied by Chou En-lai and General Wang Jo-fei, the senior Communist representative in Chungking. Intensive talks between the chiefs and their representatives took place for a period of twenty days, at the end of which an agreed communiqué was issued. This stressed that the Chinese people wished to avoid civil war, that Chiang Kai-shek was recognized as the national leader, and that a statute of equality was proclaimed between the various parties which had fought against Japan. A conference was to be called to establish a truly representative national government of all parties, the power of arrest and punishment was to be confined to official judicial and police organs, and 'patriotic' political prisoners were to be released. The help of the US Ambassador, Patrick Hurley, was specifically acknowledged.[61] There were two points on which agreement was not reached, or deferred until a later date: the Communists' claim to appoint governors and mayors in certain provinces, and the number of Communist divisions to figure in the new Chinese Army. The Communists claimed that forty-eight Communist divisions should be accepted. The Kuomintang said post-war plans envisaged a total strength of eighty to a hundred divisions, so that the Communists were asking for half, or more, of the whole. They proposed instead a Communist strength of twenty divisions: a suggestion which the Communists accepted.* Mao left for Yenan by plane on 11 October, leaving Chou En-lai and Wang Jo-fei behind in Chungking to negotiate details.

It was not long before the Communists accused the Kuomintang of violating the agreement by attacking Communist troops. They also declared that the proposed national assembly consisted largely of government officials. American troops, it was also charged, were landing at points in North China to hold them until Chiang's forces arrived.† It is estimated that General Wedemeyer transported nearly half a million Nationalist troops to key points in east and North China to ensure that the Communists were prevented from accepting the Japanese surrender in those areas. US Marines occupied Peking, Tientsin, and other cities for the same purpose.[62] Wedemeyer made public his belief that fifty thousand Marines would need to occupy North China for a considerable period.‡ He believed the Chinese

* K.C. Wu, Minister of Information in Chungking, to Hurley, via the chargé in China, 2 October 1945.[63]

† Robertson, the chargé in China, to Secretary of State, 29 October 1945.[64]

‡ War Department press conference, 22 October 1945.[65]

Nationalists were completely unprepared for occupation of Manchuria against Communist opposition. He recommended to Chiang that his troops should attempt to hold China between the Great Wall and the Yangtse in particular, and that he should consolidate his lines of communication there before going into Manchuria. The Communists were disputing Nationalist control of communications throughout North China, and attempting to rouse Chinese and American public opinion against the retention of the US Marines. On the other hand, he was aware that inept and corrupt administration by Kuomintang officials who had newly resumed office in areas liberated from the Japanese was gaining support for the Communist cause.*

The United States had no wish to withdraw completely from China. On the other hand, it was deemed 'impracticable' to intervene militarily on a major scale to assist the Nationalists in destroying the Communists.[67] A compromise solution was inevitable: mediation was attempted between the two sides. General George Marshall, the US Army Chief of Staff, was sent on 15 December 1945 to persuade the Chinese Nationalists to convene a national conference of all major political elements in China, to effect the cessation of hostilities, and to impress upon Chiang Kai-shek that a disunited China would not be considered worthy of American aid.[68] By the summer of 1946 it was clear that Marshall's mission had failed. All he achieved was the repatriation to Japan of nearly three million Japanese troops, all of whom had to be moved by means of a dilapidated transport system, disarmed, searched, and given a medical examination. To prevent them spreading Asiatic cholera in Japan, segregation camps were set up at the ports, where American units supervised inoculations. Otherwise, the American attempt to shore up the Kuomintang régime came to an end with the outbreak of the civil war that had been predicted for so long. Not all the Japanese had been repatriated, and some of them, including the ubiquitous Colonel Tsuji, served Chiang Kai-shek. But neither Japanese strategic advice nor American logistical aid saved the Kuomintang. On 8 December 1949 the Nationalist Government moved to the island of Taiwan, and a new phase in China's history began.

* Wedemeyer to General Marshall, US Army Chief of Staff, Chungking, 14 November 1945.[66]

EPILOGUE

Wars do not come to a clean end. The aftermath drags on. New situations develop, old causes produce new effects. Wrong-doing leads to retribution, retribution leads to reprisals, the chain never really breaks. So putting a line under a series of events and pretending it is a conclusion is an artistic procedure, not an historical one.

In the case of Japan, the story we have told does, in fact, lead to certain positive conclusions. For her own purposes, Japan thrust aside the hold of the European powers on East Asia. When the war was over, those powers tried to re-establish themselves, with varying degrees of coercion, and failed. The emancipation was political rather than economic. South-East Asia is still largely dependent on economic forces outside its own boundaries, even though politically its people are their own masters.

The Japanese who had committed atrocities in the campaigns were punished in some cases and went scot-free in others. Trials were held and on occasion rough justice was done. In other instances the verdict of the courts was questionable. Later jurists have queried not merely the verdict but the very basis of the International Military Tribunal of the Far East which was held in Tokyo from 3 May 1946 until judgement was rendered from 4 to 12 November 1948. Seven of the defendants were sentenced to death by hanging, sixteen to life imprisonment, one to twenty years, and one (Shigemitsu) to seven years.* Ōkawa Shūmei, secret agent of the Army General Staff in China and propagandist of a Greater East Asia, was deemed unfit to be tried, and two defendants died during the proceedings. Ōkawa achieved immortality of a kind by leaning over from his seat and smacking Tōjō's bald head with a rolled-up newspaper under the eyes of the world's cameras. There was an understandable discrepancy in the way the trial was viewed. For the Allies it was a manifestation of 'an intellectual and moral revolution which will have a profound and far-reaching influence upon the future of the

* In spite of pleas on his behalf by influential British friends such as Lord Hankey. Cf. F. S. G. Piggott, *Broken Thread*, Gale and Polden, Aldershot, 1950, pp. 382–6.

world society'.[1] For the vanquished 'this trial was a political trial. It was only victors' justice'.[2]

The Indian renegade troops who had fought against the British were tried, in the persons of three of their officers, in the Red Fort in Delhi, and the repercussions of the trial did more to help India's independence than the three years of fighting that had gone before.

The *Kempei* were brought to book in Singapore for their bestial inhumanity to the civilian internees of that city. The Double Tenth trial showed in that organization, if any proof were needed, a systematic cruelty as inhuman as that of the Gestapo.

Japan had taken around two hundred thousand prisoners. A hundred thousand of these died before rescue came. The rest returned home to pick up the threads of their lives, though it was more difficult for them than for the returning soldiers.

Japan's soldiers came home too, though the liberation armies in Asia also received their quota of Japanese deserters. Thousands of troops were kept back by the Allied armies to work as forced labour in the lands they had devastated. In Russian hands, they were spread out in camps all over Soviet Asia – some were even taken into Europe. They paid heavily for what Japan had done, and thousands of them never came back.

In South-East Asia, conditions were better, and in some cases cooperation was positively cheerful – on both sides. There were instances of ill-treatment, but it was not the savage brutality they had administered themselves. One who was ill-treated, and later became a professor in the Humanities Research Institute in the University of Kyoto, whose contact with Europe had hitherto been confined to books and works of art, and whose field of study was the art, literature, and history of the Renaissance, was brought face to face with a European reality disturbingly different from the image he had known. He came to believe that the British, in particular, were exercising upon the Japanese a deliberate policy of humiliation. He himself had been forced to kneel down while a British soldier urinated over him. The British did not work through brutalities, he thought, but through contempt. Their cold scorn for other races, the result of centuries of successful domination, was even more cruel and heart-searing than the beating which he knew the Japanese inflicted upon their prisoners.[3] But Professor Aida's reaction was perhaps idiosyncratic.

Sometimes retribution was self-inflicted. Many military leaders took the traditional *samurai* way out of an intolerable situation by committing suicide. General Anami, the War Minister, did it with a sword in the time-honoured manner. General Sugiyama, former Chief of the General Staff and former War Minister, shot himself. So did Tōjō, the wartime Prime Minister, who bungled it. American MPs found him still alive, and medical care ensured that he stood his trial. Prince Konoye took poison.

Of those who faced Allied war crimes tribunals, Homma Masaharu, accounted responsible for the death march on Bataan, was executed in 1946. Yamashita Tomoyuki, the conqueror of Singapore, was held to be guilty of crimes committed by troops under his command in the Philippines, though he claimed that at the end of the campaign his forces were so disorganized that he could not exercise control over all of them. He was hanged in February 1946. The general who lost the Burma campaign to the British, General Kimura Hyōtarō, was sentenced by the International Military Tribunal for the Far East for atrocities committed by his troops in Burma, and for his war-making role as Vice-Minister for War, and was hanged at Sugamo prison. So were several of the generals who had led Japan's invasion of the Asian mainland; Doihara Kenji, who had run Japan's intelligence service in Manchuria; Itagaki Seishirō, who had been a staff officer of the Kwantung Army, Minister of War, Chief of Staff of the China Expeditionary Force, and commander in Korea, who had surrendered to Lieutenant-General Christison in Singapore, and wept as he did so;[4] Matsui Iwane, the Commander-in-Chief in Shanghai, and victor at Nanking, who was held responsible for the atrocities committed there in December 1937; Muto Akira, chief of the Military Affairs Bureau of the War Ministry; and Tōjō himself. The trap was sprung for them all at twenty minutes past midnight on 23 December 1948. One civilian died with them, Hirota Kōki, a former Premier and Foreign Minister who was closely linked with the policy of aggression in China and who had tried desperately to make peace through the offices of the Soviet Union and its impassive ambassador, Jacob Malik, when it was far too late.

The Marquis Kido, the Emperor's confidential adviser, was sentenced to life imprisonment and released on parole in 1956. General Koiso Kuniaki, who had pointlessly negotiated with Miao Pin, was also given a life sentence, and died in prison. General Yamada Otozō, Commander-in-Chief of the Kwantung Army, was sentenced by a Russian military tribunal to twenty-five years in a labour camp in 1949, for permitting experiments to be carried out on living human beings for the purposes of bacteriological warfare.[5] Eleven others were sentenced with him to various terms ranging from two to twenty-five years. Prince Konoye's son, Konoye Fumitaka, was sentenced to twenty-five years by a Moscow tribunal for crimes against the Russians in Manchuria, and died in a Siberian prison camp in 1956.

All over the former Japanese Empire, the liberators who had become gaolers were sentenced: the railway engineers and doctors who had failed in their duty to humanity on the Siam–Burma Railway; the commanders of prisoner-of-war camps in Java, Manchuria, and Japan itself.

But there were other, stranger sentences, voluntary ones, often longer than those imposed by the victorious Allies. When the Japanese-held islands in the Pacific fell one by one to the Americans, many Japanese troops were left to die, or to survive as best they could in the jungles. Some of them never learned that Japan had surrendered and that the war was over. Some did know, and were afraid to come out of hiding. They were discovered years later, in some cases decades later.

In 1950, Japanese were found on Anatakan Island. In 1960, two (Itō Tadashi and Minagawa Bunzō) were discovered on Guam. On 24 January 1972 Sergeant Yokoi Shōichi was 'recalled to life' on Guam when two natives stumbled across his hiding place near Talorofo. He had been posted dead on 30 September 1944, but had survived the American conquest of the island with a group of ten friends. The group dwindled to three. They lived in a cave on the island. In 1964 the other two died, and for the next eight years Yokoi lived alone, eating snails and rats, and sleeping in a hole in the ground. Yokoi knew the war was over. He had learned this from a sheet of newspaper he had come across in 1946, and he had heard loudspeakers calling on stragglers to surrender. But he was sure he would be executed if he did. Until Lieutenant Onoda's surrender in the spring of 1974, Yokoi's twenty-eight years' refusal to give himself up was certainly the most spectacular of such incidents to come to light; but it is quite likely that there are other Japanese soldiers still living in isolated villages, in the Pacific islands or on the mainland of Asia, perhaps married to Polynesian, Vietnamese, or Burmese girls,* and accepted by the community.[6] Yokoi was impressed by

* If there was a chance of a deserter passing himself off as a Burmese and being able to support himself – as, say, a car mechanic or a doctor – and if it

Japan's material advances when he was flown into Haneda airport on 2 February 1972, but he had not forgotten his own traditions. One of the first things he said was that he was ashamed to come home alive, and he added, 'I have returned with the rifle I received from him' (the Emperor).[7]

A more recent and even more astounding reappearance was that of Lieutenant Onoda Hiroo,* who was brought in from the island of Lubang, off the coast of Luzon, on 10 March 1974. A graduate of the Nakano Intelligence School, Onoda had been instructed in 1945 to continue guerrilla warfare operations, and had done so for twenty-nine years, first with one or two companions, then alone. He had renewed his boots from stray pieces of rubber, made fresh clothing for himself, and had his weapons intact. The inhabitants knew there were Japanese survivors on their island, since mysterious deaths had been reported over the past two decades; but when Onoda surrendered, the President of the Philippines freely pardoned him. Onoda had been sought by members of his family, who had heard rumours that he was still alive on Lubang. But he refused to capitulate until his former commanding officer, Major Taniguchi Yoshimi, came to Lubang and read out to him the cancellation of his orders. A young Japanese drop-out, Suzuki Norio, was the instrument of Onoda's salvation. He had camped out on Lubang, displaying the Japanese flag, in the hope that the rumours of Japanese survivors would prove to be true. There can hardly have been a more polarized contrast between the new and the old Japan than the encounter between Onoda and Suzuki.

---

was possible to conceal the desertion from the British camp authorities, then the Japanese camp staff did not feel justified in preventing desertion, though its scale was infinitesimal. A case of this kind, the desertion of a medical officer named Aoyama, who declared he wanted to remain in Burma and work as a doctor, is referred to by Major-General Yamaguchi Tatsuru in a talk given to the Sittang Society in Japan and reprinted in the Society's Bulletin, *Nansō:* '"Ima da kara hanasō" ni narratte' ('On the theme "Now it can be told" '), *Nansō*, No. 34, privately printed, Tokyo, 1967. A well-known fictional account of such a desertion is Takeyama Michio's novel *Biruma no tategoto*, trans. by Howard Hibbett as *Harp of Burma*, Tuttle, Rutland and Tokyo, 1966 (filmed by Ichikawa in 1956).

* Accounts of Lt. Onoda's return, including taped interviews, and descriptions of the Nakano Intelligence School, are contained in special issues of the following periodicals: *Mainichi Gurafu*, 31 March 1974; *Shūkan Asahi*, 25 March 1974; *Sandē Mainichi*, 31 March 1974; *Shūkan Sankei*, 3 April 1974 (contains plastic recording of interview); *Bungei Shunjū*, June number, 1974.

But it would be quite wrong to end this story of Japan's capitulation on a note of retribution and expiated guilt. The end is not so simple. A Japanese civil engineer called Itō Hiroichi went out to Burma in 1954 to help build a road between Toungoo and Loikaw. The road was part of a plan to provide Burma with new sources of electric power. In the best-seller he wrote on his experience, *Toungoo Road*, he tells how, on an evening stroll through the streets of Rangoon, he was addressed by a shopkeeper with the old wartime phrase, 'Japan Master'. Coming from a Japan where feelings of defeat still lingered, he was both flattered and disturbed by this mode of address. He was glad to notice that the Burmese felt no hostility towards him, but were indebted to him, as a Japanese, a member of the nation to which, in spite of everything, they owed their independence.[8]

At its fullest extent, Japan's Empire in Asia must be one of the most short-lived in history: three and a half years. Yet its impact was very great. Either as a direct result of Japanese conquest, or in the dispositions which followed Japanese defeat, the pattern of history in Asia was irrevocably altered. Arms taken from the Japanese forces in Manchuria fed the armies of Mao Tse-tung, and enabled him to take first Manchuria and then the whole of China. The Allies' temporary divisions of Vietnam, at the 16th parallel, and of Korea, at the 38th parallel, hardened into political realities. Hesitant and belated though it was, a taste of independence was given to Burma, Vietnam, and Indonesia. Burma's wartime Prime Minister, Ba Maw, spoke of Japan being betrayed by her militarists and their racial fantasies; he said that if Japan had remained faithful to her policy of Asia for the Asians with which she began the war, nothing could have robbed her of the trust and gratitude of half of Asia. Whatever Japan's faults as a nation between 1942 and 1945, history will restore that trust and gratitude. In the long perspective, difficult and even bitter as it may be for Europeans to recognize this, the liberation of millions of people in Asia from their colonial past is Japan's lasting achievement.

REFERENCE NOTES

BOOK ONE

CHAPTER I

1 Maurice Collis, *The Journey Outward*, Faber, 1952, pp. 121–2.

2 Ba Maw, *Breakthrough in Burma: Memoirs of a Revolution 1939–1946*, Yale UP, New Haven and London, 1968, p. 78.

3 F. Tennyson Jesse, *The Story of Burma*, Macmillan, London, 1946, p. 169.

4 Cf. F. N. Trager, *Japanese and Chinese Language Sources on Burma: An Annotated Bibliography*, HRAF Press, New Haven, 1957, pp. 16, 18, 33, 45, 46, 47.

5 Ba Maw, op. cit., p. 343.

6 Ota Tsunezō, *Biruma ni okeru Nihon gunseishi no kenkyū* (Studies in the History of Japanese Military Government in Burma), Yoshikawa Kōbunkan, Tokyo, 1968, p. 567.

7 Cf. Louis Allen, 'Studies in the Japanese Occupation of South-East Asia, 1942–45 (I)', *Durham University Journal*, December 1970, pp. 1–15.

8 *Biruma Kōryaku Sakusen* (The Assault on Burma), Asagumo Shimbunsha for the Defence Agency, Tokyo, 1967, pp. 543–4.

9 Ian Morrison, *Grandfather Longlegs: The Life and Gallant Death of Major H. P. Seagrim*, Faber, London, 1947, pp. 196–7.

10 Field-Marshal Sir William Slim, *Defeat into Victory*, Cassell, London, 1956, p. 484.

11 Sawayama Yuzō, 'Hakki wo kakagete' ('Carrying the White Flag'), in *Hiroku Dai Tōa Senshi* (Secret History of the Greater East Asia War), Fuji Shobō, Tokyo, 1953, p. 370.

12 *Sittang. Mei-Go Sakusen* (The Sittang Battle, Operation Mei), Asagumo Shimbunsha for the Defence Agency, Tokyo, 1969, p. 107.

13 Cf. Slim, op. cit., pp. 516–19.

14 Ba Maw, op. cit., pp. 397–8.

15 ibid., p. 403.

16 ibid., p. 406.

17 ibid., pp. 413–14.

18 Text in Ba Maw, op. cit., pp. 389–90.

19 *Sittang. Mei-Go Sakusen*, pp. 108–9.

20 Ota Tsunezō, op. cit., Ch. VIII; L. Allen, 'Japanese Military Rule in Burma', *Modern Asian Studies*, Cambridge, III, 2, 1969, pp. 177–81; Imai Takeo, 'Ajiya dokuritsu ni hatashita meishu Nihon no kōzai' ('The Japanese Army's leadership in the achievement of Asian independence; pros and cons'), *Maru*, Tokyo, 20, 9 September 1967, pp. 212–19; Imai Takeo, *Shōwa no bōryaku* (Stratagems of the Shōwa Period), Hara Shobō, Tokyo, 1967, pp. 203–20.

21 Ba Maw, op. cit., pp. 185–6.

CHAPTER 2

1 Cf. Lennox Mills, *The New World of South-East Asia*, p. 248.
2 Sir Andrew Gilchrist, *Bangkok Top Secret*, Hutchinson, London, 1970, p. 12.
3 Cf. *For. Rel. US*, 1942, I, p. 918.
4 Cf. F. C. Jones, *Japan's New Order in East Asia*, pp. 347–9.
5 Cf. Gilchrist, op. cit., p. 23.
6 ibid., p. 19.
7 *For. Rel. US*, 1944, V, p. 1312.
8 ibid., pp. 1316–17.
9 ibid., p. 1319.
10 ibid., pp. 1319–20, letter dated 22 November 1944.
11 *For. Rel. US*, 1945, VI, p. 1241.
12 *For. Rel. US*, 1944, V, pp. 1320–1.
13 ibid., p. 1321.
14 *For. Rel. US*, 1945, VI, pp. 1243–4.
15 ibid., pp. 1246–7.
16 Gilchrist, op. cit., pp. 178–9.
17 ibid., pp. 196–7.
18 ibid., p. 197.
19 *For. Rel. US*, 1945, VI, p. 1256.
20 ibid., pp. 1260–1.
21 ibid., p. 1265.
22 *Sittang. Mei-Go Sakusen*, Asagumo Shimbunsha, Tokyo, 1969, p. 545.
23 Ba Maw, *Breakthrough in Burma: Memoirs of a Revolution 1939–46*, Yale UP, New Haven and London, 1968, pp. 336–7.
24 *Sittang. Mei-Go Sakusen*, pp. 648–9.
25 Tsuji, *Senkō Sanzenri*, p. 19; trans. *Underground Escape*, p. 16.
26 Tsuji, op. cit., p. 24.
27 J. H. H. Coombes, *Banpong Express. Malaya and After*, Darlington, n.d., p. 151.
28 ibid., p. 153.
29 ibid.
30 ibid.
31 Gilchrist, op. cit., p. 223.
32 ibid., p. 224.
33 ibid., p. 225.
34 ibid., pp. 226–7.
35 ibid., p. 230.
36 Ishida, in the English translation, *Underground Escape*, p. 33.
37 Mountbatten, *Post-Surrender Tasks*, HMSO, 1969, p. 284.
38 ibid., p. 299.

CHAPTER 3

1 Draft Statement of the Imperial Government on the Independence of Indonesia, in H. J. Benda *et al.*, *Japanese Military Administration in Indonesia: Selected Documents*, Yale University Southeast Asia Studies, 1965, p. 257.
2 In an article in 'The Hindu', cited by Willard H. Elsbree, *Japan's Role in Southeast Asian Nationalist Movements, 1940–45*, Harvard UP, 1953, p. 99.
3 Guy J. Pauker, 'The Military', in J. J. Johnson ed., *The Role of the Military in Underdeveloped Countries*, Princeton UP, 1962, p. 189.
4 G. McT. Kahin, *Nationalism and Revolution in Indonesia*, Cornell UP, Ithaca, 1962, p. 109.
5 Pauker, op. cit., pp. 188–90; and H. J. Benda, *The Crescent and the Rising Sun, Indonesian Islam under the Japanese Occupation*, Institute of Pacific Relations, New York, 1958, p. 252, n. 36. See also p. 253, n. 39, for the Islamic element in the recruitment of *Peta* officers.

6 Elsbree, op. cit., p. 83.
7 Benda, *Japanese Military Administration*, p. 201.
8 Quoted in Benda, *Japanese Military Administration*, pp. 230–4.
9 'Proclamation of the Dissolution of the Putera', in Benda, *Japanese Military Administration*, p. 144.
10 Cf. Itagaki Yōichi and Kishi Koichi, 'Japanese Islamic Policy – Sumatra/Malaya'; *Intisari*, Malayan Sociological Research Institute, Singapore, Vol. II, No. 3, pp. 11–23.
11 Benda, *The Crescent and the Rising Sun*, p. 162.
12 ibid.
13 ibid., pp. 175–6.
14 Cf. Kahin, *Nationalism and Revolution in Indonesia*, Cornell UP, Ithaca, 1962, p. 115.
15 C. B. McLane, *Soviet Strategies in Southeast Asia*, Princeton UP, 1966, pp. 279–80; Kahin, op. cit., pp. 117–19.
16 Kahin, op. cit., p. 118; McLane, op. cit., pp. 281–2.
17 Cf. Benda, *Japanese Military Administration*, p. 263.
18 ibid.
19 Text in *Haisen no kiroku* (Records of the Defeat), pp. 280–1, trans. in Benda, *Japanese Military Administration*, p. 274 (Benda omits the decision number).
20 Benda, ibid.
21 Laurens van der Post, *The Night of the New Moon*, Hogarth Press, London, 1971, p. 49.
22 ibid., p. 59.
23 Kahin, op. cit., pp. 122–7, gives an analysis of this important speech.
24 ibid.
25 Cf. Kahin, op. cit., pp. 121–2.

26 Cf. Tanaka Masaaki, 'Hikari mata kaeru' ('The Light Returns'), *Jitsuroku Taiheiyō Sensō* (The Real History of the Pacific War), Vol. 7, Chūō Kōronsha, 1960, p. 284.
27 Kahin, *Nationalism and Revolution in Indonesia*, p. 127.
28 Tanaka, op. cit., p. 284.
29 ibid., pp. 284–96.
30 *Sukarno: A Political Biography*, Allen Lane, Penguin Press, 1972; Pelican Books, 1973, p. 196.
31 Tanaka, op. cit., p. 286.
32 ibid.
33 Benda, *The Crescent and the Rising Sun*, p. 289.
34 op. cit., p. 115.
35 Cf. Kahin, op. cit., p. 113.
36 Tanaka, op. cit., p. 287.
37 ibid.
38 Kahin, op. cit., p. 136.
39 Legge, op. cit., p. 201.
40 *Dai Tōa Sensō Zenshi* (A Complete History of the Greater East Asia War), p. 1007.
41 Tanaka, op. cit., p. 288.
42 ibid.
43 Donnison, *British Military Administration in the Far East*, HMSO, 1956, p. 417.
44 P. S. Gerbrandy, *Indonesia*, Hutchinson, London, 1950, p. 70.
45 J. S. Furnivall, *Colonial Policy and Practice: A Comparative Study of Burma and Netherlands India*, Cambridge, 1948; in Gerbrandy, op. cit., p. 41.
46 Gerbrandy, op. cit., p. 28.
47 Mountbatten, *Post-Surrender Tasks*, HMSO, 1969, p. 289.
48 B. Prasad ed., *Official History of the Indian Armed Forces in the Second World War, Post-War*

Occupation Forces: Japan and South-East Asia, Orient Longmans, 1958, p. 223.

49 Donnison, op. cit., p. 424.

50 *For. Rel. US*, 1945, VI, p. 1178.

51 Woodburn-Kirby, *The War Against Japan*, Vol. 5, p. 313.

52 ibid., pp. 1160–1.

53 Mountbatten, op. cit., p. 290.

54 *For. Rel. US*, 1945, VI, p. 1166.

55 ibid., pp. 1176–7.

56 ibid.

57 Woodburn-Kirby, op. cit., p. 314.

58 Prasad, op. cit., p. 231.

59 *For. Rel. US*, 1945, VI, pp. 1163–4.

60 Tanaka, op. cit., p. 289.

61 Woodburn-Kirby, op. cit., p. 311.

62 Tanaka, op. cit., p. 289.

63 Woodburn-Kirby, op. cit., p. 321.

64 Crockett, 'How the Trouble Began – Java', *Harpers*, March 1946, quoted in Prasad, op. cit., pp. 225–6.

65 Woodburn-Kirby, op. cit., p. 322, f. 1.

66 Cf. Woodburn-Kirby, op. cit., pp. 314–15.

67 Tanaka, op. cit., p. 293.

68 Woodburn-Kirby, op. cit., pp. 323–4; and A. Brett-James, *Ball of Fire*, pp. 448–50.

69 Woodburn-Kirby, op. cit., p. 315.

70 Tanaka, op. cit., p. 295.

CHAPTER 4

1 W. D. Leahy, *I Was There*, p. 58.

2 Decoux, *A la barre de l'Indochine* (At the Helm in Indo-China), p. 196.

3 Cf. Paillat, *Vingt ans qui déchirèrent la France* (Twenty Years Which Tore France Apart), Vol. I, pp. 151–7.

4 *Sittang. Mei-Go Sakusen*, Asagumo Shimbunsha for the Defence Agency, Tokyo, 1969, p. 608.

5 ibid., p. 628.

6 Decoux, op. cit., p. 316.

7 ibid., pp. 321–3.

8 *Sittang. Mei-Go Sakusen*, p. 622.

9 ibid.

10 ibid., p. 623.

11 Decoux, op. cit., p. 329.

12 ibid., p. 330.

13 *Sittang. Mei-Go Sakusen*, p. 623.

14 Decoux, op. cit., p. 334.

15 Romanus and Sunderland, *Time Runs Out in CBI*, Washington, 1959, p. 259.

16 Raoul Salan, *Fin d'un empire* (The End of an Empire), Paris, 1970, Vol. I, p. 206. There is a useful account of the *Kempei-tai* arrests and interrogations in Saigon after the *coup de force* in Jacques Le Bourgeois, 'Prisonnier des Japonais' ('Prisoner of the Japanese'), *Revue de Paris*, juillet 1949, pp. 120–42.

17 Salan, op. cit., p. 208.

18 ibid., pp. 208–9.

19 *For. Rel. US*, 1945, VI, p. 300.

20 ibid., p. 301.

21 Paillat, op. cit., p. 158.

22 Romanus and Sunderland, op. cit., p. 260.

23 *For. Rel. US*, 1945, VI, p. 302.

24 *Sittang. Mei-Go Sakusen*, p. 659.

25 Tsuchihashi, *Futsu-in shori* (The Coup de Force in French Indo-China), in *Sittang. Mei-Go Sakusen*, pp. 659–60.

26 Cf. *Haisen no kiroku*, Hara Shobō, Tokyo, 1968, pp. 279–80.

27 Jean Lacouture, *Ho Chi Minh*, Pelican Books, 1969, p. 73.
28 Bernard Fall, *Le Viet Minh*, Armand Colin, 1960, p. 34; in Lacouture, op. cit., p. 83.
29 Lacouture, op. cit., p. 84.
30 Sainteny, *Histoire d'une paix manquée* (Story of a Peace That Failed), Amiot Dumont, Paris, 1953, pp. 53–6.
31 ibid., p. 57.
32 ibid., pp. 58–9.
33 Lacouture, op. cit., pp. 89–90.
34 Vo Nguyen Giap, Bui Lam Le Van Luong, Hoang Quoc Viet, Nguyen Luong Bang, *Récits de la résistance vietnamienne (1942–1945)* (Stories of the Vietnamese Resistance), Maspero, Paris, 1966, pp. 194–9.
35 *The Public Papers and Addresses of Franklin D. Roosevelt, 1944–5* volume, pp. 562–3; in Ellen J. Hammer, *The Struggle for Indo-China*, Stanford UP, 1954, p. 44.
36 Stimson's diary for 23 July 1945, in *For. Rel. US*, 1945 (*Potsdam*), II, p. 260, 51.
37 Cordell Hull, *Memoirs*, 1948, p. 1597; Hammer, op. cit., p. 43.
38 Memorandum by Taussig dated 15 March 1945, *For. Rel. US*, 1945, VI, p. 124.
39 C.C.S., 890/1, at Babelsberg, 17 July 1945, *For. Rel. US*, 1945 (*Potsdam*), II, pp. 1313–14.
40 ibid., p. 32.
41 ibid., pp. 1315–16.
42 ibid., p. 84.
43 Cf. Mountbatten, *Post Surrender Tasks: Section E of the Report to the Combined Chiefs of Staff by the Supreme Allied Commander South-East Asia*, HMSO, London, 1969, p. 285.
44 *For. Rel. US*, 1945 (*Potsdam*), II, pp. 1318 and 1471.
45 *For. Rel. US*, 1945 (*Potsdam*), II, p. 1321; and *For. Rel. US*, 1945, VI, p. 1275.
46 Woodburn-Kirby, *The War against Japan*, Vol. V, pp. 298–9.
47 B. Prasad ed., *Official History of the Indian Armed Forces in the Second World War, Post-War Occupation Forces: Japan and South-East Asia*, Orient Longmans, 1958, p. 164.
48 Hammer, op. cit., p. 107.
49 Devillers, *Histoire du Vietnam* (History of Vietnam), p. 153.
50 ibid., p. 155.
51 ibid., p. 157.
52 War Diary of the 100th Indian Infantry Brigade, 27 October 1945, in Prasad, op. cit., p. 199.
53 George Rosie, *The British in Vietnam*, Panther Books, London, 1970, pp. 55–6.
54 Hammer, op. cit., p. 115.
55 ibid., Rosie, op. cit., p. 55.
56 ibid., pp. 47–8.
57 Devillers, op. cit., p. 158.
58 Woodburn-Kirby, op. cit., p. 300.
59 ibid.
60 Mountbatten, *Post-Surrender Tasks*, p. 287.
61 Cf. Rosie, op. cit., pp. 59–60; Prasad, op. cit., p. 200; Hammer, op. cit., p. 116; Paillat, op. cit., p. 170; L. Allen, 'Studies in the Japanese Occupation of South-East Asia 1942–1945 (II)', *Durham University Journal*, 1971, pp. 120–32.
62 Mountbatten, *Post-Surrender Tasks*, p. 288.
63 ibid.
64 Devillers, op. cit., p. 160.

65 Devillers, op. cit., p. 159.
66 Woodburn-Kirby, op. cit., p. 300.
67 Hammer, op. cit., p. 116.
68 SACSEA Commission No. 1, *Political History of French Indo-China South of 16°, 13 September–11 October 1945*; in Hammer, op. cit., p. 117.
69 Mountbatten, *Post-Surrender Tasks*, p. 288.
70 Decoux, op. cit., p. 344.
71 ibid., p. 169.
72 Paillat, op. cit., pp. 155–6.
73 Cf. Salan, op. cit., p. 172; and Sainteny, op. cit., p. 125.
74 Salan, op. cit., p. 289.

CHAPTER 5

1 Cf. Mahmood Khan Durrani, *The Sixth Column*, Cassell, 1955, pp. 2–3; and, as a hostile witness, Shah Nawaz Khan, *INA and Its Netaji*, Delhi, 1946, pp. 3–5
2 Dr K. K. Ghosh, *The Indian National Army*, p. 7.
3 *Marē Shinkō Sakusen* (The Assault on Malaya), Asagumo Shimbunsha for the Defence Agency, Tokyo, 1966, p. 330.
4 Shah Nawaz Khan, op. cit., p. 19.
5 Cf. Tamura Yoshio, ed., *Hiroku Dai Tōa Senshi*, pp. 122–3.
6 Shah Nawaz Khan, op. cit., p. 205.
7 ibid., p. 208.
8 Wavell's diary for 24 August 1945, in Penderel Moon ed., *Wavell: The Viceroy's Journal*, OUP, 1973, p. 164.
9 For the Viceroy's reactions to the trials, cf. Penderel Moon, op. cit., Chapter 8.
10 Shah Nawaz Khan, op. cit., p. 195.
11 See in particular Appendix I, 'The Iron Curtain' (i.e. the Hindu caste system), of his book, *While Memory Serves*, London, 1950.
12 V. P. Menon, *The Transfer of Power in India*, Orient Longmans, p. 225.
13 Hugh Toye, *The Springing Tiger*, Cassell, London, 1957, p. 174.
14 John Connell, *Auchinleck*, Cassell, London, 1959, pp. 948–9.
15 R. C. Majumdar, in his Foreword (p.v.) to Ghosh's *Indian National Army*.
16 ibid., pp. 949–50; and Louis Allen, 'The Indian National Army', *History of the Second World War*, Purnell, London, Vol. 7, No. 13, pp. 3040–2.
17 K. L. Panjabi, *The Indomitable Sardar: A Political Biography of Sardar Vallabhai Patel*, Bombay, 1962, p. 113; in Ghosh, op. cit., p. 207.
18 Cf. Michael Brecher, *Nehru: A Political Biography*, OUP, London, 1959.
19 Joyce Lebra, *Jungle Alliance*, Donald Moore, Singapore, 1971, p. 207.
20 'Fujiwara Essays', SEATIC Historical Bulletin, No. 240, Singapore, 9 July 1946, p. 37.
21 Ghosh, op. cit., p. viii.

BOOK TWO

CHAPTER 1

1 Yanaga Chitoshi, *Japan since Perry*, p. 343.
2 Cf. Yanaga, op. cit., pp. 344–5.
3 R. T. Oliver, *Syngman Rhee, The*

Man behind the Myth, Dodd, Mead, New York, 1955, p. 181.

4 Oliver, op. cit., p. 12.

5 *For. Rel. US*, 1945, VI, p. 1030.

6 ibid., p. 1033.

7 ibid.

8 Oliver, op. cit., p. 200.

9 *For. Rel. US*, 1945, VI, p. 631.

10 Morita Yoshio, *Chōsen shūsen no kiroku* (The End of the War in Korea), p. 153.

11 ibid, p. 153.

12 *For. Rel. US*, 1945 (*Potsdam*), II, p. 1327 et seq.

13 ibid., p. 410.

14 Morita, op. cit., p. 158, quoting Appleman, *US Army in the Korean War*, Washington, Dept of the Army, 1961; and Feis, *The China Tangle*, Princeton UP, 1953.

15 *For. Rel. US* (1945), Vol. VI, Washington, 1969.

16 P. 1039.

17 Morita, op. cit., p. 154. Reference is made to a footnote, but this has been omitted erroneously by the Japanese author.

18 *For. Rel. US*, 1945, VI, pp. 635–6.

19 ibid., p. 659.

20 Morita, op. cit., p. 154.

21 ibid., p. 155.

22 ibid., p. 266.

23 ibid., p. 270.

24 ibid., p. 273.

25 Draft in *For. Rel. US*, 1945, VI, p. 1048.

26 ibid., p. 1052.

27 ibid., p. 1056.

28 ibid., p. 1136.

29 Oliver, op. cit., p. 204.

30 *For. Rel. US*, 1945, VI, p. 1125.

31 ibid.

32 ibid., pp. 1130–1.

33 ibid., p. 1123.

34 Morita, op. cit., pp. 354–7.

35 ibid., pp. 832–3.

36 ibid.

37 *For. Rel. US*, 1945, VI, p. 1056.

38 ibid.

39 ibid., p. 1059.

40 Morita, op. cit., p. 339.

41 ibid., p. 338.

42 ibid., p. 207.

43 ibid., p. 218.

44 ibid., pp. 220–1.

45 ibid., p. 221.

46 *Asahi Shimbun*, 14 September 1945, in Morita, op. cit., p. 222.

47 *For. Rel. US*, 1945, VI, p. 1072.

48 ibid., p. 1106.

49 ibid., p. 1121.

50 ibid.

51 ibid., pp. 1144–8.

52 ibid., p. 1146.

53 ibid., p. 1148.

54 F. C. Jones, H. Borton, and B. R. Pearn, *The Far East, 1942–6*, OUP for the Royal Institute of International Affairs, 1955, pp. 435–6.

55 *For. Rel. US*, 1945, VI, p. 1153.

56 ibid., p. 1154.

57 Borton, in Jones, Borton, and Pearn, op. cit., p. 438.

58 Oliver, op. cit., pp. 223–5.

59 Morita, op. cit., p. 899; Jones, Borton, and Pearn, op. cit., p. 451.

60 Morita, op. cit., p. 928.

61 ibid., pp. 929–30.

62 ibid., p. 931.

63 ibid., pp. 794–5.

64 M. Chanteloup, *Hokusen wa Nihon wo dō miru ka?* ('How Does North Korea View Japan?'), *Shūkan Asahi*, Tokyo, Autumn Special number 1953; in Morita, op. cit., pp. 911–12.

65 Morita, op. cit., p. 911.

66 ibid., pp. 883–90.
67 ibid., pp. 200–203.

CHAPTER 2

1 Minutes of meeting of joint chiefs of staff, 24 July 1945; in *For. Rel. US*, 1945 (*Potsdam*), II, pp. 345–53.
2 Alvin Coox, in *History of the Second World War*, Purnell, London, Vol. 8, p. 3.
3 Raymond L. Garthoff, 'Soviet Intervention in Manchuria', in Garthoff, *Sino-Soviet Military Relations*, Praeger, New York, 1966, p. 62.
4 C. Romanus and Riley Sunderland, *Time Runs Out in CBI*, Washington, 1959, p. 350.
5 *Russia at War 1941–1945*, p. 1040.
6 *Istoriya Velikoi Otechestvennoi Voiny Sovetskovo Soyuza* (History of the Great Patriotic War of the Soviet Union), Moscow, 1961, Vol. V, p. 581.
7 Cf. Joseph M. Kitagawa, *Religion in Japanese History*, Columbia UP, New York, 1966, pp. 222 et seq.
8 'Hoku-Man Kaitaku-Dan no Saiki' ('The End of the North Manchurian Settlers' Corps'), in *Jitsuroku Taiheiyō Sensō*, Vol. VII, pp. 183–95.
9 *One's Company*, p. 77.
10 ibid., p. 78.
11 *Tokyo Saiban*, Saiban Hakkōkai, Tokyo, 1962, p. 1362.
12 *The Double Patriots*, p. 117, n. 3.
13 *The Last Manchu, The Autobiography of Henry Pu Yi, Last Emperor of China*, ed. with introduction by P. Kramer, Arthur Barker, London, 1967.

14 ibid., p. 228.
15 ibid.
16 Umemoto Sutezō, *Kantōgun shimatsu-ki* (Decline and Fall of the Kwantung Army), Hara Shobō, Tokyo, 1967, p. 189.
17 ibid.
18 *The Last Manchu*, p. 274.
19 Umemoto Sutezō, op. cit., pp. 183–93.
20 ibid., p. 190.
21 Hattori Takushirō, *Dai Tōa Sensō Zenshi* (A History of the Greater East Asia War), one vol. edn., Hara Shobō, Tokyo, 1968, p. 973.

CHAPTER 3

1 The best contribution to the debate so far is J. H. Boyle's *China and Japan at War 1937–1945*, Stanford UP, 1972.
2 Jones, Borton, and Pearn, *The Far East 1942–1946*, OUP for the Royal Institute of International Affairs, 1955, p. 153.
3 C. Romanus and Riley Sunderland, *Time Runs Out in CBI*, p. 141.
4 Raymond L. Garthoff, *Sino-Soviet Military Relations*, Praeger, New York, 1966, p. 85.
5 Boyle, op. cit., p. 211.
6 Prince Higashikuni Naruhiko, *Watakushi no kiroku* (My Memoirs), p. 90; in *Shūsen Shiroku*, p. 235.
7 *For. Rel. US*, 1945, VI, p. 318.
8 Higashikuni Naruhiko, in *Shūsen Shiroku*, p. 235.
9 'Farewell Leighton Stuart', *Selected Works of Mao Tse-Tung*, Foreign Languages Press, Peking, 1969, Vol. IV, pp. 433–40.
10 Tōgō, notes of oral statement, in *Shūsen Shiroku*, pp. 235–6.

11 Robert Butow, *Japan's Decision to Surrender*, Stanford UP, 1967 reprint, p. 19.

12 Kodama Yoshio, *Ware makeraretari* (We Were Defeated), p. 202; in *Shūsen Shiroku*, p. 236.

13 Boyle, op. cit., p. 213.

14 ibid., pp. 289–93; and Imai Takeo, *Shōwa no bōryaku* (Stratagems of the Shōwa Era), Hara Shobō, Tokyo, 1967, pp. 152–67.

15 Conversation with Tawara Keiichi, staff officer at Imperial General Headquarters, *Yomiuri Weekly*, 1 October 1949; in *Shūsen Shiroku*, p. 236.

16 Hayashi Saburō, *Taiheiyō sensō rikugun gaishi* (Outline History of the Pacific War), pp. 285–6; in *Shūsen Shiroku*, p. 237.

17 *Selected Works of Mao Tse-Tung*, Vol. IV, p. 331.

18 Imai, op. cit., pp. 174–5.

19 ibid., p. 175.

20 ibid., p. 176.

21 ibid.

22 Prince Higashikuni Naruhiko, *Watakushi no kiroku* (My Memoirs), in *Shūsen Shiroku*, pp. 215–17.

23 Sanbō Honbu Shozō (Army General Staff compilation), *Haisen no kiroku* (A Record of the Defeat), p. 240.

24 *Shūsen Shiroku*, p. 225.

25 David Bergamini, *Japan's Imperial Conspiracy*, p. 1004.

26 Cf. Butow, op. cit., pp. 51–4.

27 In *Naigai hōsei kenkyūkai shiryō* (Home and Foreign Legislation Study Association materials), No. 124, for the International Military Tribunal of the Far East; in *Shūsen Shiroku*, p. 230.

28 Cf. Tsuji Masanobu, *Senkō sanzenri* (A Three Thousand-League Odyssey), Mainichi Shimbunsha, Tokyo, 1950, pp. 208–9.

29 'Shina haken-gun no kōfuku' ('The Surrender of the Expeditionary Force in China'), *Jitsuroku Taiheiyō Sensō*, VII, pp. 196–202.

30 Text in *Haisen no kiroku*, pp. 289–90.

31 Cf. Boyle, op. cit., sv. Ch'en Kung-po and Chou Fo-hai.

32 ibid., pp. 332–3; Imai, in *Jitsuroku Taiheiyō Sensō*, Vol. VII, p. 198.

33 Ho Ying-chin, *Report*, etc., in F. F. Liu, *A Military History of Modern China*, Princeton UP, 1956, p. 227.

34 *Selected Works of Mao Tse-Tung*, Vol. IV, p. 11.

35 ibid., p. 16.

36 ibid., p. 21.

37 ibid.

38 ibid.

39 ibid., p. 30; and *For. Rel. US*, 1945, VII, pp. 514–15.

40 Liu, op. cit., p. 229.

41 *Selected Works of Mao Tse-Tung*, Vol. IV, p. 28.

42 ibid., p. 29.

43 ibid.

44 *For. Rel. US*, 1945, VII, pp. 515–16.

45 Imai, in *Jitsuroku Taiheiyō Sensō*, VII, p. 198.

46 ibid., p. 520.

47 ibid., p. 521.

48 ibid., p. 530.

49 Liu, op. cit., p. 229.

50 Cf. Boyle, op. cit., pp. 328–31.

51 Liu, op. cit., p. 228.

52 *For. Rel. US*, 1945, VII, pp. 504–7.

53 S. Woodburn-Kirby, *The War*

against Japan, Vol. V, HMSO, 1969, Ch. xxvi, 'The Reoccupation of Hong Kong'.

54 ibid., p. 283.

55 *For. Rel. US*, 1945, VII, p. 511.

56 ibid., p. 512.

57 F. S. V. Donnison, *British Military Administration in the Far East*, HMSO, London, 1956, p. 199.

58 Cf. Woodburn-Kirby, op. cit., p. 284, n. 3.

59 Donnison, op. cit., p. 200.

60 Mountbatten, *Post-Surrender Tasks*, HMSO, 1969, pp. 283–4.

61 *For. Rel. US*, 1945, VII, pp. 463–5.

62 B. J. Bernstein and A. J. Matusow, *The Truman Administration*, Harper & Row, New York, 1966, p. 299.

63 *For. Rel. US*, 1945, VII, p. 470.

64 ibid., p. 481.

65 *For. Rel. US*, 1945, VII, p. 482.

66 ibid., p. 627.

67 Bernstein and Matusow, op. cit., p. 302.

68 ibid., pp. 320–1.

EPILOGUE

1 Joseph B. Keenan (the chief prosecutor) and Brendan F. Brown, in Richard H. Minear, *Victors' Justice: The Tokyo War Crimes Trial*, p. 160.

2 Tōjō, in Minear, op. cit., p. 3.

3 Aida Yūji, *Aron shūyōjo*, (Ahlone Concentration Camp), Chūō Kōronsha, Tokyo, 1963, trans. by Louis Allen and Hidé Ishiguro as *Prisoner of the British*, Cresset Press, London, 1967.

4 Cf. A. Brett-James, *Ball of Fire*, p. 431. The reference is to the surrender on 4 September 1945, not the formal ceremony of 12 September, when Mountbatten presided.

5 *Materials on the Trial of Former Servicemen of the Japanese Army Charged with Manufacturing and Employing Bacteriological Weapons*, Foreign Languages Publishing House, Moscow, 1950.

6 *Guamu ni ikita 28-nen. Yokoi Shōichi-san no kiroku*, Asahi Shimbun, Tokyo, 1972; trans. as *28 Years in the Guam Jungle*, Japan Publications, Tokyo, 1972; *The Times*, 26 January 1972; *The Japan Times Weekly*, 12 February 1972.

7 *The Japan Times Weekly*, 12 February 1972.

8 *Toungoo Road*, Iwanami Shinsho, 1963, pp. 5–6.

INTERVIEWS

Conversations with the following, either in South-East Asia in 1945 and 1946, or later in Japan, have been of considerable help to me in assessing Japanese reactions to the surrender. They are of course in no way responsible for my interpretation of these reactions. First names have been given where noted, and final ranks, where these are known to me, either in the Japanese Army or Navy, or Self-Defence Forces. In the case of a rank in the Self-Defence Forces, I have put the war-time rank in brackets.

Professor Aida Yūji
Major Fujishima Kōsaku
Major-General Fukutomi Shigeru (Lieutenant-Colonel)
Colonel Furuya Kitarō
Major Hachisuka Mitsuo
Lieutenant-General Hanaya Tadashi
Colonel Hayashi Hidezumi
Lieutenant-General Honda Masaki
Major-General Ichida Jirō
Mr Ichinose Kazutsugu
Captain Inoue Motoichi
Lieutenant Iuchi Kikuji
Mr Iwasaki Tomohiro
Colonel Kadomatsu
Major Kaetsu
Professor Kamiya Fuji
Lieutenant-General Katamura Shihachi
Major Kawaji Kenmei
Lieutenant-General Kimura Hyōtarō
Lieutenant Kitamura Kusuo
Colonel Komatsubara Yukio
Major Kōno Kōichi
Colonel Kume Matao
Captain Kurakata Inosuke
Mr Matsumoto Kaoru
Lieutenant-General Miyazaki Shigesaburō

Lieutenant-Colonel Murata Minoru
Major-General Nagazawa Kanichi
Lieutenant-General Naka Eitarō
Lieutenant-Colonel Okudaira Shōkō
Mr Osumi Hiroshi
Lieutenant-Colonel Saitō Hiroo
Lieutenant-General Sakurai Shōzō
Captain Saruta Chōichi
Lieutenant-Colonel Sumida Haruzō
Tai Seung Kim
Lieutenant-General Tanaka Nobuo
Vice-Admiral Tanaka Raizō
Professor Tanaka Toshitaka
Gunzoku (Navy Civilian) Tominaga
Lieutenant-Colonel Tsuchiya Eiichi
Captain Tsukamoto
Lieutenant-Commander Tsutsumi Shinzō
Major Wakō Hisanori
Major Wakizaka
Major-General Yamaguchi Tatsuru (Major)
Colonel Yano Masatoshi
Major-General Yoshida Gonpachi

BIBLIOGRAPHY

Books and articles are quoted in alphabetical order according to authors' names. In the case of anonymous writings or compilations, the order is that of the first word of the title.

Aida, Yūji, *Prisoner of the British*, trans. by Louis Allen and Hidé Ishiguro, Cresset Press, London, 1967, of *Aron shūyōjo* (Ahlone Concentration Camp), Chūō Kōronsha, Tokyo, 1963.

Allen, Louis, *Japan: The Years of Triumph*, Macdonald, London, 1971.

Allen, Louis, 'Japanese Military Rule in Burma', *Modern Asian Studies*, Cambridge, Vol. III, No. 2, 1969, pp. 177–81.

Allen, Louis, 'Notes on Japanese Historiography: World War II', *Military Affairs*, Kansas State University, Vol. XXXV, No. 4, 1971, pp. 133–8.

Allen, Louis, 'Postwar Burma and Malaya', *History of the Second World War*, Vol. 7, No. 4, pp. 2782–5, Purnell, London.

Allen, Louis, 'Postwar Indo-China', *History of the Second World War*, Vol. 7, No. 4, pp. 2790–3, Purnell, London.

Allen, Louis, *Sittang, The Last Battle*, Macdonald, London, 1973.

Allen, Louis, 'Studies in the Japanese Occupation of South-East Asia 1942–45, I (Burma)', *Durham University Journal*, Vol. LXIII (New Series Vol. XXXII), December 1970, pp. 1–15.

Allen, Louis, 'Studies in the Japanese Occupation of South-East Asia 1942–45, II (French Indo-China)', *Durham University Journal*, Vol. LXIV (New Series Vol. XXXIII), March 1972, pp. 120–32.

Allen, Louis, 'The Indian National Army', *History of the Second World War*, Vol. 7, No. 13, pp. 3040–2, Purnell, London.

Allen, Richard, *A Short Introduction to the History and Politics of Southeast Asia*, OUP, 1970.

'Ano 8.15 go no Nihongun' ('The Japanese Army after August 15 1945'), *Sunday Mainichi*, 30 August 1969, pp. 20–30.

Asahi Shimbun (correspondence of), *28 Years in the Guam Jungle. Sergeant Yokoi Home from World War II*, Japan Publications, Tokyo and San Francisco, 1972. A translation of *Guamu ni ikita*

28-nen. Yokoi Shoichi-san no kiroku (I Lived 28 years on Guam. The Account of Yokoi Shoichi), Asahi Shimbun, Tokyo, 1972.

Asahi Shimbun Hōtei Kisha-dan (Asahi Shimbun Court Reporters' Group), *Tokyo Saiban* (The Tokyo Trials), 3 vols., Tokyo Saiban Hakkōkai, Tokyo, 1962.

Baik Bong, *Kim Il Sung Biography.* 2 vols., Miraisha, Tokyo, 1969.

Ba Maw, *Breakthrough in Burma: Memoirs of a Revolutionary 1939–1946*, Yale UP, New Haven, Connecticut, and London, 1968.

Benda, H. J., *The Crescent and the Rising Sun. Indonesian Islam under the Japanese Occupation 1942–1945*, W. van Hoeve, The Hague and Bandung, 1958.

Benda, H. J. and others, *Japanese Military Administration in Indonesia: Selected Documents*, Yale UP, Southeast Asia Studies, 1965.

Bergamini, David, *Japan's Imperial Conspiracy*, Heinemann, London, 1971.

Bernstein, Barton J., and Matusow, Allen J., eds., *The Truman Administration: A Documentary History*, Harper and Row, New York and London, 1966.

Biruma Kōryaku Sakusen (The Assault on Burma), Asagumo Shimbunsha for the Defence Agency, Tokyo, 1967. (The first Burma volume of the official Japanese war history.)

Boorman, H. L. and others, *Biographical Dictionary of Republican China*, Columbia UP, 1970. (Biography of Henry Pu Yi in Vol. III.)

Bose, Sisir K., ed., *The International Netaji Seminar. Abstracts of Papers*, Netaji Bhawan, Calcutta, 1973.

Bose, Sisir K., ed., *The International Netaji Seminar. Official Souvenir*, Netaji Bhawan, Calcutta, 1973.

Boyle, J. H., *China and Japan at War 1937–1945*, Stanford UP, 1972.

Brecher, Michael, *Nehru, A Political Biography*, OUP, London, 1959.

Brett-James, Antony, *Ball of Fire*, Gale and Polden, Aldershot, 1951. (History of the 5th Indian Division.)

Bunker, Gerald E., *The Peace Conspiracy. Wang Ching-wei and the China War, 1937–1941*, Harvard UP, Cambridge, Mass., 1972.

Butow, R. J. C., *Japan's Decision to Surrender*, Stanford UP, 1954 (1967 reprint).

Choy, Bong-youn, *Korea. A History*, Tuttle, Rutland and Tokyo, 1971.

Coffey, Thomas M., *Imperial Tragedy. The First Days and the Last*, Pinnacle Books, New York, 1971.

Collis, Maurice, *The Journey Outward*, Faber, London, 1952.

Condominas, Georges, *L'exotique est quotidien*, Plon, Paris, 1966.

Coombes, J. H. H., *Banpong Express. Malaya and After*, Wm. Dresser & Sons (Printers), Darlington, n.d. (1949).

Coox, Alvin, 'Kwantung Army', *History of the Second World War*, Vol. 8, No. 3, pp. 3200–7, Purnell, London.

Corpe, Hilda R. (Mrs Tun Tin), *Prisoner beyond the Chindwin*, Arthur Barker, London, 1955.

Crosby, Sir Josiah (HM Minister at Bangkok, 1934–1941), *Siam: The Crossroads*, Hollis and Carter, London, 1945.

Decoux, Amiral Jean, *A la barre de l'Indochine. Histoire de mon Gouvernement Général (1940–1945)*, Plon, Paris, 1949.

Devillers, Philippe, *Histoire du Vietnam de 1940 à 1952*, Seuil, Paris, 1952.

Donnison, F. S. V., *British Military Administration in the Far East*, HMSO, London, 1956.

Dull, Paul S., and Umemura, M. T., *The Tokyo Trials: A Functional Index to the Proceedings of the International Military Tribunal for the Far East*, Univ. of Michigan Press, Ann Arbor, Michigan, 1957.

Durrani, Mahmood Khan, *The Sixth Column*, Cassell, London, 1955.

Elsbree, Willard H., *Japan's Role in Southeast Asian Nationalist Movements, 1940–45*, Harvard UP, 1953.

Eskelund, Paula and Schiff, *Squeezing Through! Shanghai Sketches 1941–1945*. Hwa Kuo Printing Co., Shanghai, 1945.

Fall, Bernard, *Indochine 1946–1962; chronique d'une guerre révolutionnaire*, Laffont, Paris, 1962.

Fall, Bernard, *Le Viet Minh*, Armand Colin, Paris, 1960.

Fall, Bernard, *Vietnam, dernières réflexions sur une guerre*, Laffont, Paris, 1968.

Fergusson, Bernard (Lord Ballantrae), 'Unfinished Tragedy of a Divided Burma', *The Times*, 2 June 1971, p. 12.

Fleming, Peter, *One's Company*, Cape, London, 1934.

Fonde, Jean-Julien, *Traitez à tout prix...Leclerc et le Viet-Nam*, Laffont, Paris, 1971.

Foreign Relations of the United States. The Conference of Berlin (The Potsdam Conference, 1945), 2 vols., Washington, 1960.

Foreign Relations of the United States (1945), Vol. VI, *The British Commonwealth, The Far East*, Washington, 1969.

Foreign Relations of the United States (1945), Vol. VII, *The Far East, China*, Washington, 1969. (I am indebted to my friend

Professor Stanley Falk for the gift of this important volume, which is very difficult to obtain.)

Fujii Shōichi, *Taiheiyō Sensōshi*, 6, *San Furanshisuko Kōwa* (A History of the Pacific War, Vol. 6, The San Francisco Conference), published for the *Rekishigaku Kenkyūkai* (Society for the Study of Historiography) by Aogi Shoten, Tokyo, 1973.

Fujiwara Iwaiichi, 'Fujiwara Essays', SEATIC (South-East Asia Translation and Interrogation Centre) Bulletin No. 240, Singapore, 1946.

Fujiwara Iwaiichi, *F Kikan* (The Fujiwara Organization), Hara Shobō, Tokyo, 1966.

Furnivall, J. S., *Colonial Policy and Practice. A Comparative Study of Burma and Netherlands India*, Cambridge, 1948.

Furuya, Kitarō (Sakurō), 'Popa-san no bōei to sono go no tenshin (Kanjō Heidan no omoide)' ('The Defence of Mount Popa and the Subsequent Retreat: Memories of Kanjō Force'), *Nansō* (Window on the South), Bulletin of the Sittang Society, No. 31, ed. Tsuchiya Eiichi, privately printed, Tokyo, 1965.

Gaichi Jōhō (Overseas Reports), publ. by Headquarters SEATIC (South-East Asia Translation and Interrogation Centre), Singapore, 1946.

Gaimushō, Ajiya Kyoku (Foreign Ministry, Asia Bureau), *Subasu Chandora Bōsu to Nihon* (Subhas Chandra Bose and Japan), Foreign Ministry, Tokyo, 1956.

Garthoff, Raymond L., ed., *Sino-Soviet Military Relations*, Frederick A. Praeger, New York, Washington and London, 1966.

Gerbrandy, P. S., *Indonesia*, Hutchinson, London, 1951.

Ghosh, K. K., 'The Indian National Army – Motives, Problems and Significance', *Asian Studies*, Quezon City, Philippines, Vol. VII, No. 1, 1969, pp. 4–30.

Ghosh, K. K., *The Indian National Army. Second Front of the Indian Independence Movement*, Meenakshi Prakashan, Meerut, 1969.

Giap, Vo Nguyen, and others (Bui Lam Le Van Luong, Hoang Quoc Viet, Nguyen Luong Bang), *Récits de la résistance vietnamienne (1942–1945)*, Maspéro, Paris, 1966.

Gilchrist, Sir Andrew, *Bangkok Top Secret; Being the Experiences of a British Officer in the Siam Country Section of Force 136*, Hutchinson, London, 1970.

Gilmour, O. W., *With Freedom to Singapore*, Ernest Benn, London, 1950.

Giuglaris, Marcel, *Le Japon perd la guerre du Pacifique. De Pearl Harbour à Hiroshima*, Fayard, Paris, 1958.

Hammer, Ellen J., *The Struggle for Indochina*, Stanford UP, 1954.

Hanayama, Shinshō, *The Way of Deliverance. Three Years with the Condemned Japanese War Criminals*, Gollancz, London, 1955.

Hattori, Takushirō, *Dai Tōa Sensō Zenshi* (A History of the Greater East Asia War). One vol. edn., with folder of maps and charts, Hara Shobō, Tokyo, 1965.

Hayashi, Fusao, 'Dai Tōa Sensō Kōtei-ron' ('An Affirmative Theory of the Greater East Asia War'), *Chūō Kōron*, Tokyo, April 1964, pp. 168–85 (fifth in a series of articles later published in book form by Bancho Shobō, Tokyo, 1965).

Hayashida Tatsuo, *Higeki no eiyū. Chandora Bōsu no shōgai* (Tragic Hero: The Life of Subhas Chandra Bose), Shinjusha, Tokyo, 1968.

Hayashi, Shigeru; Andō, Yoshio; Imai Seiichi; and Oshima, Tarō, *Nihon Shūsenshi* (A History of the End of Japan's War), Yomiuri Shimbunsha, Tokyo, 1965.

Higashikuni, Prince Naruhiko, *Watakushi no kiroku* (My Memoirs), Tōhō Shobō, Tokyo, 1947.

Hsu Long-hsuen and Chang Ming-kai (compilers), *History of the Sino–Japanese War (1937–1945)*, translated by Wen Ha-hsiung, Chung Wu Publishing Co., Taipei, Taiwan, Republic of China, 1971.

Iijima, Shirō, 'Hoku-Man kaitaku-dan no saiki' ("The Last Days of the North Manchurian Settlers' Corps'), in *Jitsuroku Taiheiyō Sensō*, Vol. 7, pp. 183–95.

Imai, Takeo, 'Ajiya dokuritsu ni hatashita meishu Nihon no kōzai' ('The Japanese Army's leadership in the achievement of Asian independence; pros and cons'), *Maru*, Tokyo, Vol. 20, September 1967, pp. 212–19.

Imai, Takeo, 'Shina haken-gun no kōfuku' ('The Surrender of the China Expeditionary Force'), in *Jitsuroku Taiheiyō Sensō*, Vol. 7, pp. 196–202.

Imai, Takeo, *Shōwa no bōryaku* (Stratagems of the Shōwa Era), Hara Shobō, Tokyo, 1967.

Istoriya Velikoi Otechestvennoi Voiny Sovetskovo Soyuza (*History of the Great Patriotic War of the Soviet Union*), 5 vols., Moscow, 1961 (only the final volume concerns the events in this book).

Itagaki, Yōichi, and Kishi, Kōichi, 'Japanese Islamic Policy

Sumatra/Malaya', *Intisari*, Malayan Sociological Research Institute, Singapore, Vol. II, No. 3, pp. 11–23.

Itō, Hiroichi, *Tongū Rōdo* (Toungoo Road). *Biruma baishō kōji no go-nenkan.* (Five years' work on behalf of the indemnity to Burma), Iwanami Shinsho, Tokyo, 1963.

Itō, Masanori; Tomioka, Sadatoshi; and Inada, Masazumi, *Jitsuroku Taiheiyō Sensō* (Authentic Records of the Pacific War), 7 vols., Chūō Kōronsha, Tokyo, 1960. (Contains abridgements and extracts from a great variety of books on the subject; Vol. 7 deals with the surrender period.)

Itō, Masanori, *Teikoku rikugun no saigo* (The End of the Imperial Japanese Army), 4 vols., Bungei Shunjū, Tokyo, 1959; 14th impression, 5 vols., 1969.

Johnson, J. J., ed., *The Role of the Military in Underdeveloped Countries*, Princeton UP, 1962. Cf. in particular G. J. Pauker, 'The Role of the Military in Indonesia', pp. 185–230; Lucian W. Pye, 'The Army in Burmese Politics', pp. 231–51; and David A. Wilson, 'The Military in Thai Politics', pp. 253–75.

Johnston, Reginald F., *Twilight in the Forbidden City*, Gollancz, London, 1934.

Jones, F. C., *Japan's New Order in East Asia. Its Rise and Fall 1937–45*, OUP, 1954.

Jones, F. C., Borton, H., and Pearn, B. R., *The Far East 1942–1946*, OUP for the Royal Institute of International Affairs, 1955.

Junod, Marcel, *Warrior without Weapons*, trans. from the French *Le troisième combattant* by E. Fitzgerald, The Non-Fiction Book Club, London, n.d.

Kahin, G. M., *Nationalism and Revolution in Indonesia*, Cornell UP, Ithaca, New York, 1952 (3rd printing 1955).

Khin, U (recorded by), *U Hla Pe's Narrative of the Japanese Occupation of Burma*, Dept. of Far Eastern Studies, Cornell University, Ithaca, 1961.

Kido, Kōichi, *Kido Kōichi Nikki* (*The Diary of Kido Kōichi*), Tokyo UP, Tokyo, 1966. The diary is in 2 vols., and there is a third vol. of related documents, *Kido Kōichi Kankei Bunsho*.

(Kim Il Sung), *Brief History of the Revolutionary Activities of Comrade Kim Il Sung*, compiled by the Party History Institute of the Central Committee of the Workers' Party of Korea, Foreign Languages Publishing House, Pyongyang, Korea, 1969.

Kurowa, Shigeru, *Taiheiyō wo meguru Nichi-Bei kōsō-shi* (A History of the Japanese–American Struggle for the Pacific), Nansōsha, Tokyo, 1968.

Lartéguy, Jean, ed., *Le Japon et ses morts. Ces voix qui nous viennent de la mer*, Lettres recueillies, adaptées et présentées par Jean Lartéguy. Traduit du japonais en collaboration avec Suzanne Audrey et Ko Iwasé, Gallimard, Paris, 1954. A translation of *Kike wadatsumi no koe* (Listen to the Voices from the Sea), diaries of Japanese university students killed during the war, Tokyo UP, Tokyo, 1952.

Leahy, W. D., Fleet Admiral, *I Was There; The Personal Story of the Chief of Staff to Presidents Roosevelt and Truman Based on His Notes and Diaries Made at the Time*, McGraw-Hill, New York, 1950.

Le Bourgeois, Jacques, 'Prisonnier des Japonais', *Revue de Paris*, juillet 1949, pp. 120–42.

Lebra, Joyce, 'Japanese and Western Models for the Indian National Army', *The Japan Interpreter*, Vol. V, pp. 364–75, Tokyo, 1972.

Lebra, Joyce, 'Japanese Policy and the Indian National Army', *Asian Studies*, Quezon City, Philippines, Vol. VII, No. 1, April 1969, pp. 31–49.

Lebra, Joyce, *Jungle Alliance. Japan and the Indian National Army*. Donald Moore, Singapore, 1971.

Léger, François, *Les influences occidentales dans la révolution de l'Orient. Inde-Malaisie-Chine. 1850–1950*, 2 vols., Plon, Paris, 1955.

Legge, J. D., *Sukarno. A Political Biography*, Allen Lane, Penguin Press, 1972; Pelican Books, 1973.

Lensen, G. A., *The Strange Neutrality. Soviet-Japanese Relations during the Second World War, 1941–1945*, The Diplomatic Press, Tallahassee, Florida, 1972.

Liu, F. F., *A Military History of Modern China 1924–1949*, Princeton UP, 1956.

McAleavy, Henry, *A Dream of Tartary: The Origins and Misfortunes of Henry Pu Yi*, Allen and Unwin, London, 1963.

McAleavy, Henry, 'China: Before the Explosion', *History of the Second World War*, Vol. 7, No. 4, pp. 2778–81, Purnell, London.

McLane, C. B., *Soviet Strategies in Southeast Asia. An Exploration of Eastern Policy under Lenin and Stalin*, Princeton UP, 1966.

Mainichi Shimbunsha, publ., *Ichioku-nin no Shōwashi. 5. Senryō kara kōwa e* (A popular History of the Showa era. 5. From Occupation to Peace), Tokyo, 1975.

Mao Tse-tung, *Selected Works of Mao Tse-Tung*, Vol. IV, Foreign Languages Press, Peking, 1969 (1st ed. 1961; translated from the first Chinese ed., Sept. 1960).

Materials on the Trial of Former Servicemen of the Japanese Army Charged with Manufacturing and Employing Bacteriological Weapons, Foreign Languages Publishing House, Moscow, 1950.

Matsumoto Shunichi and Andō Yoshirō, *Nihon Gaikōshi* (History of Japanese Diplomacy), Vol. 25, ed. Kajima Morinosuke, Kajima Kenkyūjo Shuppankai, Tokyo, 1973.

Mayer, S. L., 'Postwar Indonesia', *History of the Second World War*, Vol. 7, No. 4, pp. 2794–800, Purnell, London.

Menon, V. P., *The Transfer of Power in India*, Orient Longmans, Bombay, 1957.

Mills, Lennox A., and others, *The New World of Southeast Asia*, University of Minnesota Press, Minneapolis, and OUP, London, 1949.

Minear, Richard H., *Victors' Justice. The Tokyo War Crimes Trial*, Princeton UP, 1971.

Mitra, Nripendra Nath, ed., *The Indian Annual Register: An Annual Digest of Public Affairs of India*, Calcutta, 1945, Vol. 2 (reports on the INA trials).

Miyamoto, Shizuo, *Jawa shūsen shori-ki* (An account of the End of the War in Java), Jawa shūsen shori-ki kankōkai, Tokyo, 1973.

Morita, Yoshio, *Chōsen shūsen no kiroku* (The End of the War in Korea), Iwanami, Tokyo, 1964 (1967 reprint).

Morrison, Ian, *Grandfather Longlegs: The Life and Gallant Death of Major H. P. Seagrim*, Faber, London, 1947.

Mountbatten of Burma, Vice-Admiral the Viscount (later Earl), *Report to the Combined Chiefs of Staff by the Supreme Allied Commander South-East Asia 1943–1945*, HMSO, London, 1951.

Mountbatten of Burma, Vice-Admiral the Viscount (later Earl), *Post Surrender Tasks. Section E of the Report to the Combined Chiefs of Staff by the Supreme Allied Commander South-East Asia 1943–1945*, HMSO, London, 1969.

Nakamura Akihito, Lt.-Gen., *Chū-Tai shi-nen kaisō-roku* (Recollections of Four Years in Occupied Thailand). Unpublished manuscript in the archive of the War History Room, The Defence Agency, Ichigaya, Tokyo.

Nihon Senbotsu Gakusei Shuki Henshū Yūinkai (Committee for the editing of diaries of Japanese students killed in the war) compilers, *Kike wadatsumi no koe* (Listen to the Voices from the Sea). *Nihon senbotsu gakusei no shuki* (Diaries of Japanese Students Killed in the War), Tokyo UP, Tokyo, 1952 (1954 reprint). And cf. under Lartéguy.

Notosusanto, Nugroho, 'The Revolt of a PETA Battalion in Blitar, February 14, 1945', *Asian Studies*, Quezon City, Philippines, Vol. VII, No. 1, April 1969, pp. 111–23.

Nu, Thakin (later U Nu), *Burma under the Japanese*, Macmillan, London, 1954.

Oliver, Robert T., *Syngman Rhee. The Man behind the Myth*, Dodd, Mead, New York, 1955.

Onada Hirō, *Waga Ruban-tō no 30-nen sensō* (My Thirty years' War on Lubang Island), Kodansha, Tokyo, 1974.

Ōta, Tsunezō, *Biruma ni okeru Nihon gunseishi no kenkyū* (Studies in the History of the Japanese Military Government in Burma), Yoshikawa Kōbunkan, Tokyo, 1968.

The Pacific War Research Society, *Japan's Longest Day. The Story of Japan's Struggle to Surrender – August 1945*, Souvenir Press, 1968; Corgi Books, 1969 (original text published by Bungei Shunjū, Tokyo, 1968).

Paillat, Claude, *Vingt ans qui déchirèrent la France* (Twenty Years Which Tore France Apart), 2 vols., Laffont, Paris, 1969. (t.i, *Le Guêpier* (The Wasps' Nest).

Palmier, L. H., *Indonesia and the Dutch*, OUP for the Institute of Race Relations, 1962 (1965 reprint).

Piggott, F. S. G., *Broken Thread*, Gale and Polden, Aldershot, 1950.

Pu Yi, Aisin Gioro, *From Emperor to Citizen*, 2 vols., Foreign Languages Press, Peking, 1964–5.

Pu Yi, Henry, *The Last Manchu. The Autobiography of Henry Pu Yi, Last Emperor of China*, ed. with intro. by P. Kramer, Arthur Barker, London, 1967.

Rand, Christopher, 'That Was the War. Rip Van Winkle and Fu Manchu', *New Yorker*, 19 April 1947, pp. 62–9.

Romanus, C. F., and Sunderland, R., *Time Runs Out in CBI*, Office of the Chief of Military History, Department of the Army, Washington, D.C., 1959. (I am deeply indebted to Dr Sunderland for his gift of this volume, together with its two predecessors, constituting a history of the American war effort in the China–Burma–India Theatre.)

Rosecrance, R. N., *Australian Diplomacy and Japan. 1945–1951*, Cambridge UP for Melbourne UP, 1962.

Rosie, George, *The British in Vietnam*, Panther Books, London, 1970.

Sabattier, General, G., *Le destin de l'Indochine: souvenirs et documents 1941–1951*, Plon, Paris, 1952.

Sainteny, Jean, *Face à Ho Chi Minh*, Seghers, Paris, 1970.

Sainteny, Jean, *Histoire d'une paix manquée*, Amiot Dumont, Paris, 1953.

Salan, General Raoul, *Mémoires. Fin d'un empire*, 2 vols., Presses de la Cité, Paris, 1970, 1971. (t.i, Le sens d'un engagement; juin 1889–septembre 1946.)

Sanbō Honbu Shozō (Army General Staff Compilation), *Haisen no kiroku (Records of the Defeat)*, Hara Shobō, Tokyo, 1967.

Shah Nawaz Khan, *I.N.A. and its Netaji*, Rajkamal Publications, Delhi, 1946.

Shaplen, Robert, *The Lost Revolution: Vietnam 1945–1965*, André Deutsch, London, 1966, 2 vols. (Cf. ch. I, The Return of the French, 1945–1946 and ch. II, Ho Chi Minh – the Untried Gamble.)

Shewmaker, Kenneth E., *Americans and Chinese Communists, 1927–1945 – A Persuading Encounter*, Cornell UP, Ithaca, and London, 1971.

Shigemitsu, Mamoru, *Japan and Her Destiny: My Struggle for Peace*, E. P. Dutton, New York, 1958.

Shūsen Shiroku (Records of the End of the War), compiled by the Foreign Ministry, Tokyo, 1952.

Singh, Rajendra, *Official History of the Indian Armed Forces in the Second World War. Post-War Occupation Forces: Japan and South-East Asia*, Orient Longmans, 1958.

Sittang. Mei-Go Sakusen (The Sittang Battle; the *Coup de Force* in French Indo-China), Asagumo Shimbunsha for the Defence Agency, Tokyo, 1969 (the final Burma volume of the official war history; deals also with French Indo-China and Siam).

Slim, Field-Marshal Sir William (later Viscount Slim), *Defeat into Victory*, Cassell, London, 1956.

Snow, Edgar, *Red Star over China*, Gollancz, London, 1937.

Sparrow, Gerald, *The Golden Orchid*, Jarrolds, London, 1963. (Memories of wartime Siam.)

Stimson, H. L. and Bundy, McGeorge, *On Active Service in Peace and War*, Harper, New York, 1948.

Storry, Richard, *The Double Patriots. A Study of Japanese Nationalism*, Chatto and Windus, London, 1957.

Stuart, John Leighton, *Fifty Years in China*, Random House, New York, 1954.

Sugiyama, General (Field-Marshal), *Sugiyama Memo* (The Sugiyama Memoranda), 2 vols., Hara Shobō, Tokyo, 1967.

Takami, Jun, *Nikki* (Diary), Vol. 4, *Genbaku tōka* (The Dropping of the Atomic Bomb), Keiso Shobō, Tokyo, 1964.

Takami, Jun, *Nikki* (Diary), Vol. 5, *Haisen no hyōjō* (The Face of Defeat), Keiso Shobō, Tokyo, 1965.

Tamura, Yoshio, ed., *Hiroku Dai Tōa Senshi. Biruma-hen* (Secret History of the Greater East Asia War. Burma volume), Fuji Shoen, Tokyo, 1953. (1 vol. of 12, compilations of accounts by Japanese war correspondents from all theatres.)

Tanaka, Masaaki, *Hikari mata kaeru* (The Light will Return), Nihon Shūhōsha, Tokyo, 1958 (also extracts in *Jitsuroku Taiheiyō Sensō*, Vol. 7. Page refs. given in this book are to these easily accessible extracts).

Tennyson Jesse, F., *The Story of Burma*, Macmillan, London, 1946.

Tewksbury, Donald G. (compiler), *Source Materials on Korean Politics and Ideologies*, Institute of Pacific Relations, New York, 1950 (mimeographed).

Tinker, Hugh, *The Union of Burma*, OUP, 1957.

Toland, John, *The Rising Sun*, Random House, New York, 1970.

Toye, Hugh, *The Springing Tiger. A Study of a Revolutionary*, Cassell, London, 1959.

Trager, F. N., ed., *Burma: Japanese Military Administration. Selected Documents, 1941–1945*, trans. by Won Zoon Yoon, ass. by T. T. Winant, Univ. of Pennsylvania Press, 1971. (The documents are those provided by Ota Tsunezō, listed above.)

Trager, F. N., *Japanese and Chinese Language Sources on Burma: An Annotated Bibliography*, HRAF Press, New Haven, Connecticut, 1957.

Tsuchihashi Yūichi, Lt.-Gen., *Futsu-In Shori* (The *Coup de Force* in French Indo-China). Manuscript in the archive of the War History Room, The Defence Agency, Ichigaya, Tokyo.

Tsuchiya Eiichi, ed., 'Dai Nijūhachi-gun Sengoshi' ('Post-war History of 28 Army'), in *Nanso* (Window on the South), Bulletin of the Sittang Society, Nos. 36 and 37, privately printed, Tokyo, 1969, 1970.

Tsuji, Masanobu, *Jūgo tai ichi: Biruma no shitō* (Fifteen to One: a Fight to the Death in Burma), Kantō-sha, Tokyo, 1950, reprinted by Hara Shobō, Tokyo, 1968.

Tsuji, Masanobu, *Senkō sanzenri* (A Three-thousand League Odyssey), Mainichi Shimbunsha, Tokyo, 1950. Trans. as *Underground Escape*, an Asian Publication, Robert Booth and Taro Fukuda, Tokyo, 1952.

Tsutsumi, Shinzō, *Tenshin: Biruma haken kaigun Fukami butai zen-metsu no ki* (Retreat: A Record of the Annihilation of Fukami Unit – 13 Naval Guard Force – in Burma), first published in *Nanso*, privately printed, Tokyo, Nos. 34 and 35, 1967 and 1968; then separately, also privately printed; and lastly in *Kai-gun shukeika shikan senki* (War Memories of Officers of the Naval Intendance Department), eds. Ichigawa Kōnosuke and Arakawa Masayoshi, Seikyōsha, Tokyo, 1970. (Not commercially distributed; I am indebted to Mr Tsutsumi, now of Mitsui & Co., for the gift of these items.)

Tuchman, Barbara W., *Sand against the Wind. Stilwell and the American Experience in China, 1941–1945*, Macmillan, London, 1970.

Tuker, Major-General F. S., *While Memory Serves*, London, 1950.

Umemoto, Sutezō, *Kantōgun shimatsuki* (Decline and Fall of the Kwantung Army), Hara Shobō, Tokyo, 1967.

van der Post, Laurens, *The Night of the New Moon*, Hogarth Press, London, 1971.

Vasiljevova, Z., 'Le nationalisme japonais et la seconde guerre mondiale' ('Japanese Nationalism and the Second World War'), *La pensée*, nouvelle série, no. 128, août 1966, pp. 102–88. (A discussion of the theories of Hayashi Fusao, listed above.)

Weinberg, Gerhard L., *The Foreign Policy of Hitler's Germany*, Univ. of Chicago Press, Chicago and London, 1970.

Werth, Alexander, *Russia at War 1941–1945*, Barrie and Rockliff, London, 1964.

Westerling, Raymond, *Mes aventures en Indonésie*, Hachette, Paris, 1952.

Wild, C. H. D., 'Expedition to Singkep', *Blackwood's Magazine*, No. 1572, October 1946, pp. 217–23.

Wild, C. H. D., Note on the Capitulation of Singapore. MS written in New Delhi, 30 November 1945, and now in the possession of the Very Rev. J. H. S. Wild, Colonel Wild's brother and formerly Dean of Durham, to whom I am indebted for the loan of this manuscript.

Wildes, Harry Emerson, *Typhoon in Tokyo. The Occupation and Its Aftermath*, Allen and Unwin, London, 1954.

Woodburn-Kirby, Major-General S. (with Brig. M. R. Roberts, Col. G. T. Wards, Air Vice-Maʾshal N. L. Desoer), *The War against Japan*, Vol. V, *The Surrender of Japan*, HMSO, London, 1969.

Yamaguchi, Tatsuru, Major-General, ' "Ima da kara hanasō" ni naratte' ('On the Theme "Now It Can Be Told" '), *Nanso* (Window on the South), Bulletin of the Sittang Society, No. 34, privately printed, Tokyo, 1967.

Yanaga, Chitoshi, *Japan since Perry*, Archon Books, Hamden, Connecticut, 1966.

Yasuda Takeshi and Fukushima Shurō, eds., *Shōgen Shōwa ni-jū nen hachi-gatsu ju-go nichi-haisenka no Nihonjin* (15 August 1945: Eyewitness Accounts. The Japanese in Defeat), Shin-jinbutsu Orai-sha, Tokyo, 1973.

Yoshihashi, Takehiko, *Conspiracy at Mukden: The Rise of the Japanese Military*, Yale UP, 1963.

INDEX

Grew, Joseph, 37
Guadalcanal, 39
Guam, 260
Gubbins, Major-General (later Sir), 26
Guerrilla Regiment, Fifth (Indian National Army), 145
Gurkhas, 7, 8, 11, 13, 123, 155

Ha Giang, 112
Ha' adyai, 135
Hachijō Village (Halahei), 205
Hachiya, Teruo, 150
Hagiwara, Mrs, 209
Hague, The, 85, 94
Hague Agreement, 93
Hague Conference, Second, 159
Hainan Island, 15, 24
Haiphong, 15, 97, 110, 115, 130, 131
Halahei, 200, 202, 203, 206, 209
Halifax, Lord, 32
Halon-Arshan, 203
Hamada, Minoru, Major-General (later Lieutenant-General), 39, 40, 44, 48, 50, 55, 56, 57, 60
Hamaguchi (Japanese Premier), 177
Hamgyung, 167
Hamgyung-Namdo (South Province), 167
Hamgyung-Pukto (North Province), 163, 167
Hammer, Ellen, 105, 123
Hanaya, Tadashi, Lieutenant-General, 48
Haneda Airport, 261
Hangchow, 244
Hankey, Lord, 257
Hankow, 222
Hanoi, 64, 99, 100, 105-7, 109-11, 114-16, 121, 127, 129-31, 225
Hantō Hotel, 169
Harada, 177
Harbin, 198, 199
Harcourt, Rear-Admiral C. H. J., 252, 254
Hardinge, Lord (Viceroy of India), 133
Harriman, Averell (US Ambassador to Moscow), 186
Harris, Brigadier General Charles, 167, 168, 179

Harvard, 223
Hashimoto, Kenzō, 204
Hashimoto, Toranosuke, 216
Hata, Hikosaburō, Lieutenant-General, 196-7
Hata, Shunroku, Field-Marshal, 227
Hatada, Yoshio, 190
Hatta, Mohammed, 69, 71, 72, 76-81, 87
Hattori, Takushirō, Colonel, 81, 218
Hawthorn, Major-General D.C., 92, 93
Hayashi, Hidezumi, Colonel, 49
Hayashida, Tatsuo (*Higeki no eiyū*), 132, 140, 144
Hei-ho (Military Auxiliaries), 70, 90
Helfrich, Admiral, 91
Helliwell, Colonel, 113
Higashikuni, Naruhiko, Prince, 22, 223, 230-32
Hikari Kikan, 56, 59, 136, 138-9, 149
Hindi, 134
Hiranuma, Kiichirō, Baron (former Japanese Premier), 223
Hirokane, Torao (Hirokane Hospital), 170
Hiroshima, xi, 49, 75
Hirota, Kōki (former Japanese Premier and Foreign Minister), 29, 259
Historical Policy Research (US State Department), Division of, 163
Hitler, Adolf, 137
Hla Pe, Thakin (Bo Let Ya), 24
Ho Chi Minh, 110-13, 115, 120, 130, 131
Ho Chu-kuo, 233
Ho Ping-yin, 241
Ho Shih-chen, 225
Ho Ying-chin, 238-9, 241-2
Hoa Hao, 121
Hoang Quoc Viet, 116
Hōantai (Unit for the Preservation of Public Order), 170-71
Hodge, Lieutenant-General J. R., 167-72, 174-8, 186, 187, 189
Hodzumi, 174-5
Hokkaido, 162, 163
Hokkekyō (Lotus Sutra), 202
Holland, 82, 86
Homma, Masaharu, General, 259